Preaching Through the Psalms
Sermon Outlines and Helpful Homiletic Tips for all 150 Psalms!
By Charles H. Spurgeon

Edited by Barry L. Davis, D.Min.

Copyright©2013 Barry L. Davis

www.pastorshelper.com

Please check out some of our other Sermon Titles:

52 Sermons About Jesus
http://www.amazon.com/dp/B00AVLEQG2

52 Sermons from the Gospel of John
http://www.amazon.com/dp/B00BI1DAWA

Originally published as a part of *The Treasury of David* under the "Hints to Preachers" section.

Table of Contents

INTRODUCTION 9
PSALM 1 11
PSALM 2 13
PSALM 3 15
PSALM 4 16
PSALM 5 18
PSALM 6 19
PSALM 7 20
PSALM 8 22
PSALM 9 23
PSALM 10 25
PSALM 11 27
PSALM 12 28
PSALM 13 30
PSALM 14 31
PSALM 15 33
PSALM 16 35
PSALM 17 39
PSALM 18 41
PSALM 19 43
PSALM 20 45
PSALM 21 47
PSALM 22 49
PSALM 23 51
PSALM 24 52
PSALM 25 54
PSALM 26 57

PSALM 27	59
PSALM 28	61
PSALM 29	62
PSALM 30	63
PSALM 31	65
PSALM 32	69
PSALM 33	71
PSALM 34	74
PSALM 35	76
PSALM 36	78
PSALM 37	80
PSALM 38	85
PSALM 39	87
PSALM 40	91
PSALM 41	96
PSALM 42	98
PSALM 43	102
PSALM 44	104
PSALM 45	107
PSALM 46	110
PSALM 47	112
PSALM 48	114
PSALM 49	117
PSALM 50	119
PSALM 51	123
PSALM 52	126
PSALM 53	127
PSALM 54	129
PSALM 55	130
PSALM 56	133

PSALM 57	135
PSALM 58	139
PSALM 59	140
PSALM 60	141
PSALM 61	143
PSALM 62	145
PSALM 63	146
PSALM 64	148
PSALM 65	150
PSALM 66	152
PSALM 67	156
PSALM 68	158
PSALM 69	165
PSALM 70	169
PSALM 71	170
PSALM 72	174
PSALM 73	177
PSALM 74	181
PSALM 75	184
PSALM 76	186
PSALM 77	188
PSALM 78	191
PSALM 79	196
PSALM 80	198
PSALM 81	199
PSALM 82	201
PSALM 83	202
PSALM 84	203
PSALM 85	208
PSALM 86	212

PSALM 87	215
PSALM 88	219
PSALM 89	222
PSALM 90	228
PSALM 91	232
PSALM 92	235
PSALM 93	238
PSALM 94	240
PSALM 95	244
PSALM 96	247
PSALM 97	250
PSALM 98	253
PSALM 99	256
PSALM 100	258
PSALM 101	260
PSALM 102	263
PSALM 103	268
PSALM 104	273
PSALM 105	280
PSALM 106	284
PSALM 107	290
PSALM 108	293
PSALM 109	295
PSALM 110	297
PSALM 111	300
PSALM 112	303
PSALM 113	306
PSALM 114	309
PSALM 115	311
PSALM 116	315

PSALM 117	320
PSALM 118	321
PSALM 119 (part 1 vv. 1-56)	325
PSALM 119 (part 2 vv. 57-120)	352
PSALM 119 (part 3 vv. 121-176)	387
PSALM 120	423
PSALM 121	425
PSALM 122	428
PSALM 123	433
PSALM 124	435
PSALM 125	438
PSALM 126	441
PSALM 127	445
PSALM 128	447
PSALM 129	449
PSALM 130	452
PSALM 131	457
PSALM 132	460
PSALM 133	466
PSALM 134	469
PSALM 135	471
PSALM 136	476
PSALM 137	479
PSALM 138	482
PSALM 139	487
PSALM 140	493
PSALM 141	498
PSALM 142	500
PSALM 143	504
PSALM 144	508

PSALM 145 513
PSALM 146 518
PSALM 147 520
PSALM 148 524
PSALM 149 527
PSALM 150 530

INTRODUCTION

In my opinion, as well as the estimation of many other preachers down through the years, Charles H. Spurgeon is the greatest preacher to ever stand behind a pulpit in the post-New Testament era.

The massive volume of his sermon material is itself astounding and without compare, but when you consider the *content* of his messages he stands head and shoulders above the rest. Spurgeon was a preacher's preacher, and those of us who stand behind the sacred desk would do well to learn from him.

Spurgeon would join the Apostle Paul in exhorting us to:

> *Preach the word; be instant in season, out of season; reprove, rebuke, exhort with all longsuffering and doctrine. For the time will come when they will not endure sound doctrine; but after their own lusts shall they heap to themselves teachers, having itching ears; And they shall turn away their ears from the truth, and shall be turned unto fables.* – 2 Timothy 4:2-4 (KJV)

We have compiled this wonderful collection of sermon outlines and preaching tips on the Psalms to help you do exactly that! Contained in the following pages you will find the sermon material that Spurgeon himself found most useful to those in ministry.

It was originally a part of Spurgeon's vast commentary on the Psalms, *The Treasury of David*. We have taken all of the sections specifically designed to help preachers and put it in this one extremely practical volume.

If you are preaching on one Psalm, doing a series through the Psalms, or merely wanting to learn more about the Psalms, this will become your most valuable resource. There is more material here for preaching on the Psalms than any other book that I am aware of. Please free to use any of the following material in your preaching or teaching ministry. Use it "as is" or feel free to adapt it to your own style.

May God bless you as you continue to serve Him!

In Christ,
Barry L. Davis, Editor

PSALM 1

SERMON OUTLINES AND HELPFUL TIPS

Verse 1. May furnish an excellent text upon "Progress in Sin," or "The Purity of the Christian," or "The Blessedness of the Righteous." Upon the last subject speak of the believer as BLESSED—
1. By God;
2. In Christ;
3. With all blessings;
4. In all circumstances;
5. Through time and eternity;
6. To the highest degree.

Verse 1. Teaches a godly man to beware, (1) of the opinions, (2) of the practical life, and (3) of the company and association of sinful men. Show how meditation upon the Word will assist us in keeping aloof from these three evils.
The insinuating and progressive nature of sin. *J. Morrison.*

Verse 1. *in connection with the whole Psalm.* The wide difference between the righteous and the wicked.

Verse 2. THE WORD OF GOD.
1. The believer's delight in it.
2. The believer's acquaintance with it.

We long to be in the company of those we love.

Verse 2.
1. What is meant by "the law of the Lord."
2. What there is in it for the believer to delight in.
3. How he shows his delight, thinks of it, reads much, speaks of it, obeys it, does not delight in evil.

Verse 2. *(last clause).* The benefits, helps, and hindrances of meditation.

Verse 3. *"The fruitful tree."*
1. Where it grows.
2. How it came there.
3. What it yields.
4. How to be like it.

Verse 3. *"Planted by the rivers of water."*
1. The origination of Christian life, *"planted."*
2. The streams which support it.
3. The fruit expected from it.

Verse 3. Influence of religion upon prosperity.—*Blair.*

The nature, causes, signs, and results of true prosperity.

"*Fruit in his season;*" virtues to be exhibited at certain seasons— patience in affliction; gratitude in prosperity; zeal in opportunity, etc.

"*His leaf also shall not wither;*" the blessing of retaining an unwithered profession.

Verses 3, 4. See No. 280 of "Spurgeon's Sermons." "The Chaff Driven Away."

Sin puts a negative on every blessing.

Verse 5. The sinner's double doom.
    1. Condemned at the judgment-bar.
    2. Separated from the saints.
Reasonableness of these penalties, "therefore," and the way to escape them.

"*The congregation of the righteous*" viewed as the church of the first-born above. This may furnish a noble topic.

Verse 6. (*first sentence*). A sweet encouragement to the tried people of God. The knowledge here meant.
    1. *Its character.*—It is a knowledge of observation and approbation.
    2. *Its source.*—It is caused by omniscience and infinite love.
    3. *Its results.*—Support, deliverance, acceptance, and glory at last.

Verse 6. (*last clause*). His way of pleasure, of pride, of unbelief, of profanity, of persecution, of procrastinating, of self-deception, etc.: all these shall come to an end.

PSALM 2

SERMON OUTLINES AND HELPFUL TIPS

Whole Psalm. Shows us the nature of sin, and the terrible results of it if it could reign.

Verse 1. *Nothing is more irrational than irreligion.* A weighty theme.
   The reasons why sinners rebel against God, stated, refuted, lamented, and repented of.
   The crowning display of human sin in man's hatred of the Mediator.

Verses 1 *and* 2. Opposition to the gospel, unreasonable and ineffectual. *Two sermons by John Newton.*

Verses 1 *and* 2. These **Verse**s show that all trust in man in the service of God is vain. Inasmuch as men oppose Christ, it is not good to hang our trust upon *the multitude* for their number, *the earnest* for their zeal, *the mighty* for their countenance, or *the wise* for their counsel, since all these are far oftener against Christ than for him.

Verse 2. "Spurgeon's Sermons," No. 495, "The Greatest Trial on Record."

Verse 3. The true reason of the opposition of sinners to Christ's truth, viz.: their hatred of the restraints of godliness.

Verse 4. God's derision of the rebellious, both now and hereafter.

Verse 5. *The voice of wrath.* One of a series of sermons upon the voices of the divine attributes.

Verse 6. *Christ's Sovereignty.*
   1. The opposition to it: "*yet.*"
   2. The certainty of its existence: "*Yet have I set.*"
   3. The power which maintains it: "*have I set.*"
   4. The place of its manifestation: "*my holy hill of Zion.*"
   5. The blessings flowing from it.

Verse 7. The divine decree concerning Christ, in connection with the decrees of election and providence. The Sonship of Jesus.
   This **Verse** teaches us faithfully to declare, and humbly to claim, the gifts and calling that God hath bestowed upon us. *Thomas Wilcocks.*

Verse 8. Christ's inheritance. *William Jay.*
   Prayer indispensable. — *Jesus must ask.*

Verse 9. *The ruin of the wicked.* Certain, irresistible, terrible, complete, irretrievable, "like a potter's vessel."
   The destruction of systems of error and oppression to be expected. The gospel an iron rod quite able to break mere pots of man's making.

Verse 10. True wisdom, fit for kings and judges, lies in obeying Christ.

The gospel, a school for those who would learn how to rule and judge well. They may consider its principles, its exemplar, its spirit, etc.

Verse 11. *Mingled experience.* See the case of the women returning from the sepulchre. Matthew 28:8. This may be rendered a very comforting subject, if the Holy Spirit direct the mind of the preacher.

True religion, a compound of many virtues and emotions.

Verse 12. *An earnest invitation.*
1. *The command.*
2. *The argument.*
3. *The benediction* upon the obedient. "Spurgeon's Sermons," No. 260.

Last clause.—Nature, object, and blessedness of saving faith.

PSALM 3

SERMON OUTLINES AND HELPFUL TIPS

Verse 1. *The saint telling his griefs to his God.*
   (1) His right to do so.
   (2) The proper manner of telling them.
   (3) The fair results of such holy communications with the Lord.

When may we expect increased troubles? Why are they sent? What is our wisdom in reference to them?

Verse 2. The lie against the saint and the libel upon his God.

Verse 3. The threefold blessing which God affords to his suffering ones—Defense, Honor, Joy. Show how all these may be enjoyed by faith, even in our worst estate.

Verse 4.
   (1) In dangers we should pray.
   (2) God will graciously hear.
   (3) We should record his answers of grace.
   (4) We may strengthen ourselves for the future by remembering the deliverances of the past.

Verse 5.
   (1) Describe sweet sleeping.
   (2) Describe happy waking.
   (3) Show how both are to be enjoyed, "*for the Lord sustained me.*"

Verse 6. Faith surrounded by enemies and yet triumphant.

Verse 7.
   (1) Describe the Lord's past dealing with his enemies; "thou hast."
   (2) Show that the Lord should be our constant resort, "O Lord," "O my God."
   (3) Enlarge upon the fact that the Lord is to be stirred up: "Arise."
   (4) Urge believers to use the Lord's past victories as an argument with which to prevail with him.

Verse 7. (*last clause*). Our enemies vanquished foes, toothless lions.

Verse 8. (*first clause*). Salvation of God from first to last. (See the exposition.)

Verse 8. (*last clause*). They were blessed *in* Christ, *through* Christ, and shall be blessed *with* Christ. The blessing rests upon their persons, comforts, trials, labors, families, etc. It flows from grace, is enjoyed by faith, and is insured by oath, etc. *James Smith's Portions*, 1802-1862.

PSALM 4

SERMON OUTLINES AND HELPFUL TIPS

Verse 1. Is full of matter for a sermon upon, *past mercies a plea for present help.* The first sentence shows that believers desire, expect, and believe in a God that heareth prayer. The title— *God of my righteousness,* may furnish a text (see exposition), and the last sentence may suggest a sermon upon, "The best of saints must still appeal to God's mercy and sovereign grace."

Verse 2. *Depravity of man* as evinced
    (1) by continuance in despising Christ,
    (2) by loving vanity in his heart, and
    (3) seeking lies in his daily life.

Verse 2. The length of the sinner's sin. "How long?" May be bounded by repentance, shall be by death, and yet shall continue in eternity.

Verse 3. *Election.* Its aspects toward God, our enemies, and ourselves.

Verse 3. "*The Lord will hear when I call unto him.*" Answers to prayer certain to special persons. Mark out those who can claim the Favor.

Verse 3. *The gracious Separatist.* Who is he? Who separated him? With what end? How to make men know it?

Verse 4. The sinner directed to review himself, that he may be convinced of sin. *Andrew Fuller, 1754-1815.*

Verse 4. "*Be still.*" Advice—good, practical, but hard to follow. Times when seasonable. Graces needed to enable one to be still. Results of quietness. Persons who most need the advice. Instances of its practice. here is much material for a sermon.

Verse 5. The nature of those sacrifices of righteousness which the Lord's people are expected to offer. *William Ford Vance,* 1827.

Verse 6. The cry of the world and the church contrasted. *Vox populi* not always *Vox Dei.*

Verse 6. The cravings of the soul all satisfied in God.

Verses 6, 7. An assurance of the Savior's love, the source of unrivalled joy.

Verse 7. The believer's joys.
    (1) Their source, "*Thou;*"
    (2) Their season—even now—"*Thou hast;*"
    (3) Their position, "*in my heart;*"
    (4) Their excellence, "*more than in the time that their corn and their wine increased.*"
    Another excellent theme suggests itself— "The superiority of the joys of grace to the joys of earth;" or, "Two sorts of prosperity—which is to be the more desired?"

Verse 8. The peace and safety of the good man. *Joseph Lathrop, D.D., 1805.*

Verse 8. A bedchamber for believers, a vesper song to sing in it, and a guard to keep the door.

Verse 8. The Christian's good night.

Verses 2 *to* 8. The means which a believer should use to win the ungodly to Christ.
    (1) Expostulation, **Verse 2.**
    (2) Instruction, **Verse 3.**
    (3) Exhortation, **Verse**s 4, 5.
    (4) Testimony to the blessedness of true religion as in **Verse**s 6, 7.
    (5) Exemplification of that testimony by the peace of faith, **Verse 8.**

PSALM 5

SERMON OUTLINES AND HELPFUL TIPS

Verses 1, 2. Prayer in its threefold form. "*Words, meditation, cry.*" Showing how utterance is of no avail without heart, but that fervent longings and silent desires are accepted, even when unexpressed.

Verse 3. The excellence of morning devotion.

Verse 3. (*last two clauses*)
   1. Prayer directed.
   2. Answers expected.

Verse 4. God's hatred of sin an example to his people.

Verse 5. "*The foolish.*" Show why sinners are justly called fools.

Verse 7. "*Multitude of thy nercy.*" Dwell upon the varied grace and goodness of God.

Verse 7. The devout resolution

Verse 7.
   1. Observe the *singularity* of the resolution.
   2. Mark the *object* of the resolution. It regards the service of God in the sanctuary. "I will come into thine *house. . .* in thy fear will I *worship* towards thy holy *temple.*"
   3. The *manner* in which he would accomplish the resolution.
   (1) Impressed with a sense of the divine goodness: "I will come into thy house in *the multitude of thy mercy.*"
   (2) Filled with holy veneration: "And *in thy fear* will I worship." *William Jay, 1842.*

Verse 8. God's guidance needed always and especially when enemies are watching us.

Verse 10. Viewed as a threatening. The sentence, "Cast them out in the multitude of their transgressions," is specially fitted to be the groundwork of a very solemn discourse.

Verse 11.
   1. The character of the righteous: *faith and love.*
   2. The privileges of the righteous.
   (1) *Joy*—great, pure, satisfying, triumphant, (*shout*) constant (*ever*).
   (2) *Defense*—by power, providence, angels, grace, etc.

Verse 11. Joy in the Lord both a duty and a privilege.

Verse 12. (*first clause*). *The divine blessing upon the righteous.* It is ancient, effectual, constant, extensive, irreversible, surpassing, eternal, infinite.

Verse 12. (*second clause*). A sense of divine Favor a defense to the soul.

PSALM 6

SERMON OUTLINES AND HELPFUL TIPS

Verse 1. *A sermon for afflicted souls.*
   1. God's twofold dealings.
   (1) *Rebuke,* by a telling sermon, a judgment on another, a slight trial in our own person, or a solemn monition in our conscience by the Spirit.
   (2) *Chastening.* This follows the other when the first is disregarded. Pain, losses, bereavements, melancholy, and other trials.
   2. The evils in them to be most dreaded, anger and hot displeasure.
   3. The means to avert these ills. Humiliation, confession, amendment, faith in the Lord, etc.

Verse 2. *The argumentum ad misericordiam.*

Verse 2. *First sentence – Divine healing.*
   (1) What precedes it, *my bones are vexed.*
   (2) How it is wrought.
   (3) What succeeds it.

Verse 3. The impatience of sorrow; its sins, mischief, and cure.

Verse 3. A fruitful topic may be found in considering the question, How long will God continue afflictions to the righteous?

Verse 4. "Return, O Lord." A prayer suggested by a sense of the Lord's absence, excited by grace, attended with heart searching and repentance, backed by pressing danger, guaranteed as to its answer, and containing a request for all mercies.

Verse 4. The praying of the deserted saint.

   1. *His state:* his soul is evidently in bondage and danger;
   2. *His hope:* it is in the Lord's return.
   3. *His plea:* mercy only.

Verse 5. The final suspension of earthly service considered in various practical aspects.

Verse 5. The duty of praising God while we live.

Verse 6. Saint's tears in quality, abundance, influence, assuagement, and final end.

Verse 7. The voice of weeping. What it is.

Verse 8. The pardoned sinner forsaking his bad companions.

Verse 9. Past answers the ground of present confidence. He *hath,* he *will.*

Verse 10. The shame reserved for the wicked.

PSALM 7

SERMON OUTLINES AND HELPFUL TIPS

Verse 1. The necessity of faith when we address ourselves to God. Show the worthlessness of prayer without trust in the Lord.

Verses 1, 2. Viewed as a prayer for deliverance from all enemies, especially Satan the lion.

Verse 3. Self-vindication before men. When possible, judicious, or serviceable. With remarks upon the spirit in which it should be attempted.

Verse 4. "*The best revenge.*" Evil for good is devil-like, evil for evil is beast-like, good for good is man-like, good for evil is God-like.

Verse 6. How and in what sense divine anger may become the hope of the righteous.
   Fire fought by fire, or man's anger overcome by God's anger.

Verse 7. *The congregation of the people."*
   1. Who they are.
   2. Why they congregate together with one another.
   3. Where they congregate.
   4. Why they choose such a person to be the centre of their congregation.

Verse 7. The gathering of the saints around the Lord Jesus.

Verse 7 (*last clause*). The coming of Christ to judgment for the good of his saints.

Verse 8. The character of the Judge before whom we all must stand.

Verse 9 (*first clause*).

   (1) By changing their hearts; or
   (2) by restraining their wills,
   (3) or depriving them of power,
   (4) or removing them.

Show the times when, the reasons why, such a prayer should be offered, and how, in the first sense, we may labor for its accomplishment.

Verse 9. This **Verse** contains two grand prayers, and a noble proof that the Lord can grant them.

Verse 9. The period of sin, and the perpetuity of the righteous. *Matthew Henry.*

Verse 9. "*Establish the just.*" By what means and in what sense the just are established, or, the true established church.

Verse 9 (*last clause*). God's trial of men's hearts.

Verse 10. "*Upright in heart.*" Explain the character.

Verse 10. The believer's trust in God, and God's care over him. Show the action of faith in procuring defense and protection, and of that defense upon our faith by strengthening it, etc.

Verse 11. The Judge, and the two persons upon their trial.

Verse 11 (*second clause*). God's present, daily, constant, and vehement anger, against the wicked.

Verse 12. See "Spurgeon's Sermons," No. 106. "Turn or Burn."

None.

Verses 14, 15, 16. Illustrate by three figures the devices and defeat of persecutors.

Verse 17. The excellent duty of praise.

Verse 17. View the **Verse** in connection with the subject of the Psalm, and show how the deliverance of the righteous, and the destruction of the wicked are themes for song.

PSALM 8

SERMON OUTLINES AND HELPFUL TIPS

Verse 1. "*O Lord, our Lord.*" Personal appropriation of the Lord as ours. The privilege of holding such a portion.

"*How excellent*", etc. The excellence of the name and nature of God in all places, and under all circumstances.

Sermon or lecture upon the glory of God in creation and providence.

"*In all the earth.*" The universal revelation of God in nature and its excellency.

"*Thy glory above the heavens.*" The incomprehensible and infinite glory of God.

"*Above the heavens.*" The glory of God outsoaring the intellect of angels, and the splendour of heaven.

Verse 2. Infant piety, its possibility, potency, "strength," and influence, "that thou mightest still," etc.

The strength of the gospel not the result of eloquence or wisdom in the speaker.
Great results from small causes when the Lord ordains to work.
Great things which can be said and claimed by babes in grace.
The stilling of the powers of evil by the testimony of feeble believers.
The stilling of the Great Enemy by the conquests of grace.

Verse 4. Man's insignificance. God's mindfulness of man. Divine visits. The question, "What is man?" Each of these themes may suffice for a discourse, or they may be handled in one sermon.

Verse 5. Man's relation to the angels.
The position Jesus assumed for our sakes.
Manhood's crown—the glory of our nature in the person of the Lord Jesus.

Verses 5, 6, 7, 8. The universal providential dominion of our Lord Jesus.

Verse 6. Man's rights and responsibilities towards the lower animals.

Verse 6. Man's dominion over the lower animals, and how he should exercise it.

Verse 6 (*second clause*). The proper place for all worldly things, "*under his feet.*"

Verse 9. The wanderer in many climes enjoying the sweetness of his Lord's name in every condition.

PSALM 9

SERMON OUTLINES AND HELPFUL TIPS

    1. The only object of our praise—"thee, O Lord."
    2. The abundant themes of praise—"all thy marvelous works."
    3. The proper nature of praise—"with my whole heart." *B. Davies.*

Verse 1. "*I will show forth.*" Endless employment and enjoyment.

Verse 1. "*Thy marvelous works.*" Creation, Providence, Redemption, are all marvelous, as exhibiting the attributes of God in such a degree as to excite the wonder of all God's uni**Verse**. A very suggestive topic.

Verse 2. Sacred song: its connection with holy gladness.

Verse 4.

    (1) The rights of the righteous are sure to be assailed,
    (2) but equally sure to be defended.

Verse 6.

    1. The great enemy.
    2. The destruction he has caused.
    3. The means of his overthrow.
    4. The rest which shall ensue.

Verse 7 (*first clause*). The eternity of God—the comfort of saints, the terror of sinners.

Verse 8. The justice of God's moral government, especially in relation to the last great day.

Verse 9. Needy people, needy times, all-sufficient provision.

Verse 10.

    1. All-important knowledge—"know thy name."
    2. Blessed result—"will put their trust in thee."
    3. Sufficient reason—"for thou, Lord, hast not forsaken them that seek thee." *T. W. Medhurst.*

Knowledge, Faith, Experience, the connection of the three.

Verse 10. The names of God inspire trust. JEHOVAH *Jireh, Tsidkenu, Rophi, Shammah, Nissi,* ELOHIM, SHADDAI, ADONAI, etc.

Verse 11.

1. Zion, what is it?
   2. Her glorious inhabitant, what doth he?
   3. The twofold occupation of her sons—"sing praises," "declare among the people his doings."
   4. Arguments from the first part of the subject to encourage us in the double duty.

Verse 12.

   1. God on awful business.
   2. Remembers his people; to spare, Honor, bless, and avenge them.
   3. Fulfils their cries, in their own salvation, and overthrow of enemies. A consolatory sermon for times of war or pestilence.

Verse 13. "*Have mercy upon me, O Lord.*" The publican's prayer expounded, commended, presented, and fulfilled.

Verse 14. "*I will rejoice in thy salvation.*" Especially because it is *thine*, O God, and therefore Honors thee. In its freeness, fulness, suitability, certainty, everlastingness. Who can rejoice in this? Reasons why they should always do so.

Verse 15. *Lex talionis.* Memorable instances.

Verse 16. Awful knowledge; a tremendous alternative as compared with **Verse 10.**

Verse 17. A warning to forgetters of God.

Verse 18. Delays in deliverance.

   1. Unbelief's estimate of the—"forgotten," "perish."
   2. God's promise—"not always."
   3. Faith's duty—wait.

Verse 19. "*Let not man prevail.*" A powerful plea. Cases when employed in Scripture. The reason of its power. Times for its use.

Verse 20. A needful lesson, and how it is taught.

PSALM 10

SERMON OUTLINES AND HELPFUL TIPS

Verse 1. The answer to these questions furnishes a noble topic for an experimental sermon. Let me suggest that the question is not to be answered in the same manner in all cases. Past sin, trials of graces, strengthening of faith, discovery of depravity, instruction, etc., etc., are varied reasons for the hiding of our Father's face.

Verse 2. Religious persecution in all its phases based on pride.

Verse 3. God's hatred of covetousness: show its justice.

Verse 4. Pride the barrier in the way of conversion.

Verse 4 (*last clause*). Thoughts in which God is not, weighed and condemned.

Verse 5. "*Thy judgments are far above out of his sight.*" Moral inability of men to appreciate the character and acts of God.

Verse 6. The vain confidence of sinners.

Verse 8. Dangers of godly men, or the snares in the way of believers.

Verse 9. The ferocity, craftiness, strength, and activity of Satan.

Verse 9 (*last clause*). The Satanic fisherman, his art, diligence, success, etc.

Verse 10. Designing humility unmasked.

Verse 11. Divine omniscience and the astounding presumption of sinners.

Verse 12. "*Arise, O Lord.*" A prayer needful, allowable, seasonable, etc.

Verse 13 (*first clause*). An astounding fact, and a reasonable enquiry.

Verse 13. Future retribution: doubts concerning it.
    1. By whom indulged: "*the wicked.*"
    2. Where fostered: "*in his heart.*"
    3. For what purpose: *quieting of conscience*, etc.
    4. With what practical tendency: "*contemn God.*" He who disbelieves hell, distrusts heaven.

Verses 13, 14. Divine government in the world.
    1. Who doubt it? and why?
    2. Who believe it? and what does this faith cause them to do?

Verse 14 (*last clause*). A plea for orphans.

Verse 16. The Eternal Kingship of Jehovah.

Verse 17 (*first clause*).

    1. The Christian's character — "*humble.*"

    2. An attribute of the Christian's whole life — "*desire:*" he desires more holiness, communion, knowledge, grace, and usefulness; and then he desires glory.

    3. The Christian's great blessedness — "*Lord, thou hast heard the desire of the humble.*"

Verse 17 (*whole* **Verse**).

    1. Consider the *nature* of gracious desires.

    2. Their *origin.*

    3. Their *result.*

The three sentences readily suggest these divisions, and the subject may be very profitable.

PSALM 11

SERMON OUTLINES AND HELPFUL TIPS

Verse 1. Faith's bold avowal, and brave refusal.

Verse 1. Teacheth us to trust in God, how great soever our dangers be; also that we shall be many times assaulted to make us put far from us this trust, but yet that we must cleave unto it, as the anchor of our souls, sure and steadfast. *Thomas Wilcocks.*

Verse 1. The advice of cowardice, and the jeer of insolence, both answered by faith. Lesson — Attempt no other answer.

Verse 2. The craftiness of our spiritual enemies.

Verse 3. This may furnish a double discourse.
    1. *If God's oath and promise could remove*, what could we do? Here the answer is easy.
    2. *If all earthly things fail*, and the very State fall to pieces, what can we do? We can suffer joyfully, hope cheerfully, wait patiently, pray earnestly, believe confidently, and triumph finally.

Verse 3. Necessity of holding and preaching foundation truths.

Verse 4. The elevation, mystery, supremacy, purity, everlastingness, invisibility, etc., of the throne of God.

Verses 4, 5. In these **Verses** mark the fact that the children of men, as well as the righteous, are tried; work out the contrast between the two trials in their designs and results, etc.

Verse 5. *"The Lord trieth the righteous."*
    1. Who are tried?
    2. What in them is tried? — Faith, love, etc.
    3. In what manner? — Trials of every sort.
    4. How long?
    5. For what purpose?

Verse 5. *"His soul hateth."* The thoroughness of God's hatred of sin. Illustrate by providential judgments, threatenings, sufferings of the Surety, and the terrors of hell.

Verse 5. The trying of the gold, and the sweeping out of the refuse.

Verse 6. *"He shall rain."* Gracious rain and destroying rain.

Verse 6. The portion of the impenitent.

Verse 7. The Lord possesses righteousness as a personal attribute, loves it in the abstract, and blesses those who practice it.

PSALM 12

SERMON OUTLINES AND HELPFUL TIPS

Verse 1. *"Help, Lord."*
   1. The Prayer itself, short, suggestive, seasonable, rightly directed, vehement.
   2. Occasions for its use.
   3. Modes of its answer.
   4. Reasons for expecting gracious reply.

Verse 1. *First two clauses*. Text for funeral of an eminent believer.

Verse 1. *Whole* **Verse**.
   1. *The fact bewailed*—describe godly and faithful, and show how they fail.
   2. *The feeling excited.* Mourning the loss, fears for church, personal need of such companions, appeal to God.
   3. *The forebodings aroused.* Failure of the cause, judgments impending, etc.
   4. *The faith remaining:* "Help, Lord."

Verse 1. Intimate connection between yielding Honor to God and honesty to man, since they decline together.

Verse 2. (*first clause*). A discourse upon the prevalence and perniciousness of vain talk.

Verse 2. *The whole* **Verse**. Connection between flattery and treachery.

Verse 2. *"A double heart."* Right and wrong kinds of hearts, and the disease of duplicity.

Verse 3. God's hatred of those twin sins of the lips—Flattery and Pride (which is self flattery). Why he hates them. How he shows his hatred. In whom he hates them most. How to be cleansed from them.

Verses 3, 4.
   1. *The revolt of the tongue.* Its claim of power, self-possession, and liberty. Contrast this and the believer's confession, "we are not our own."
   2. *The method of its rebellion*— "flattery, and speaking proud things."
   3. *The end of its treason*—"cut off."

Verse 5. The Lord aroused—How! Why! What to do! When!

Verse 5. *Last clause.* Peculiar danger of believers from those who despise them and their special safety. Good practical topic.

Verse 6. The purity, trial, and permanency of the words of the Lord.

Seven crucibles in which believers try the word. A little thought will suggest these.

Verse 7. Preservation from one's generation in this life and forever A very suggestive theme.

Verse 8. *Sin in high places specially infectious.* Call to the rich and prominent to remember their responsibility. Thankfulness for Honorable rulers. Discrimination to be used in choice of our representatives, or civic magistrates.

PSALM 13

SERMON OUTLINES AND HELPFUL TIPS

Verse 1. The apparent length of sorrow, only apparent. Contrast with days of joy, with eternal misery and eternal joy. Impatience, and other evil passions, cause the seeming length. Means of shortening, by refusing to forestall, or to repine afterwards.

Verse 1 (*second clause*). Hiding of the divine face. Why at all? Why from me? Why so long?

Verse 2. Advice to the dejected, or the soul directed to look out of itself for consolation. *A. Fuller.*

Verse 2 (*first clause*).— *Self-torture*, its cause, curse, crime, and cure.

Verse 2. "*Having sorrow in my heart daily.*"
    1. The cause of daily sorrow. Great enemy, unbelief, sin, trial, loss of Jesus' presence, sympathy with others, mourning for human ruin.
    2. The necessity of daily sorrow. Purge corruptions, excite graces, raise desires heavenward.
    3. The cure of daily sorrow. Good food from God's table, old wine of promises, walks with Jesus, exercise in good works, avoidance of everything unhealthy. *B. Davies.*

Verse 2 (*second clause*).— Time anticipated when defeat shall be turned into victory.

Verse 3. By accomodating the text to the believer.
    1. True character of Satan, "enemy."
    2. Remarkable fact that this enemy is exalted over us.
    3. Pressing enquiry, "How long?" *B. Davies.*

Verse 3. "*Lighten mine eyes.*" A prayer fit for (1) Every benighted sinner. (2) Every seeker of salvation. (3) Every learner in Christ's school. (4) Every tried believer. (5) Every dying saint. *B. Davies.*

Verse 4. Noteth the nature of the wicked two ways; namely, the more they prevail the more insolent they are; they wonderfully exult over those that are afflicted. *T. Wilcocks.*

Verse 5. Experience and perseverance. "I have," "my heart shall."

Verse 6. The bountiful giver and the hearty singer.

The whole Psalm would make a good subject, showing the stages from mourning to rejoicing, dwelling especially upon the turning point, prayer. There are two **Verses** for each, mourning, praying, rejoicing. *A. G. Brown.*

PSALM 14

SERMON OUTLINES AND HELPFUL TIPS

Verse 1 (*first clause*). The folly of atheism.

Verse 1. Atheism of the heart. *Jamieson's Sermons on the Heart.*

Verse 1 (*whole* **Verse**). Describe:
    1. The creed of the fool.
    2. The fool who holds the creed: or thus, Atheism.
    1. Its source: "*the heart.*"
    2. Its creed: "*no God.*"
    3. Its fruits: "*corrupt,*" etc.

Verse 1.
    1. The great source of sin—alienation from God.
    2. Its place of dominion—the heart.
    3. Its effect upon the intellect— makes man a fool.
    4. Its manifestations in the life—acts of commission and omission.

Verse 1 (*last clause*). The lantern of Diogenes. Hold it up upon all classes, and denounce their sins.

Verse 2.
    1. Condescending search.
    2. Favored subjects.
    3. Generous intentions.

Verse 2. What God looks for, and what we should look for. Men usually are quick to see things congruous to their own character.

Verses 2, 3. God's search for a naturally good man; the result; lessons to be learned therefrom.

Verse 3. Total depravity of the race.

Verse 4. "*Have all the workers of iniquity no knowledge?*" If men rightly knew God, his law, the evil of sin, the torment of hell, and other great truths, would they sin as they do? Or if they know these and yet continue in their iniquities, how guilty and foolish they are! Answer the question both positively and negatively, and it supplies material for a searching discourse.

Verse 4 (*first clause*). The crying sin of transgressing against light and knowledge.

Verse 4 (*last clause*). Absence of prayer, a sure mark of a graceless state.

Verse 5. The foolish fears of those who have no fear of God.

Verse 5. The Lord's nearness to the righteous, its consequences to the persecutor, and its encouragement to saints.

Verse 6. The wisdom of making the Lord our refuge. *John Owen.*

Verse 6. Describe,
    1. The poor man here intended.
    2. His counsel.
    3. His reproach.
    4. His refuge.

Verse 6. Trust in God, a theme for mockery to fools only. Show its wisdom.

Verse 7. Longings for the advent.

Verse 7. "*Out of Zion.*" The church, the channel of blessings to men.

Verse 7. Discourse to promote revival.
    1. Frequent condition of the church, "*captivity.*"
    2. Means of revival—the Lord's coming in grace.
    3. Consequences, "*rejoice,*" "*be glad.*"

Verse 7. Captivity of soul. What it is. How provided for. How accomplished. With what results.

PSALM 15

SERMON OUTLINES AND HELPFUL TIPS

Verse 1. Qualifications for church membership on earth and in heaven. A subject for self-examination.

Verse 1.
   1. *Comparison of the church to the tabernacle.* God's presence manifested, sacrifice offered, and vessels of grace preserved in it;mean externally, glorious within.
   2. *Comparison of its double position to that of the tabernacle.* Moving in the wilderness, and fixed on the hill.
   3. Enquire into qualification for admittance into church and tabernacle. Parallel with the priests, etc.

Verse 1. The great question. Asked by idle curiosity, despair, godly fear, earnest enquirer, soul troubled by falls of others, holy faith. Give answer to each.

Verse 1. The citizen of Zion described. *Thomas Boston's Sermons.*

Verse 1. Anxiety to know the true saints, how far lawful and profitable.

Verse 1. God the only infallible discerner of true saints.

Verse 2. "*He that walketh uprightly.*"
   1. What he must be. He must be upright in heart. A man himself bent double cannot walk uprightly.
   2. How he must act. Neither from impulse, ambition, gain, fear, or flattery. He must not be warped in any direction, but stand perpendicularly.
   3. What he must expect. Snares, etc., to trip him.
   4. Where he must walk. Path of duty, the only one in which he can walk uprightly.
   5. Where he must look. Up, right-up, and then he will be upright.

Verse 2. "*Speaketh the truth in his heart.*" Subject:— Heart falsehood and heart truth.

Verse 2 (*first clause*). The citizen of Zion, an upright walker.

Verse 2 (*middle clause*). The citizen of Zion, a worker of righteousness.

Verse 2 (*last clause*). The citizen of Zion, a speaker of truth. *Four Sermons in Thomas Boston's Works.*

Verse 3. The evils of detraction. It affects three persons here mentioned: the backbiter, the suffering neighbour, and the taker-up of the reproach.

Verse 3. "*Nor taketh up a reproach.*" The sin of being too ready to believe ill reports. Common, cruel, foolish, injurious, wicked.

Verse 4. The duty of practically Honoring those who fear the Lord. Commendation, deference, assistance, imitation, etc.

Verse 4. The sin of estimating persons other than by their practical characters.

Verse 4 (*last clause*). The Lord Jesus as our unchanging Surety, his oath and his hurt.

Verse 5. The evidences and privileges of godly men.

Verse 5 (*last clause*). The fixedness and safety of the godly.

PSALM 16

SERMON OUTLINES AND HELPFUL TIPS

Michtam of David. Under the title of "The Golden Psalm," Mr. Canon Dale has published a small volume, which is valuable as a series of good simple discourses, but ought hardly to have been styled "an exposition." We have thought it right to give the headings of the chapters into which his volume is divided, for there is much showiness, and may be some solidity in the suggestions.

Verse 1. *The seeking of the gold.* The believer conscious of danger, trusting in God only for deliverance.

Verses 2, 3. *The possessing of the gol.d* The believer looking for justification to the righteousness of God alone, while maintaining personal holiness by companionship with the saints.

Verses 4, 5. *The testing of the gold.* The believer finding his present portion, and expecting his eternal inheritance in the Lord.

Verse 6. *The prizing or valuing of the gold.* The believer congratulating himself on the pleasantness of his dwelling and the goodness of his heritage.

Verses 7, 8. *The occupying of the gold.* The believer seeking instruction from the counsels of the Lord by night, and realising his promise by day.

Verses 9, 10. *The summing or reckoning of the gold.* The believer rejoicing and praising God for the promise of a rest in hope and resurrection into glory.

Verse 11. *The perfecting of the gold.* The believer realising at God's right hand the fulness of joy and the pleasures for evermore.

Upon this suggestive Psalm we offer the following few hints out of many—

Verse 1. The prayer and the plea. The preserver and the truster. The dangers of the saints and the place of their confidence.

Verse 2. *"Thou art my Lord."* The soul's appropriation, allegiance, assurance, and avowal.

Verses 2, 3. The influence and sphere of goodness. No profit to God, or departed saints or sinners, but to living men. Need of promptness, etc.

Verse 2, 3. Evidences of true faith.

    1. Allegiance to divine authority.

    2. Rejection of self-righteousness.

    3. Doing good to the saints.

    4. Appreciation of saintly excellence.

    5. Delight in their society.

Verse 3. *Excellent of the earth.* May be translated noble, wonderful, magnificent. They are so in their new birth, nature, clothing, attendance, heritage, etc., etc.

Verse 3. "*In whom is all my delight.*" Why Christians should be objects of our delight. Why we do not delight in them more. Why they do not delight in us. How to make our fellowship more delightful.

Verse 3. Collection sermon for poor believers.

    1. Saints.

    2. Saints on the earth.

    3. These are excellent.

    4. We must delight in them.

    5. We must extend our goodness to them.

—*Matthew Henry.* **Verse** 4. Sorrows of idolatry illustrated in heathens and ourselves.

Verse 4 (*Second clause*). The duty of complete separation from sinners in life and lip.

Verse 5. Future inheritance and present cup found in God. (See exposition.)

Verse 6.

    1. "*Pleasant places.*" Bethlehem, Calvary, Olivet, Tabor, Zion, Paradise, etc.

    2. *Pleasant purposes,* which made these lines fall to me.

    3. *Pleasant praises.* By service, sacrifice, and song.

Verse 6 *(second clause).*

    1. A heritage.

    2. A goodly heritage.

    3. I have it.

    4. Yea, or the Spirit's witness.

Verse 6. "*A goodly heritage.*" That which makes our portion good is—

  1. The Favor of God with it.

  2. That it is from a Father's hand.

  3. That it comes through the covenant of grace.

  4. That it is the purchase of Christ's blood.

  5. That it is an answer to prayer, and a blessing from above upon honest endeavors.

Verse 6. We may put this acknowledgment into the mouth of—

  1. *An indulged child of providence.*

  2. *An inhabitant of this Favored country.*

  3. *A Christian with regard to his spiritual condition.*

—*William Jay.*

Verse 7. Taking counsel's opinion. Of whom? Upon what? Why? When? How? What then?

Verse 7. Upward and inward, or two schools of instruction.

Verse 8. Set the Lord always before you as—

  1. Your *protector.*

  2. Your *leader.*

  3. Your *example.*

  4. Your *observance*

—*William Jay.*

Verses 8, 9. A sense of the divine presence our best support. It yields,

  1. Good confidence concerning things without. "*I shall not be moved.*"

  2. Good cheer within. "*My heart is glad.*"

  3. Good music for the living tongue. "*My glory rejoiceth.*"

  4. Good hope for the dying body. "*My flesh also,*" etc.

Verse 9. *(last clause).*

  1. The saint's Sabbath *(rest).*

  2. His sarcophagus *(in hope).*

  3. His salvation (for which he *hopes*).

Verses 9, 10. Jesus cheered in prospect of death by the safety of his soul and body; our consolation in him as to the same.

Verse 10. Jesus dead, the place of his soul and his body. A difficult but interesting topic.

Verses 10, 11. Because he lives we shall live also. The believers, therefore, can also say, "Thou wilt show *me* the path of life." This life means the blessedness reserved in heaven for the people of God after the resurrection. It has three characters. The first regards its *source* — it flows from "*his presence.*" The second regards its plenitude — it is "*fulness*" of joy." The third regards its *permanency* — the pleasures are "*for evermore.*" — *William Jay.*

Verse 11. A sweet picture of heaven.

PSALM 17

SERMON OUTLINES AND HELPFUL TIPS

Verse 1. The voice of Jesus—our Righteousness, and our own voice. Work out the thought of both coming up to the ear of heaven, noting the qualities of our prayer as indicated by the psalmist's language, such as earnestness, perseverance, sincerity, etc.

Verse 2. "*Let my sentence come forth from thy presence.*"
    1. When it will come.
    2. Who dare meet it *now*.
    3. How to be among them.

Verse 3. "*Thou hast proved mine heart.*" The metal, the furnace, the refiner, etc.

Verse 3. "*Thou hast visited me in the night.*"
    1. Glorious visitor.
    2. Favored individual.
    3. Peculiar season.
    4. Refreshing remembrance.
    5. Practical result.

Verse 3 (*last sentence*). Transgressions of the lip, and how to avoid them.

Verse 4. The highway and the by-paths. *The world and sin.* "*The paths of the destroyer*"—a significant name for transgression.

Verse 5. "*Hold up.*"
    1. Who? God.
    2. What? "*My goings.*"
    3. When? Present tense.
    4. Where? "*In thy paths.*"
    5. Why? "*That my footsteps slip not.*"

Verse 5. Let me observe David and learn to pray as he prayed, "Hold up my goings in thy paths, that my footsteps slip not."

    1. See his *course*. He speaks of his "goings." Religion does not allow a man to sit still. He speaks of his goings "in God's paths." These are threefold.
        (1). The path of his *commands*.
        (2). The path of his *ordinances*.
        (3). The path of his *dispensations*.

    2. His *concern* respecting this course. It is the language of—
        (1). *Conviction*;
        (2). of *apprehension*;

(3). of *weakness;*
(4). of *confidence.* —William Jay.

Verse 6. *Two words*, both great, though little, "call" and "hear." *Two persons*, one little and the other great, "I," "Thee, O God." *Two tenses:* past, "I have;" future, "Thou wilt." *Two wonders,* that we do not call more, and that God hears such unworthy prayers.

Verse 7. (*first sentence*). See Exposition. A view of divine lovingkindness desired.

Verse 7. "*O thou,*" etc. God, the Savior of believers.

Verse 8. Two most suggestive emblems of tenderness and care. Involving in the one case *living unity,* as the eye with the body, and in the other, *loving relationship,* as the bird and its young.

Verse 14. "*Men of the world, which have their portion in this life.*" Who they are? What they have? Where they have it? What next?

Verse 14. "*Men which are thy hand.*" Providential control and use of wicked men.

Verse 15. This is the language
    (1). of a man whose mind is made up; who has decided for himself; who does not suspend his conduct upon the resolution of others.
    (2). Of a man rising in life, and with great prospects before him.
    (3). It is the language of a Jew.

Verse 15. *The beholding of God's face* signifies two things.
    1. The enjoyment of his Favor.
    2. Intimate communions with him. —*William Jay.*

Verse 15. See "Spurgeon's Sermons," No. 25. Title, "The Hope of Future Bliss." Divisions.
    1. The Spirit of this utterance.
    2. The matter of it.
    3. The contrast implied in it.

Verse 15. To see God and to be like him, the believer's desire. —*J. Fawcett.*

PSALM 18

SERMON OUTLINES AND HELPFUL TIPS

Verse 1. Love's resolve, love's logic, love's trials, love's victories.

James Hervey has two sermons upon "Love to God" from this text.

Verse 2. The many excellences of Jehovah to his people.

Verse 2. God the all-sufficient portion of his people. — *C. Simeon's Works,* Vol. 5, Page 85.

Verse 3. Prayer resolved upon; praise rendered; result anticipated.

Verses 4-6. Graphic picture of a distressed soul, and its resorts in the hour of extremity.

Verse 5 (*first clause*). The condition of a soul convinced of sin.

Verse 5 (*second clause*). The way in which snares and temptations are, by Satanic craft, arranged so as to forestall or prevent us.

Verse 6. The time, the manner, the hearing, and the answering of prayer.

Verse 7. The quaking of all things in the presence of an angry God.

Verse 10. Celestial and terrestrial agencies subservient to the divine purposes.

Verse 11. The darkness in which Jehovah hides, Why? When? What then? etc.

Verse 13. "*Hailstones and coals of fire.*" The terrific in its relation to Jehovah.

Verse 16. The Christian, like Moses, "one taken out of the water." The whole **Verse** a noble subject; may be illustrated by life of Moses.

Verse 17. The saint's paean of victory over Satan, and all other foes.

Verse 17 (*last clause*). Singular but sound reason for expecting divine help.

Verse 18. The enemy's "craft," "*They prevented me in the day of my calamity.*" The enemy chained. "*But the Lord was my stay.*"

Verse 19. The reason of grace, and the position in which it places its chosen ones.

Verse 21. Integrity of life, its measure, source, benefit, and dangers.

Verse 22. The need of considering sacred things, and the wickedness of carelessly neglecting them.

Verse 23. The upright heart and its darling sin. *W. Strong's Sermons.*

Verse 23. *Peccata in deliciis;* a discourse of bosom sins. *P. Newcome.*

Verse 23. The sure trial of uprightness. *Dr. Bates.*

Verse 25. Equity of the divine procedure.—*C. Simeon.*

Verse 26. Echoes, in providence, grace, and judgment.

Verse 27. Consolation for the humble, and desolation for the proud.

Verse 27 (*second clause*). The bringing down of high looks. In a way of grace and justice. Among saints and sinner, etc. A wide theme.

Verse 28. A comfortable hope for an uncomfortable state.

Verse 29. Believing exploits recounted. Variety, difficulty in themselves, ease in performance, completeness, impunity, and dependance upon divine working.

Verse 30. God's way, word, and warfare.

Verse 31. A challenge.
    1. To the *gods.* World, pleasure, etc. Which among these deserve the name?
    2. To the *rocks,* self-confidence, superstition, etc. On which can we trust?

Verses 32-34. Trying positions, gracious adaptations, graceful accomplishments, secure abidings, grateful acknowledgment.

Verse 35. "*The shield of thy salvation.*" What is it? Faith. Whence it comes? "Thou hast given." What it secures? "Salvation." Who have received it?

Verse 35. See Spurgeon's Sermons," No. 683. "Divine Gentleness Acknowledged."

Verse 36. Divine benevolence in the arranging of our lot.

Verse 39. The Red Cross Knight armed for the fray.

Verse 41. Unavailing prayers—on earth and in hell.

Verse 42. The sure overthrow, final shame, and ruin of evil.

Verse 43 (*last clause*). Our natural and sinful distance from Christ, no bar to grace.

Verse 44. Rapid advances of the gospel in some places, slow progress in others. Solemn considerations.

Verse 46. The living God, and how to bless and exalt him.

Verse 50. The greatness of salvation, "*great deliverances;*" its channel, "*the King;*" and its perpetuity, "*for evermore.*"

PSALM 19

SERMON OUTLINES AND HELPFUL TIPS

Verse 1. "Chalmers' Astronomical Discourses" will suggest to the preacher many ways of handling this theme. The power, wisdom, goodness, punctuality, faithfulness, greatness, and glory of God are very visible in the heavens.

Verses 1-5. Parallel between the heavens and the revelation of Scripture, dwelling upon Christ as the central Sun of Scripture.

Verse 1. "*The heavens declare the glory of God.*" Work in which we may unite, the nobility, pleasure, usefulness, and duty of such service.

Verse 2. Voices of the day and of the night. Day and night thoughts.

Verse 3. The marginal reading, coupled with **Verse** four, suggests the eloquence of an unobtrusive life—silent, yet heard.

Verse 4. In what sense God is revealed to all men.

Verses 4, 5, 6. The Sun of Righteousness.
    1. His tabernacle.
    2. His appearance as a Bridegroom.
    3. His joy as a champion.
    4. His circuit and his influence.

Verse 5. "*Rejoiceth as a strong man,*" etc. The joy of strength, the joy of holy labor, the joy of the anticipated reward.

Verse 6. The permeating power of the gospel.

Verse 7(*first clause*). Holy Scripture.
    1. What it is—"law."
    2. Whose it is—"of the Lord."
    3. What is its character—"perfect."
    4. What its result—"converting the soul."

Verse 7 (*second clause*).
    1. Scholars.
    2. Class-book.
    3. Teacher.
    4. Progress.

Verses 7, 8, 9. The Hexapla. *See notes.*

Verse 7 (*last clause*). The wisdom of a simple faith.

Verse 8 (*first clause*). The heart-cheering power of the Word.
    1. Founded in its righteousness.

    2. Real in its quality.
    3. Constant in its operation.

Verse 8 (*second clause*). Golden ointment for the eyes.

Verse 9. The purity and permanence of true religion, and the truth and justice of the principles upon which it is founded.

Verse 10. Two arguments for loving God's statutes—Profit and Pleasure.

Verse 10. The inexpressible delights of meditation on Scripture.

Verse 11 (*first clause*).—
    1. What? "Warned."
    2. How? "By them."
    3. Who? "Thy servant."
    4. When? "Is"—present.

Verse 11 (*second clause*). Evangelical rewards—"*In,*" not *for* keeping.

Verse 12. See "Spurgeon's Sermons," No. 116. "Secret Sins."

Verses 12, 13. The three grades of sin—secret, presumptuous, unpardonable.

Verse 13. See "Surgeon's Sermons," No. 135. "Presumptuous Sins."

Verse 13 (*last clause*). "*The great transgression.*" What it is not, may be, involves, and suggests.

Verse 14. A prayer concerning our holy things.

Verse 14. All wish to please. Some please *themselves*. Some please *men*. Some seek to please *God*. Such was David.
    1. The prayer shows his *humility*.
    2. The prayer show his *affection*.
    3. The prayer shows a *consciousness of duty*.
    4. The prayer shows a *regard to self-interest. William Jay.*

Verse 14. The harmony of heart and lips needful for acceptance.

PSALM 20

SERMON OUTLINES AND HELPFUL TIPS

This Psalm has been much used for coronation, thanksgiving, and fast sermons, and no end of nonsense and sickening flattery has been tacked thereto by the trencher-chaplains of the world's church. If kings had been devils, some of these gentry would have praised their horns and hoofs; for although some of their royal highnesses have been very obedient servants of the prince of darkness, these false prophets have dubbed them "most gracious sovereigns," and have been as much dazzled in their presence as if they had beheld the beatific vision. — C. H. S.

Whole Psalm. A loyal song and prayer for subjects of King Jesus.

Verse 1. Two great mercies in great trouble — hearing at the throne, and defense from the throne.

Verses 1, 2.
    1. The Lord's trouble in its nature and its cause.
    2. How the Lord exercised himself in his trouble.
    3. We ought not to be unmoved spectators of the trouble of Jesus.
Hamilton Verschoyle.

Verses 1-3. A model of good wishes for our friends.
    1. *They include personal piety.* The person who is spoken of prays, goes to the sanctuary, and offers sacrifice. We must wish our friend grace.
    2. *They point upward.* The blessings are distinctly recognized as divine.
    3. *They do not exclude trouble.*
    4. *They are eminently spiritual.* Acceptance, etc.

Verse 2. Sanctuary help — a suggestive topic.

Verse 3. God's ceaseless respect to the sacrifice of Jesus.

Verses 3, 4. The great privilege of this fourfold acceptance in the Beloved.

Verse 5. Joy in salvation, to be resolved on and practiced.

Verse 5. *Setting up the banner.* Open avowal of allegiance, declaration of war, index of perseverance, claim of possession, signal of triumph.

Verse 5 (*last clause*). The prevalence of our Lord's intercession, and the acceptance of our prayers through him.

Verse 6. "*His anointed.*" Our Lord as the Anointed. When? With what unction? How? For what offices? etc.

Verse 6. "*He will hear him.*" The ever-prevalent Intercessor.

Verse 6. God's "*saving strength;*" the strength of his most used and most skilful hand.

Verse 6 (*first clause*). "*Now know I.*" The moment when faith in Jesus fills the soul. The time when assurance is given. The period when a truth gleams into the soul. etc.

Verse 7. *Creature confidence.* Apparently mighty, well adapted, showy, noisy, etc. *Faithful trust.* Silent, spiritual, divine, etc.

Verse 7. "*The name of the Lord our God.*" Comfortable reflections from the name and character of the true God.

Verse 8. *Tables turned.*

Verse 9. "*Save, Lord.*" One of the shortest and most pithy prayers in the Bible.

Verse 9. (*last clause*).
    1. To whom we come, and what then. "*To a king.*"
    2. How we come, and what it means. "*We call.*"
    3. What we want, and what it implies. "*Hear us.*"

PSALM 21

SERMON OUTLINES AND HELPFUL TIPS

Verse 1. The joy of Jesus and of his people in the strength and salvation of God.

Verses 1, 2. The doctrine of the resurrection of Jesus Christ contained in the text, may be considered under three heads:
   1. *As an answer to prayer.*
   2. *His joy therein – even in the resurrection.*
   3. As a necessary appendage to this—*our own individual concern in his glory and in his joy.* Hamilton Verschoyle.

Verse 2. The successful Advocate.

Verse 3 (*first clause*). Preventing mercies.

Verse 3 (*first clause*). GOD GOING BEFORE US, or God's anticipation of our necessities by his merciful dispensations. God prevents us with the blessings of his goodness:
   1. When we come into the world.
   2. When we become personal transgressors.
   3. When we enter upon the duties and upon the cares of mature life.
   4. When, in the general course of life, we enter upon new paths.
   5. In the dark "valley of the shadow of death."
   6. By giving us many mercies without our asking for them; and thus creating occasion, not for prayer, but for praise only.
   7. By opening to us the gate of heaven, and by storing heaven with every provision for our blessedness.—*Samuel Martin.*

Verse 3 (*second clause*). Jesus crowned.
   1. His previous labors.
   2. The dominion bestowed.
   3. The character of the crown.
   4. The divine coronant.

Verse 4. Jesus ever living.

Verse 5. The glory of the Mediator.

Verse 6. The blessedness of Jesus.

Verse 7. Jesus, and example of faith and of its results.

Verse 8. The secret sinner unearthed, and deprived of all hope of concealment.

Verses 8, 9. The certainty and terror of the punishment of the wicked.

Verses 11, 12. The guilt and punishment of evil intentions.

Verse 12. The retreat of the grand army of hell.

Verse 13. *A devout Doxology.*
- **1.** God exalted.
- **2.** God alone exalted.
- **3.** God exalted by his own strength.
- **4.** His people singing his praise.

PSALM 22

SERMON OUTLINES AND HELPFUL TIPS

Whole Psalm. The volume entitled "Christ on the Cross," by Rev. J. Stevenson, has a sermon upon every **Verse**. We give the headings, they are suggestive. **Verse** 1. The Cry. 2. The Complaint. 3. The Acknowledgment. 4-6. The Contrast. 6. The Reproach. 7. The Mockery. 8. The Taunt. 9, 10. The Appeal. 11. The Entreaty. 12, 13. The Assault. 14. The Faintness. 15. The Exhaustion. 16. The Piercing. 17. The Emaciation. 17. The Insulting Gaze. 18. The Partition of the Garments and Casting Lots. 19-21. The Importunity. 21. The Deliverance. 22. The Gratitude. 23. The Invitation. 24. The Testimony. 25. The Vow. 26. The Satisfaction of the Meek; the Seekers of the Lord Praising Him; the Eternal Life. 27. The Conversion of the World. 28. The Enthronement. 29. The Author of the Faith. 30. The Seed. 31. The Everlasting Theme and Occupation. The Finish of the Faith.

Verse 1. The Savior's dying cry.

Verse 2. *Unanswered prayer.* Enquire the reason for it; encourage our hope concerning it; urge to continue in importunity.

Verse 3. Whatever God may do, we must settle it in our minds that he is holy and to be praised.

Verse 4. God's faithfulness in past ages a plea for the present.

Verses 4, 5. Ancient saints.
   1. Their life. "*They trusted.*"
   2. Their practice. "*They cried.*"
   3. Their experience. "*Were not confounded.*"
   4. Their voice to us.

Verses 6-18. Full of striking sentences upon our Lord's suffering.

Verse 11. A saint's troubles, his arguments in prayer.

Verse 20. "*My darling.*" A man's soul to be very dear to him.

Verse 21 (*first clause*). "*Lion's mouth.*" Men of cruelty. The devil. Sin. Death. Hell.

Verse 22. Christ as a brother, a preacher, and a presenter.

Verse 22. A sweet subject, a glorious preacher, a loving relationship, a heavenly exercise.

Verse 23. *A threefold duty,* "praise him, "glorify him;" "fear him;" *towards one object,* "the Lord;" *for three characters,* "ye that fear him, seed of Jacob, seed of Israel," *which are but one person.*

Verse 23. Glory to God the fruit of the tree on which Jesus died.

Verse 24. A consoling fact in history attested by universal experience.

Verse 24. (*first clause*). A common fear dispelled.

Verse 25. Public praise.
   1. A delightful exercise—"praise."
   2. A personal participation—"My praise."
   3. A fitting object—"of thee."
   4. A special source—"from thee."
   5. An appropriate place—"in the great congregation."

Verse 25. (*second clause*). *Vows.* What vows to make, when and how to make them, and the importance of paying them.

Verse 26. *Spiritual feasting.* The guests, the food, the host, and the satisfaction.

Verse 26. (*second clause*). *Seekers who shall be singers.* Who they are? What they shall do? When? and what is the reason for expecting that they shall?

Verse 27. (*last clause*). *Life everlasting.* What lives? Source of life. Manner of life. Why for ever? What occupation? What comfort to be derived from it?

Verse 27. Nature of true conversion, and extent of it under the reign of the Messiah. *Andrew Fuller.*

Verse 27. The universal triumph of Christianity certain.

Verse 27. The order of conversion. See the Exposition.

Verse 28. The empire of the King of kings as it is, and as it shall be.

Verse 29. Grace for the rich, grace for the poor, but all lost without it.

Verse 29 (*last clause*). A weighty text upon the vanity of self-confidence.

Verse 30. The perpetuity of the church.

Verse 30 (*last clause*). Church history, the marrow of all history.

Verse 31. Future prospects for the church.
   1. Conversions certain.
   2. Preachers promised.
   3. Succeeding generations blest.
   4. Gospel published.
   5. Christ exalted.

PSALM 23

SERMON OUTLINES AND HELPFUL TIPS

Verse 1. Work out the similitude of a shepherd and his sheep. He rules, guides, feeds, and protects them; and they follow, obey, love and trust him. Examine as to whether we are sheep; show the lot of the goats who feed side by side with the sheep.

Verse 1. (*second clause*). The man who is beyond the reach of want for time and eternity.

Verse 2. (*first clause*). Believing rest.
    1. Comes from God — "*He maketh.*"
    2. Is deep and profound — "*lie down.*"
    3. Has solid sustenance — "*in green pastures.*"
    4. Is subject for constant praise.

Verse 2. The contemplative and the active element provided for.

Verse 2. The freshness and richness of Holy Scripture.

Verse 2. (*second clause*). Onward. The Leader, the way, the comforts of the road, and the traveler in it.

Verse 3. Gracious restoration, holy guidance, and divine motives.

Verse 4. The soft silence of the Spirit's work.

Verse 4. God's presence the only sure support in death.

Verse 4. Life in death and light in darkness.

Verse 4. (*second clause*). The calm and quiet of the good man's end.

Verse 4. (*last clause*). The tokens of divine government — the consolation of the obedient.

Verse 5. The warrior feasted, the priest anointed, the guest satisfied.

Verse 5. The means and uses of the continual anointing of the Holy Spirit.

Verse 5. Providential super-aboundings, and what is our duty concerning them.

Verse 6. (*first clause*). The blessedness of content.

Verse 6. On the road and at home, or heavenly attendants and heavenly mansions.

PSALM 24

SERMON OUTLINES AND HELPFUL TIPS

Verse 1. The great Proprietor, his estates and his servants, his rights and wrongs.

Verse 1. *"The earth is the Lord's."*
   1. *Mention other claimants — idols: pope, man, devil, etc.,*
   2. *Try the suit.*
   3. *Carry out the verdict.* Use our substance, preach everywhere, claim all things for God.
   4. *See how glorious the earth looks when she bears her Master's name.*

Verse 1 (*last clause*). All men belong to God. His sons or his subjects, his servants or his serfs, his sheep or his goats, etc.

Verse 2. Divine purposes accomplished by singular means.

Verse 2. *Founded on the seas.* Instability of terrestrial things.

Verse 3. The all-important question.

Verse 4 (*first clause*). Connection between outward morality and inward purity.

Verse 4 (*second clause*). Men judged by their delights.

Verse 4. *"Clean hands."*
   1. How to get them clean.
   2. How to keep them clean.
   3. How to defile them
   4. How to get them clean again.

Verses 4, 5. Character manifested and Favor received.

Verse 5 (*second clause*). The good man receiving righteousness and needing salvation, or the evangelical meaning of apparently legal passages.

Verse 6. Those who truly seek fellowship with God. **Verse** 7. Accommodate the text to the entrance of Jesus Christ into our hearts.
   1. There are obstacles, *"gates,"* *"doors."*
   2. We must will to remove them: *"lift up."*
   3. Grace must enable us: *"be ye lift up."*
   4. Our Lord will enter.
   5. He enters as *"King,"* and *"King of glory."*

Verse 7. The ascension and its teachings. **Verse**s 7-10. —
   1. His title — the Lord of hosts.
   2. His victories, implied in the expression. The Lord strong and mighty in battle.
   3. His mediatorial title, The King of glory.
   4. His authoritative entrance into the holy place.

John Newton's "Messiah."

Verse 8. The mighty Hero. His pedigree, his power, his battles, his victories.

Verse 10. The sovereignty and glory of God in Christ.

PSALM 25

SERMON OUTLINES AND HELPFUL TIPS

Verse 1. Heavenly machinery for uplifting an earthbound soul.

Verse 1. Genuine devotion described and commended.

Verse 2. The soul at anchor, and the two rocks from which it would be delivered.

Verse 3. Shame out of place and in place.

Verse 4. Practical divinity the best study; God the best teacher; Prayer the mode of entrance into the school.

Verses 4-5. Shew. Teach. Lead. Three classes in the school of grace.

Verse 5.

1. Sanctification desired.
2. Knowledge sought.
3. Assurance enjoyed.
4. Patience exercised.

Verse 5. *Thou art the God of my salvation.* A rich and overflowing text.

Verse 5 (*last clause*). How to spend the day with God. *Matthew Henry.*

Verse 6. The antiquity of mercy.

Verses 6-7. The Three Remembers.

Verse 7 (*first clause*). The best Act of Oblivion. *Thomas Fuller.*

Verse 7. Oblivion desired and remembrance entreated. Note "*my*", and "*thy.*"

Verse 8. Opposing attributes working together. God teaching sinners—a great wonder.

Verse 9. The meek. Who are they? What are their privileges? How to be like them?

Verse 9 (*first clause*). Moral purity needful to a well-balanced judgment.

Verse 10. God's mercy and faithfulness in providence, and the persons who may derive comfort therefrom.

Verse 11. A model prayer. Confession, argument, entreaty, etc.

Verse 11. Great guilt no obstacle to the pardon of the returning sinner. *Jonathan Edwards.*

Verse 12. Holiness the best security for a well ordered life. Free will at school, questioned and instructed.

Verse 13. A man at ease for time and eternity.

Verse 14. 1. A secret, and who know it.
2. A wonder, and who see it.

Verse 15. 1. What we are like. A silly bird.

2. What is our danger? "Net."

3. Who is our friend? "The Lord."

4. What is our wisdom? "Mine eyes," etc.

Verse 16. A desolate soul seeking heavenly company, and an afflicted spirit crying for divine mercy. Our God the balm of all our wounds.

Verses 16-18. David is a petitioner as well as a sufferer; and those sorrows will never injure us that bring us near to God. Three things he prays for:—1. *Deliverance.* This we are called to desire, consistently with resignation to the divine will.

2. *Notice.* A kind look from God is desirable at any time in any circumstances; but in affliction and pain, it is like life from the dead.

3. *Pardon.* Trials are apt to revive a sense of guilt. *William Jay.*

Verse 18. Two things are here taught us:

1. That a kind look from God is very desirable in affliction:

    (a) It is a look of special observation;

    (b) It is a look of tender compassion;

    (c) It is a look of support and assistance (with God, power and compassion go together).

2. The sweetest cordial under trouble would be an assurance of divine forgiveness:

    (a) Because trouble is very apt to bring our sins to remembrance;

    (b) Because a sense of pardon will in great measure remove all distressing fears of death and judgment.

Improvement 1. Let us adore the goodness of God, that one so great and glorious should bestow a Favorable look upon any of our sinful race.

Improvement 2. Let the benefit we have received from the Lord's looking upon us in *former* afflictions, engage us to *pray,* and encourage us to *hope,* that he will now look upon us again.

3. If a kind look from God be so comfortable, what must *heaven* be! *Samuel Lavington.*

Verse 18. 1. It is well when our sorrows remind us of our sins.

2. When we are as earnest to be forgiven as to be delivered.

3. When we bring both to the right place in prayer.

4. When we are submissive about our sorrows—"*Look,*"etc.—but very explicit about our sins—"*forgive,*" etc.

Verse 19. The spiritual enemies of the saint. Their number, malice, craft, power, etc.

Verse 20. Soul preservation. 1. Its twofold character, "Keep, "and "deli**Verse**"

2. Its dreadful alternative, "Let me not be ashamed."

3. Its effectual guarantee, "I put my trust in thee."

Verse 20. A superhuman keeping, a natural fear, a spiritual trust.

Verse 21. The open way of safety in action, and the secret way of safety in devotion.

Verse 22. Jacob's life, as typical of ours, may illustrate this prayer.

Verse 22. A prayer for the church militant.

PSALM 26

SERMON OUTLINES AND HELPFUL TIPS

Verse 1.

1. *Two inseparable companions*—faith and holiness.

2. *The blessedness of the man who possesses them.* He needs not fear the judgment, nor the danger of the way.

3. *The only means of procuring them.*

Verse 1. (*last sentence*). The upholding power of trust in God.

Verse 2. *Divine examinations.* Their variety, severity, searching nature, accuracy, certainty: when to be desired, and when to be dreaded.

Verse 3. Delight for the eyes and safety for the feet; or the good man's sweet contemplation and holy practice; or the heavenly compound of godliness—motive, and motion, enjoying and acting, love and truth, free grace and good works.

Verse 3. *Thy lovingkindness is before mine eyes.* It might be well to follow David and to keep the lovingkindness of God before *our* eyes. This should be done in four ways:

1. As a subject of contemplation.
2. As the source of encouragement.
3. As an incitement to praise.
4. As an example for imitation.
—*William Jay.*

Verse 4. *Vain persons.* Who they are. Why they are to be avoided. What will become of them. *Dissemblers.* Describe this numerous family. Show what their objects are. The mischief done to believers by their craftiness. The need of shunning them, and their fearful end.

Verse 5. *Bad company.* Cases of its evil results, excuses for it answered, warnings given, motives urged for relinquishing.

Verse 6. The necessity of personal holiness in order to acceptable worship.

Verse 7. 1. The believer's calling—a publisher.

2. The author selected, and the quality of his works. "*Thy wondrous works.*"

3. The mode of advertising—"voice of thanksgiving", "tell", etc.

Verse 8. God's house. Why we love it. What we love in it. How we show our love. How our love will be rewarded.

Verse 9. See "Spurgeon's Sermons, "No. 524. "The Saints' Horror at the Sinners' Hell."

Verse 11. The best men needing redemption and mercy; or the outward walk before men, and the secret walk with God.

Verse 12. Secure standing, honored position, grateful praise.

Verse 12 (*last clause*). Congregational Psalmody, and our personal share in it.

PSALM 27

SERMON OUTLINES AND HELPFUL TIPS

Verse 1. (*first clause*). The relation of illumination to salvation, or the need of light if men would be saved.

Verse 1. The Christian hero, and the secret springs of his courage.

Verse 1. The believer's fearless challenge.

Verse 2. The character, number, power, and cruelty of the enemies of the church, and the mysterious way in which they have been defeated.

Verse 3. Christian peace.

1. Exhibited in the calm foresight of trouble.

2. Displayed in the confident endurance of affliction.

3. Sustained by divine help and past experience Ps 27:1-2.

4. Producing the richest results, glory to God, etc.

Verse 4. Model Christian life.

1. Unity of desire.
2. Earnestness of action.
3. Nearness of communion.
4. Heavenliness of contemplation.
5. Progress in divine education.

Verse 4. The affection of moral esteem towards God. *Thomas Chalmers.*

Verse 4. A breathing after God. *R. Sibbes's Sermon.*

Verse 4. (*last clause*). Sabbath occupations and heavenly delights.

Verse 4. (*final clause*). Matters for enquiry in the Temple of old opened up in the light of the New Testament.

Verse 6. The saint's present triumph over his spiritual foes, his practical gratitude, and his vocal praises.

Verse 7. Prayer. To whom addressed? How? *Cry*, etc. When? *Left indefinite.* On what is it based? *Mercy.* What it needs? *Hear, answer.*

Verse 8. The heart in tune with its God. Note, the promptness, heartiness, personality, unreservedness, accuracy, and resolution of the response to the precept.

Verse 8. The successful seeker. *R. Sibbe's Sermon.*

Verse 8. The echo. See Spurgeon's Sermons. No. 767.

Verse 9.

1. Desertion deprecated in all its forms.
2. Experience pleaded.
3. Divine aid implored.

Verse 9. The horror of saints at the hell of sinners. *James Scot.*

Verse 10. The portion of the orphan, the comfort of the persecuted, the paradise of the departing.

Verse 11. The plain man's pathway desired, described, divinely approved, "*thy way*", "*a plain way*", and divinely taught, "*teach me, O Lord,* ""*lead me.*"

Verse 13. Faith, its precedence of sight, its objects, its sustaining power.

Verse 13. Believing to see. See Spurgeon's Sermons. No. 766.

Verse 14. The believer's position," *wait;*" his condition, "*good courage;*" his support," *he shall,*" etc.; his perseverance, "*wait*" repeated a second time; his reward.

PSALM 28

SERMON OUTLINES AND HELPFUL TIPS

Verse 1. *(first clause).* A sinner's wise resolution in the hour of despondency.

Verse 1. The saint's fear of becoming like the ungodly.

Verse 1. God's silence—what terror may lie in it.

Verse 1. *(last clause).* How low a soul may sink when God hides his face.

Verses 1-2. Prayer.

1. *Its nature — a "cry":*
   - (a) The utterance of life,
   - (b) The expression of pain,
   - (c) The pleading of need,
   - (d) The voice of deep earnestness.

2. *Its object —* "*O Lord, my rock.*" God as our Foundation, Refuge, and immutable Friend.

3. *Its aim —* "*Hear,*" "*Be not silent.*" We expect an answer, a clear and manifest answer, a speedy answer, a suitable answer, an effectual answer.

4. *Its medium —* "*Towards thy holy oracle.*" Our Lord Jesus, the true mercy seat, etc.

Verse 3. The characters to be avoided, the doom to be dreaded, the grace to keep us from both.

Verse 4. Measure for measure, or punishment proportioned to desert.

Verse 4. Endeavour the measure of sin rather than mere result. Hence some are guilty of sins which they were unable to commit.

Verse 5. Culpable negligence constantly persisted in, losing much blessing, and involving terrible condemnation.

Verse 6. Answered prayers, a retrospect and song.

Verse 7. The heart's possessions, confidence, experience, joy, and music.

Verse 7. Adoring God for his mercies. 1. What God is to the believer.

2. What should be the disposition of our hearts towards him. — *C. Simeon.*

Verse 8. All power given to believers because of their union with Jesus.

Verse 9. "A prayer for the church militant." See Exposition and Spurgeon's Sermons, No. 768.

PSALM 29

SERMON OUTLINES AND HELPFUL TIPS

Verse 1. The duty of ascribing our strength and the Honor of it to God; the penalty of neglecting to do so; the pleasure of so doing.

Verse 1. National glorying should be in the Lord.

Verse 2. (*first clause*). Royal dues, the royal treasury, loyal subjects paying their dues, the king receiving them. Smugglers and preventive men.

Verse 2. (*second clause*). Inspired ritualism. What to do? *Worship.* Whom? *The Lord.* How? *In the beauty of holiness.* Absence of all allusions to place, time, order, words, form, vestments, etc.

Verse 3. God's voice heard in trouble and above trouble, or in great personal and national calamities.

Verse 4. Power and majesty of the gospel. Illustrate by succeeding **Verse**s.

Verse 4. (*last clause*). "The majestic voice." See Spurgeon's Sermons, No. 87.

Verse 5. The breaking power of the gospel.

Verse 6. The unsettling power of the gospel.

Verse 7. The fire which goes with the word. This is a wide subject.

Verse 8. The arousing and alarming of godless places by the preaching of the word.

Verse 9. The revealing power of the word of God in the secrets of man's heart, and its regenerating force.

Verse 9 (*last clause*).

1. Matchless temple.
2. Unanimous worship.
3. Forcible motive.
4. General enthusiasm, "*glory.*"

Verse 10. The ever present and undisturbed government of God.

Verse 11. The twin blessings from the same source; their connection, and their consummation.

Verse 11. The two wills, the two blessings, the one people, the one Lord.

PSALM 30

SERMON OUTLINES AND HELPFUL TIPS

Title. House dedication, and how to arrange it.

Whole Psalm. In this ode we may see the workings of David's mind before, and under, and after, the affliction.

1. *Before* the affliction: Ps 30:6.
2. *Under* the affliction: Ps 30:7-10.
3. *After* the affliction: Ps 30:11-12.
—William Jay.

Verse 1. (*first clause*). God and his people exalting each other.

Verse 1. (*second clause*). The happiness of being preserved so as not to be the scorn of our enemies.

Verse 1. The disappointment of the devil.

Verse 2. The sick man, the physician, the night bell, the medicine, and the cure; or, a covenant God, a sick saint, a crying heart, a healing hand.

Verse 3. *Upbringing and preservation,* two choice mercies; made the more illustrious by two terrible evils, *grave,* and *pit*; traced immediately to the Lord, *thou hast.*

Verse 4. *Song,* a sacred service; *saints* especially called to it; *divine holiness,* a choice subject for it; *Memory,* an admirable aid in it.

Verse 5. The anger of God in relation to his people.

Verse 5. *The night of weeping, and the morning of joy.*

Verse 5. *Life* in God's *Favor.*

Verse 5. The transient nature of the believer's trouble, and the permanence of his joy.

Verse 6. The peculiar dangers of *prosperity*.

Verses 6-12. David's prosperity had lulled him into a state of undue security; God sent him this affliction to rouse him from it. The successive frames of his mind are here clearly marked; and must successively be considered as they are here presented to our view.

1. His carnal security.
2. His spiritual dereliction.
3. His fervent prayers.
4. His speedy recovery.
5. His grateful acknowledgments.
— Charles Simeon.

Verse 7. (*first clause*). Carnal security; its causes, dangers, and cures.

Verse 7. (*last clause*). The gracious bemoanings of a soul in spiritual darkness.

Verse 8., in connection with **Verse** 3 *prayer the universal remedy.*

Verse 9. (*first clause*). Arguments with God for continued life and renewed Favor.

Verse 9. (*last clause*). The resurrection, a time in which the *dust* shall *praise* God, and *declare* his *truth*.

Verse 10. Two gems of prayer; short, but full and needful.

Verse 10. *Lord, be thou my helper.* I see many fall; I shall fall too except thou hold me up. I am weak; I am exposed to temptation. My heart is deceitful. My enemies are strong. I cannot trust in man; I dare not trust in myself. The grace I have received will not keep me without thee. *Lord, be thou my helper.* In every duty; in every conflict; in every trial; in every effort to promote the Lord's cause; in every season of prosperity; in every hour we live, this short and inspired prayer is suitable. May it flow from our hearts, be often on our lips, and be answered in our experience. For if the Lord help us, there is no duty which we cannot perform; there is no foe which we cannot overcome; there is no difficulty which we cannot surmount. *James Smith's Daily Remembrancer.*

Verse 11. *Transformations.* Sudden; complete; divine, *thou;* personal, "*for me;* "gracious.

Verse 11. *Holy dancing:* open up the metaphor.

Verse 11. The believer's change of raiment: illustrate by life of Mordecai or Joseph; mention all the garbs the believer is made to wear, as a mourner, a beggar, a criminal, &c.

Verse 12. Our *glory*, and its relation to God's glory.

Verse 12. The end of gracious dispensations.

Verse 12. Silence—when sinful.

Verse 12. (*last clause*). The believer's vow and the time for making it. See the whole Psalm.

PSALM 31

SERMON OUTLINES AND HELPFUL TIPS

Verse 1. Faith expressed, confusion deprecated, deliverance sought.

Verse 1. (*first clause*). *Open avowal of faith.*

1. Duties which precede it, self-examination, etc.

2. Modes of making the confession.

3. Conduct incumbent on those who have made the profession.

Verse 1. (*last clause*). How far the righteousness of God is involved in the salvation of a believer.

Verse 2. (*first clause*). God's hearing prayer a great condescension.

Verse 2 (*second clause*). How far we may be urgent with God as to time.

Verses 2-3 (*last and first clauses*). That which we have we may yet seek for.

Verses 2-3. (*last and first clauses*). That which we have we may yet seek for.

Verse 3. Work out the metaphor of God as a rocky fastness of the soul.

Verse 3. (*last clause*).

1. A blessing needed, *lead me*.

2. A blessing obtainable.

3. An argument for its being granted, *for thy name's sake*.

Verse 4. *The rescue of the ensnared.*

1. The fowlers.
2. The laying of the net.
3. The capture of the bird.
4. The cry of the captive.
5. The rescue.

Verse 4. (*last clause*). The weak one girt with omnipotence.

Verse 5.

1. Dying, in a saint's account, is a difficult work.

2. The children of God, when considering themselves as dying, are chiefly concerned for their departing immortal spirits.

3. Such having chosen God for their God, have abundant encouragement when dying, to commit their departing spirits into his hand, with hopes of their being safe and happy forever with him. — *Daniel Wilcox.*

Verse 5. The believer's requiem. Redemption the foundation of our repose in God.

1. What we do — *commit ourselves to God.*

2. What God has done — *redeemed us.*

Verse 6. Holy detestation, as a virtue discriminated from bigotry: or, the good hater.

Verse 7.

1. An endearing attribute rejoiced in.

2. An interesting experience related.

3. A directly personal Favor from God delighted in.

Verse 7. (*centre clause*). *Consider* the measure, the effects, the time, the tempering, the ending, and the recompense.

Verse 7. (*last clause*). The Lord's familiarity with his afflicted.

Verse 8. Christian liberty, a theme for gladness.

Verse 9. The mourner's lament.

Verse 9. (*last clause*). Excessive sorrow, its injurious effects on the body, the understanding, and the spiritual nature. Sin of it, cure of it.

Verses 9-10. The sick man's moan, a reminder to those who enjoy good health.

Verses 9-10. The sick man's moan, a reminder to those who enjoy good health.

Verse 10. *My strength faileth because of mine iniquity.* The weakening influence of sin.

Verse 11.. The good man evil spoken of.

Verses 12-15.

Forgot as those who in the grave abide,
And as a broken vessel past repair,
Slandered by many, fear on every side.
Who counsel take and would my life ensnare.
But, Lord, my hopes on thee are fixed: I said,
Thou art my God, my days are in thy hand;
Against my furious foes oppose thy aid,
And those who persecute my soul withstand.
— *George Sandys.*

Verse 12. The world's treatment of its best friends.

Verse 14. Faith peculiarly glorious in season of great trial.

Verse 15. The believer the peculiar care of providence.

Verse 15. (*first clause*).

1. The character of the earthly experience of the saints, "My times, "that is, the changes I shall pass through, etc.

2. The advantage of this variety.

    (a) Changes reveal the various aspects of the Christian character.
    (b) Changes strengthen the Christian character.
    (c) Changes lead us to admire an unchanging God.

3. Comfort for all seasons.

    (a) This implies the changes of life are subject to the divine control.
    (b) That God will support his people under them.
    (c) And, consequently, they shall result in our being abundantly profited.

4. The deportment which should characterize us. Courageous devotion to God in times of persecution; resignation and contentment in times of poverty and suffering; zeal and hope in times of labor. – *From Stems and Twigs, or Sermon Framework.*

Verse 16. A sense of divine Favor.

1. Its value.
2. How to lose it.
3. How to obtain a renewal of it.
4. How to retain it.

The heavenly servant's best reward.

Verse 16. (*last clause*). A prayer for saints in all stages. Note its object, *save me*; and its plea, *Thy mercies' sake*. Suitable to the penitent, the sick, the doubting, the tried, the advanced believer, the dying saint.

Verse 17. The shame and silence of the wicked in eternity. The silence of the grave, its grave eloquence.

Verse 19. See "Spurgeon's Sermons," No. 773." David's Holy Wonder at the Lord's Great Goodness."

Verse 20. The believer preserved from the sneers of arrogance by a sense of the divine presence, and kept from the bitterness of slander by the glory of the King whom he serves.

Verse 21. *Marvelous kindness.* Marvelous that it should come to me in such a way, at such a time, in such a measure, for so long.

Verse 21. Memorable events in life to be observed, recorded, meditated on, repeated, made the subject of gratitude, and the ground of confidence.

Verse 22. Unbelief confessed and faithfulness adored. The mischief of hasty speeches.

Verse 23. An exhortation to love the Lord.

1. The matter of it, *love the Lord.*

2. To whom addressed, *all ye his saints.*

3. By whom spoken.

4. With what arguments supported, *for the Lord preserveth*, etc.

Verse 24. Holy courage. Its excellences, difficulties, encouragements, and triumphs.

PSALM 32

SERMON OUTLINES AND HELPFUL TIPS

Verse 1. Gospel benedictions. Take the first Psalm with thirty-second, show the doctrinal and practical harmoniously blended. Or, take the first, the thirty-second, and the forty-first, and show how we go from reading the word, to feeling its power, and thence to living charitably towards men.

Verse 1. *Evangelical Blessedness.*

1. The original condition of its possessor.
2. The nature of the benefit received.
3. The channel by which it came.
4. The means by which it may be obtained by us.

Verses 1-2. The nature of sin and the modes of pardon.

Verse 2. Non imputation, a remarkable doctrine.—Prove, explain, and improve it.

Verse 2. *No guile.* The honesty of heart of the pardoned man.

Verse 3. *Retention of our griefs to ourselves.* Natural tendency of timidity and despair; danger of it; means of divulging grief; encouragements to do so; the blessed person who is ready to hear confession. The silent mourner the greatest sufferer.

Verses 3-4. "Terrible Conviction and Gentle Drawings." See "Spurgeon's Sermons, "No. 313.

Verse 4. The sorrows of a convinced soul. Daily, nightly, from God, heavy, weakening, destroying.

Verse 4. (*last clause*) Spiritual drought.

Verse 5. The gracious results of a full confession; or, confession and absolution scripturally explained.

Verse 6. The *godly* man's picture, drawn with a Scripture pencil. *Thomas Watson.*

Verse 6. The experience of one, the encouragement of all.

Verse 6. (*first clause*).—The day of grace, how to improve it.

Verse 6. (*whole* **Verse**).—Pardon of sin the guarantee that other mercies shall be given.

Verse 6. (*last clause*).—Imminent troubles, eminent deliverances.

Verse 6. (*last clause*).—The felicity of the faithful. *Thomas Playfere.*

Verse 7. Danger felt, refuge known, possession claimed, joy experienced.

Verse 7. (*first sentence*).—Christ, a hiding place from sin, Satan, and sorrow, in death and at judgment.

Verse 7. (*second sentence*).—Troubles from which saints shall be preserved.

Verse 7. (*last sentence*).—The circle of song—who draws the circle, what is the circumference, who is in the centre.

Verse 7. *Songs of deliverance.* From guilt, hell, death, enemies, doubts, temptations, accidents, plots, etc. The divine schoolmaster, his pupils, their lessons, their chastisements and their rewards.

Verse 8. The power of the eye. *Henry Melvill.* In which he vainly tries to prove infant baptism and episcopacy, which he admits are not expressly taught in Scripture, but declares them to be hinted at as with the divine eye.

Verse 9. God's bits and bridles, the mules who need them, and reasons why we ought not to be of the number.

Verse 9. How far in our actions we are better, and how far worse than horses and mules.

Verse 10. The many sorrows which result from sin. The encompassing mercy of the believer's life even in his most troublesome times. The portion of the wicked, and the lot of the faithful.

Verse 11. A believer's gladness. *Its spring,* "in the Lord; " *its vivacity,* "shout; " *its propriety,* it is commanded; *its beautiful results and its abundant reasons.*

Verse 11. *Upright in heart,* an instructive description. Not horizontal or grovelling, nor bent, nor inclined, but vertical in heart.

PSALM 33

SERMON OUTLINES AND HELPFUL TIPS

Whole Psalm. This Psalm is *Eucharistic:* the contents are:

1. *An exhortation to praise God* Ps 33:1-3.

2. The *arguments* to enforce the duty Ps 33:4-19.

3. The *confidence* of God's people in his name, their happiness, and petition Ps 33:20-22.

—Adam Clarke.

Verse 1. Rejoicing—the soul of praise; the Lord—a wellspring of joy. Character—indispensable to true enjoyment.

Verse 1. (*last clause*). Praise comely. What? Vocal, meditative, habitual praise. Why? It is comely as wings to an angel, we mount with it; as flowers to a tree, it is our fruit; as a robe to a priest, it is our office; as long hair to a woman, it is our beauty; as a crown to a king, it is our highest Honor. When? Evermore, but chiefly amid blasphemy, persecution, sickness, poverty, death. Whom? Not from the ungodly, hypocritical, or thoughtless. To be without praise is to miss our comeliest adornment.

Verse 2. Instrumental music. Is it lawful? Is it expedient? If so, its uses, limits, and laws. A sermon to improve congregational music.

Verse 3. (*first clause*). The duty of maintaining the freshness of our devotions. Freshness, skill, and heartiness, to be combined in our congregational psalmody.

Verse 4. God's word and works, their rightness, and agreement, and our view of both.

Verse 4. (*first clause*). The word doctrinal, preceptive, historical, prophetic, promissory, and experimental, always right, *i.e.,* free from error or evil.

Verse 4. (*second clause*). God's work of creation, providence, and grace, always in conformity with truth. His hatred of everything like a sham.

Verses 4-5. A fourfold argument for praise, from the *truth,* the *faithfulness* the *justice,* and *goodness* of God:

1. *For the word of the Lord is right.*
2. *All his works are done in truth.*
3. *He loveth righteousness and judgment.*
4. *The earth is full of his goodness.*
—Adam Clarke.

Verse 5. Justice and goodness equally conspicuous in the divine action.

Verse 5. (*last clause*). A matchless theme for an observant eye and an eloquent tongue.

Verse 6. The power of the Word and the Spirit in the old and new creations.

Verse 7. God's control of destructive and reconstructive agencies.

Verse 7. The storehouses of the Great Husbandman.

Verse 8. Reasons for universal worship, obstacles to it, future prospects of it, our duty in relation to it.

Verse 8. (*last clause*). Awe—the soul of worship.

Verse 9. *The irresistible word of Jehovah* in creation, in calling his people, in their comfort and deliverance, in their entrance to glory.

Verse 10. Educated and philosophical heathen within the reach of missions.

Verses 10-11. The opposing counsels.

Verse 11. The eternity, immutability, efficiency, and wisdom of the divine decrees. God's purposes, "the thoughts of his heart," hence their wisdom, and yet more their love.

Verse 12. Two elections made by a blessed people and a gracious God, and their happy result. The happiness of the church of God. God's delight in his people, and their delight in him.

Verse 13. Omniscience and its lessons.

Verses 13-15. The doctrine of providence.

Verse 15. God's acquaintance with men hearts, and his estimate of their actions. The similarity of human nature.

Verses 16-18. The fallacy of human trust, and the security of faith in God.

Verse 18. Hoping in the mercy of God—false and true forms distinguished.

Verse 18.

1. The eyes of God's *knowledge* are upon them.
2. The eyes of his *affection* are upon them.
3. The eyes of his *providence* are upon them.
—*William Jay.*

Verse 19. Life in famine, natural and spiritual, especially a famine of inward hope and legal satisfaction.

Verse 20. *Waiting for the Lord,* includes:

1. Conviction—a persuasion that the Lord is the supreme good.
2. Desire—it is expressed by hungering and thirsting after righteousness.
3. Hope.

4. Patience—God is never slack concerning his promise.
—*William Jay.*

Verse 20. (*first clause*). The believer's hourly position.

Verse 21. Joy, the outflow of faith.

Verse 22. A prayer for believers only.

Verse 22. Measure for measure, or mercy proportioned to faith.

PSALM 34

SERMON OUTLINES AND HELPFUL TIPS

Verse 1. Firm resolution, serious difficulties in carrying it out, helps for its performance, excellent consequences of so doing. Six questions.—*Who?* "I." *What?* "Will bless." *Whom?* "The Lord." *When?* "At all times." *How? Why?*

Verse 1. Direction for making a heaven below.

Verse 2. The commendable boaster and his gratified audience. We may boast of the Lord, in himself, his manifestations of himself, his relationship to us, our interest in him, our expectations from him, etc. The duty of believers to relate their experience for the benefit of others.

Verse 3. Invitation to united praise.

Verse 3. *Magnifying*—or making great the work of God, a noble exercise.

Verse 4. *Confessions of a ransomed soul.* Simple, Honoring to God, exclude merit, and encourage others to seek also.

Verse 4. *Four stages,* "fears," "sought," "heard," "delivered."

Verse 5. The power of a faith look.

Verse 6.

1. The poor man's heritage, "troubles."
2. The poor man's friend.
3. The poor man's cry.
4. The poor man's salvation.

Verse 6. The poor man's wealth.

The position of prayer in the economy of grace, or the natural history of mercy in the soul.

Verse 7. *Castra angelorum, salvatio bonorum.*

Verse 7. The ministry of angels. In what sense Jesus is "The angel of the Lord."

Verse 8. Experience the only true test of religious truth.

Verse 8. *Taste.* The sanctified palate, the *recherche* provision, the gratified verdict, the celestial host.

Verse 9. The blest estate of a God fearing man.

Verse 9. Fear expelling fear. *Similia similibus curantur.*

Verse 10. Lions lacking, but the children satisfied. See "Spurgeon's Sermons, "No. 65.

1. Description of a true Christian, "seek the Lord."
2. The promise set forth by a contract.
3. The promise fulfilled.

Verse 10. What is a good thing?

Verse 11. A royal teacher, his youthful disciples, his mode of instruction, "Come; "his choice subject.

Verse 11. Sunday school work.

Verses 12-14. How to make the best of both worlds.

Verse 13. Sins of the tongue—their mischief, their cause, and their cure.

Verse 14. (*first clause*). The relation between the negative and positive virtues.

Verse 14. (*second clause*). *The royal hunt.* The game, the difficulties of the chase, the hunters, their methods, and their rewards.

Verse 15. Our observant God. Eyes and ears both set on us.

Verse 16. The evil man checkmated in life, and forgotten in death.

Verse 17. *Afflictions and their threefold blessing.*

1. They make us pray.

2. They bring us the Lord's hearing ear.

3. They afford room for joyful experience of deliverance.

Verse 18. The nearness of God to broken hearts, and the certainty of their salvation.

Verse 19. Black and white, or bane and antidote. Special people, special trials, special deliverances, special faith as a duty.

Verse 20. The real safety of a believer when in great perils. His soul, his spiritual life, his faith, hope, love, etc.; his interest in Jesus, his adoption, justification, these all kept.

Verse 21. Wickedness, its own executioner, illustrated by scriptural cases, by history, by the lost in hell. Lessons from the solemn fact. The forlorn condition of a man of malicious spirit.

Verses 21-22. Who shall and who shall not be desolate.

Verse 22. *Redemption* in its various meanings; *faith* in its universal preservation; *the Lord* in his unrivalled glory in the work of grace.

PSALM 35

SERMON OUTLINES AND HELPFUL TIPS

Verse 1. Jesus our Advocate and Champion; our friend in the courts of heaven and the battles of earth.

Verse 2. Jesus armed as the defender of the faithful.

Verse 3. Enemies kept at arm's length. How the Lord does this, and the blessedness of it to us.

Verse 3. (*last clause*). Full assurance. An assurance positive, personal, spiritual, present, divine, complete, coming by a word from God.

Verse 3. (*last clause*). Heaven made sure. *Thomas Adams' Sermon.*

Verse 4. The everlasting confusion of the devil.

Verse 5. Let them be as chaff before the wind. They were swift enough to attack, let them be as swift to flee. Let their own fears and the alarms of their consciences unman them so that the least breeze of trouble shall carry them hither and thither. Ungodly men are worthless in character, and light in their behavior, being destitute of solidity and fixedness; it is but just that those that make themselves chaff should be treated as such. When this imprecation is fulfilled in graceless men, they will find it an awful thing to be forever without rest, without peace of mind, or stay of soul, hurried from fear to fear, and from misery to misery. *And let the angel of the Lord chase them.* Fallen angels shall haunt them, good angels shall afflict them. To be pursued by avenging spirits will be the lot of those who delight in persecution. Observe the whole scene as the psalmist sketches it: the furious foe is first held at bay, then turned back, then driven to headlong flight, and chased by fiery messengers from whom there is no escape, while his pathway becomes dark and dangerous, and his destruction overwhelming.

Verse 6. The horrible pilgrimage of the ungodly.

Verse 6. The trinity of dangers in the pathway of the wicked, their way dark with ignorance, and slippery with temptation, while behind them is the avenger.

Verse 8. Destruction at unawares, an awful topic.

Verse 9. Joy in God and in his salvation.

Verse 10. A matchless God, and his matchless grace—these are the themes. An experienced heart, thoroughly quickened—this is the songster; and from this cometh matchless music. The music of a shattered harp.

Verse 11. The meanness, cruelty, sinfulness, and commonness of slander.

Verse 12. How a soul may be robbed.

Verse 13. Christian sympathy even for the froward.

Verse 13. (*last clause*). Personal benefit of intercessory prayer.

Verses 13-14. Compassion to the sick. *C. Simeon.*

Verse 15. The shameful conspiracy of men against our Lord Jesus at his passion.

Verse 17. *The limit of divine endurance.* Reference: The Treasury of David, by Charles Haddon Spurgeon. Published by Guardian Press, 1976, Vol. II, Page 173.

Verse 18. "*I will give thee thanks in the great congregation.*" Notable deliverances must be recorded, and their fame emblazoned. All the saints should be informed of the Lord's goodness. The theme is worthy of the largest assembly, the experience of a believer is a subject fit for an assembled universe to hear of. Most men publish their griefs, good men should proclaim their mercies. ["I will praise thee among much people."] Among friends and foes will I glorify the God of my salvation. Praise—personal praise, public praise, perpetual praise—should be the daily revenue of the King of heaven. Thus, for the second time, David's prayer ends in praise, as indeed all prayers should. Reference: The Treasury of David, by Charles Haddon Spurgeon. Published by Guardian Press, 1976, Vol. II, Page 159.

Verse 18. *The duty, blessedness, and seasonableness of public praise.* Reference: The Treasury of David, by Charles Haddon Spurgeon. Published by Guardian Press, 1976, Vol. II, Page 173.

Verse 19. He earnestly prays that as they have no cause for their enmity, they may have no cause for triumph either in his folly, sin, or overthrow. ["Neither let them wink with the eye that hate me without a cause."] The winking of the eye was the low-bred sign of congratulation at the ruin of their victim, and it may also have been one of their scornful gestures as they gazed upon him whom they despised. To cause hatred is the mark of the wicked, to suffer it causelessly is the lot of the righteous. God is the natural Protector of all who are wronged, and he is the enemy of all oppressors. Reference: The Treasury of David, by Charles Haddon Spurgeon. Published by Guardian Press, 1976, Vol. II, Page 160.

Verse 22. Omniscience pleaded, a word sought for, presence requested, action entreated, affiance urged as a claim. Reference: The Treasury of David, by Charles Haddon Spurgeon. Published by Guardian Press, 1976, Vol. II, Page 173.

Verse 25. The ungodly man's delight, and the righteous, man's refuge. Reference: The Treasury of David, by Charles Haddon Spurgeon. Published by Guardian Press, 1976, Vol. II, Page 173.

Verse 26. The convict dress of the wicked - ["clothed with shame,"] etc. Reference: The Treasury of David, by Charles Haddon Spurgeon. Published by Guardian Press, 1976, Vol. II, Page 173.

Verse 27 (last clause). What is that prosperity in which the Lord hath pleasure? Reference: The Treasury of David, by Charles Haddon Spurgeon. Published by Guardian Press, 1976, Vol. II, Page 173.

Verse 28. A blessed theme, a fitting tongue, an endless speech.

PSALM 36

SERMON OUTLINES AND HELPFUL TIPS

Verse 1. What is the fear of God? How does it operate? What is the effect of its absence? What should we learn from seeing such evil results? Or the atheism underlying transgression.

Verse 2. The arts, motives, assistances, results, and punishments of self-flattery, and the discovery which concludes it.

Verse 2. Self-flatteries. *Jonathan Edwards' Sermon.*

Verse 2. On the deceitfulness of the heart, with regard to the commission of sin. *Two Sermons, in Jamieson's "Sermons on the Heart."*

Verse 3. Bad words. Two out of many kinds.

Verse 3. (*second clause*). The relation between true wisdom and practical goodness.

Verse 4. Diligence in doing evil, a mark of deep depravity. *W.S. Plumer.*

Verse 4. The abuse of retirement to wicked purposes, a sure characteristic of an habitual sinner. *N. Marshall.*

Verse 4. The sinner on his bed, in his conduct, in his heart; and to this, in his death, and in his doom.

Verse 4. (*second clause*). Ways which are not good.

Verse 4. (*last clause*). Neutrality condemned.

Verses 5-6. Four glorious similes of the mercy, faithfulness, and providence of God. The preacher has here a wealth of poetic imagery never surpassed.

Verse 6. God's word and works mysterious. *C. Simeon.*

Verse 6. (*second clause*). God's judgments are—

1. Often unfathomable—we cannot discover the foundation or cause, and spring of them.

2. They are safe sailing. Ships never strike on rocks out in the great deeps.

3. They conceal great treasure.

4. They work much good—the great deep, though ignorance thinks it to be all waste, a salt and barren wilderness, is one of the greatest blessings to this round world.

5. They become a highway of communion with God. The sea is today the great highway of the world.

Verse 6. (*last clause*). Kindness of God to the lower animals, as well as man.

Verse 7. The object, reasons, nature, and experience of faith.

Verses 7-8. Admiration! Confidence! Expectation! Realisation!

Verse 8. (*first clause*). *The provisions of the Lord's house.* What they are, their excellence and abundance, and for whom provided.

Verse 8. (*second clause*). *The heavenly Hiddekel*—Its source, its flood, the happy drinkers, how they came to drink.

Verse 9. (*first clause*). LIFE, natural, mental, spiritual, proceeds from God, is sustained, restored, purified, and perfected by him. In him it dwells with permanency, from him it flows freely, with freshness, abundance, and purity; to him it should be consecrated.

Verse 9. (*second clause*). LIGHT, what it is to see it. *Divine* light, what it is; how it is the medium by which we see other light. The experience here described, and the duty here hinted at.

Verse 10.

1. *The character of the righteous*—he knows God, and is upright in heart.

2. *His privilege*—lovingkindness and righteousness.

3. *His prayer*, continue, etc.

Verse 10. The need of daily supplies of grace.

Verse 12. A view of the overthrow of evil powers, principles, and men.

PSALM 37

SERMON OUTLINES AND HELPFUL TIPS

Verse 1. The art of tranquillity. *W. Jones.*

Verses 1-2. A frequent temptation, and a double corrective—a sight of sinners in death and hell.

Verse 2. How and when the wicked perish.

Verse 3.

1. A combination descriptive of holy living.

2. A combination descriptive of happy living.

Verse 3. The believer portrayed.

1. His object of trust.

2. His mode of life.

3. His place of abode.

4. His certainty of provision.

Verse 3. (*last clause*). Read it in four ways.

1. "Certainly fed, "or the certainty of supply.

2. "Fed in verity, "or the sufficiency of the provision for soul and body.

3. "Fed on truth, "or the spirituality of the provision.

4. "Feed on truth, "or the duty of choosing such provision.

Verse 4. Explain the delight and the desire of the believer, and show the connection between them.

Verses 5-6. The higher life.

1. Based on hearty resignation.

2. Sustained by faith.

3. Constantly unfolded by the Lord.

4. Consummated in meridian splendor.

Verses 5-6. The higher life.

1. Based on hearty resignation.

2. Sustained by faith.

3. Constantly unfolded by the Lord.

4. Consummated in meridian splendor.

Verse 6. Sweet comfort for slandered saints. Where their character now is. Who shall reveal it. The gradual yet sure manner of the revelation, and the glorious conclusion.

Verse 7. *Rest in the Lord.* What? Where? When? Why? How?

Verse 7. Peace, patience, self-possession.

Verse 7. Stillness in God. *Bishop Wilberforce.*

Verse 7. *Rest in the Lord.*

1. Rest in the *will* of God, for whatever he wills is for your good, your highest good.

2. Rest in the *love* of God, and often meditate on the words of Jesus on this point, "Thou hast loved them as thou hast loved me."

3. Rest in the *mercy* of God.

4. Rest in the *word* of God.

5. Rest in the *relation* thy God fills to thee; he is the Father.

6. Rest in the Lord as he is manifested in Jesus, thy God *in covenant*.

James Smith.

Verse 8. A SERMON FOR THE FRETFUL.

1. *Cease* from present anger. It is madness, it is sin; it shuts out our prayers; it will grow into malice; it may lead to worse.

2. *Forsake it* for the future. Repent of it, watch temper, discipline thy passions, etc.

3. *Avoid* all kindred feelings of fretfulness, impatience, envy, etc., for they lead to evil.

Verse 9. How the humble are the true lords of the land.

Verse 10.

1. Consider what the departed sinner has left. Possessions, joys, Honors, aims, hopes, etc.

2. Consider where he has gone.

3. Consider whether you will share the same lot.

Verses 10-11. Terror to the wicked: comfort for believers. *A. Farindon.*

Verse 11. The meek man's delight, or "the harvest of a quiet eye."

Verse 14. *Upright conversation.*

1. What it excludes. The horizontal or earthly, the crooked or crafty, the slanting or sinister.

2. What it includes. Motive, object, language, action.

3. What it achieves. It stands like a pillar; it supports like a column; it ascends like a tower; it adorns like a monument; it illuminates like a Pharos.

Verse 15. The self-destructive nature of evil.

Verse 16. How to make much of a little.

Verses 16-17.

1. The owners contrasted.

2. The possessions compared.

3. The preference given.

4. The reasons declared.

Verse 17. (*last clause*).

1. The Favored persons.

2. Their evident need, "upholding."

3. Their singular blessedness, "upheld, "above trial, under trial, after trial.

4. Their august Patron.

Verse 18. The comforts derivable from a consideration of the divine knowledge. The eternity of the righteous man's possessions.

Verse 18.

1. The *persons,* "the upright."

2. The *period,* "their days." These are known to God. (1) He knows them *kindly* and *graciously;* (2) He knows their *number;* (3) He knows the *nature* of them.

3. The *portion,* "their inheritance shall be forever."

—William Jay.

Verse 18 (*last clause*). What it is. How they come by it. How long they hold it.

Verse 19. Good words for hard times.

Verse 21. Monetary transactions tests of character.

Verse 22. The divine blessing the secret of happiness. The divine displeasure the essence of misery.

Verses 23-24.

1. The divine predestination.
2. The divine delight.
3. The divine support.

Verse 24. Temporary trials.

1. To be expected.
2. Have their limit.
3. Have their results.
4. Our secret comfort under them.

What may be. What cannot be. What shall be.

Verse 25. Memorandum of an aged observer.

Verse 26. The righteous man's merciful disposition, generous action, and rich reward.

Verse 26. The benediction of the good man's family: what it is, and what it is not.

Verse 27. Negative, positive, remunerative.

Verse 28.

1. The Lord's love of right.

2. His faithfulness to the righteous.

3. Their sure preservation thus doubly guaranteed.

4. The doom of the wicked thus certified.

Verse 29. Canaan as a type of the righteous man's inheritance.

Verse 30. *Our speech* as a test of godliness.

Verse 31.

1. The best thing.
2. In the best place.
3. With the best of results.

Verses 32-33. Our enemies; their inveterate malice; our safeguard and justification.

Verse 34.

1. A twofold admonition: (a) *Wait on the Lord.* (b) *And keep his way;* wait and work, wait and walk, get grace and exercise it.

2. A twofold promise: (a) *He shall exalt thee to inherit the land;* God is the source of all elevation and Honor. (b) *When the wicked are cut off, thou shalt see it;* and they will be cut off. *William Jay.*

Verse 34. Patient faith, persevering holiness, and promised exaltation.

Verse 34 (*last clause*). Emotions caused in the godly by a sight of the sinner's doom.

Verse 34. (*last clause*). The wicked are often cut off 1. Even *in life*, from their places, and riches, and prospects. 2. At *death* they are cut off from all their possessions and comforts. 3. In *the last day* they will be cut off from "the resurrection of life." *William Jay.*

Verses 35-37. Three memorable scenes.

1. The imposing spectacle.
2. The astounding disappearance.
3. The delightful exit.

Verses 35-37. Three memorable scenes.

1. The imposing spectacle.
2. The astounding disappearance.
3. The delightful exit.

Verses 39-40.

1. The doctrines of grace condensed.

2. The experience of the gracious epitomized.

3. The promises of grace summarized.

4. The grandest evidence of grace declared: *because they trust in him.*

PSALM 38

SERMON OUTLINES AND HELPFUL TIPS

TITLE. The art of memory. Holy memorabilia. The usefulness of sacred remembrance.

Verse 1. The rebuke of God's wrath.

1. Richly deserved.
2. Reasonably dreaded.
3. Earnestly deprecated.
— *B. Davies.*

Verse 1. The evil consequences of sin in this world. *J. J. Blunt.*

Verse 1. The bitterest of bitters, *thy wrath;* why deprecated; and how escaped.

Verse 2. God sharply chasteneth many of his children, and yet for all that he loves them never a whit the less, nor withholdeth in good time his mercy from them. *Thomas Wilcocks.*

Verse 3. (*last clause*). Sin causes *unrest.* He who cures it alone gives rest. Dwell on both facts.

Verse 4. (*first clause*). Sin in its relations to us. To the *eye* pleasing. To the *heart* disappointing. In the *bones* vexing. Over the *head* overwhelming.

Verse 4. The confession of an awakened sinner.

Verse 4. (*last clause*). Sin.

1. Heavy — *a burden.*
2. Very heavy — *A heavy burden.*
3. Superlatively heavy — *too heavy for me.*
4. Not immoveable, for though too heavy *for me,* yet Jesus bore it.

Verse 5. *Foolishness.* The folly of sin. Everything that a man has to do with sin shows his folly.

1. Dallying with sin.
2. Committing it.
3. Continuing in it.
4. Hiding it.
5. Palliating it.
— *B. Davies.*

Verse 6. Conviction of sin. Its grief, its depth, its continuance.

Verse 6. *I go mourning.*

1. Unlawful reasons for mourning.
2. Legitimate themes for sorrow.
3. Valuable alleviations of grief.

Verse 9. The many desires of God's children: the fact that God understands them even when unexpressed; and the certainty that he will grant them.

Verse 9. Omniscience, a source of consolation to the desponding.

Verse 13. The wisdom, dignity, power, and difficulty of silence.

Verse 15. Prayer, the offspring of hope. Hope strengthened by confidence in God's answering prayer.

Verse 17. Mr. Ready to halt. His pedigree, and infirmity; his crutches, and his cure; his history, and safe departure.

Verse 18. The excellence of penitent confession.

Verse 18. The twin children of grace—confession and contrition: their mutual revelation and reaction.

Verse 18. (*last clause*). There is good reason for such sorrow, God is well pleased with it. It benefits the mourner.

Verse 19. The terrible energy and industry of the powers of evil.

Verse 22. Faith tried, faith trembling, faith crying, faith grasping, faith conquering.

PSALM 39

SERMON OUTLINES AND HELPFUL TIPS

Verses 1-2. I was dumb, etc.

1. **There is a time to be silent**. He had been enabled to do this when reproached and unjustly accused by others. He did it for good; others might attribute it to sullenness, or pride, or timidity, or conscious guilt; but he did it for good. Breathe upon a polished mirror and it will evaporate and leave it brighter than before; endeavor to wipe it off, and the mark will remain.

2. **There is a time to meditate in silence**. The greater the silence without, often the greater commotion within. "*His heart was hot.*" The more he thought, the warmer he grew. The fire of pity and compassion, the fire of love, the fire of holy zeal burned within him.

3. **There is a time to speak**. "*Then spake I.*" The time to speak is when the truth is clear and strong in the mind, and the feeling of the truth is burning in the heart. The emotions burst forth as from a volcano. Jer 20:8-9. The language should always be a faithful representation of the mind and the heart. *G. Rogers, Tutor of the Metropolitan Tabernacle College.*

Verse 2. There is a sevenfold silence.

1. A *stoical* silence.
2. A *politic* silence.
3. A *foolish* silence.
4. A *sullen* silence.
5. A *forced* silence.
6. A *despairing* silence.
7. A *prudent*, a *holy*, a *gracious* silence.
—Thomas Brooks' "Mute Christian."

Verse 4. *Make me to know mine end.*

1. *What we may desire to know about our end.* Not its *date, place, circumstances,* but

   (a). *Its nature.* Will it be the end of saint or sinner?

   (b). *Its certainty.*

   (c). *Its nearness.*

   (d). *Its issues.*

   (e). *Its requirements.* In the shape of attention, preparation, passport.

2. *Why ask God to make us know it?* Because *the* knowledge is important, difficult to acquire, and can be *effectually imparted by the Lord only. W. Jackson.*

Verse 4. David prays,

1. That he may be enabled continually to keep in view the end of life: all things should be judged by their *end*. "Then understood I their end." Life may be Honorable, and cheerful, and virtuous here; but the *end!* What will it be?

2. That he may be diligent in the performance of all the duties of this life. The measure of his days, how short, how much to be done, how little time to do it in!

3. He prays that he may gain much instruction and benefit from the frailties of life. *That I may know,* etc. My frailties may make me more humble, more diligent, while I am able for active service; more dependent upon divine strength, more patient and submissive to the divine will, more ripe for heaven. —G. Rogers.

Verse 5. (*last clause*). Man is vanity, *i.e.,* he is mortal, he is mutable. Observe how emphatically this truth is expressed here.

1. *Every* man is vanity, without exception, high and low, rich and poor.

2. He is so at his *best estate;* when he is young, and strong, and healthful, in wealth and honor, etc.

3. He is *altogether* vanity, as vain as you can imagine.

4. *Verily* he is so.

5. *Selah* is annexed, as a note commanding observation. —Matthew Henry.

Verse 6. The vanity of man, as mortal, is here instanced in three things, and the vanity of each shown.

1. The vanity of our joys and honors: *Surely every man walketh in a vain show.*

2. The vanity of our griefs and fears: *Surely they are disquieted in vain.*

3. The vanity of our cares and toils: *He heapeth up riches, and knoweth not who shall gather them.* —Matthew Henry.

Verse 6. The world's trinity consists, 1. In fruitless honors: what appears to them to be substantial honors are but *a vain show.* 2. In needless cares. *They are disquieted in vain.* Imaginary cares are substituted for real ones. 3. In useless riches; such as yield no lasting satisfaction to themselves, or in their descent to others. *G. Rogers.*

Verse 7. *What wait I for?* 1. *For what salvation as a sinner?* Of works or grace—from Sinai or Calvary? 2. *For what consolation as a sufferer?* Earthly or heavenly? 3. *For what supply as a suppliant?* Meager or bountiful? Present or future? 4. *For what communication as a servant?* Miraculous or ordinary? Pleasing or unacceptable? 5. *For what instruction as a pupil?* Mental or spiritual? Elating or humbling? Ornamental or useful? 6. *For what inheritance as an heir?* Sublunary or celestial? *W. Jackson.*

Verse 7.

1. An urgent occasion. *And now Lord,* etc. There are seasons that should lead us specially to look up to God, and say, *Now, Lord.* "Father, the hour is come."

2. A devout exclamation, *Now, Lord, what wait I for?* Where is my expectation? where my confidence? To whom shall I look? I am nothing, the world is nothing, all earthly sources of confidence and consolation fail: *What wait I for?* In life, in death, in a dying world, in a coming judgment, in an eternity at hand; what is it that I need? —G. Rogers.

Verse 8.

1. Prayer should be *general*: *Deliver me from all my transgressions.* We often need anew to say, "God be merciful to me a sinner." Afflictions should remind us of our sins. If we pray to be delivered from all transgressions, we are sure to be delivered from the one for which affliction was sent.

2. Prayer should be *particular*: *Make me not the reproach of the foolish.* Suffer me not so to speak or show impatience in affliction as to give occasion even to the foolish to blaspheme. The thought that many watch for our halting should be a preservative from sin. —G. Rogers.

Verse 9.

1. The *occasion* referred to. *I was dumb,* etc. We are not told what the particular trial was, that each one may apply it to his own affliction, and because all are to be viewed in the same light.

2. The *conduct* of the psalmist upon that particular occasion: *I opened not my mouth.* (a) Not in anger and rebellion against God in murmurs or complaints. (b) Not in impatience, or complaining, or angry feelings against men. (c) The *reason* he assigns for this conduct: *Because thou didst it. G. Rogers.*

Verse 10.

1. *Afflictions are sent by God. Thy strokes.* They are strokes of *his* hand, not of the rod of the law, but of the shepherd's rod. Every affliction is *his* stroke.

2. *Afflictions are removed by God. Remove.* He asks not for miracles, but that God in his own way, in the use of natural means, would interpose for his deliverance. We should seek his blessing upon the means employed for our deliverance both by ourselves and others. "*Cause to remove,* "etc.

3. *Afflictions have their end from God. I am consumed by the conflict,* etc. God hath a controversy with his people. It is a conflict between his will and their wills. The psalmist owns himself conquered and subdued in the struggle. We should be more anxious that this end should be accomplished than that the affliction should be removed, and when this is accomplished the affliction will be removed. *G. Rogers.*

Verse 10.

1. The *cause* of our trials: "*for iniquity.*" Oh, this trial is come to take away my comforts, my peace of mind, and the divine smile! No, this is all the fruit to take away their sin—the dross, none of the gold—sin, nothing but sin.

2. The *effect* of our trials. All that he counted desirable in this life, but not for his real good, is *consumed.* His robes which are beautiful in men's esteem are moth eaten, but the robe of righteousness upon his soul cannot decay.

3. The *design* of our trials. They are not penal inflictions, but friendly *rebukes* and fatherly *corrections.* On Christ our Surety the penal consequences were laid, upon us their paternal chastisements only.

4. The *reasonableness* of our trials. "*Surely every man is vanity.*" How in a world like this could any expect to be exempt from trials! The world is the same to the Christian as before, and his body is the same. He has a converted soul in an unconverted body, and how can he escape the external ills of life? *G. Rogers.*

Verse 12. David pleads the good impressions made upon him by his affliction.

1. It had set him a weeping.
2. It had set him a praying.
3. It had helped to wean him from the world.
— *Matthew Henry.*

Verse 12. (*last clause*). Am I a stranger and a sojourner with God? Let me realise, let me exemplify the condition.

1. Let me look for *the treatment* such characters commonly meet with.

2. And surely if any of my own nation be near me, I shall *be intimate with them.*

3. Let me *not be entangled* in the affairs of this life.

4. Let my affection be *set on things that are above,* and my conversation be always *in heaven.*

5. Let me be *not impatient for home;* but *prizing* it. —W. Jay.

Verse 13.

1. The *subject* of his petition—not that he may escape death and live always in this life, because he knows that he must go hence; but 1. That he may be recovered from his afflictions; and, 2. That he may continue longer in this life. Such a prayer is lawful when offered in submission to the will of God.

2. The *reasons* for this petition. 1. That he may remove by his future life, the calumnies that had been heaped upon him. 2. That he may have brighter evidences of his interest in the divine Favor. 3. That he may become a blessing to others, his family and nation. 4. That he might have greater peace and comfort in death; and, 5. That he might "have an entrance ministered more abundantly, "etc. —G. Rogers.

PSALM 40

SERMON OUTLINES AND HELPFUL TIPS

Verse 1.

1. *My part*—praying and waiting.
2. *God's part*—condescension and reply.

Verse 2.

1. The *depth* of God's goodness to his people. It finds them often in a horrible pit and miry clay. There is a certain spider which forms a pit in sand, and lies concealed at the bottom, in order to seize upon other insects that fall into it. Thus David's enemies tried to bring him into a pit.

2. The *height* of his goodness. He brought me out and set my feet upon a rock. That rock is Christ. Those feet are faith and hope.

3. The *breadth* of his goodness establisheth my *goings,* restored me to my former place in his love, showing me still to have been his during my low estate. He was the same to me, though I felt not the same to him. My goings refer both to the past and the future.

4. The *strength* of his goodness *established* my goings, making me stand firmer after every fall. — George Rogers.

Verses 2-3. The sinner's position by nature, and his rescue by grace.

Verses 2-3. By one and the same act the Lord works our salvation, our enemies' confusion, and the church's edification. *J. P. Lange's Commentary.*

Verse 3. The new song, the singer, the teacher.

Verse 4. (*last clause*).

1. Find out who turn aside to lies—Atheists, Papists, self-righteous, lovers of sin.

2. Show their folly in turning aside from God and truth, and in turning to fallacies which lead to death.

3. Show how to be preserved from the like folly, by choosing truth, truthful persons, and above all the service of God.

Verse 5.

1. *There are works of God in his people and for his people.* There are his works of creation, of providence, and of redemption, and also his works of grace, wrought in them by his Spirit, and around them by his providence, as well as for them by his Son.

2. *These are wonderful works;* wonderful in their variety, their tenderness, their adaptation to their need, their cooperation with outward means and their power.

3. *They are the result of the divine thoughts respecting us.* They come not by chance, not by men, but by the hand of God, and that hand is moved by his will, and that will by his thought respecting us. Every mercy, even the least, represents some kind thought in the mind of God respecting us. God thinks of each one of his people, and every moment.

4. They are innumerable. *They cannot be reckoned up.* Could we see all the mercies of God to us and his wonderful works wrought for us individually, they would be countless as the sands, and all these countless mercies represent countless thoughts in the mind and heart of God to each one of his people. —George Rogers.

Verse 5. The multitude of God's thoughts, and deeds of grace; beginning in eternity, continuing forever; and dealing with this life, heaven, hell, sin, angels, devils, and indeed all things.

Verse 6. Here David goes beyond himself, and speaks the language of David's Son. This was naturally suggested by God's wonderful works, and innumerable thoughts of love to man.

1. *The sacrifices that were not required.* These were the sacrifices and burnt offerings under the law. (a) When required? From Adam to the coming of Christ. (b) When not required? (c) Why required before? As types of the one method of redemption. (d) Why not now required? Because the great Antitype had come.

2. *The sacrifice that was required.* This was the sacrifice offered on Calvary. (a) It was required by God by his justice, his wisdom, his faithfulness, his love, his Honor, his glory. (b) It was required by man to give him salvation and confidence in that salvation. (c) It was required for the Honor of the moral government of God throughout the uni**Verse**.

3. *The person by whom this sacrifice was offered. Mine ears hast thou opened.* This is the language of Christ, prospectively denoting—(a) Knowledge of the sacrifice required. (b) Consecration of himself as a servant for that end. —George Rogers.

Verse 6. *Mine ears hast thou opened.* Readiness to hear, fixity of purpose, perfection of obedience, entireness of consecration.

Verses 6-8. The Lord gives an ear to hear his word, a mouth to confess it, a heart to love it, and power to keep it. —James Merrick, M.A., 1720-1769.

Verses 6-8. The Lord gives an ear to hear his word, a mouth to confess it, a heart to love it, and power to keep it.

Verse 7.

1. The time of Christ's coming. *Then said I.* When types were exhausted, when prophecies looked for their fulfillment, when worldly wisdom had done its utmost, when the world was almost entirely united under one empire, when the time appointed by the Father had come.

2. The design of his coming. *In the volume* was written—(a) The constitution of his person. (b) His teaching. (c) The manner of his life. (d) The design of his death. (e) His resurrection and ascension. (f) The kingdom he would establish.

3. The voluntariness of his coming, *Lo, I come*. Though sent by the Father, he came of his own accord. "Christ Jesus came into the world." Men do not come into the world, they are sent into it. *Lo, I come*, denotes pre-existence, pre-determination, pre-operation. —George Rogers.

Verses 6-8. The Lord gives an ear to hear his word, a mouth to confess it, a heart to love it, and power to keep it.

Verse 8. *To do thy will, O God.*

1. The will of God is seen in the fact of salvation. It has its origin in the will of God.

2. The will of God is seen in the plan of salvation. All things have proceeded, are proceeding, and will proceed according to that plan.

3. It is seen in the provision of salvation, in the appointment of his own Son to become the mediator the atoning sacrifice, the law fulfiller, the head of the church, that his plan required.

4. It is seen in the accomplishment of salvation.

Verse 9. Referring to our Lord; a great preacher, a great subject, a great congregation, and his great faithfulness in the work.

Verse 10. (*first clause*).

1. The righteousness *possessed* by God.
2. The righteousness *prescribed* by God.
3. The righteousness *provided* by God. *James Frame.*

Verse 10.

1. The preacher must reveal his whole message. 2. He must not conceal any part: (a) Not of the righteousness of the law or the gospel; (b) Not of the loving kindness of grace; (c) Not of any portion of the truth with flowers of rhetoric; (d) To give a partial representation; (e) To put one truth in the place of another; (f) To give the letter without the spirit. **G.R.**

Verse 10. The great sin of concealing what we know of God.

Verse 11. Enrichment and preservation sought. The true riches are from God, gifts of his sovereignty, fruits of his mercy, marked with his tenderness. The best preservations are divine love and faithfulness.

Verses 11-13. As an instance of clerical ingenuity, it may be well to mention that Canon Wordsworth has a sermon from these **Verses** upon "the duty of making responses in public prayer."

"Came at length the dreadful night.
Vengeance with its iron rod
Stood, and with collected might
Bruised the harmless Lamb of God,

> See, my soul, thy Savior see,
> Prostrate in Gethsemane!"

> "There my God bore all my guilt,
> This through grace can be believed;
> But the horrors which he felt
> Are too vast to be conceived.
> None can penetrate through thee,
> Doleful, dark Gethsemane."

> "Sins against a holy God;
> Sins against his righteous laws;
> Sins against his love, his blood;
> Sins against his name and cause;
> Sins immense as is the sea—
> Hide me, O Gethsemane!"

Verses 11-13. As an instance of clerical ingenuity, it may be well to mention that Canon Wordsworth has a sermon from these **Verse**s upon "the duty of making responses in public prayer."

Verse 12. Compare this with Ps 40:5. The number of our sins, and the number of his thoughts of love.

Verse 12. (*second clause*).

1. The soul arrested—"taken hold."
2. The soul bewildered—"cannot look up."
3. The soul's only refuge—prayer, Ps 40:13.

Verses 11-13. As an instance of clerical ingenuity, it may be well to mention that Canon Wordsworth has a sermon from these verses upon "the duty of making responses in public prayer."

Verse 13.

1. The language of believing prayer—deliver me, help me; looking for deliverance and help to God only.

2. Of earnest prayer—make haste to help me.

3. Of submissive prayer—be pleased, O Lord, if according to thy good pleasure.

4. Of consistent prayer. Help me, which implies efforts for his own deliverance, putting his own shoulder to the wheel.

Verse 14. *Honi soit mal y pense;* or, the reward of malignity.

Verse 16. (*last clause*). An everyday saying. Who can use it? What does it mean? Why should *they* say it? Why say it continually?

Verse 17. The humble *But,* and the believing *Yet.* The little *I am,* and the great *Thou art.* The fitting prayer.

Verse 17. *The Lord thinketh upon me.* Admire the condescension, and then consider that this is—

1. A promised blessing.

2. A practical blessing—he thinks upon us to supply, protect, direct, sanctify, &c.

3. A precious blessing—kind thoughts, continual, greatly good. He thinks of us as his creatures with pity, as his children with love, as his friends with pleasure.

4. A present blessing—promises, providences, visitations of grace.

Verse 17.

1. The less we think of ourselves the more God will think upon us.

2. The less we put trust in ourselves the more we may trust in God for help and deliverance.

3. The less delay in prayer and active efforts the sooner God will appear for us.

PSALM 41

SERMON OUTLINES AND HELPFUL TIPS

Verse 1. (*first clause*). The incidental blessings resulting from considering the pious poor.

1. We learn gratitude.

2. We see patience.

3. We often remark the triumphs of great grace.

4. We obtain light on Christian experience.

5. We have their prayers.

6. We feel the pleasure of beneficence.

7. We enter into communion with the lowly Savior.

Verse 1. The support of the Small pox Hospitals recommended. *Bishop Squire*, 1760. Scores of sermons of this kind have been preached from this text.

Verse 2. *Blessed upon the earth.* What blessings of an earthly character godly character secures, and in general what it is to be blessed with regard to this life.

Verse 2. (*second clause*). What it is to be delivered *in* trouble. From impatience, from despair, from sinful expedients, from violent attacks, from losing fellowship with God.

Verse 3. Strength in weakness. Inward strength, divinely given, continuously sustained, enduring to the end, triumphant in death, glorifying to God, proving the reality of grace, winning others to the faith.

Verse 3. (*last clause*). The heavenly bed making.

Verse 4. (*first clause*). A saying worth repeating: *I said*. It expresses penitence, humility, earnestness, faith, importunity, fear of God, etc.

Verse 4. *Heal my soul.*

1. The hereditary disease, breaking out in many disorders—open sin, unbelief, decline of grace, etc.

2. Spiritual health struggling with it; shown in spiritual pain, desire, prayer, effort.

3. The well proved Physician. Has healed, and will, by his word, his blood, his Spirit, &c.

Verse 4. *I have sinned against thee.* This confession is personal, plain, without pretense of excuse, comprehensive and intelligent, for it reveals the very heart of sin—"against thee."

Verse 5. What we may expect. What our enemies desire. What we may therefore prize, *i.e.*, the power of Christian life and name. What we should do—tell the Lord all in prayer. What good will then come of the evil.

Verse 6. (*first clause*). The folly and sin of frivolous visits.

Verse 6. (*second and third clauses*). Like to like, or the way in which character draws its like to itself. The same subject might be treated under the title of *The Chiffonnier*, or the rag collector. What he gathers; where he puts it—in his *heart*; what he does with it; what he gets for it; and what will become of him.

Verses 7-12. On a sick bed a man discovers not only his enemies and his friends, but himself and his God, more intimately.

Verse 9. The treachery of Judas.

Verse 11. Deliverance from temptation a token of divine Favor.

Verse 12. This text reveals the insignia of those whom grace has distinguished.

1. Their integrity is manifest.

2. Their character is divinely sustained.

3. They dwell in the Favor of God.

4. Their position is stable and continues.

5. Their eternal future is secure.

Verse 13.

1. The object of praise—Jehovah, the covenant God.

2. The nature of the praise—without beginning or end.

3. Our participation in the praise—"Amen and Amen."

The ancient rabbis saw in the Five Books of the Psalter the image of the Five Books of the Law. This way of looking on the Psalms as a second Pentateuch, the echo of the first, passed over into the Christian church, and found Favor with some early fathers. It has commended itself to the acceptance of good recent expositors, like Dr. Delitzsch, who calls the Psalter "the congregation's fivefold word to the Lord, even as the *Thora* (the Law) is the Lord's fivefold word to the Congregation." This mat be mere fancy, but its existence from ancient times shows that the fivefold division attracted early notice. *William Binnie, D.D.*

God presented Israel with the Law, a Pentateuch, and grateful Israel responded with a Psalter, a Pentateuch of praise. *F.L.K.*

PSALM 42

SERMON OUTLINES AND HELPFUL TIPS

Verse 1. The longing heart and the panting hart compared.

Verses 1,2. Those who have enjoyed the presence of God in the public ordinances of religion will greatly desire, if deprived of them, to be favored with them again...Prevention from attending the public ordinances of God's house may be made the means of great benefit to the soul.

1. By renewing our relish for the provisions of the Lord's house, which so soon and so often palls.

2. By making us to prize the means of grace more highly. There is, through human degeneracy, a proneness to value things less, however excellent in themselves, because of their being common, or plentiful, or of easy attainment.

3. By driving us more directly from God. *H. March.*

Verses 1-3. The home sickness of the soul. What awakens it in the soul? To what is it directed, or does it point or tend? Wherewith can it be satisfied? By the bitter, but ofttimes wholesome food of tears. *J. P. Lange.*

Verses 1-2. Those who have enjoyed the presence of God in the public ordinances of religion will greatly desire, if deprived of them, to be Favored with them again...Prevention from attending the public ordinances of God's house may be

Verse 2.

1. What thirsts? "my soul."
2. For what? "for God."
3. In what way? "when shall I come."

Or, the cause, incentives, excellences, and privileges of spiritual thirst.

Verse 2. *(last clause).* The true view of public worship.

Verse 2. *(last clause).* Appearance before God here and hereafter. *Isaac Watts, D.D., Two Sermons.*

Verses 1-3. The home sickness of the soul. What awakens it in the soul? To what is it directed, or does it point or tend? Wherewith can it be satisfied? By the bitter, but ofttimes wholesome food of tears. *J. P. Lange.*

Verse 3. The believer's Lent, and its salt meats.

1. What causes the sorrow?
2. What will remove it?
3. What benefit will come of it?

Verses 3, 10. The carriage of David's enemies.

1. The *nature* of it, and that was *reproach*.

2. The *expression* of it, *They say unto me*.

3. The *constancy* of it: *daily*, or, *all the day long*.

4. The *specification* of it, in a scornful and opprobrious question: *Where is (now) thy God?* Thomas Horton.

Verse 4.

1. It is common for the mind, in seasons of sorrow, to seek relief from the present in recollections of the past.

2. In recollections of past enjoyments, those that relate to social worship will be peculiarly dear to the servant of God.

3. Man is a social being, hence he derives help from united worship.

Verse 4. *I pour out my soul in me.* The uselessness of mistrustful introspection.

Verse 4. *I had gone with the multitude,* etc. Company, if it be that which is good, is a very blessed and comfortable accommodation in sundry respects.

1. It is an exercise of men's faculties, and the powers and abilities of the mind.

2. It is a fence against danger, and a preservative against sadness and various temptations.

3. An opportunity of doing more good. *Thomas Horton.*

Verse 4. *I had gone,* etc. Sunny memories, their lessons of gratitude and hope.

Verse 4. *(last clause).* Not Chaucer's tales of the Canterbury pilgrims, but David's tales of the Jerusalem pilgrims.

Verse 4. *With the voice,* etc. Congregational singing defended, extolled, discriminated, and urged.

Verse 5. Sorrow put to the question, or the Consolatory Catechism.

Verse 5. The sweetness, safety, and rightness of hope *in* God. Good grip for the anchor.

Verse 5. The music of the future, *I shall yet praise him.*

Verse 5. *The help of his countenance,* or the sustaining power of God's presence.

Verse 5. *Why art thou cast down?*

1. The mind, even of a holy man, may be unduly cast down and disquieted.

2. In cases of undue dejection and disquietude, the proper remedy is to expostulate with the soul, and to direct it to the *only true source* of relief.

3. Expostulation with the soul in times of distress, is then productive of its proper end, when it leads to an immediate application to God. *H. March.*

Verse 5. An emphasis of *enquiry or examination;* David calls himself to account for his present passion and trouble of mind. An emphasis of *reproof or objurgation;* David chides and rebukes himself for his present distemper. "*Why art thou thus?*" *Thomas Horton.*

Verses 5, 11. or *help* and *health.*

Verse 6. *Remember thee.* The consolation derivable from thoughts of God.

Verse 6. *Therefore will I remember thee.* There are two ways of understanding this; each of them instructive and profitable...

1. It may be considered as an expression of *determined remembrance of God* should he ever be found in such places and conditions. Believers can suppose the worst, and yet hope for the best.

2. The language may be considered as an expression of *encouragement derived from reflection.* He had been in these situations and circumstances, and had experienced in them displays of divine providence and grace. *W. Jay.*

Verse 6. Ebenezers, many, varied, remembered, helpful.

Verse 7. *Deep calleth unto deep.* See Spurgeon's Sermons, No. 865.

Verse 7. *Deep calleth unto deep.* One evil inviting another.

1. The *variety* of evils—one evil to another.

2. The *conjunction* of evils—one evil with another.

3. The *connection* of evils, or dependence and mutual reference—one evil upon another. *T. Horton.*

Verse 7. The threefold depth which the saints and servants of God are subject to here in this life.

1. The depth of *temptation.*

2. The depth of *desertion.*

3. The depth of *affliction and human calamities. T. Horton.*

Verses 7, 8. In seasons of affliction the servants of God will be distinguished from others by their ready perception and acknowledgment of the hand of God in their trials. *H. March.*

Verse 8. Daily mercy and nightly song; the mercies of sunshine and shade.

Verse 8. *(last clause).* The blessed alternation between praise and prayer.

Verse 8. *God of my life.* Author, sustainer, comforter, object, crown, consummation.

Verse 8. *The God of my life.* There is a threefold life whereof we partake, and God is the God of each unto us. First, the life of *nature*; secondly, the life of *grace*; thirdly, the life of *glory*. T. Horton.

Verse 9. *God my rock.* Appellations of God, suited to circumstances.

Verse 9. *My rock.* See Keach in his metaphors.

Verse 9.

1. Why *thou?*

2. Why *I?*

3. Why *he?* It is a *why* to all three. To God, *Why has thou forgotten me?* To David himself, *Why do I go mourning?* To David's *adversary*, whoever he was, *Why does the enemy oppress me?* — T. Horton.

Verse 10. The most grievous of taunts.

Verse 11. *My God.*

1. It's a word of *interest* — *My God,* as in covenant with him.

2. A word of *compliance* — *My God,* as submitting to him.

3. A word of affection — *My God,* as taking delight, and rejoicing in him. T. Horton.

Verse 11. A catechism, a consolation, a commendation.

Verse 11.

1. David's *experience* of God. *He is the health*, or *help of my countenance.*

2. His *relation* to God, and *interest* in him — *And my God.* T. Horton.

PSALM 43

SERMON OUTLINES AND HELPFUL TIPS

Verse 1. We apply to God—

1. As our *Judge*: *Judge me.*

2. As our *Advocate*: *Plead my cause.*

3. As our *Deliverer*: *O deliver me.*

Verse 1. Popular opinion outweighed by divine approbation.

Verse 1. How the Lord pleads the cause of his people.

Verse 1. Deceit and injustice twin vipers; their origin, their character, their folly, their end.

Verses 1-2, 4-5. *Five mys:*

1. My cause—"*plead it.*"
2. My strength—"*thou art.*"
3. My joy—God is.
4. My soul—"*why disquieted.*"
5. My God.

Verse 3. *O send out thy light and thy truth.*

1. What is truth?

2. How truth is to be diffused.

3. Why it should be diffused.

4. Who must be the main agent of it. *Varied from Dr. Bogue.* 1800.

Verse 3. The blessings desired; the guidance sought; the end longed for.

Verse 3. Under what influence we should resort to divine worship.

Verse 4.

1. The good man's duty—expressed by *going to God.*

2. His *blessedness*—expressed by *rejoicing in God. Samuel Lavington.*

Verse 4. (*first clause*). When? *Then.* Where? *Altar of God.* Who? *I.* Why? *My exceeding joy.*

Verse 4. (*second clause*). It is God alone who can be an exceeding joy to his creatures. *W. Dunlop's Sermons.*

Verse 4. The joy of joy. The soul of soul joy.

Verse 4. The great object of public worship, its bliss, and the praise resulting from attaining it.

Verse 4.

1. *The medium of joy*, the altar of God, or God in Christ Jesus.

2. *The springs of joy*, or the attributes of God—mercy, justice, power, holiness, as seen in the atonement.

3. *The value of joy*, as comfort, strength, etc.

Verse 4. *God my exceeding joy.* A most rich and precious title.

Verse 4. *(last clause).* Possession, praise, resolution.

Verse 5. Discouragement's recovery. *R. Sibbes Sermons.*

Verse 5. *I shall yet praise him. I,* even *I; shall,* sooner or later, most assuredly; *yet,* despite troubles, foes, devils; *praise* with gratitude, confidence, exultation; *him* above all other helpers, though now afflicting me.

Verse 5. *Health of my countenance,* removing that which mars it—sin, shame, fear, care, sorrow, weakness, etc.

PSALM 44

SERMON OUTLINES AND HELPFUL TIPS

Verse 1. The encouraging traditions of church history. The days of yore.

Verse 1. The parent's duty, and the children's privilege.

Verse 1. Family conversation, the most profitable subject for it.

Verse 2. The contrast; or, the dealings of God with saints and sinners.

Verse 3. Free grace exalted.

1. In putting a negative upon human power.
2. In manifestations of divine energy.
3. In its secret source, *Because thou hadst a Favor unto them.*

Verse 3.

1. The creature laid low.
2. The Lord exalted.
3. Discriminating grace revealed.

Verse 3. *(last clause)*. The eternal well spring of all mercy.

Verse 4.

1. Divine royalty acknowledged.

2. Royal interposition entreated.

3. Divine covenant hinted at, *Jacob;* or, the loyal subject seeking royal aid for the royal seed.

Verse 4. Personal allegiance and pleading intercession.

Verse 4. *My King.* This intends—

1. My Ruler.
2. My Honor.
3. My Leader.
4. My Defender.

Verse 4. The deliverances of Jacob, illustrated by his eventful life.

Verse 5. Our enemies, their activity, the closeness of their approach, the certainty of their overthrow, the secret of our strength.

Verse 6. Relinquishment of outward trusts. *My bow* may miss its aim, may be broken, may be snatched away. *My sword* may snap, or grow blunt, or slip from my hold. We may not trust in our abilities, our experience, our shrewdness, our wealth, etc.

Verse 6. Self-renunciation—the duty of saint and sinner.

Verse 7. Accomplished salvation. How never achieved, *But.* By whom wrought, *thou.* When performed, *hast.* For whom, *us.* To what extent, *from our enemies.*

Verse 7. Salvation completed, hell confounded, Christ exalted.

Verse 8. Praise, its continuance—how to make it continual, how to manifest it perpetually, influence of its continuance, and reasons to compel us to abide in it.

Verse 9. A lament for the declension of the church.

Verse 9. In what sense God casts off his people, and why.

Verse 12. The human and divine estimate of the results of persecution.

Verse 12. In answer to this complaint.

1. God's people lose nothing eventually by their privations.

2. The wicked gain nothing by their triumphs.

3. God loses none of his glory in his dealings with either. —*George Rogers.*

Verse 13. Trial of cruel mockings; our conduct under them, comfort in them, and crown from them.

Verse 14. Unholy proverbs or godless bywords.

Verse 15. Confessions of a penitent.

Verse 17. The trial, truth, and triumph of the godly.

Verse 17. The faithful soul holding fast his integrity.

Verse 17. What it is to be false to our covenant with God.

Verse 18. *(first clause).* When we may be sure that our heart has not apostatised.

Verse 18.

1. The position of the heart in religion—it comes first.

2. The position of the outer moral life in religion—it follows the heart.

3. Necessity of the agreement of the two.

4. The need that both should be faithful to God.

Verse 18. Connection between the heart and the life, both in constancy and apostasy.

Verse 18. God's delight in the progress of the upright. *Thomas Brooks.*

Upright hearts will hold on in the ways of God, and in the ways of well doing, notwithstanding all afflictions, troubles, and discouragements, they meet withal. *Thomas Brooks.*

Verse 18. *Thy ways.* The ways of God are

(1) *righteous* ways;
(2) *blessed* ways;
(3) *soul refreshing* ways;
(4) *transcendent* ways—ways that transcend all other ways;
(5) *soul strengthening* ways; and
(6) sometimes *afflicted, perplexed,* and *persecuted* ways. — *Thomas Brooks.*

Verse 21. Can he not? Will he not?

Verse 21. A question and an assertion.

Verse 22.

1. Innocence in the midst of suffering, *sheep.*
2. Honor in the midst of shame, *for thy sake.* G. Rogers.

Verse 23. The cry of a church in sad circumstances. The complaint of a deserted soul.

Verse 24. Reasons for the withdrawal of divine comfort.

Verse 25. The great need, the great prayer, the great plea.

Verse 26. A fit prayer for souls under conviction, for saints under trial or persecution, and for the church under oppression or decay.

PSALM 45

SERMON OUTLINES AND HELPFUL TIPS

Verse 1. In the preface, the prophet commends the subject he is to treat of, signifying,

1. That it is *a good matter* — *good* as speaking of the Son of God, who is the *chief good*.

2. *Good for us*; for upon the marriage of Christ to his church depends our good. *Bishop Nicholson.*

Verse 1. Character read by heart writing.

1. The true lover of Christ is sincere — *my heart*?
2. He is a man of emotion.
3. A man of holy meditation.
4. A man of experience — *things I have made*.
5. A man who bears witness for his Lord.

Verse 1. Three things requisite for Christian teaching:

1. That the matter be good; and concerning the best of all subjects, *touching the King*.

2. That the language be fluent like the pen, etc. — (a) Partly from nature, (b) Partly from cultivation, (c) Partly from the Spirit of God.

3. That the heart be absorbed in it — *My heart is inditing*. G. R.

Verse 2. In what respects Jesus is fairer than the best of men.

Verse 2. Jesus — his person, his gospel, his fulness of blessing.

Verse 2.

1. We may and ought to praise Christ. Angels do, God does, Scripture does, Old Testament saints and New, so should we. It is the work of heaven begun on earth.

2. For what should we praise him? (a) For his beauty. Is wisdom beauty? Is righteousness? Is love? Is meekness? All are found in him supremely — "All human beauties, all divine, In our Redeemer meet and shine." (b) For his grace. Grace of God treasured up in him.

3. For his blessedness — of God and forever. **G.R.**

Verses 2-5. In these **Verses** the Lord Jesus is presented,

1. As most amiable in himself.
2. As the great Favorite of heaven.
3. As victorious over his enemies.
— *Matthew Henry.*

Verses 3-5. Messiah's victory predicted and desired. *E. Payson's Sermon.*

Verse 5.

1. Arrows of judicial wrath are sharp.

2. Arrows of providential goodness are sharper still.

3. Arrows of subduing grace are sharpest of all. The quiver of the Almighty is full of these arrows. *G.R.*

Verse 5. Arrows—what they are; whose they are; whom they strike; where they strike; what they do; and what follows.

Verse 6. The God, the King, his throne, its duration, his sceptre. Let us worship, obey, trust, acquiesce, rejoice.

Verses 6-7. Empire, Eternity, Equity, Establishment, Exultation.

Verse 7. *Thou hatest wickedness.* He hated it when it assailed him in his temptation, hated it in others, denounced it, died to slay it, will come to condemn it.

Verse 7. Christ's love and hate.

Verse 8. Christ's garments—his offices, his two natures, his ordinances, his Honors, all are full of fragrance.

Verse 8. *Whereby they have made thee glad.* We make Jesus glad by our love, our praise, our service, our gifts, our holiness, our fellowship with him.

Verse 8.

1. The odor of his garments, not of blood and battle, but of sweet perfume.

2. The splendor of his palaces—ivory for rareness, purity, durability, etc.

3. The source of his delight. (a) Himself, the sweet odor of his own graces. (b) His people, the savor of those who are saved. (c) His enemies, "even in them that perish." (d) All holy happy creatures who unite to make him glad. *G.R.*

Verses 9-10. The connections of the Bridegroom are to be remembered, those of the Bride to be forgotten.

Verse 10. "Christ the best husband: or, an earnest invitation to young women to come and see Christ." *George Whitefield's "Sermon, Preached to a Society of Young Women, in Fetter Lane."*

Verse 11. *So shall the king greatly desire thy beauty.* Christ delighting in the Beauty of the Righteous. *Martin Luther.* (Select Works, by H. Cole. I. 281.)

Verses 13-15.

1. The Bride's *new name*—"The king's daughter." She is the king's daughter for two reasons. (a) She is *born* of God; and (b) She is *espoused* to the Son of God.

2. The Bride's *character*—"All glorious within." (a) Because *Christ reigns on the throne of her heart.* (b) Because *she is the temple of the Holy Ghost.*

3. The Bride's *raiment*—"wrought gold, " "needlework:" this is the *righteousness of Christ;* in other words, His *perfect obedience,* and His *atoning death.*

4. The Bride's *companion*—"Virgins that follow her."

5. The Bride's *home going*—"She shall be brought unto the king in raiment of needlework...With gladness and rejoicing shall they be brought: they shall enter into the king's palace." (a) *She shall see the king in his beauty.* (b) *There will be an open declaration of his love to her before all worlds.* Duncan Macgregor, M.A.

Verse 17.

1. Christ is the Father's delight. "*I will make,* "etc.
2. He is the church's theme—his name shall be remembered; and
3. He is heaven's glory, "Shall praise thee, "etc. **G.R.**

PSALM 46

SERMON OUTLINES AND HELPFUL TIPS

Verse 1. The song of faith in troubled times.

1. *Our refuge.* Our only, impregnable, accessible, delightful place of retreat is our God.

2. *Our strength.* Our all sufficient, unconquerable, honorable, and emboldening strength is our God.

3. *Our help.* Ever near, sympathizing, faithful, real, and potent is our God.

Verse 1. *A very present help in trouble.* Religion never so valuable as in seasons of trouble, sickness, and death. God is present helping us to bear trouble, to improve it, and to survive it. Present by gracious communications and sweet manifestations; present most when he seems absent, restraining, overruling, and sanctifying trouble. Trust and wait. *James Smith.*

Verse 2. The reasons, advantages, and glory of holy courage.

Verses 2-3.

1. The great and many causes for fear.

    (a) What might come—mountains, waters, etc., persecution, pestilence, etc.

    (b) What must come—afflictions, death, judgment.

2. The great and one cause for not fearing. Fearlessness under such circumstances should be well grounded. God himself is our refuge, and we confiding in him are fearless. *G. Rogers.*

Verse 4. Glad tidings in sad times; or, the city of God in the times of trouble and confusion, watered with the river of consolation. *Ralph Erskine.*

Verse 4. What can this *river* be but that blessed covenant to which David himself repaired in the time of trouble? ...And what are *the streams* of this river, but the outgoings and effects of this divine constitution?

1. The blood of Jesus.
2. The influences of the Holy Spirit.
3. The doctrines and promises of the gospel.
4. The ordinances of religion.
5. All the means of grace. *W. Jay.*

Verse 4. *Make glad the city of God.* There are four ways in which the streams of a river would gladden the citizens.

1. The first regards *prospect.*
2. The second regards *traffic.*
3. The third regards *fertility.*
4. The fourth regards *supply. W. Jay.*

Verse 4. *City of God.* The church may be called "the city *of God*" because, 1. He dwells in it (see Ps 44:5). 2. He *founded* it and *built* it. 3. It derives all *privileges* and *immunities* from him. 4. He is the chief Ruler or Governor there. 5. It is his property. 6. He draws the *rent* of it. *Ralph Erskine.*

Verses 4-5. To the church, Joy, Establishment, Deliverance.

Verse 6. What man did and what God did.

Verse 8. *Behold the works of the Lord.*

1. They are worth beholding, for they are like himself; well becoming his infinite power, wisdom, justice,

2. Our eyes were given us for this very purpose—not for the beholding of vanity, not for the ensnaring or wounding of the soul; but for the use and Honor of the Creator.

3. The Lord delights to have his works beheld; he knows their excellency and perfection, and that the more they are seen and noted the more Honor will accrue to the Maker of them.

4. None but we can do it; there is great reason then that we should carefully *behold,* etc.

5. This shall be of great benefit to ourselves. *Bishop Hall.*

Verse 8. The desolations of the Lord, the consolation of his saints.

1. A declaration of what has happened.

2. A promise of what shall be achieved. *Spurgeon's Sermons, No. 190.*

Verse 9. The Great Peacemaker, or the principle of the gospel our only hope, for the total abolition of war.

Verse 10. *Be still, and know that I am God.* The sole consideration that God is God, sufficient to still all objections to his sovereignty. *Jonathan Edwards.*

Verse 10. *I am God.* 1. In that he is God, he is an absolutely and infinitely *perfect* being. 2. As he is God, he is so *great,* that he is infinitely above all comprehension. 3. As he is God, all things are his *own.* 4. In that he is God, he is *worthy* to be sovereign over all things. 5. In that he is God, he *will* be sovereign, and *will* act as such. 6. In that he is God, he is able to *avenge* himself on those who oppose his sovereignty. *Jonathan Edwards.*

PSALM 47

SERMON OUTLINES AND HELPFUL TIPS

Verse 1. Unusual and enthusiastic expressions of joy when justifiable and even desirable.

Verses 1-4. Joy the true spirit of worship.

1. Joy in God's character.
2. In his reign.
3. In the triumphs of his gospel.
4. In his Favor to his saints.

Verse 2. The terrors of the Lord viewed by faith as a subject of joy.

Verse 2 (*second clause*). The universal reign of Christ as it is and is to be.

Verse 3. The hope of victory to the church. What shall be subdued? By whose instrumentality? Us. By whose power? He. When shall it be accomplished? What is the token of it? The ascension, Ps 47:5.

Verse 3.

1. The final triumph of the saints. All enemies subdued under them in earth and hell, within and without—(a) gradually, (b) completely.

2. The power by which it is accomplished. He shall, etc.

    (a) Not without means.
    (b) Not by means only.
    (c) But by appointed means made potent by divine energy. G. R.

Verse 4. This comprehends time and eternity. It is a matter of fact, of holy acquiescence, of desire, of thankfulness.

Verse 4.
1. God is willing to choose our inheritance for us in time and eternity.
2. His choice is better than ours—the excellency of Jacob.
3. He will leave us to the consequences of our own choice.
4. He will help us in obtaining that which he chooses for us. G. R.

Verse 5. The ascension. Its publicity, solemnity, triumph, joy. Who went up. Where he went up. To what he went up. For what purpose. With what result.

Verse 6. The importance of holy song. The repetition rebukes our slackness, and implies that earnestness, frequency, delight, and universality should characterise the praises offered.

Verse 7 (*last clause*). The psalmody of the instructed, and instruction by psalmody; praise should be both the fruit and the vehicle of teaching.

Verse 8 (*last clause*). Divine sovereignty always connected with holiness.

Verse 8.

1. God has a throne of holiness, for which he is to be feared by all men.
2. A throne of grace, for which he is to be loved by his redeemed.
3. A throne of glory, for which he is to be praised by his whole creation.

Verse 9.

1. A shield is a *merciful* weapon, none more so.

2. A shield is a *venturous* weapon, a kind of surety, which bears the blows and receives the injuries which were intended for another.

3. A shield is a *strong* weapon, to repel the darts of wickedness and break them in pieces.

4. A shield is an honorable weapon, none more: taking away of shields was a sign of victory; preserving them a sign of glory.

5. Remember, a shield must ever *have an eye to guide it*—you the shields, the law the eye. *Bishop Reynolds.*

PSALM 48

SERMON OUTLINES AND HELPFUL TIPS

All the suggestions under this Psalm except those otherwise designated, are by our beloved friend, Rev. George Rogers, Tutor of the Pastor's College.

Verse 1.

1. *What the church is to God.*

   (a) His "*city:*" not a lawless rabble, but a well-organized community.

   (b) A mountain of holiness, for the display of justifying righteousness, of sanctifying grace.

2. *What God is to the church.*

   (a) Its inhabitant. It is *his* city, his mountain. There he is great. There was no room for the whole of God in Paradise, there is no room for him in his law, no room for him in the heaven of angels: in the church only is there room for all his perfections, for a triune Jehovah. Great everywhere, he is peculiarly great here.

   (b) The object of its praises. As he is greatest here, so are his praises, and through the universe on this account.

Verse 2.

1. *Was the ancient Zion beautiful for situation?* So is the New Testament church founded upon a rock, upon eternal purpose and grace.

2. *Was it the joy of the whole earth?* So the New Testament church will become.

3. *Was it the special joy of the tribes of Israel* that were almost entirely to the north of Jerusalem? So the church is to the saints.

4. *Was it a royal as well as a holy city?* So is the church. "Yet I have set, "etc.

Verse 3.

1. God is a refuge in his church. The church is a city of refuge, but the refuge is not in its church, but its God.

   (a) For sinners from wrath.

   (b) For saints from trials and fears.

   (c) God is there known as such, known to thousands, not known as such elsewhere. "They that know thy name, "etc.

Verses 4-7.

1. The opposition of worldly powers to the church. "The kings, "etc.

2. The manner in which they are subdued—by their own fears; conscience has persecuted those who have persecuted the church of God. They who have seized the ark of God have been glad to return it with an offering.

3. The completeness of their overthrow, As a fleet of ships of Tarshish, dispersed, broken, and engulfed by the east wind.

Verse 8.

1. God has ever been to his people what he now is; the same *heard* as *seen*.

2. He is now what he ever has been: the same *seen* as *heard*.

3. He will ever be what he now is. "Will establish it forever."

Verse 9.

1. What are the loving kindnesses of God? Pity to the wretched, pardon to the penitent, help to the prayerful, comfort to the afflicted, etc.

2. Where are they to be found? "In the midst of, "etc.

    (a) Here they are revealed.
    (b) Here they are dispensed.
    (c) Here they are sought.
    (d) Here they are enjoyed.

Verse 10. As the name of God, so his praises are—

1. Supreme.
2. Unqualified.
3. Universal.
4. Everlasting.

Verse 10. *Thy right hand,* etc.

1. The justice of omnipotence.
2. Omnipotence controlled by justice.
3. The omnipotence of justice.

Verse 11.

1. The subjects of his peoples' joy. Not mercies merely, but judgments

2. Reasons: (a) Because they are holy—needful to the purity of moral government; (b) Just—needful to vindicate law; (c) Good—needful for the greatest amount of good.

Verse 12.

1. What is to be understood by the preservation and protection of the church?

2. What is meant by searching into, and considering of, these causes and means of the church's preservation?

3. What are those causes and means of the church's preservation, those towers and bulwarks which will not fail?

4. What reason is there why we should thus search into and consider these causes of the church's preservation and protection?

5. What is the testimony which we have to give concerning this matter to the ensuing generation? *John Owen's Sermon.*

Verse 14. (*first clause*). This is the language of a *proprietary* in God: 1. Of an *assured* proprietary—"This God is *our* God." 2. Of a *permanent* proprietary—*forever and ever* 3. Of an *exulting* proprietary. *W. Jay.*

Verse 14.

1. The language of discrimination. *This* God. *This* God in Christ, in the church.

2. The language of Faith—*our* God.

3. Of Hope—*For ever and ever*

4. Of Resignation—*He will be our guide,* etc.

PSALM 49

SERMON OUTLINES AND HELPFUL TIPS

Verse 2.

1. The common needs of rich and poor men.
2. The common privileges of rich and poor saints.
3. Their common service.
4. Their common heaven.

Verse 3. The deep things of God are intended,

1. To exercise our minds to understand them.

2. To try our faith by believing them—"incline" implies a submissive mind.

3. To excite our joy as we grasp them—"upon the harp."

4. To employ our faculties in explaining them to others.

Verse 5.

1. The effects of our sin remain—(a) In ourselves, (b) In others.

2. In a time of conviction they *compass us about:* better to do so in this life, than to haunt us as ghosts for *ever.*

3. When they are pardoned we have nothing to fear. **G.R.**

Verse 7.

1. *Implied.* The soul needs redeeming.
2. *Denied.* Wealth, power, learning, none can redeem.
3. *Supplied*—a ransom by Jesus.
4. *Applied*—by the Spirit to our actual deliverance.

Verse 12. (*last clause*). Wherein the ungodly are like beasts, and wherein different.

Verse 12. Here is a twofold thwarting or crossing of the purposes of the ungodly worldling.

1. The first is, *he shall not be that which he ever wished to be:* he shall not continue in Honor.

2. The other is this, *he shall be that which he never desired to be:* he shall be like the beasts that die. He shall miss of that which he sought for, and he shall have that which he looked not for. — S. Hieron.

Verse 13.

1. In secular things men imitate the *wisdom* of others.

2. In spiritual things they imitate *their folly.* G. R.

Verse 14.

1. In proportion to the prosperity of the ungodly here, will be their misery hereafter: as sheep from the fat pasture led to the slaughterhouse.

2. In proportion to the luxury here, will be their corruption hereafter—*Death shall feed on them:* they have become well fed for death to feed on them.

3. In proportion to their dignity here, will be their degradation hereafter—*The upright shall have,* etc. Oh, what a contrast between the rich man and Lazarus then!

4. In proportion to their beauty here, will be their deformity hereafter. "Art thou become like one of us?" G. R.

Verse 14. Sheep, how far they image the wicked.

Verse 14. *In the morning.* See the various Biblical prophecies of what will happen "in the morning."

Verse 15.

1. *Return* to the dust I shall.
2. *Redeem* from the dust he will.
3. *Receive* into heaven he will.
4. *Rejoice* forever I shall.

Verse 17. The loaded and unloaded sinner.

Verse 20.

1. Men of spiritual understanding without worldly Honor are higher than the angels of God in heaven.

2. Men in worldly Honor without the true wisdom are worse than the beasts that perish. *G. R.*

PSALM 50

SERMON OUTLINES AND HELPFUL TIPS

Verse 1. It unspeakably concerns *all* men to know what God has spoken. *W. S. Plumer.*

Verse 1.

1. Who has spoken? The Mighty, not men or angels, but God himself.

2. To whom has he spoken? To all nations—all ranks—all characters. This calls for,

    (a) Reverence—it is the voice of God.
    (b) Hope—because he condescends to speak to rebels.

3. Where has he spoken?

    (a) In creation.
    (b) In providence.
    (c) In his word. *G. R.*

Verses 1-6.

1. The court called in the name of the King of kings.

2. The judgment set, and the judge taking his seat; Ps 50:2-3.

3. The parties summoned; Ps 50:8.

4. The issue of this solemn trial foretold; Ps 50:6. — *Matthew Henry.*

Verses 1-15.

1. God's call to man.
2. Man's call to God.

Verse 2.

1. The internal beauty of Zion.

(a) *Positive* beauty of wisdom—holiness—love.
(b) *Comparative* with the beauty of Paradise and the heaven of angels.
(c) *Superlative*—all the perfections of God combined.

2. Its external glory. Out of it God hath shined.

(a) On this world.
(b) On gracious souls.
(c) On angels who desire to look, etc.
(d) On the universe. "All the creatures heard I, "etc.

Verse 4.

1. What God will do for his people. He will judge them. (a) Deli**Verse** (b) Defend. (c) Uphold.

2. The means at his disposal for this purpose. "He shall call, "etc.—Heaven and earth are subservient to him for the good of his church. G. R.

Verse 4. The judgment of the visible church. It will be by God himself, public, searching—with fire and wind, exact, final.

Verse 5. The great family gathering.

>   (a) Who are gathered.
>   (b) How they are gathered.
>   (c) To whom.
>   (d) When they are gathered.

Verse 5 (*last clause*).

1. The covenant.
2. The sacrifice which ratifies it.
3. How we may be said to make it.

Verse 6 (*last clause*). Then slander will not pervert the sentence, undue severity will not embitter it, partiality will not excuse, falsehood will not deceive, justice will surely be done.

Verse 7. Sins of God's people specially against God, and only known to God. A searching subject.

Verses 13-15. What sacrifices are not, and what are acceptable with God.

Verse 15.

1. The occasion—"trouble."
2. The command—"call upon me."
3. The promise—"I will deliver thee."
4. The design—"Thou shalt, "etc. G. R.

Verse 15. *Thou shalt glorify me.* This we do by praying, and by praising when prayer is heard; as also by confidence in his promises, submission to his chastisements, concern for his Honor, attachment to his cause, affection to his people, and by continual obedience to his commands.

Verse 15.

1. A special invitation as to person and time.
2. Special promise to those accepting it.
3. Special duty involved when the promise is fulfilled.

Verses 16-17.

1. The prohibition given.

>   (a) The prohibited *things*—"declare my statutes." "Take my covenant, "etc. (1.) Preaching. (2.) Teaching, as in Sunday schools. (3.) Praying. (4.) Attending ordinances.
>   (b) Prohibited *persons*. Wicked preachers, etc., while they continue in wickedness.

2. The reason assigned; Ps 50:17.

    (a) No self application of the truth.
    (b) Inward hatred of it.
    (c) Outward rejection. —G. R.

Verse 17.

1. *The fatal sign.* (a) Hating to be taught. (b) Hating what is taught.

2. *What it indicates:* (a) Pride. (b) Contempt of God. (c) Indifference to truth. (d) Atheism at heart. (e) Deadness of conscience.

3. *What it leads to.* See Ps 50:22.

Verses 17-18. Rejection of salutary instruction leads sooner or later to open transgression. Instances, reasons, inferential warnings.

Verses 20-21.

1. Man speaking and God silent.
2. God speaking and man silent.

Verse 21.

1. God leaves men for a time to themselves.

2. They judge of God on this account by themselves.

3. He will in due time reveal their whole selves to themselves. "I will reprove, "etc. G. R.

Verses 21, 23. Note the alternative; a life rightly ordered now, or sins set in order hereafter.

Verse 22.

1. The accusation—"Ye that forget God, "his omniscience, his power, his justice, his goodness, his mercy, his word, his great salvation.

2. The admonition—"Consider this, "rouse yourselves from your forgetfulness into serious reflection.

3. The condemnation—"Lest, "etc. (a) The awfulness. "Tear, "as a lion or eagle its prey—tear body and soul. (b) Its irresistibleness—"None to deliver." —G. R.

Verses 21, 23. Note the alternative; a life rightly ordered now, or sins set in order hereafter.

Verse 23.

1. Salvation is the work of God.

2. The evidence of salvation is holiness of heart and life.

3. The effect of that evidence is praise.

4. The tendency of that praise is to glorify God. God is not glorified by the doubts, and fears, and murmurings of his people, but by their praise. *G. R.*

Verse 23. (*last clause*). The true order of life.

1. That first which is first.
2. That most which is most.
3. That ever which is ever.
4. That all which is all.

PSALM 51

SERMON OUTLINES AND HELPFUL TIPS

The Psalm is upon its surface so full of suggestions for sermons that I have not attempted to offer any of my own, but have merely inserted a selection from Mr. G. Rogers and others.

Verse 1.

1. The Prayer.

    (a) For mercy, not justice. Mercy is the sinner's attribute—as much a part of the divine nature as justice. The possibility of sin is implied in its existence. The actual commission of sin is implied in its display.

    (b) For pardon, not pity merely, but forgiveness.

2. The plea.

    (a) For the pardon of great sins on account of great mercies, and loving kindness.

    (b) Many sins on account of multitude of mercies.

3. Hell deserving sins on account of tender mercies. We who have sinned are human, he who pardons is divine.

"Great God, thy *nature* hath no bound,
So let thy pardoning love be found."

Verse 3.

1. Confession. "I acknowledge, "etc.

2. Humiliation, not a mere confession with the lips, but ever before me—in its guilt—defilement—consequences in this life and hereafter.

Verses 3-4, 11-12, 17.

1. Scripture estimate of sin.

    (a) Personal accountability—*My sin.*

    (b) Estimated as hateful to God—*Against thee,* etc.

    (c) Sin estimated as separation from God.

2. Spiritual restoration. First step—Sacrifice of a broken spirit. Last step—Spirit of liberty. *Thy free spirit.* F. W. Robertson.

Verse 6. See T. Goodwin's Treatise, entitled, "An Unregenerate Man's Guiltiness before God, in respect of Sin and Punishment." Book 9 cap. 1-2. (Nichol's edition, Vol. X., p. 324 *et seq.*)

Verse 7. Here is,

1. Faith in the act of an atonement for sin. "I shall be clean."

2. Faith in the method of its application. "Purge me, "etc. Sprinkled as the blood of sacrifices.

3. Faith in its efficacy. "I shall be whiter, "etc.

Verse 10.

1. The change to be effected.

    (a) A clean heart.
    (b) A right spirit.

2. The power by which it is accomplished.

    (a) A creative power, such as created the world at first.
    (b) A renewing power, such as continually renews the face of the earth.
    (c) The acquirement of these blessings. The prayer, "Create, "etc.

Verses 12-13. A threefold desire.

1. To be *happy*—"Restore," etc.
2. To be *consistent*—"Uphold," etc.
3. To be *useful*—"Then will I teach," etc. —*W. Jackson.*

Verse 13.

1. It is not our duty to seek the conversion of others until we are converted ourselves.

2. The greater enjoyment we have in the ways of God, the more faithfully and earnestly we shall make them known to others.

3. The more faithfully and earnestly we make them known to others the more they will be influenced by them.

Verse 15.

1. Confession. His lips are sealed on account—

    (a) Of his fall—and well they might be.
    (b) Of natural timidity.
    (c) Of want of zeal.

2. Petition, "Open thou, "etc. Not my understanding merely and heart, but "lips."

3. Resolution. Then he would speak freely in God's praise.

Verse 15.

1. When God does not open our lips we had better keep them closed.

2. When he does open them we ought not to close them.

3. When he opens them it is not to speak in our own praise, and seldom in praise of others, but always in his own praise.

4. We should use this prayer whenever we are about to speak in his name. "O Lord, open, "etc.

Verses 16-17.

1. Men would gladly do something towards their own salvation if they could. "Thou desirest not, "etc., else would I give it.

2. All that they can do is not of the least avail. All the ceremonial observances of Jewish or Gentile churches could not procure pardon for the least transgression of the moral law.

3. The only offering of man which God will not despise is a broken and a contrite heart.

4. All other requirement for his salvation God himself will provide.

Verse 18.

1. For whom is the prayer offered—for the church or Zion?

   (a) Next to our own welfare we should seek the welfare of Zion.

   (b) All should seek it by prayer.

2. For what is the prayer offered?

   (a) The kind of good, not worldly or ecclesiastical, but spiritual.

   (b) The measure of good. "In thy good pleasure." Thine own love to it, and what thou hast already done for it.

   (c) The continuance of good. "Build, "etc. Its doctrines, graces, zeal.

Verse 19.

1. When we are accepted of God our offerings are accepted." Then," etc.

2. We should then make the richest offerings in our power, our time, talents, influence, etc.

   (a) Holy obedience.

   (b) Self sacrifices, not half offerings, but whole "burnt offerings; "not lambs merely, but "bullocks."

   (c) Zeal for divine ordinances. "Upon thine altar."

3. God will take pleasure in such services. "Then shalt thou be pleased."

1. Because from his own redeemed.

2. Because given in the name of the Redeemer. With such sacrifices God is well pleased.

PSALM 52

SERMON OUTLINES AND HELPFUL TIPS

Verse 1. The confidence of faith.

1. *The circumstances were distressing.*

    (a) David was misjudged.
    (b) David exiled.
    (c) A bad man in power.
    (d) God's priests slain.

2. *The consolation was abiding.*

    (a) There is a God.
    (b) He is good.
    (c) His goodness continues.
    (d) Good will therefore overcome.

3. *The rejoinder was triumphant. Why boasteth thou?*

    (a) The mischief did not touch the main point.
    (b) It would be overruled.
    (c) It would recoil.
    (d) It would expose the perpetrators to scorn.

Verse 3. In what cases men clearly love evil more than good.

Verses 7-8. The worldling like an uprooted tree, the believer a vigorous well planted olive.

Verse 8. The believer's character, position, confidence, and continuance.

Verse 9. The double duty, and the double reason: the single heart and its single object.

Verse 9. What God has done, what we will do, and why.

PSALM 53

SERMON OUTLINES AND HELPFUL TIPS

See the tips on Psalm 14.

Verse 1. The fool's inside and outside.

Verse 1.

1. The folly of atheism. He who says there is no God is a fool.

>   (a) No reason for the assertion.
>   (b) All reason against it.

2. The seat of atheism is the heart; it is a moral unbelief not an intellectual, the language of the will not of the understanding.

3. Cause of atheism.

>   (a) Loving evil.
>   (b) Hating good. G. R.

Verse 2.

1. God has not left the world to itself.

2. He takes particular notice of all that is in it.

3. The only thing he values in it is the knowledge of himself. G. R.

Verse 4. How far knowledge is and is not a restraint upon ungodliness.

Verse 4. It is a sin not to call upon God.

1. What is it to call upon God? Three things required in it.

>   (a) A drawing near to him.
>   (b) A speaking to him. 1Sa 1:12-13.
>   (c) A praying to him.

2. How should we call upon God?

>   (a) Reverently, considering (1) God's holiness and greatness; (2) our own sin and weakness. Ge 18:27.
>
>   (b) Understandingly. 1Co 14:15. (1) Of what we ask. (2) Of whom we ask it.
>
>   (c) Submissively.
>
>   (d) Believingly. Mr 11:24 Jas 1:6.
>
>   (e) Sincerely. Jas 4:3.

(f) Constantly. (1) So as to be always in a praying frame. (2) So as to take all occasions of pouring forth our souls in prayer to God. (3) So as to let no day slip without prayer.

3. How it appears to be a sin not to call upon God.

(a) He hath commanded it. Isa 55:6 1Ti 2:8.

(b) Because praying is one of the principal parts of worship we owe to God.

4. Who are guilty of this sin?

(a) All who pray to any one else but God.

(b) All who neglect either public, private, or family prayer.

(c) All who pray, but not aright. *William Beveridge (1636-1708), in "Thesaurus Theologicus."*

Verse 5.

1. What persecutors are to themselves-their own tormentors, full even of groundless fears.

2. What they are to one another-though in concert here, their bones are scattered hereafter.

3. What they are to those whom they persecute—made ashamed before them.

4. What they are to God-a contempt and derision. G. R.

Verse 6.

1. There is salvation for Israel.

2. That salvation is in Zion.

3. Their salvation remains there when they are banished from it.

4. Their joy becomes greater when they return. G. R.

PSALM 54

SERMON OUTLINES AND HELPFUL TIPS

Verse 1. In the deliverance of the saints the Honor and power of God are concerned.

1. Their failure would dishonor both.

2. Their salvation glorifies both.

3. Both are immutable, therefore we have a sure plea at all times.

Verse 2. Our main concern in prayer.

1. What is meant by God's hearing prayer.
2. How we may know that he has done so.
3. What is to be done when this is doubtful.
4. What is due to him when the hearing is given.

Verse 3. Strange trials.

1. They are not altogether strange.

    (a) Not so to God.
    (b) Not so in the history of the church.
    (c) Not so to the provisions of grace wherein they are anticipated.

2. Wherein they are strange.

    (a) They reveal God anew.
    (b) Endear forgotten promises.
    (c) Train unused graces.
    (d) Being new praises, etc.

Verse 3. (*last clause*). The root of sin: if they remembered his authority they dared not, if they tasted his love they would not, if they were conformed to his nature they could not.

Verse 4. A theme for wonder.

1. At his unmerited grace, that he should side with *me*.
2. At his gracious power, for who can resist him?
3. At his practical help, for he has upheld my soul.

Verse 6. We should sacrifice voluntarily, liberally, joyfully, continuously, with pure motive.

Verse 6. The goodness of praising the good name.

Verse 7. (*first clause*). The exclamation of the newly pardoned penitent, the cry of the delivered saint, the song of the ripe Christian, the shout of the glorified believer.

PSALM 55

SERMON OUTLINES AND HELPFUL TIPS

Verse 1. (*second clause*).

1. An evil to be dreaded: *Hide not thyself,* etc.

    (a) By long delay in an urgent case.

    (b) In the sinner's case by refusing to hear altogether.

2. Causes which may produce it.

    (a) In the man.

    (b) In the prayer itself.

    (c) In the manner of the prayer.

3. Evils which will follow a list which the preacher can readily think of.

4. Remedies for the evil. There is none of it should continue; but heart searching, repentance, importunity, pleading the name of Jesus, etc., will lead to its removal.

Verse 2. The Great Hearer.

1. What address shall we present to him?

2. What sort of attention do we desire?

3. How shall we secure it?

4. What is the reflex duty on our part? To attend and hear him.

Verse 2. (*second clause*). Allowable complaining.

1. Not *of* God but *to* God.

2. Mainly of ourselves.

3. Of the world as against God and right.

4. Ever with holy grief, and not selfish vexation.

Verse 4. The terrors of death. See Sermon by *Grove* in the Notes.

Verse 7. Solitude.

1. Its fancied benefits.
2. Its sore temptations.
3. Its occasional benefits.
4. Its sweet solaces.

Verse 8. Too hasty a flight from trial.

1. Would show rebellion against God.

2. Would manifest cowardly want of faith.

3. Would involve loss of useful experience.

4. Would land us in other and worse trials.

5. Would prevent our glorifying God.

6. Would mar our conformity to Christ and fellowship with his people.

7. Would lessen the value of heaven.

Verse 9. (*first clause*). The Babel of heresies. *Essential,* for truth is one. *Inevitable,* for the motives of heretics clash. *Providential,* for so they weaken each other. *Judicial,* for so they torment each other.

Verse 10. (*first clause*). The activity of evil.

Verse 10. (*second clause*). The diabolical twins, or cause and effect.

Verse 14. The social companionships which grow out of religion.

1. They are on a good foundation.
2. They yield profit—*counsel.*
3. They yield pleasure—*sweet.*
4. They lead to enthusiasm—*walked in company.*
5. They ought to be sacredly maintained.
6. But they need to be carefully watched.

Verse 16. The contrast.

1. A child of God will not wrong others as they do him.

2. He will call upon God as they do not.

3. God will hear him as he does not the wicked.

4. God will deal with him at last otherwise than with them.

Verse 17.

1. David will pray fervently; *I will pray and cry aloud.*

2. He will pray frequently; every day, and three times a day, evening, and morning, and at noon. *Matthew Henry.*

Verse 18. Our battles, our almost rout, our helper, our deliverances, our praise.

Verse 19. The eternal government of God a threat to the ungodly.

Verse 19. (*second part*). Prosperity creating atheism. This involves—

1. Ingratitude—they ought to be the more devout.

2. Impudence—they think themselves as God.

3. Forgetfulness—they forget that changes will come.

4. Ignorance—they know not that unbroken prosperity is often for awhile the portion of the accursed.

5. Insanity—for there is no reason in their conduct.

6. Rottenness—preparing them to be cast away forever.

Verse 21. The hypocrite's mouth.

1. It has many words.
2. They are only from his mouth.
3. They are very smooth.
4. They conceal rather than reveal his purpose.
5. They are cutting and killing.
6. They will kill himself.

Verse 22. (*first clause*). Here we see the believer has—

1. A *burden* to try him.

2. A *duty* to engage him, "Cast thy burden, "etc.

3. A *promise* to encourage him, "He shall sustain, "etc. *Ebenezer Temple,* 1850.

Verse 22. (*last clause*). Who are the righteous? What is meant by their being moved? Whose permission is needful to accomplish it? Will he give it? "Ne**Verse**" Why not?

Verse 23. (*last clause*). The grand "I WILL." Sum up the Psalm.—

1. When I pray, Ps 55:1-3.
2. When I faint, Ps 55:4-7.
3. When I am sore beset, Ps 55:9-11.
4. When I am betrayed, Ps 55:12-14,20-21.
5. When others perish, Ps 55:15.
6. After I am delivered, Ps 55:18.
7. In every condition, Ps 55:22.

PSALM 56

SERMON OUTLINES AND HELPFUL TIPS

Verses 2-3.

1. *Fears are common to all men,* at one time or another.
2. *Improper and inefficacious means* of removing fear are often resorted to.
3. There is here suggested *a true and effectual* method of removing fear.
— Robert Morrison (1782-1834), in "A Parting Memorial."

Verse 3. *What time I am afraid, I will trust in thee.* Whensoever we are afraid of any evil, we are still to put our trust in God.

1. What is it to put our trust in God?

   (a) To keep our hearts from desponding or sinking down under any fears.

   (b) To comfort ourselves in God.

   (c) To expect deliverance from him.

2. What is there in God we ought to put our trust in?

   (a) In his promises.

   (b) In his properties. His power, wisdom, justice, mercy, all sufficiency.

3. Why should we in all our fears put our trust in God?

   (a) Because there is none else can secure us from our fears. Whereas,

   (b) There are no fears but God can secure us from them, either by removing the thing feared, or by subduing the fear of the thing. *Bishop Beveridge.*

Verse 3.

1. There is fear without trust.
2. There is trust without fear.
3. There is fear and trust united. *G. R.*

Verse 7.

1. From iniquity there is an escape.

2. By iniquity there is no escape. The mercy of God secures the one. The justice of God prevents the other. *G. R.*

Verse 8. Here are —

1. Manifold mercies, to reclaim from wanderings.
2. Tender mercies, putting tears in a bottle.
3. Covenant mercies, "Are they not, "etc. G. R.

Verse 9.

1. God is on the side of his people.
2. He is known to be on their side.
3. In answer to prayer he appears on their side.
4. When he appears enemies flee.

Or—

1. The fact, God is for me.
2. The knowledge of that fact—*This I know.*
3. The use of that knowledge—*When I cry,* etc.
4. The consequence of that use—*Mine enemies turn back.* G. R.

Verse 10.

1. "I will praise God *for* his word."
2. *In* his word, as he is there revealed.
3. *By* his word. "Thou hast put a song, "etc.

Verse 12. Here is—

1. Past dedication.
2. Present consecration.
3. Future glorification. G. R.

Verses 12-13. You have here—

1. The commemoration of former mercies: *Thou hast delivered.*

2. The confidence of future: *Wilt not thou.*

3. The end of all: *To walk before God in the light of the living.* Stephen Charnock.

Verse 13.

1. The language of Gratitude—*Thou hast,* etc.
2. Of Faith—*Wilt not thou,* etc.
3. Of Hope—*That I may walk,* etc. G. R.

PSALM 57

SERMON OUTLINES AND HELPFUL TIPS

Verse 1. (*first clause*). *Repetition in prayer.*

1. Its dangers. May degenerate into "vain repetitions." Carried to excess painfully suggests the idea, God is unwilling.

2. Its uses. Eases the soul like tears. Manifests intense emotion. Enables those of less mental activity to join in the general supplication. *R. A. Griffin.*

Verse 1. Here are—

1. Calamities:

    (a) War.
    (b) Pestilence.
    (c) Privations.
    (d) Sin, greatest of all.
    (e) Death.
    (f) Curse of a broken law.

2. Here is a refuge from these calamities.

    (a) In God.
    (b) Specially in the mercy of God.

3. There is flying to that refuge.

    (a) By faith; *My soul trusteth in thee; Under the shadow,* etc.
    (b) By prayer; "*Be* "etc.

4. Here is continuance both in faith and prayer; *until,* etc. G. R.

Verses 1, 4, 6-7. Note the varying condition of the same heart, at the same time. *My soul trusteth in thee... My soul is among lions... My soul is bowed down... My heart is fixed.*

Verse 2. Prayer to the performing God. He performs all his promises, all my salvation, all my preservation, all needed between here and heaven. Here he reveals his omnipotence, his grace, his faithfulness, his immutability; and we are bound to show our faith, patience, joy, and gratitude.

Verse 2. Strange reasons.

1. The psalmist in the depth of distress, cries to God, because he is most high in glory. Surely this thought might well paralyse him with the fear of divine inaccessibility, but the soul quickened with suffering, sees through and beyond the metaphor, rejoices in the truth, "Though the Lord be high, yet hath he respect unto the lowly."

2. He cries to God for help, because God *is* performing all things for him. Why urge him then? Prayer is the music to which "the mighty man of war" goes forth to battle. *R. A. G.*

Verse 3. The saints comfort in adversity.

1. All contingencies are provided for: *He shall* (or will) *send.*

2. The highest resources are available: *from* heaven.

3. The worst foes will be overcome in the end: *him* that would swallow me up.

4. By the holiest means: *mercy and truth. R. A. G.*

Verse 3. The celestial messengers. What they are. The certainty of their being sent. Their efficient operation. The grateful receive

Verse 3. (*last clause*). The harmony of the divine attributes in salvation. Mercy founded on truth, truth vindicating mercy. Mercy without injustice, justice honored in mercy.

Verse 5.

1. The end which God has in view, both in heaven and earth, in a sinful and in sinless worlds—his own glory.

2. Our duty to acquiesce in that end: *Be thou,* etc.—Not self, not men, not angels—*Be thou exalted,* etc. In this we should acquiesce—

    (a) Actively, by seeking that end.

    (b) Passively, by submission to his will. *G. R.*

Verse 7. (*first clause*). It is implied that the *heart* is the main thing required in all acts of devotion; nothing is done to purpose in religion further than it is done with the heart. The heart must be *fixed*; fixed *for* the duty, fitted and put in frame for it; fixed *in* the duty by a close application; *attending on the Lord* without distraction. *Matthew Henry.*

Verse 7.

1. What is fixed? the heart, not the mind merely, but the will, the conscience, the affections, which draw the mind after them: *My heart is fixed*—found an anchorage, a resting place, not therefore at the mercy of every gale, etc.

2. The objects upon which it is fixed.

    (a) Upon God.
    (b) Upon his word.
    (c) Upon his salvation.
    (d) Upon heaven.

3. The fixedness of the heart upon these objects, denotes—

(a) Singleness of aim.
(b) Uniformity of action.
(c) Perseverance to the end. *G. R.*

Verses 7-9.

1. He that will be thankful must treasure up in his heart and memory the courtesy that is done him; so had David done, and therefore he mentions *his heart;* and to make it more emphatic, he names it again, *My heart.*

2. After he remembers it, he must be affected with it, and resolve upon it; so doth David: *My heart is ready,* or else, *My heart is fixed;* confirmed I am in it to be thankful, and I cannot be altered.

3. It is not enough that a man carry about with him a thankful heart he must *anunciare,* tell it abroad, and make it known publicly what God hath done for him; yea, and do it joyfully too: *I will,* saith David, *sing and give praise.*

4. He must use all means he can to make it known—"tongue, ""psaltery, "and "harp, "all are little enough. Whence, by an apostrophe, David turns to these. *Awake, my glory:* i.e., Tongue, awake; lute and harp, awake; I myself will awake.

5. He must not do it in a sleepy manner, but with intention and earnestness of spirit: "Awake, awake, I will awake."

6. He must take the first opportunity to do it, and not hang off and delay it. *I will awake early.*

7. He must do it in such a place, and such an assembly as may most redound to God's Honor: *I will praise thee, O Lord, among the people: I will sing unto thee among the nations. William Nicholson.*

Verse 9. Who? *I.* What? *Will praise.* Whom? *Thee, O Lord.* Where? *Among the people.* Why?

Verse 9. Public profession.

1. A necessity.
2. A privilege.
3. A duty. *R. A. G.*

Verse 10. The mercy of God reaches to the heavens.

1. As a throne. God is exalted in our eyes by his mercy.

2. As a ladder. By mercy we ascend from earth to heaven.

3. As a rainbow. Present and past mercies argue exemption for the saints from the wrath of heaven.

4. As a mountain. Its base is on the earth though its summit is lost in clouds. The influence of the cross towers to the heaven of heavens. Who can tell the glory of the summit of this mountain, whose *base* is refulgent with glory! *R. A. G.*

Verse 10. The amazing greatness of mercy.

1. It is not said merely that it is high as heaven, but great unto the heavens. It is *high* as the heavens, overtopping the greatest sin, and highest thought of man.

2. It is *wide* as the far reaching sky, compassing men of all ages, countries, classes, etc.

3. It is *deep*. Everything of God is proportionate; this, therefore, is deep in abiding foundation, and infinite wisdom.

PSALM 58

SERMON OUTLINES AND HELPFUL TIPS

Verse 3.

1. The natural effects of original sin are seen in early suffering and death.

2. Its moral effects are seen in the early commission of actual sin.

3. Early depravity is evinced in the conscious guilt of telling lies. *G. R.*

Verse 3. (*first clause*). The inner pandemonium, or the calendar of the heart's crime.

Verse 4. (*first clause*). A generation of serpents. *T. Adams's Sermon.*

Verse 4. Sin as a poison. Poisons may be attractive in colour and taste, slow or rapid in action, painful in effect, withering, soporific or maddening. In all cases deadly.

Verse 5. The serpent charmer.

1. He charms with moral persuasion, promise, threatening, etc.

2. He charms wisely, earnestly, affectionately, argumentively.

3. He charms in vain; the will is a**Verse**. Hence the need of divine grace and of the gospel.

Verse 8. The snail like course of ungodly men. Their sin destroys their property, health, time, influence, life.

Verse 11. Remarkable cases of divine judgments and their results.

PSALM 59

SERMON OUTLINES AND HELPFUL TIPS

Verse 1. (*first clause*). Deliver me from temptation, uphold me in temptation, cleanse me from the result of temptation. The world, the flesh, the devil, and chiefly sin, these are our enemies. We cannot escape them of ourselves, but the Lord by providence and grace can rescue us.

Verse 2. (*first clause*). From being tempted by their promises, cowed by their threats, corrupted by their teaching, influenced by their example, injured by their slander, hindered in usefulness by their opposition.

Verse 3. (*first clause*). The subtleties of Satan. Watches for places, times, states, and ways in which to assail us. Errors in doctrine, practice, spirit, set forth to entrap us. "Ye are not ignorant of his devices." Or, the diabolical ambush, discovered by watchfulness, and defeated by faith.

Verse 4. The activity of the evil a rebuke for the good.

1. Their activity, *run.*
2. Unanimity—*they run.*
3. Their care—*prepare themselves.*
4. Their readiness—*without my fault.*

Verse 5. *O Lord God of hosts, the God of Israel.* This title furnishes an admirable topic.

Verse 9. The greatness of difficulty a reason for prayer and faith.

Verse 10. (*first clause*). The divine forwardness to bless.

Verse 11. The continuance of our enemies a salutary ordinance of God for the prevention of an evil to which we are very liable.

Verse 13 (*last clause*). God as the God of the church, his government as such, known in all human history.

Verse 16. The heavenly chorister.

1. His song is sweet in contrast with the revilings of others—*but I.*
2. It treats of subjects which terrify others—*thy power.*
3. It grows louder on tender themes—*thy mercy.*
4. It has its choice seasons—*in the morning.*
5. It is tuned by experience—*for thou hast.*
6. It is all to God's glory—*thy power, thy mercy, thou hast.*

Verse 17.

1. *A doctrine*—God is his people's strength.
2. *An appropriation*—"my strength."
3. *A resolution.* The song of gratitude for the past, faith for the present, hope for the future, of bliss for eternity.

PSALM 60

SERMON OUTLINES AND HELPFUL TIPS

Verse 1. Prayer of a church in low condition.

1. *Complaint.*

    (a) Left of God's Spirit.
    (b) Scattered.

2. *Cause.* Something displeasing to God. Neglect or actual sin; a subject for self examination.

3. *Cure.* The Lord's return to us and ours to him. In our version it is a prayer; in the Septuagint an expression of faith—"Thou wilt return."

Verse 2. The perturbation, the prayer, the plea. *G. R.*

Verse 3. That God does afflict his people severely, and that he has good reason for the same.

Verse 3. *The wine of astonishment.* A purgative, a tonic. Astonishing sin followed by astonishing chastisements, discoveries of corruption, of the spirituality of the law, of the terrors of divine wrath, and by astonishing depressions, temptations, and conflicts.

Verse 4. The banner of the gospel.

1. Why a banner? A rallying point, meant to fight under, etc.

2. By whom given. *Thou.*

3. To whom. *To them that fear thee.*

4. What is to be done with it. *To be displayed.*

5. For what cause. *Because of the truth.* Truth promotes truth.

Verse 5. The deliverance of the elect needs a saving God, a mighty God (*right hand*), and a prayer hearing God.

Verse 5. (*last clause*). *Save... and hear.* The remarkable order of these words suggests that—

1. In the purpose of God.

2. In the first works of grace.

3. Often under trial.

4. And specially in fierce temptations, Gods saving precedes man's praying.

Verse 6. God's holy promise, ground for present joy, and for boldly taking possession of the promised good.

Verse 7. *Gilead is mine, and Manasseh is mine.* How, and in what respect this world is the Christian's.

Verse 7. *Judah is my lawgiver.* The believer owning no law but that which comes from Christ.

Verse 8. *Moab is my washpot.* How we may make sinners subservient to our sanctification. We are warned by their sin, and punishment, etc. See "Spurgeon's Sermons," "No. 983, "Moab is my washpot."

Verse 9. The soul winner's question.

1. The object of attack; the strong city of man's heart, barricaded by depravity, ignorance, prejudice, custom, etc.

2. Our main design. To penetrate, to reach the citadel for Jesus.

3. Our great enquiry. Eloquence, learning, wit, none of these can force the gate, but there is One who can.

Verse 12. Divine operation a reason for human activity.

PSALM 61

SERMON OUTLINES AND HELPFUL TIPS

Whole Psalm. The progressive *I wills*.

1. I will cry.
2. I will abide in thy tabernacle.
3. I will trust.
4. I will sing praise.

Verse 1. Answers to prayer to be earnestly sought.

1. What hinders the answer of prayer?

2. What is our duty when answers are denied?

3. What encouragements we have to believe that the delay is only temporary.

Verse 2. *Lead me.*

1. Show me the way: reveal Jesus.

2. Enable me to tread it: work faith in me.

3. Uplift me when I cannot tread: do for me what is beyond me.

Verse 2. *Higher than I.* Jesus greater than our highest efforts, attainments, desires, expectations, conceptions.

Verse 2. God, the saint's rock. *John Owen's Two Sermons.* Works. Vol. 9, pp. 237-256.

Verse 2. The heart's cry and desire.

1. A recognition of a place of safety; then,

2. We have this place brought before us, as abundantly sufficient, when personal weakness has been realized.

3. This place cannot be attained without the help of another's hand.

4. The character of this refuge, and the position of a believer when availing himself of it: the place of refuge is "a rock, "and the position of the believer is "upon a rock." *P. B. Power.*

Verses 2-3.

1. *How* would he pray? *I will cry unto thee.*

2. *Where* would he pray? *From the ends of the earth.*

3. *When* would he pray? *When my heart is overwhelmed.*

4. *For what* would he pray? *Lead me to the rock that is higher than I.*

5. *Whence* does he derive his encouragement to pray? For thou hast been, etc. (Ps 61:3). *William Jay.*

Verse 3. *A shelter* from the rain of trouble, the storm of persecution, the floods of Satanic temptation, the heat of divine wrath, the blast of death. The ark, Lot's mountain, the blood stained door in Egypt, the city of refuge, the cave Adullam. *A strong tower:* lasting in itself, impregnable against foes, secure for the occupant.

Verse 5. (*second clause*). Enquire whether or no it fares with us as with the saints.

Verses 5, 8.

1. Vows heard in heaven.
2. Vows to be carefully fulfilled on earth.

Verse 5. (*second clause*).

1. They that fear God have a "heritage."
2. This heritage is "given."
3. We may know that we possess it. *William Jay.*

Verse 6. Our King, his eternal existence, our personal joy in this, and our joy for our descendants.

Verses 4, 7.

1. My privilege, *I will abide* (Ps 61:4).
2. The ground of it, *He shall abide,* etc. (Ps 61:7).

Verses 5, 8.

1. Vows heard in heaven.
2. Vows to be carefully fulfilled on earth.

PSALM 62

SERMON OUTLINES AND HELPFUL TIPS

Verse 1.

1. *What* he did? *Waited upon God.* Believed, was patient, was silent in resignation, was obedient.

2. To whom he did it? To his God, who is true, a sovereign, gracious, etc.

3. How he did it? With his soul, truly and only.

4. What came of it? Salvation present, personal, eternal, etc.

Verse 2. *God a rock.* David speaks of him as high and strong, and as a rock to stand upon, a rock of defense and refuge, a rock of habitation (Ps 71:3, in Hebrew), and a rock to be praised. Ps 95:1. See the Concordance for many hints. "Christ the Rock:" a Sermon on 1Co 10:4. By RALPH ROBINSON, in "*Christ All and in All.*"

Verse 2. (*first clause*). See "SPURGEON'S *Sermons*", No. 80, "*God alone the Salvation of His People.*"

Verse 2, 6. I shall not be greatly moved. I shall not be moved. Growth in faith. How it is produced, preserved, and evidenced.

Verse 4. Wherein lies a believer's excellency? Who would cast him down, and why, and how they seek to do it?

Verse 4. *They delight in lies.* Those who invent them, or spread them, or laugh at them, or readily believe them. Romanists, self-righteous persons, the presumptuous, persecutors, zealous errorists, etc.

Verse 5. (*second clause*). Great expectations from a great God; because of great promises, great provisions, and great foretastes.

Verse 5. (*last clause*). What we expect from God, and why and when?

Verse 2, 6. I shall not be greatly moved. I shall not be moved. Growth in faith. How it is produced, preserved, and evidenced.

Verse 10. Evils usually connected with the love of riches. Idolatry, covetousness, carking, care, meanness, forgetfulness of God and spiritual truth, neglect of charity, hardness of heart, tendency to injustice, etc. Means for escaping this seductive sin.

Verse 11.

1. How God speaks. "*Once,* "plainly, powerfully, immutably, etc.

2. How we should hear. *Twice,* continually, in heart as well as ear, observantly in practice, in spirit as well as in letter.

Verses 11-12. The constant union of power and mercy in the language of Scripture.

PSALM 63

SERMON OUTLINES AND HELPFUL TIPS

Verse 1. (*first clause*). While the Atheist says, "No God, "and the heathen worship "gods many, "the true believer says, "O God, thou art my God." He is so,

1. By choice.
2. By covenant.
3. By confession.

Verse 1. (*second clause*). Seeking God *early*.

1. Early in respect of *life*.
2. Early in respect of *diligence*.
3. Early in respect of (*fervor.*)
4. Early in respect of *times* or *continuance. Alexander Shanks.*

Verse 1. (*second clause*). *Earnest seeking.* That which is longed for will be eagerly sought.

1. The soul is *resolute. I will seek.*
2. The soul is *reasonable. I will seek.*
3. The soul is *ready. Early* will I.
4. The soul is *persevering.*

Let this be the resolution of both saved and unsaved. *G. J. K.*

Verse 3.

1. *Love's resolution. My lips shall praise thee.*

   (a) *To praise.* This is congenial to the renewed nature. It delights not in grumbling, reproaching, or scolding. Praise expresses appreciation, gratitude, happiness, affection.
   (b) *To praise God.*
   (c) *To praise God practically. My lips.* By speaking well *to* him; by speaking well *of* him; of his wisdom, justice, love, grace, etc.
   (d) *To praise God continually.* As long as I live, etc.

2. *Love's reason. Because thy lovingkindness.* Love must praise God because—

   (a) It owes its existence to him. "We love him because he first loved us."
   (b) Because it is fostered by him. "The love of God is shed abroad, "etc.
   (c) Because the expressions of his love demand praise. "Kindness" to needy, helpless, lost. *Lovingkindness,* not wounding our natures. *Better than life;* either the principle, pleasures, or pursuits of life. *G. J. K.*

Verse 3. *Thy lovingkindness is better than life.*

1. *Love enjoyed with life.*
2. *Love compared with life.*
3. *Love preferred to life. G. J. K.*

Verses 5-6.

1. *The empty vessel filled.* How? By meditation. With what? God's goodness as marrow and fatness. To what extent? Satisfaction.

2. *The full vessel running o***Verse** *My mouth shall praise thee with joyful lips.* The soul overflows with praise—joyful praise. G. J. K.

Verses 5-6. Describe the nature of, and show the intimate connection between 1. the believer's employments and 2. his enjoyments. J. S. Bruce.

Verse 7. A well founded resolve.

1. Upon what based.
2. How expressed. J. S. B.

Verse 8.

1. *The soul's pursuit after God.* It follows, (a) In desire. (b) In action. (c) Earnestly. (d) Quickly. (e) Closely.

2. *The soul's support. Thy right hand upholdeth me,* the arm of strength. In doing and bearing. G. J. K.

Verse 8. "A mighty hunter before the Lord."

1. The object of pursuit: *Thee.*
2. The manner of pursuit: *Hard after.*
3. The dangers encountered. J. S. B.

Verse 8. (*second clause*). God's right hand upholds his people three ways.

1. As to *sin;* lest they should fall by it.
2. As to *suffering;* lest they should sink under it.
3. As to *duty;* lest they should decline from it. W. Jay.

Verses 9-10.

1. The enemies of the Christian. Evil spirits, evil men, evil habits, etc., etc.
2. Their intent. To destroy the soul.
3. Their fall. Certain, shameful, destructive.
4. Their future. Hell is reserved for them G. J. K.

Verse 11. Three topics.

1. Royal rejoicing.
2. Lawful swearing.
3. Evil speaking.

PSALM 64

SERMON OUTLINES AND HELPFUL TIPS

Verse 1.

1. *The preservation of life desired.*

   (a) The desire expressed.
   (b) Qualified—from violent death, from fear of, etc.

2. *The preservation of life prayed for.*

   (a) For self-improvement.
   (b) For usefulness.
   (c) For the divine glory. *G. R.*

Verse 2. (*first clause*). Applied to Satan.

1. *The danger considered.*

   (a) The enemy, wicked, mighty, malicious, experienced.
   (b) His counsel. He tempts cunningly, and with deliberation.
   (c) The secrecy of it. He may be exciting others against me, or sowing evil in myself.

2. *The deliverance implored. Hide me.*

   (a) Keep me from being tempted.
   (b) Keep me from evil when tempted.
   (c) Bring me out of it all unharmed.
   (d) Meanwhile, let me be in thy secret place.

3. *The consolation of faith.*

   (a) God does preserve praying ones.
   (b) Our enemy is *his* enemy.
   (c) He has preserved us.
   (d) We are his own.
   (e) His Honor is involved.

Verse 3. *Bitter words.* An excellent topic in reference both to the sinner and to professed saints.

Verse 3. *The whetting of the tongue.* Fresh faults discovered, evil motives imputed, exaggerations invented, lies forged, innuendoes suggested, old slanders furnished, and ancient hatreds rekindled.

Verse 6. (*two first clauses*). The fault hunter; his motive, his character, his pretences, and his punishment.

Verse 9.

1. *The subject for consideration*—Judgments upon the wicked.

    (a) As Judgments.
    (b) As judgments from God—that work of God—his doing.

2. *The consideration of the subject.*

    (a) They are intended to be considered by others.
    (b) They are to be considered wisely.

3. *The effect of this consideration.*

    (a) Fear of God.
    (b) Praise to God; shall declare, etc. G. R.

Verses 9-10.

1. An act of God; something of his doing.
2. Its effect upon men in general: *All men shall fear, and shall declare*, etc.
3. A special duty resulting from it, incumbent on good men: *The righteous,* etc. H. Dove.

Verse 10.

1. *The persons.*
(a) What they are, in distinction from others; the righteous; the justified.
(b) What they are in themselves; upright in heart; not perfect, but sincere.

2. *Their privilege.*
(a) Amidst all their persecutions to joy in God.
(b) Amidst all their dangers to trust in God. G. R.

PSALM 65

SERMON OUTLINES AND HELPFUL TIPS

Verse 1. The fitness, place, use, and power of silence in worship.

Verse 1. The limitations, advantages, and obligations of vows.

Verse 2. (*first clause*). The hearing and granting of prayer is the Lord's property, his usual practice, his pleasure, his nature, and his glory. *David Dickson.*

Verse 3.

1. *The humble confession.* Sins prevail against us.

    (a) *When* we are not alert, or go into temptation, and even after most sacred engagements.

    (b) *How.* Through our inbred corruption, natural constitution, suddenness of temptation, neglect of means of grace, and want of fellowship.

    (c) In *whom.* In the best of men: David says, *against me.* Let us take home the caution.

2. *The reassuring confidence.* Sin is forgiven.

    (a) By God: *Thou.*
    (b) By atonement: covering all.
    (c) Effectually: *purge away.*
    (d) Comprehensively: *our transgressions.*

Verse 3.

1. *A cry of distress.* Man soul besieged: *Iniquities prevail against me.*

2. *A shout of delight.* Man soul relieved: *Thou shalt purge them away.* E. G. Gange.

Verse 4. Nearness to God is the foundation of a creature's happiness. This doctrine appears in full evidence, while we consider the three chief ingredients of true felicity, *viz.,* the contemplation of the noblest object, to satisfy all the powers of the understanding; the love of the supreme good, to answer the utmost propensities of the will, and the sweet and everlasting sensation and assurance of the love of an Almighty Friend, who will free us from all the evils which our nature can fear, and confer upon us all the good which a wise and innocent creature can desire. Thus all the capacities of man are employed in their highest and sweetest exercises and enjoyments. *Isaac Watts.*

Verse 4. Election, effectual calling, access, adoption, final perseverance, satisfaction. This **Verse** is a body of divinity in miniature.

Verse 5. Treat the first clause experimentally, and show how prayers for our own sanctification are answered by trial; for God's glory, by our persecution; for our babes' salvation, by their death; for the good of others, by their sickness, etc.

Verse 7. The Lord, the giver, creator, and preserver of peace.

Verse 8. Tokens of God's presence; those causing terror, and those inspiring joy.

Verse 8. (*last clause*). The peculiar joys of morning and evening.

Verse 9. *The river of God.* John Bunyan's treatise on "The Water of Life" would be suggestive on this topic.

Verse 9. Divine visits and their consequences.

Verses 9-13. A Harvest Sermon.

1. *The general goodness of God,* Visiting the earth in rotation of seasons: "Seed time and harvest, "etc.

2. *The greatness of his resources:* The river of God, which is full of water; not like Elijah's brook, which dried up.

3. *The variety of his benefactions:* Corn; Water; Blessest the springing thereof, etc.

4. *The perpetuity of his blessings;* Crownest the year. *E. G. G.*

Verse 13. The song of nature and the ear which hears it.

PSALM 66

SERMON OUTLINES AND HELPFUL TIPS

Verse 3. The terrible in God's works of nature and providence.

Verse 4.

1. *Who?* All the earth.

    (a) All, collectively, all classes and tribes.
    (b) All numerically.
    (c) All harmoniously.

2. *What?* Shall worship and sing.

    (a) Humiliation; then,
    (b) Exultation.

3. *When?* Shall, &c. Denotes

    (a) Futurity.
    (b) Certainty. God has spoken it. All things are tending towards it. *G. R.*

Verse 5. Here is—

1. A subject for general study: the *Works of God*.

2. For particular study: *his doings towards*, etc.

    (a) These are the most wonderful.
    (b) In these we are most concerned.

Verse 7. Sovereignty, immutability ("forever"), and omniscience,—the enemies of proud rebels.

Verse 8. (*last clause*). To get a hearing for the gospel—difficult, necessary, and possible. Ways and means for so doing.

Verses 8-9.

1. Praise *to*.

    (a) As God.
    (b) As *our* God.

2. Praise *for*. Preservation.

    (a) Of natural life.
    (b) Of spiritual life.

3. Praise *by, ye people*.

(a) On your own account.
(b) On account of others.
Or
(a) Individually.
(b) Unitedly. *G. R.*

Verse 9. Perseverance the subject of gratitude.

1. The maintenance of the inner life.

2. The integrity of the outward character.

Verse 10. The assaying of the saints.

Verse 10.

1. The design of the afflictions.

> (a) To prove them.
> (b) To reprove them.

2. The illustration of that design. As silver, etc.

3. The issue of the trial.

Verses 11-12. The hand of God should be acknowledged.

1. In our temptations: *Thou broughtest us.*
2. In our bodily afflictions: *Thou laidest,* etc.
3. In our persecutions: *Thou hast caused,* etc.
4. In our deliverances: *Thou broughtest us out,* etc. *G. R.*

Verse 12. *Fire and water.* Varied trials.

1. Discover different evils.
2. Test all parts of manhood.
3. Educate varied graces.
4. Endear many promises.
5. Illustrate divine attributes.
6. Afford extensive knowledge.
7. Create capacity for the varied joys of heaven.

Verse 12. (*first clause*). The rage of oppression. *Thomas Adam's Sermon.*

Verse 12. (*last clause*). A plentiful place, free from penury; a pleasant place, void of sorrow; a safe place, free from dangers and distresses. *Daniel Wilcocks.*

Verse 12. (*last clause*). The victory of patience, with the expiration of malice. *Thomas Adams' Sermon.*

Verse 12. (*last clause*). The wealth of a soul whom God has tried and delivered. Among other riches he has the wealth of experience, of strengthened graces, of confirmed faith, and of sympathy for others.

Verse 13. God's house; or, the place of praises. *Thomas Adams' Sermon.*

Verses 13-15.

1. Resolutions made (Ps 66:13).

>   (a) What? To offer praise.
>   (b) Why? For deliverance.
>   (c) Where? In thy house.

2. Resolutions uttered (Ps 66:14).

>   (a) To God.
>   (b) Before men.

3. Resolutions fulfilled.

>   (a) In public acknowledgment.
>   (b) In heartfelt gratitude.
>   (c) In more frequent attendance at the house of God.
>   (d) The renewed self dedication.
>   (e) In increased liberality. *G. R.*

Verse 16.

1. What has God done for the soul of every Christian?

2. Why does the Christian wish to declare what God has done for his soul?

3. Why does he wish to make this declaration to those who only fear God?

>   (a) Because they alone can understand such a declaration.

>   (b) They alone will really believe him.

>   (c) They only will listen with interest, or join with him in praising his Benefactor. *E. Payson.*

Verse 16.

1. Religious teaching should be *simple: I will declare.*
2. *Earnest: Come and hear.*
3. *Seasonable: All ye that.*
4. *Discriminating: Fear God.*
5. *Experimental: What he hath, etc.*

Verse 17.

1. The two principal parts of devotion. Prayer and praise.

2. Their degree. In prayer, crying. In praise, extolling.

3. Their order.

    (a) Prayer.

    (b) Then praise. What is won by prayer is worn in praise.

Verses 18-19.

1. The test admitted.
2. The test applied.
3. The test approved.

Verse 19. The fact that God has heard prayer.

Verse 20. The mercy of God.

1. In permitting prayer.
2. In inclining to prayer.
3. In hearing prayer.

PSALM 67

SERMON OUTLINES AND HELPFUL TIPS

Verse 1.

1. Here is mercy in God the Father.

2. Here is blessing as the fruit of that mercy in God the Son.

3. Here is the experience of that blessing in the comfort of the Holy Ghost.

Verse 1. The need of seeking a blessing for ourselves.

Verses 1-2. The prosperity of the church at home, the hope for missions abroad.

Verse 2.

1. The way of God towards the earth.

   (a) A way of mercy.
   (b) Of blessing.
   (c) Of comfort.

2. The knowledge of that way.

   (a) By outward means.
   (b) By inward teaching.

3. The effect of that knowledge. Salvation among all nations.

Verse 2. What is the true health of men?

Verse 3. Viewed,

1. As the desire of every renewed heart.
2. As a prayer.
3. As a prophecy.

Verse 4.

1. The reign of God in the world: it is not left to itself.

2. The joy of the world on that account: *Let the* nations, etc.

3. The reason of that joy: *He will judge righteously.*

(a) As faithful to his law.

(b) Faithful to his promises of mercy.

Verses 5-7.

1. The prayer (Ps 67:5).
2. The promise (Ps 67:6).
   (a) Of temporal good.
   (b) Of spiritual good.
3. The prediction (Ps 67:7).

Verses 6-7. See "Spurgeon's Sermons, "No. 819: "The Minstrelsy of Hope."

Verse 7.

1. God to man: *shall bless us.*
2. Man to God: *shall fear him.*

PSALM 68

SERMON OUTLINES AND HELPFUL TIPS

Verses 1-2.

First. The church of God ever had, and will have, enemies and haters; for against these doth the psalmist arm himself and the church with this prayer.

Secondly. The church's enemies are God's enemies; they that hate the church, hate God. *Thine* enemies, them that hate thee.

Thirdly. God sometimes seems to sleep or lie still, and let these enemies and haters do what they will for a season, This, also, is implied: he to whom we say, *Arise* is either asleep or lies still.

Fourthly. There is a time when God will arise.

Fifthly. God's rising time is the enemies' scattering time, his hater's flying time.

Sixthly. It is the duty of God's people to pray him up when he seems to be down, and to exalt him in their praises when he doth arise to their rescue and redemption; for these words are both a prayer and a triumph as they are used both by Moses and David. Thomas Case, in a Fast Sermon, preached before the House of Commons, *entitled*, "*God's Rising, his Enemies' Scattering.*" 1644.

Verses 1-3. Prayer for the Second Advent. *A. Macaul.*

Verse 4.

1. The name that inspires the song: *Jah.*

    (a) Self existent.
    (b) Immutable.
    (c) Eternal.

2. The song inspired by that name.

    (a) Of exultation.
    (b) Of confidence.
    (c) Of joy. *G. R.*

Verse 5. The claims of widows and orphans upon the church of God, from God's relation to them and his indwelling in the church.

Verse 6. Comparison of churches to families. See extract from *Dr. Gill.*

Verse 6.

1. Two curable evils: "solitary", "bound with chains."

2. Two rich blessings: "set in families, ""bringeth out."

3. One monster evil, and its miserable consequences.

Verses 7-8.

1. God has his seasons for delivering his people from their troubles: *When thou,* etc.

2. His deliverance is complete: *The earth shook,* etc.; all things gave way before him.

3. The deliverance is greater for the delay.

    (a) It is so in itself.

    (b) It is more prized: as in the case of Job, Abraham, Israel at the Red Sea, Daniel, his three companions, etc. *G. R.*

Verses 7-9.

1. The presence of God in his church.

    (a) His preeminence: "before."
    (b) As covenant God of Israel.
    (c) As active and making active.
    (d) His rule within: they follow.
    (e) His design without: marching for war.

2. The blessed consequences.

    (a) The most stolid shake.
    (b) The lofty bow.
    (c) Difficulties removed: "Sinai."
    (d) Blessings plenteous.
    (e) Church revived.

Verse 9.

1. God's mercy compared to a shower.

    (a) It is direct from heaven; not through priests.

    (b) It is pure and unmixed.

    (c) No one has a monopoly of it.

    (d) There is no substitute for it.

    (e) It is sovereignly dispensed, as to (1) time; (2) place; (3) manner; and (4) measure.

    (f) It works efficiently. Isa 55:10.

    (g) Prayer can get it.

2. There are seasons when these showers fall.

(a) In the house of God.

(b) In the means of grace.

(c) In prayer.

(d) In affliction.

(e) When saints are weary (1) through working; (2) through sickness; (3) through non success.

(f) By the Holy Spirit refreshing the heart.

3. These showers are meant to "confirm God's people."

4. They are wanted *now*.

Verse 9.

1. The church is God's inheritance.

 (a) Chosen.
 (b) Purchased.
 (c) Acquired.

2. Though his inheritance, at times it may be weary.

3. When weary, it will be refreshed by him. *G. R.*

Verse 10. (*second clause*). Special goodness, for a special people, specially prepared.

Verse 10. (*second clause*). It is spoken in reference to the *poor,* because,

1. They are the larger mass of mankind; and, whatever pride may think, in the eye of reason, policy, and revelation, by far the most important, useful, and necessary part.

2. They would be more peculiarly affected by deficiency.

3. To encourage those in humble and trying life to depend upon him.

4. To enforce our attention to them from the divine example. *W. Jay.*

Verse 11. The divinity of the gospel; the divers ways and agents for its publication.

Verses 11-12.

1. The word given: "The Lord." etc.

2. The word proclaimed: "Great, "etc.

3. The word obeyed: "Kings, "etc. Thus it was in Old Testament times, when to Joshua, to Gideon, to David, etc., the Lord gave the word, and it ran through the hosts, and "kings of

armies, "etc. Thus it was in apostolic times, when the word of reconciliation was given. Thus it is still, and will be more signally than ever hereafter. G. R.

Verse 12. (*last clause*). The church in redemption as a spouse tarrying at home; her home duties; the spoil of her Lord's glorious and finished work, and her dividing it.

Verse 13.

1. The contrast.

    (a) Instead of humiliation, exaltation.
    (b) Instead of pollution, purity.
    (c) Instead of inertness, activity.
    (d) Instead of deformity, beauty.

2. Its application.

    (a) To penitence and pardon.
    (b) To depravity and regeneration.
    (c) To affliction and recovery.
    (d) To desertion and consolation.
    (e) To death and glory. G. R.

Verse 14.

1. Where earth's greatest battles are fought. "Scattered, ""in it, "*i.e.*, in Zion. "There brake he, "etc.

2. By whom? The Almighty.

3. When? In answer to his people's faith and prayer.

4. How?

    (a) Without noise, gently: as the fall of snow.

    (b) Without human aid: as untrodden snow.

    (c) Without violence: "All bloodless lay the untrodden snow." G. R.

Verse 15-16.

1. The superiority of the hill of Zion.

    (a) In fertility, to the hill of Bashan; to earthly pleasures.

    (b) In glory, to other hills; to human heights of learning and power.

2. The reason of that superiority.

    (a) The place of God's choice.
    (b) Of his delight

(c) Of his abode.
(d) Of his continuance forever. *G. R.*

Verse 16.

1. The church the dwelling place of God.

    (a) Elected of old.
    (b) Favored forever.
    (c) Affording rest, etc., as a home for God.
    (d) Receiving Honor, etc., for herself.

2. The church, therefore, envied by others.

    (a) They feel their own greatness outdone.
    (b) They leap with rage.
    (c) They are unreasonable in so doing.

Verses 17-18.

1. The comparison between Zion and Sinai.

    (a) The same Lord is there: "The Lord is among, "etc.

    (b) The same attendants: "The chariots," etc.

2. The contrast.

    (a) God descended at Sinai, ascended from near Zion.

    (b) Put a yoke upon them at Sinai, leads captivity captive at Zion.

    (c) At Sinai demanded obedience, in Zion bestows gifts.

    (d) In Sinai spoke terror, in Zion receives gifts for the rebellious.

    (e) In Sinai appeared for a short season, in Zion dwells forever. *G. R.*

Verse 18.

1. Christ's *ascension*.

2. His *victories*.

3. The *gifts* he received for men; and

4. The great *end* for which he bestows them. *John Newton.*

Verse 18. *That the Lord God might dwell among them.* It is ground for devout wonder that God should dwell among men, when we contemplate his *immensity, loftiness, independence, holiness,* and *sovereignty;* yet he does so—

1. In the coming of Christ into the world.
2. In the residence of his Spirit in the heart.
3. In the presence of God in his churches.
—*William Staughton, D.D. 1770-1829.*

Verse 19.

1. The load of benefits.
2. The load of obligation.
3. The load of praise due in return.

Verse 19.

1. Salvation is not to be forgotten in the midst of daily mercies.
2. Daily mercies are not to be forgotten in the enjoyment of salvation. *G. R.*

Verse 20. Death in God's hand.

1. Escapes from it.

2. Entrances to it.

3. The exit out of it beyond.

4. The gate which, when closed, shuts us in it forever.

Verse 20.

1. What God has been to his people.

    (a) Their salvation.
    (b) Their portion: "Our God."

2. What he will be: With them.

    (a) Until death.
    (b) In death.
    (c) After death. *G. R.*

Verse 21. The power, pride, wisdom, and very life of evil, to be conquered by God.

Verse 22.

1. Where his people may be driven.
2. The certainty of their return.
3. The reasons for being assured of this.

Verse 24. *The allowable procession in the sanctuary.* The marshaled order of doctrine, the holy walk of believers, the banners of joy, the music of devotions, the shouts to the King.

Verse 25. (*last clause*). Work for holy women in the church.

Verse 27.

1. The variety of song.

    (a) The royal tribe of Benjamin in the time of Saul.

    (b) The princely tribe of Judah, as David was prince regent in the time of Saul.

    (c) The literary tribe of Zebulun: "Out of Zebulun" they that handle the pen of the writer.

    (d) The eloquent tribe: "Naphtali giveth goodly words."

2. The harmony of song. Let all unite in praising the Lord, the fountain of Israel. "Ten thousand thousand are their tongues, "etc. *G. R.*

Verse 30-31.

1. Hindrances to the progress of divine truth.

    (a) Idolatry. Worship of the crocodile—*beasts of the reeds,* (LXX)—of bulls and calves, as in Egypt.

    (b) Covetousness.

    (c) War.

2. The means for their removal. Prayer and the divine *rebuke. Scatter thou,* etc.

3. The consequences of this removal; Ps 68:31.

Verse 35.

1. Consider God's jealousy towards his people for his holiness in the three "holy places."

    (a) In the outer court of profession.
    (b) In the holy place of our priesthood.
    (c) In the holy of holies with his Son.

2. Consider his terribleness to his foes, as inferred from those "holy places."

Verse 35. *Blessed be God.* A brief, but very suggestive text.

PSALM 69

SERMON OUTLINES AND HELPFUL TIPS

Verse 1. Our trials like waters.

1. They should be kept out of the heart.
2. There are, however, leaks which admit them.
3. Take note when the hold is filling.
4. Use the pumps, and cry for help.

Verses 2-3. The sinner aware of his position, unable to hope, overwhelmed with fear, finding no comfort in prayer, unvisited with divine consolation. Direct and console him.

Verse 3.

1. Here is faith in the midst of trouble: *My God.*

2. Hope in the midst of disappointment: *Mine eyes fail, etc.*

3. Prayer in the midst of discouragement: *I am weary,* etc.; *My throat,* etc. Or, (a) There is praying beyond prayer: *I am weary,* etc.; (b) Hoping beyond hope: *Mine eyes,* etc. G. R.

Verse 4. Jesus as the Restorer, the Christian imitating him in the same office; Christianity a power which will do this for the whole race in due season.

Verse 5. *Our foolishness.* Wherein it appears generally, how it may display itself in individuals, what it occasions, and what are the divine provisions to meet it.

Verse 5.

1. God's knowledge of sin is an inducement to repent.

    (a) Because it is foolish to endeavor to hide any sin from him.

    (b) Because it is impossible to confess all our sin to him.

2. It is an encouragement to hope for pardon.

    (a) Because, in the full knowledge of sin, he has declared himself to be merciful and ready to forgive.

    (b) Because he has made provision for pardon, not according to our knowledge of sin, but his own.

Verses 8-9.

1. A grievous trial.
2. An Honorable reason for it: for Christ's sake.
3. Consoling supports under it.

Verse 9.

1. The object of zeal: *thy house;* thy Zion; thy Church.

2. The degree of zeal: *hath eaten me up.* Our Lord was consumed by his own zeal. So Paul: *And I if I be offered up, etc.*

3. The manifestation of zeal: *The reproaches,* etc.; of thy justice; of thy law; of thy moral government; of thy lovingkindness. "Who himself bare our sins," etc. G. R.

Verses 10-12. A prophecy.

1. Of the Savior's tears: *When I wept.*

2. Of his fasting.

3. Of reproach.

4. Of his humiliation: *I made sackcloth,* etc.

5. Of the perversion of his words: as, "I will destroy this temple, "etc.

6. Of the opposition of the Pharisees, and rulers: *They that sit in the gate, etc.*

7. Of the contempt of the lowest of the people: *I was the song, etc.* G. R.

Verse 11. Proverbial sayings of a scoffing character.

Verse 13. *An acceptable time.* While life lasts usually, and especially when we are repentant, feel our need, are importunate, give all glory to God, have faith in his promise, and expect a gracious reply.

Verse 13. *Multitude of thy mercy.* Seen in many forbearances before conversion, countless pardons, innumerable gifts, many promises, frequent visits, and abundant deliverances. Of all these who can count the thousandth part?

Verse 13. *The truth of thy salvation.* An instructive topic. Its reality, certainty, completeness, eternity, etc., all illustrate its *truth* under various aspects.

Verses 14-16.

1. The depth from which prayer may rise.

2. The height to which it may ascend. Thus Jonah, when at the bottom of the sea, says, "My prayer came up," etc. G. R.

Verse 17.

1. Prayer: *Hide not thy face.*
2. Person: *Thy servant.*
3. Plea: *For I am in trouble.*
4. Pressure: *Hear me speedily.*

Verse 19.

1. God knows what his people suffer; how much, how long, from whom, for what.

2. His people should find consolation in this knowledge.

>(a) That trial is permitted by him.
>(b) That it is apportioned by him.
>(c) That it has its design from him.
>(d) That when the design is accomplished, it will be removed by him. *G. R.*

Verse 20. The Savior's broken heart. Broken hearts, such as are sentimental, caused by disappointed pride, penitence, persecution, sympathy, etc.

Verse 21. The conduct of men to Jesus throughout his entire life, rendering to him evil for all his good, and where good would have seemed to be the inevitable return.

Verse 22. *The table a snare.* Excess in feasting; looseness in conversation; want of principal in confederate councils; superstition in religion.

Verse 23. The judicial curse which falls on some despisers of Christ; their understandings fail to perceive the truth; and they tremble because they are unable to receive strengthening comforts.

Verse 29.

1. The humiliation that precedes exaltation.

>(a) Deep: *I am poor and sorrowful.*
>(b) Confessed: *I am poor,* etc.

2. The exaltation that follows humiliation.

>(a) Divine: *Thy salvation, O Lord. Though the Lord be high,* etc.
>(b) Complete: God does nothing by halves.
>(c) Preeminent: *Set me up on high. G. R.*

Verse 30-31.

1. The effect of deliverance upon the people of God. It fills them with praise and thanksgiving.

2. The effect in relation to God. He is more pleased with it than with any other offerings: "Whoso offereth praise, "etc. *G. R.*

Verse 32.

1. The joy of a good man's heart is in the experience of others.

2. The life of his heart is in God.

Verse 33.

1. What the people of God are in their own esteem: "poor" and "prisoners."

2. What they are in the divine esteem: not unnoticed; not unheard; not despised.

Verse 34. *The sea,* etc. How God is, should be, and shall be praised by the sea.

Verse 35. Salvation, edification, preservation, peace, full assurance.

Verses 35-36. Observe the sequence: — "Save," "build," "dwell and have," "inherit," "love and dwell."

Verse 36.

1. The sure evidence of grace: "love his name."
2. The blessing given.
3. The enduring character of it: "shall dwell."

Verse 36.

1. The inheritance: "Inherit it;" "we reign with Christ on earth, then in heaven.

2. The title.

    (a) Legal: "Seed of his servants" — Abraham, Jacob, David — David's Lord and Son.

    (b) Moral: "They that love his name." *G. R.*

PSALM 70

SERMON OUTLINES AND HELPFUL TIPS

Verse 1.

1. Occasion of his prayer.
    (a) Affliction.
    (b) Helplessness.
2. Subject of his prayer. Deliverance, help.
3. Importunity of his prayer. The time of deliverance may be an answer to prayer, as well as deliverance itself.

Verse 1.

1. Times when such urgent prayer is allowable, praiseworthy, or faulty.
2. Reasons for expecting a speedy reply.
3. Consolations if delay should occur.

Verse 2.

1. There are those who seek our soul's hurt.
2. We must oppose them, not dally or yield.
3. Our best weapon is prayer to God.
4. Their defeat is here described.

Verse 3.

1. Who are these who cry "shame"?
2. What master do they serve?
3. What shall their wages be?

Verse 4. Joy for seekers, and employment for finders.

Verse 4. (*last clause*).

1. The character.
2. The saying.
3. The wish.

Verse 5.

1. Who needs help?
2. Who renders help?
3. What it comes to: "deliver"
4. What prayer it suggests.

Verse 5.

1. Confession! *I am poor and needy.*
2. Profession: *Thou art my help,* etc.
3. Supplication: *Make haste; Make no tarrying.*

PSALM 71

SERMON OUTLINES AND HELPFUL TIPS

Arguments used to induce to Lord to hear, drawn,

1. From his *justice* and *equity:* *Deliver me in thy righteousness.*

2. From his *word* and *promise:* *Thou hast given commandment, etc.*

3. From his *power:* *Thou art my rock.* etc.

4. From his *relation* to him: *My God, my hope.*

5. From the *qualities* of his *adversaries:* *They were wicked, unrighteous, and cruel.*

6. From his *confidence:* *Thou art my hope.*

7. From his *gracious providence:* *By thee have I been holden up, etc.*

8. From his *thankful heart:* *My praise shall be continually, etc.*

9. He had *none to trust to* but God: *Thou art my refuge.* Adam Clarke.

Verse 1. Faith is a present act; faith is a personal act, faith deals only with God, faith knows what she is about, faith kills her fears by prayer.

Verse 2. An appeal.

1. To the power of God: *Deliver me.*

2. To the faithfulness of God: *In thy righteousness.*

3. To the providence of God: *Cause me to escape.*

4. To the condescension of God: *Incline thine ear.*

5. To the mercy of God: *Save me.*

Verse 2. *Cause me to escape.* From whom? From what? How? By what power? For what end?

Verse 3. (*first two clauses*). The believer abiding in God and continually resorting to him.

Verse 3. (*Third clause*). A command based on the divine promise, clothed with divine power, addressed to all necessary agencies, and embracing all exigencies.

Verse 4.

1. When God is for us, the wicked are against us.

2. When the wicked are against us, God is for us.

Verse 5. God the essence of hope and faith.

Verse 7. (*first clause*). may be accommodated to,

1. *The Savior.*

2. *The Saint.* He is a *wonder* in reference to

>   (a) What he once was;
>   (b) What he now is;
>   (c) What he will hereafter be.

3. *The sinner* is "a wonder unto many;" a wonder to three worlds: to

>   (a) angels;
>   (b) saints;
>   (c) devils and lost souls.
>   —*Warwell Fenn.* 1830.

Verse 7. Consider the text, with reference to *David,* to *Christ,* and to the *Christian.*

1. With reference to *David.*

>   (a) David was a wonder as a man.
>   (b) As a king.
>   (c) As a servant of God.

2. With respect to *Christ.*

>   (a) Christ was a wonder in his person.
>   (b) In his life.
>   (c) In his miracles.
>   (d) In his teaching.
>   (e) In his sufferings.
>   (f) In his ascension and mediatorial glory.

3. With regard to the *Christian.*

>   (a) The Christian is a wonder to himself.
>   (b) To the world.
>   (c) To wicked spirits.
>   (d) To the angels in heaven.
>   —*John Cawood.* 1830.

Verse 8.

1. What? filled with what?—murmurings? doubts? fears? No! Praise. My own?—of men? No. *Thy praise. Thy Honor.*

2. When? *All the day.*

>   (a) The whole day.

(b) Every day; a good preparation for heaven.

Verse 9. There are some peculiar circumstances of old age which render this blessing—the Favor and presence of God—necessary.

1. Old age is a time of but little natural enjoyment, as Barzillai acknowledged, 2Sa 19:35.

2. It is a time of life in which the troubles of life are often known to increase.

3. Old age is a time in which the troubles of life not only increase, but become less tolerable.

4. Old age is a time which ought to command respect, and does so among dutiful children and all serious Christians: but it is often known to be attended with neglect. This is the case especially where they are poor and dependent. It has been the case where public characters have lost their youthful vivacity, and the brilliancy of their talents. *A. Fuller.*

Verse 9. There is,

1. Fear, mixed with faith.

    (a) Natural to old age.
    (b) Suggested by the usage of the world.

2. Faith mixed with fear: "Cast me not, "etc.

    (a) Old age is not a sin.
    (b) It is a crown of glory if found, etc.

Verses 11-12. Two great lies and two sweet prayers.

Verses 13-14.

1. What the wicked gain by opposing the righteous: Let them, etc. Ps 71:13.

2. What the righteous gain from being opposed by them, Ps 71:14: *But I,* etc.

Verse 14. See "Spurgeon's Sermons, "No. 998; "More and More."

Verse 15.

1. The determination avowed.

    (a) To recount the instances of the divine faithfulness in his deliverances.

    (b) To recount them publicly: *My mouth,* etc.

    (c) Constantly: *All the day.*

2. The reason assigned: *For I know not,* etc. "Eternity's too short to utter all thy praise." Therefore I begin it now, and will continue it.

Verse 16.

1. The resolution: *I will go.*

2. The reservation: *Thy strength only — thy righteousness only.*

Verse 17. *O God, thou hast taught me.* None but God can teach us experimentally; and the lessons he teaches are always useful and important. He teaches all his scholars to know themselves — their depravity, poverty, and slavery. He teaches them his law — its purity, claims, and penalty. He teaches them his gospel — its fulness, freeness, and sensibility. He teaches them to know himself; as a reconciled God, as their Father and faithful friend. His teaching is accompanied with power and authority. We may know divine teaching by its effects: it always produces humility — they sit as his feet; dependence upon him; abhorrence of sin; love to God as a teacher; obedience to the lessons taught; thirst for further attainments; and it brings us daily to Jesus. *James Smith.*

Verse 18. The peculiar testimony of pious old age, what it is based upon, to whom it should be directed, and what we may hope from it.

Verse 19. A sermon might be instructively worked out upon "the high things of God."

Verse 20.

1. The future benefit of present trials: "Hereafter," said Aneas to his shipwrecked companions. "It will delight us to think of these things."

2. The present benefit of future mercies: "Glory to thee for all the grace we have not tasted yet."

Verse 22. A choice subject for song — "thy truth, "which may mean either doctrinal truth, or the attribute of faithfulness, its manifestation in history, and in our own experience.

Verse 22-23.

1. The soul of music: Not in the instrument or the voice, but in the soul. "I will sing with the understanding also." "Making melody in the heart, "etc.

2. The music of the soul. The *soul which thou hast redeemed.* Redemption is the music of souls once lost. Their only song in heaven.

Verse 24. How to make familiar talk edifying and useful.

PSALM 72

SERMON OUTLINES AND HELPFUL TIPS

Whole Psalm.

1. He shall.

2. They shall. Ring the changes on these, as the Psalm does.

Verse 1. The prayer of the ancient church now fulfilled.

1. Our Lord's titles.

    (a) King, by divine nature.

    (b) King's Son, in both natures. Thus we see his power innate and derived.

2. Our Lord's authority: "Judgments."

    (a) To rule his people.
    (b) To rule the world for his people's benefit.
    (c) To judge mankind.
    (d) To judge devils.

3. Our Lord's character. He is righteous in rewarding and punishing, righteous towards God and man.

4. Our loyal prayer. This asks for his rule over ourselves and the uni**Verse**.

Verse 2. The rule of Christ in his church.

1. The subjects.

    (a) Thy people, the elect, called, etc.
    (b) Thy poor, through conviction and consciousness of sin.

2. The ruler. He, only, truly, constantly, etc.

3. The rule.—Righteous, impartial, gentle, prudent, etc. Lesson. Desire this rule.

Verse 3. Mountains of divine decree, of immutable truth, of almighty power, of eternal grace, etc. These mountains of God are securities of peace.

Verse 4. The poor man's King, or the benefits derived by the poor from the reign of Jesus.

Verse 5. The perpetuity of the gospel, reasons for it, things which threaten it, and lessons derived from it.

Verse 6. The field, the shower, the result. This **Verse** is easily enough handled in a variety of ways.

Verse 7.

1. The righteous flourish more at one season than another.

2. They flourish most when Jesus is with them: *in his days, etc.*

3. The fruit of their growth is proportionately abundant: *and abundance,* etc. *G. Rogers.*

Verse 7. *Abundance of peace.* Abundant overtures of peace, abundant redemption making peace, abundant pardon conferring peace, abundant influences of the Spirit sealing peace, abundant promises guaranteeing peace, abundant love spreading peace, etc.

Verse 8. The universal spread of the gospel. Other theories as to the future overturned, and their evil influence exposed; while the benefit and certainty of this truth is vindicated.

Verse 9 (*last clause*). The ignoble end of Christ's enemies.

Verse 10. Christian finance; voluntary but abundant are the gifts presented to Jesus.

Verse 12. Christ's peculiar care of the poor.

Verse 12.

1. Pitiable characters.
2. Abject conditions: "cry;" "no helper."
3. Natural resort: "crieth."
4. Glorious interposition. *G. Rogers.*

Verse 14. The martyr's hope in life and comfort in death. *G. Rogers.*

Verse 14 (*last clause*). The martyr's blood.

1. Seen of God when shed.
2. Remembered by him.
3. Honored by being a benefit to the church.
4. Rewarded especially in heaven.

Verse 15. *Prayer shall be made for him.* We are to pray for Jesus Christ. Owing to the interest he has in certain objects, what is done for them is done for himself and so he esteems it. We, therefore, pray for him when we pray for his ministers, his ordinances, his gospel, his church—in a word, his *cause.* But what should we pray for on his behalf?

1. The degree of its resources; that there be always a sufficiency of suitable and able instruments to carry on the work.

2. The freedom of its administration; that whatever opposes or hinders its progress may be removed.

3. The diffusion of its principles; that they may become general and universal.

4. The increase of its glory, as well as its extent. *W. Jay.*

Verse 15. Prayer for Jesus, a suggestive topic. Daily praise, a Christian duty.

Verse 15. A living Savior, a giving people; the connection between the two. Or, Christ in the church fills the exchequer, fosters the prayer meeting, and sanctifies the service of song.

Verse 16.

1. A happy description of the gospel: it is *a handful of corn.*

2. The places where it is sown.

3. The blessed effects which this gospel, when thus sown, will produce in the world. *J. Sherman.*

Verse 16.

1. Commencement.
2. Publicity.
3. Growth.
4. Result.

Verse 16.

1. What? *Corn.*

2. How much? *A handful.*

3. Where? *In the earth upon the top of the mountains.*

4. Will it grow? *The fruits,* etc.

5. What then? *They of the city,* etc.

Verse 17.

1. Christ glorified in the Church: *men shall be* blessed, etc.

2. Glorified in the world: *all nations,* etc.

3. Glorified in worlds to come: *endure, be continued, etc.*

4. Glorified forever. *G. Rogers.*

Verses 17-19. The Four Blesseds, their meaning and order.

Verse 20.

1. Prayer should be frequent: *The prayers.*

2. Should be individual: *Of David.*

3. Should be early commenced: *the son of Jesse.*

4. Should be continued till they are no more needed.

PSALM 73

SERMON OUTLINES AND HELPFUL TIPS

Whole Psalm. It containeth the godly man's *trial,* in the former part of it, and his *triumph,* in the latter part of it. We have,

1. The grievous conflict between the flesh and the spirit, to the 15th **Verse**.

2. The glorious conquest of the spirit over the flesh, to the end. *G. Swinnock*.

Whole Psalm.

1. The cause of his distemper.
2. The cure of it.
3. The psalmist's carriage after it.
— *G. Swinnock.*

Verse 1. The true Israel, the great blessing, and the sureness of it: or, the proposition of the text expounded, enforced, and applied.

Verse 1. (*first clause*). Israel's receipts from God are,

1. For quantity, the greatest;
2. For variety, the choicest;
3. For quality, the sweetest;
4. For security, the surest;
5. For duration, the most lasting.
— *Simeon Ash.*

Verse 2.

1. How far a believer may fall.
2. How far he shall not fall.
3. What fears are and what are not allowable.

Verse 2. A retrospect of our slips; prospect of future danger; present preparation for it.

Verse 4. Quiet death; the cases of the godly and ungodly distinguished by the causes of the quiet, and the unreliability of mere feelings shown.

Verse 5. The bastard's portion contrasted with that of the true son.

Verse 7. The dangers of opulence and luxury.

Verse 8. Connection between a corrupt heart and a proud tongue.

Verse 10.

1. The believer's cup is bitter.

2. It is full.

3. Its contents are varied *waters.*

4. It is but a *cup,* measured and limited.

5. It is the cup of *his people,* and, consequently, works good in the highest degree.

Verse 11. The atheists open question; the oppressor's practical question; the careless man's secret question; and the fearful saint's fainting question. The reasons why it is ever asked, and the conclusive reasons which put the matter beyond question.

Verse 12. This **Verse** suggests solemn enquiries for persons who are growing rich.

Verse 14. The frequent and even constant chastisement of the righteous; the necessity and design thereof; and the consolations connected therewith.

Verse 15. How we may bring injury on the saints; why we should avoid so doing, and how.

Verse 17.

1. Entrance into the place of fellowship with God, it privileges, and the way thereto.

2. Lessons learned in that hallowed place; the text mentions one.

3. Practical influence of the fellowship, and the instruction.

Verses 17-18. The sinner's end; See "Spurgeon's Sermons," No. 486.

Verse 18. *Thou didst set them in slippery places.*

1. It implies that they were always exposed to *sudden, unexpected destruction.* As he that walks in slippery places is every moment liable to fall, he cannot foresee one moment whether he shall stand or fall the next; and when he does fall, he falls at once without warning.

2. They are liable to fall *of* themselves, without being thrown down by the hand of another; as he that stands or walks on slippery ground needs nothing but his own weight to throw him down.

3. There is nothing that keeps wicked men at any one moment out of hell but the mere pleasure of God. *Jonathan Edwards.*

Verses 18-20. The end of the wicked is,

1. Near: *Thou hast set,* etc. It may happen at any time.

2. Judicial: *Thou bringest,* etc.

3. Sudden: *How are they,* etc.

4. Tormenting: *They are utterly consumed,* etc.

5. Eternal: Left to themselves; gone from the mind of God; and disregarded as a dream when one awaketh. No after act respecting them, either for deliverance or annihilation.

Verse 19. The first sight and sense of hell by a proud and wealthy sinner, who has just died in peace.

Verse 20. The contemptible object:—a self-righteous, or boastful, or persecuting, or caviling, or wealthy sinner when his soul is called before God.

Verse 22. Our folly, ignorance, and brutishness. When displayed. What effect the fact should have upon us; and how greatly it illustrates divine grace.

Verse 22-25.

1. The psalmist's confession concerning the flesh.

2. The faithful expressions of the spirit.

3. The conclusion of the whole matter. See "Spurgeon's Sermons, "No. 467.

Verse 25. God the best portion of the Christian. *Jonathan Edwards' Works, Vol. 2, pp. 104-7.*

Verse 25. Heaven and earth ransacked to find a joy equal to the Lord himself. Let the preacher take up various joys and show the inferiority.

Verse 26.

1. The psalmist's complaint: *My flesh and my heart faileth.*

2. His comfort: *But God,* etc. Or, we may take notice, (a) Of the frailty of his flesh; (b) Of the flourishing of his faith.

Doctrine 1. That man's flesh will fail him. The highest, the holiest man's heart will not always hold out. The prophet was great and gracious, yet his flesh failed him.

Doctrine 2. That it is the comfort of a Christian, in his saddest condition, that God is his portion. *G. Swinnock.*

Verse 26. "The Fading of the Flesh, " *Swinnock's Treatise. (Nichol's Puritan Series.)*

Verse 26. Where we fail and where we cannot fail.

Verse 27.

1. The sad conditions.
2. The terrible punishments.
3. The implied consolations.

Verse 28. To draw near to God is our wisdom, our Honor, our safety, our peace, our riches. *Thomas Watson's Sermon,* "*The Happiness of Drawing near to God.*" 1669. See also, "*The Saint's Happiness,* "R. Sibbes's Sermons.

Verse 28. David's conclusion; or, the saint's resolution. *R. Sibbes.*

Verse 28.

1. The language of prayer: *It is good,* etc.

2. Of faith: *I have put,* etc.

3. Of praise: *That I may declare.* G. R.

Verse 28. See "Spurgeon's Sermons," Nos. 287-8, "Let us pray." No. 879, "An assuredly good thing."

PSALM 74

SERMON OUTLINES AND HELPFUL TIPS

Verse 1.

1. The divine displeasure a fact.

2. It is but in measure, and we are very liable to exaggerate it.

3. Even while it lasts our relation to him is unaffected: *Sheep of thy pasture.*

4. Our business is to enquire the reason of it, and act accordingly.

Verse 1. *(second clause).* The Lord's anger with his people compared to smoke.

1. It is not a consuming fire.
2. It suggests fear of the fire.
3. It darkens the light of joy.
4. It blinds the eyes of faith.
5. It checks the breath of life.
6. It blackens the beauty of our worldly comforts.

Verse 2.

1. The Lord's relation to his people.

    (a) Election.
    (b) Redemption.
    (c) Indwelling.

2. The prayer arising from it: *Remember.*

Verse 3. Church mischief.

1. The church has enemies.

2. Wickedness in the church is their great weapon.

3. This causes much desolation to weak saints, to enquirers, to peace, to prayer, to usefulness.

4. The cure for it is God's interposition.

Verses 3-4. The power of prayer.

1. On one side were,

    (a) Desolation: *perpetual,* etc.
    (b) Desecration.
    (c) Declamation: *enemies roar.*
    (d) Demonstration: *they set up.*

2. On the other side is,

    (a) Supplication.
    (b) This brings God to the rescue effectually and quickly.

Verse 4. *Ensigns for signs.* The craft of Satan is supplanting truth with deceptive counterfeits.

Verse 5. True fame. To build for God with labor, daring, diligence, skill, etc.

Verse 6. Vandal work against the truth of God.

Verses 6-7. Things feared by a church.

1. Injury to her doctrines or ordinances: *carved work.*

2. The fire of strife, division, etc.

3. The defilement of sin. Either of these three will throw a church down; let her guard and pray against them.

Verse 8. The destruction of rural churches, the aim of our enemies: the injury they would so do, and our duty to prevent it: the means the destroyers use: bribery, oppression, etc. Our proper method for sustaining such churches.

Verse 9. (*first clause*).

1. There are such things as *signs,* that is, tokens and marks of God's special Favor to the soul.

2. There is also *a seeing* those signs when God, the Holy Ghost, is pleased to shine upon them.

3. There is a third state, where there is *not seeing* the signs, those signs being enveloped in darkness, dimness, and obscurity. *J. C. Philpot.*

Verse 10. A prayer for revival.

1. How God is reproached.
2. What are the ill effects of it.
3. When we may expect him to arise.

Verse 11.

1. The patience of God with man: He 'withdraws his hand, even,' etc., he hesitates to strike.

2. The impatience of man with God: "pluck it, "etc. *G. R.*

Verse 12.

1. The sovereignty of God.
2. Its antiquity.
3. Our loyalty to it.
4. The practical character of his reign: *working.*

5. The graciousness of it: *working salvation.*
6. The place of its operation: *in the midst of the earth.*

Verse 14. God's defeat of our enemies, and the benefit accruing to ourselves.

Verse 15. The wonderful nature of gracious supplies, illustrated by the smitten rock.

Verse 16. God present alike in all dispensations of providence.

Verses 16-17.

1. The God of grace is the God of nature: *The day in thine,* etc.

2. The God of nature is the God of grace: the wisdom, the power, the faithfulness the same. See Psalm 19. *G. R.*

Verse 19. The soul of the believer compared to a turtledove.

Verse 20.

1. The title given to heathen nations: *dark places of the earth.* Not without the light of nature, or of reason, or of natural conscience, or of philosophy, as of Greece and Rome; but without the light of revelation.

2. Their condition: *full of,* etc.: cruelty in their public, social, and private relationships. See Romans 1: "without natural affection, implacable, unmerciful."

3. Their part in the covenant. This is known from their part in its promises, and in prophecies: *I will give thee the heathen,* etc.

4. The prayer of others on their behalf: *Have respect,* etc.; *Oh send forth thy light,* etc.

The conversion of the world will be in answer to the prayers of the church.

Verse 22. God pleading his own cause in providential visitations of nations and individuals, as also in remarkable conversions and awakenings.

Verse 22.

1. The glory of our cause: it is the Lord's own.

2. The hope of our cause: he will plead it himself.

3. The hope thus derivable from the violence of man: it will move the Lord to arise.

PSALM 75

SERMON OUTLINES AND HELPFUL TIPS

Verse 1. The unceasing thanksgiving of the church, her grand cause for adoration: the nearness of her God, and the evident proof thereof in the displays of his power.

Verse 1.

1. Do we give thanks?
2. We do give thanks.
3. What thanks do we give.?
4. When do we give thanks?
5. Let us give thanks again.

Good resolutions commendable, how they should be made, strengthened, and performed.

Verse 3. The Lord the stay of his people under the worst circumstances.

Verse 3. Teacheth us that no disorder or confusion should hinder us from doing that which God requireth of us; nay, rather, the more things are out of order the more readily should we labor to redress them. *Thomas Wilcocks.*

Verse 4.

1. Who spoke to them? *I.*

2. Who were they? *Fools, wicked.*

3. What did you say?

4. What was the good of it? Or, Rebuke of sin, a duty.

Verse 4. The unhallowed trio:—wickedness, folly, pride.

Verse 5. Arguments against pride in heart, appearance, and speech.

Verses 6-7. The changes of providence not the tricks of fortune.

Verse 7. God acts as a judge and not arbitrarily in his providential arrangements.

Verse 8. *In the hand of the Lord there is a cup,* etc.

1. As to matter of *preparation,* consider it so, and thus it is *in the hand of the Lord.*

2. By way of *qualification:* it is he that tempers it; it was *full of mixture.*

3. By way of *distribution,* as giving to every one his share and portion in it. *Thomas Horton.*

Verse 8. The cup of wrath. Where it is, what it is, how full it is, who brings it, who must drink it.

Verse 8. *Full of mixture.* Wrath of God, remorse, memory of lost joy, fear of future, recriminations, despair, shame, etc., all these are ingredients of the mingled cup.

Verse 8. (*last clause*).

1. "The dregs" of the cup: the wrath of wrath, the gall of bitterness.

2. The dregs of the people: "all wicked."

Verse 9. Our life work: to declare and to sing.

PSALM 76

SERMON OUTLINES AND HELPFUL TIPS

Verse 1. Reverence for God's name proportionate to true knowledge of it.

Verse 2. The peculiar relation of God to his church.

Verse 2. (*first clause*). A peaceful church the tabernacle of God. The benefits peace confers, the evils of strife, the causes of dissension, and the means of promoting unity.

Verse 3. Christian glories, or the victories vouchsafed to the church over heathenism, heresy, persecution, etc.

Verse 3.

1. Where enemies are conquered; "There; "not on the battlefield so much as in the house of God; as Amalek by Moses on the Mount; Sennacherib by Hezekiah in the Sanctuary.

2. How there?

    (a) By faith.

    (b) By prayer. "The weapons of our warfare, "etc.

Verse 4. The Lord, our portion, compared with the treasures of empires.

Verse 4.

1. What the world is, compared with the church: Mountains of prey.

    (a) Cruelty instead of love.
    (b) Violence instead of peace.

2. What the church is compared with the world.

    (a) *More glorious,* because *more excellent.*

    (b) *More excellent,* because *more glorious.* Both are more real and abiding. G. R.

Verse 5. *They have slept their sleep.* Divers kinds of deaths or sleeps for the various classes of men.

Verse 7. The anger of God. A very suggestive subject.

Verses 8-9.

1. The characters described: *the meek of the earth.*

2. The need implied.

    (a) To be vindicated.
    (b) To be saved.

3. The divine interposition on their behalf: *Thou didst cause,* etc. *When God arose,* etc.

4. The effect of their deliverance: *The earth feared,* etc. G. R.

Verse 10.

1. Evil permitted for good: *the wrath,* etc.
2. Restrained for good: *The remainder,* etc.

Or,

1. Ruled.
2. Overruled. G. R.

Verse 11.

1. To whom vows may be made. Not to man, but God.

2. What vows should be thus made.

> (a) Of self dedication.
> (b) Of self service.
> (c) Of self-sacrifice.

3. How kept: *Vow and pay.*

> (a) From duty.
> (b) From fear of his displeasure. G. R.

Verse 11. The propriety, obligation, pleasure, and profit of presenting gifts unto the Lord.

PSALM 77

SERMON OUTLINES AND HELPFUL TIPS

Verse 1. The benefit of using the voice in private prayer.

Verses 1, 3, 5, 10. Note the wise man's progress out of his soul trouble.

1. I cried.
2. I remembered.
3. I considered.
4. I said.

Verse 2. See "Spurgeon's Sermons, "No. 853. "A Sermon for the Most Miserable of Men."

Verse 2.

1. Special prayer: *In the days,* etc.

2. Persevering prayer: hands lifted up to God by night as well as by day.

3. Agonizing prayer: *my soul refused to be comforted, until the answer came*. "Being in an agony, he prayed, "etc.

Verse 2. (*last clause*). When this is wise, and when it is censurable.

Verse 4.

1. A good man cannot rest on his bed until his soul rests on God.

2. He cannot speak freely to others until God speaks peace to his soul. *G. R.*

Verse 4. Occupation for the sleepless, and consolation for the speechless.

Verses 5-6. There are four rules for obtaining comfort in affliction.

1. The consideration of God's goodness to his people of old.

2. Remembrance of our own past experience.

3. Self-examination.

4. The diligent study of the word. *G. R.*

Verse 6. *Remembrance.* A good memory is very helpful and useful.

1. It is a great means of *knowledge:* for what signifies your reading or hearing, if you remember nothing?

2. It is a means of *faith:* 1Co 15:2.

3. It is a means of *comfort*. If a poor Christian in distress could remember God's promises they would inspire him with new life; but when they are forgotten, his spirits sink.

4. It is a means of *thankfulness.*

5. It is a means of *hope;* for "experience worketh hope" (Ro 5:4), and the memory is the storehouse of experience.

6. It is a means of *repentance;* for, how can we repent or mourn for that which we have forgotten?

7. It is a means of *usefulness.* When one spark of grace is truly kindled in the heart, it will quickly endeavor to heat others also. *R. Steele.*

Verse 7. (*first clause*). To place the question in a strong light, let us consider,

1. Of whom is the question raised? *the Lord.*

2. What course of action is in question? *cast off forever.*

3. Towards whom would the action be performed?

Verse 8. These questions,

1. Suppose a change in the immutable Jehovah in two glorious attributes.

2. Are contrary to all past evidence.

3. Can only arise from the flesh and Satan; and, therefore,

4. Are to be met in the power of the Spirit, with strong faith in the Eternal God.

Verse 10. A confession applicable to many other matters. Such as, fear of death, fear of desertion, dread of public service, sensitiveness of neglect, etc.

Verse 10. *My infirmity.* Different meanings of this word. These would furnish a good subject. Some infirmities are to be patiently endured, others gloried in, others taken in prayer to God for his Spirit's help, and others lamented and repented of.

Verses 10-12. Remember, meditate, talk.

Verses 11-12.
1. Consolation derived from the remembrance of the past.
2. Consolation increased by meditation.
3. Consolation strengthened by communication: "and talk," etc. *G. R.*

Verses 11-12.

1. Consolation derived from the remembrance of the past.
2. Consolation increased by meditation.
3. Consolation strengthened by communication: "and talk," etc. *G. R.*

Verse 12. Themes for thought and topics for conversation. Creation, Providence, Redemption, etc.

Verses 13, 19. *In the sea, in the sanctuary.* God's way incomprehensible, though undoubtedly right: in his holiness lies the answer to its enigmas.

Verse 14. *Thaumaturgeis,* or the Great Wonder worker.

Verse 15. *And Joseph.* The Honor of nourishing those who have been begotten of God by other men's labors.

Verse 15. Redemption thy power, the consequence, evidence, and necessary attendant of redemption by price.

Verse 15.

1. The redeemed: *thy people; the sons of,* etc.

    (a) In captivity though they are his people.
    (b) His people though they are in captivity.

2. The redemption: from Egyptian bondage.

3. The Redeemer: *Thou, with thine arm,* etc. God by Christ, his arm: *Mine own arm brought,* etc. *To whom is the arm of the Lord revealed?* G. R.

Verses 16-18.
1. The homage of nature to the God of grace.
2. Its subserviency to his designs. *G. R.*

Verse 19.

1. The ways of God to men are peculiar: *In the sea: thy path, etc.*
2. They are uniform, they lie in regular *footsteps.*
3. They are inscrutable: like the path of the ship upon the waters, not of the ploughshare on the land.

Verse 19. God's way is in the sea. In things changeable, ungovernable, vast, unfathomable, terrible, overwhelming, the Lord has the ruling power.

Verse 20.

1. The subjects of divine guidance: *thy people.*

2. The manner of their guidance: *like a flock*—separated, united, dependent.

3. The agents employed: *by the hand*; the Great Shepherd leads by the hand of under shepherds. "May every under shepherd keep his eye intent on Thee."

Verse 20. Church history.

1. The church a flock.
2. God seen as leading it on.
3. Instrumentality always used.

PSALM 78

SERMON OUTLINES AND HELPFUL TIPS

Verse 1. The duty of attending to God's word. Modes of neglecting the duty; ways of fulfilment; reasons for obedience; evils of inattention.

Verse 2. (*first clause*). Preach on the "Parable of the Prodigal Nation, "as given in the whole Psalm. *C. A. Davies, of Chesterfield.*

Verses 2-3.

1. Truths are none the worse for being old: *sayings of* old. "Old wood, "says Lord Bacon, "is best to burn; old books are best to read; and old friends are best to trust."

2. Truths are none the worse for being concealed under metaphors: *I will open,* etc., *in a parable; dark sayings.*

3. Truths are none the worse for being often repeated.

     (a) They are more tested.
     (b) They are better testified. *G. R.*

Verse 3. The connection between what we have "heard, "and what we have personally "known" in religion.

Verse 4. A good resolution, and a blessed result. *C. D.*

Verse 4.

1. What is to be made known? *The praises of the Lord; his strength and his wonderful works.*

2. To whom are they to be made known? *To the generations to come.*

3. By whom? Parents—one generation to another.

4. How made known?

     (a) By hiding nothing.
     (b) By declaring everything God has done. *G. R.*

Verse 5. Scriptural tradition, or the heirloom of the gospel.

Verses 5-8. Family religion.

1. The fathers' knowledge the children's heritage—Ps 78:5-6.
2. The fathers' fall the children's preservation—Ps 78:7-8.

Verses 5-8.

1. Truth once started can never be arrested—Ps 78:5-6.
2. Truth received binds the soul to God—Ps 78:7.
3. Truth rejected lights up beacons for others—Ps 78:8.

Verses 7-8. On the deceitfulness of the heart, in disregarding providential dispensations in general. *John Jamieson's "Sermons on the Heart," I. 430.*

Verse 8. Stubbornness not steadfastness, or the difference between a natural vice and a gracious quality.

Verse 8. The false heart (*middle clause*), with its left hand, "Stubbornness in the wrong" (*first clause*), and its right hand, "Fickleness in the right" (*last clause*). C. D.

Verse 9. Who were they? What had they? What did they? When did they do it?

Verses 9, 67. The backsliding of prominent believers.

1. The Lord's soldiers: who they were; belonging to God's chosen people; were distinguished by grace. Ge 48:17-20. Strong by God's blessing. De 33:17. Honorable place among their brethren. Favored with the tabernacle at Shiloh—Ps 78:60.

2. Their equipment: armor defensive and offensive; like that of others who triumphed.

3. Their behavior in battle: to turn back was traitorous, cowardly, dangerous, disastrous, dishonorable.

4. Their punishment—Ps 78:57. Deprived of their special Honor. Re 3:11. C. D.

Verses 10-11. The gradations of sin: neglecting, rejecting, forgetting God. C. D.

Verses 12-16. God revealed in his deeds. The wonder working God—Ps 78:12-16. The avenging God—Ps 78:12. The interposing God—Ps 78:13. The guiding God—Ps 78:14. The Father God—Ps 78:14-16. C. D.

Verses 12-17. Obstinacy of unbelief. It makes head against God's majesty—Ps 78:17; his gracious providence—Ps 78:14-16; his interposing care—Ps 78:13; his avenging justice—Ps 78:12; his distinguishing grace—Ps 78:12-16. C. D.

Verses 12-17. Prodigies cannot convert the soul. Lu 16:31. C. D.

Verses 15-16. Divine supplies seasonable, plentiful, of the best, marvelous.

Verse 16. Streams from the Rock Christ Jesus.

I. Their source.
2. Their variety.
3. Their abundance.
—*B. Davies, of Greenwich.*

Verses 12-17. Obstinacy of unbelief. It makes head against God's majesty—Ps 78:17; his gracious providence—Ps 78:14-16; his interposing care—Ps 78:13; his avenging justice—Ps 78:12; his distinguishing grace—Ps 78:12-16. *C. D.*

Verses 12-17. Prodigies cannot convert the soul. Lu 16:31. *C. D.*

Verse 17. Sin in its progress feeds upon divine mercies to aid its advance, as also every other surrounding circumstance.

Verses 17-21.

1. They tempted God's patience; Ps 78:17.
2. They tempted God's wisdom; Ps 78:18.
3. They tempted God's power; Ps 78:19-20.
4. They tempted God's wrath; Ps 78:21.
—*E. G. Gange, of Bristol.*

Verses 18-21. The progress of evil.

1. They are drawn away by their lust: Ps 78:18.
2. Lust having conceived bringeth forth sin: Ps 78:19-20.
3. Sin being finished bringeth forth death: Ps 78:21.

"Their carcasses fell." *C. D.*

Verses 21-22. Evil consequences of unbelief.

1. The sin itself: they doubted the ultimate certainty, completeness, and reality of God's salvation from Egypt.

2. The aggravation of it: the object of it was God; they who entertained it were God's people: The aids to faith were overlooked: "though."

3. What it led them to; inward sin—Ps 78:18; outward sin—Ps 78:19, etc.

4. What it brought upon them; Ps 78:21. Fiery serpents, etc. *C. D.*

Verse 25. Different kinds of food. Beast's food, Lu 15:16. Sinners' food, Ho 4:8. Formalists' food, Ho 12:1. Saints' food, Jer 15:16 Joh 6:53-57. Angels' food. Christ's food, Joh 4:34. *C. D.*

Verse 29-31. Dangerous prayers. When lust dictates, wrath may answer. Let grace dictate, and mercy will answer. *C. D.*

Verses 34-37. The hypocrite's feet, Ps 78:34. The hypocrite's memory, Ps 78:35. The hypocrite's tongue, Ps 78:36. The hypocrite's heart, Ps 78:37. Or, the hypocrite's cloak and the hypocrite's heart. *C. D.*

Verse 38. (*last clause*) and Ps 78:50 (*first clause*). God's anger as exercised against his people and against his foes. *C. D.*

Verses 39, 35. God's memory of his people and their memory of God.

Verse 42. The day of days.

1. The enemy encountered on that day.
2. The conflict endured.
3. The deliverance accomplished.
4. The joy experienced. *B. D.*

Verse 45. The power of little things when commissioned to plague us.

Verse 47. (*last clause*). Sometimes it will not shoot. Sometimes it will. And when it does, it misses the mark.

Verse 52.

1. God has a people in the world.
2. He brings them away from others.
3. He brings them into fellowship with himself.
4. He brings them into fellowship with each other.
5. He guides them to their rest.

Verse 55. Divine supplanting. He supplants the fallen angels in heaven. One nation of earth by another (see all history). The thoughts and affections of the heart in regeneration, etc.—*Isa 55:13*. *C. D.*

Verses 56-57. On the deceitfulness of the heart, with respect to the performance of duty. *J. Jamieson*. I. 326. On the deceitfulness of the heart, with respect to the omission of duty. *J. Jamieson*. I. 353.

Verses 59-72.

1. A gloomy sunset, *Ps 78:59-60*.
2. A baleful might, *Ps 78:60-64*.
3. A blessed sunrise, *Ps 78:65-72*. *C. D.*

Verses 9, 67. The backsliding of prominent believers.

1. The Lord's soldiers: who they were; belonging to God's chosen people; were distinguished by grace. *Ge 48:17-20*. Strong by God's blessing. *De 33:17*. Honorable place among their brethren. Favored with the tabernacle at Shiloh—*Ps 78:60*.

2. Their equipment: armor defensive and offensive; like that of others who triumphed.

3. Their behavior in battle: to turn back was traitorous, cowardly, dangerous, disastrous, dishonorable.

4. Their punishment—*Ps 78:57*. Deprived of their special Honor. *Re 3:11*. *C. D.*

Verses 70-72. Spiritual promotions.

Verses 72. In spite of his transgressions, which he always bitterly repented of and which were therefore blotted out of the Book of God, he remains to all princes and rulers of the earth as the noblest pattern. In perfect inward truth he knew and felt himself to be "*King by the grace of God.*" The crown and scepter he bore merely in trust from the King of all kings; and to his latest breath he endeavored with all his earnestness to be found as a genuine theocratic king, who in everything must conduct his earthly government according to the ordinances and directions of God. Therefore the Lord made all that he took in hand prosper, and nothing was clearer to the people than that the Lord was *truly with the king. Frederick William Krummacher, in "David, the King of Israel."* 1867.

PSALM 79

SERMON OUTLINES AND HELPFUL TIPS

Verse 4. Saints the subject of derision to sinners. When justly so. When unjustly. What do they see to excite ridicule; what shall we do under the trial; how will it end?

Verse 5.

1. The cause of anger: jealousy.

2. The moderation of it. If it continued forever, the people would perish, the promises be unfulfilled, the covenant fail, and the Lord's Honor be impeached.

3. The staying of it. By prayer; by pleading his name, his glory, and the blood of Jesus.

Verse 8. A sinner's confession, petition, and plea.

Verse 9. I. A threefold prayer. II. An encouraging title: "God of our salvation." III. A victorious plea.

Verse 10.
I. The Prayer. "Help us," etc.
　1. Purge away sin.
　2. Deliver us from our troubles.
　3. Help us to serve thee in future.
2. The Plea.
　1. For thy name's sake.
　2. The glory of thy name.
　3. The glory of thy name as our salvation. The order in both cases is inverted. —G. R.

Verse 10. The revenge for the martyrs, which it is lawful and incumbent upon us to desire.

Verse 11.
I. The prisoner.
　1. Under forced bondage to sin.
　2. Under the bondage of conviction.
　3. In the dungeon of despair.
2. The prisoner's application for relief.
3. The source from which he looked for help. —P. B. Power.

Verse 11.
I. The degree of protection solicited: "According to the greatness of thy power."
2. The protection itself: "Preserve thou."
3. The objects of it: "Those that are appointed to die." —W. C. Le Breton.

Verse 11.
I. Mournful condition. A prisoner, sighing, appointed to die.
2. Hopeful facts: a God, a God hearing sighs, a God of great power.
3. Suitable prayers: "come before thee": "preserve."

Verse 11. "*Appointed to die,*" used as a description of deep spiritual distress. Fears of the divine decree, of having apostatised, of having sinned away the day of grace, of the sin which is unto death, etc. How these cases can be effectually met.

Verse 13. The obligations of the Protestant church based on her martyrs' blood, her great deliverances, her nearness to God. She ought to secure gospel teaching to coming generations.

Verse 13.
I. Relation claimed: "We thy people, the sheep of," etc.
2. Obligation admitted: "So we," etc., when thou hast interposed for our deliverance, we will praise thee.
3. Resolution formed.   1. To give thanks for ever;   2. To transmit his praise to generations following. — G. R

PSALM 80

SERMON OUTLINES AND HELPFUL TIPS

Verse 1. In what respects the Lord acted as a Shepherd to Israel, as illustrative of his dealings with his Church.

Verse 2. Salvation expected in connection with the people of God, their prayers, labors, and daily service.

Verse 3. The double work in salvation, (1) Turn us; (2) Turn to us.

Verse 4. What prayers they are which make God angry.

Verse 5. Unpalatable provender.

1. Analyze the Provision.
2. Note the hand which sends it.
3. Consider the healthfulness of the diet.
4. Remember the alleviating accompaniments.

Verse 7. Conversion, communion, confidence of salvation.

Verses 8-15. Parallel between the Church and a vine.

Verse 12.

1. The hedges of the Church.
2. Their removal.
3. The deplorable consequences.

Verse 13. What are the greatest enemies of the Church? Where do they come from? How shall we defeat them?

Verses 17-18. The power of God seen in Jesus, the cause of the perseverance of the saints.

Verse 18 (*last clause*). The need of quickening in order to acceptable worship.

PSALM 81

SERMON OUTLINES AND HELPFUL TIPS

Verse 1. Congregational singing should be general, hearty, joyful. The reasons for this, and the benefits of it.

Verses 1-3.

1. Praise should be sincere. It can come from the people of God only.

2. It should be constant: they should praise God at all times.

3. It should be special. There should be seasons of special praise.

    (a) Appointed by God, as Sabbaths and solemn feasts.

    (b) Demanded by providence on occasion of special

deliverances and special mercies.

4. It should be public: "sing aloud:" "bring hither, "etc. *G. R.*

Verse 4. The rule of ordinances and worship; pleas for going beyond it; instances in various churches; the sin and danger of such will worship.

Verse 5. What there is in the language of the world which is unintelligible to the sons of God.

Verse 6. The emancipation of believers. Law work is burdensome, servile, never completed, unrewarded, more and more irksome. Only the Lord can deliver us from this slavish toil, and he does it by grace and by power. We do well to remember the time of our liberation, exhibit gratitude for it, and live consistently with it.

Verse 7.

1. Answered prayers,—bonds of gratitude.

2. Former testing times,—warning memories.

3. The present a time for new answers as it is also for fresh tests.

Verse 7. *Waters of Meribah.* The various test points of the believer's life.

Verses 8-10.

1. A compassionate Father, calling to his child: *O my people, and I will testify unto thee: O Israel, if thou wilt hearken unto me.*

2. A jealous sovereign, laying down his law: *There shall no strange god be in thee.*

3. An all sufficient Friend, challenging confidence: *I am the Lord thy God: open thy mouth wide, and I will fill it. Richard Cecil.* 1748-1810.

Verses 8, 11, 13. The command, the disobedience, the regret.

Verses 11, 12.

1. The sin of Israel. They would not hearken. The mouth is opened in attentive hearing: *open thy mouth wide; but* my people, etc. Their sin was greatly aggravated

1. By what God had done for them.
2. By the gods they had preferred to him.
2. The punishment.

1. Its greatness: *I gave them up,* etc.
2. Its justice: *They would none of me.* G. R.

Verses 8, 11, 13. The command, the disobedience, the regret.

Verse 13. The excellent estate of an obedient believer.

1. Enemies subdued.
2. Enjoyments perpetuated.
3. Abundance possessed.

Verses 13-14. The sin and loss of the backslider.

Verse 14. Spiritual enemies best combatted by an obedient life.

Verse 16.

1. Spiritual dainties.
2. By whom provided.
3. To whom given.
4. With what result—"satisfied."

PSALM 82

SERMON OUTLINES AND HELPFUL TIPS

Verse 1. The sovereignty of God over the most powerful and exalted. How that sovereignty reveals itself, and what we may expect from it.

Verse 1. The Lord's presence in cabinets and senates.

Verse 2. A common sin. Regard for the persons of men often influences our judgment of their opinions, virtues, vices, and general bearing; this involves injustice to others, as well as deep injury to the flattered.

Verse 3. A plea for orphans.

Verse 5.

1. The characters of wicked princes.

   (a) Ignorance: *They know not.*
   (b) Willful blindness: *Neither will they,* etc.
   (c) Unrestrained perverseness: *They walk on,* etc.

2. The consequences to others: *All the foundations,* etc.

   (a) Of personal security.
   (b) Of social comfort.
   (c) Of commercial prosperity.
   (d) Of national tranquility.
   (e) Of religious liberty; all are out of course. G. R.

Verse 5. (*middle clause*). A description of the pilgrimage of presumptuous sinners.

Verse 6. *Ye are gods.* The passage in the Old Testament which involves the doctrine of the divinity of Christ. J. P. Lange.

Verse 8.

1. The invocation: *Arise,* etc.
2. The prediction: *For thou shalt,* etc. —G. R.

PSALM 83

SERMON OUTLINES AND HELPFUL TIPS

Verse 1. The long silence of God, the reasons for it, and our reasons for desiring him to end it.

Verse 3. Thy hidden ones.

1. Hidden as to their new nature, which is an enigma to men.
2. Hidden for protection, as precious things.
3. Hidden, for solace and rest.
4. Hidden, because not yet fully revealed.

Verse 4. The immortality of the church.

Verse 5. The confederacies of evils against the saints.

Verses 13-15. The instability, restlessness and impotence of the wicked; their horror when God deals with them in justice.

Verse 16. A prayer for the Pope and his priests.

Verse 17. The righteous fate of persecutors, and troublers.

Verse 18. The Golden Lesson: how taught, to whom, by whom, through whom?

PSALM 84

SERMON OUTLINES AND HELPFUL TIPS

Verse 1.

1. Why called Tabernacles? To include

   (a) the holiest of all;
   (b) The holy place;
   (c) The court and precincts of the Tabernacle. Amiable is predicated of these. The courts amiable—the holy place more amiable—the holiest of all most amiable.

2. Why called the Tabernacles of the Lord of Hosts? To denote

   (a) Its connection with the boundless univers.
   (b) Its distinction from it. Present everywhere where God is peculiarly present here.

3. Why called *amiable?*

   (a) Because of the character in which God dwells here. Is condescension amiable? Is love? Is mercy? Is grace? These are displayed here.
   (b) Because of the purpose for which he resides here. To save sinners: to comfort saints.

Verses 1-3. The Titles for God in these three **Verse**s are worth dwelling upon. *Jehovah of Hosts; the living God; my King and my God. G. R.*

Verse 3.

1. The Eloquence of Grief. David in his banishment envies the sparrows and the swallows that had built their nests by the house of God, more than Absalom who had usurped his palace and his throne.

2. The Ingenuity of Prayer. Why should sparrows and swallows be nearer to thy altars than I am, O Lord of hosts, my King and my God! "Fear not, ye are of more value than many sparrows." *G. R.*

Verse 4.

1. The Privilege suggested—dwelling in the house of God. Some birds fly over the house of God—some occasionally alight upon it—others build their nests and train up their young there. This was the privilege which the Psalmist desired.

2. The Fact asserted. *Blessed are they that dwell,* etc., who make it the spiritual home of themselves and their children.

3. The Reason given. *They will be still,* etc.

   (a) They will have much for which to praise God;
   (b) They will see much to praise in God. *G. R.*

Verse 5. Man is blessed,

1. When his strength is in God. Strength to believe, strength to obey, strength to suffer.

2. When God's ways are in him. *In whose heart,* etc. When the doctrines, precepts, and promises of God are deeply engraved upon the heart. *G. R.*

Verse 5. The preciousness of intensity and enthusiasm in religious belief, worship, and life.

Verses 5-7. The blessed people are described,

1. By their earnest desire and resolution to take this journey, though they dwelt far off from the tabernacle, Ps 84:5.

2. By their painful passage, yet some refreshments by the way, Ps 84:6.

3. By their constant progress, till they came to the place they aimed at, Ps 84:7. *T. Manton.*

Verse 6. As the valley of weeping symbolizes dejection, so a "well" symbolizes ever flowing salvation and comfort (compare Joh 4:14 Isa 12:3).

Verse 6.

1. *The valley of Baca.* Of this valley we may observe,

> (a) It is much frequented.
> (b) Unpleasant to flesh and blood.
> (c) Very healthful.
> (d) Very safe.
> (e) Very profitable.

2. The toilsome effort: *make it a well.*

> (a) Comfort may be obtained in the deepest trouble.
> (b) Comfort must be obtained by exertion.
> (c) Comfort obtained by one is of use to others, as a well may be.

3. The heavenly supply. *The rain also filleth the pools.* All is from God; effort is of no avail without him.

Verse 7.

1. Trusting God in trouble brings present comfort—Who passing, etc.

2. Present comfort ensures still larger supplies—*The rain also,* etc. *G. R.*

Verse 8. There is,

1. Progression. *They go;*

(a) The people of God cannot remain stationary;
(b) They must not recede;
(c) They should always be advancing.

2. Invigoration. *From strength to strength.*

(a) From one ordinance to another;

(b) from one duty to another;

(c) from one grace to another;

(d) from one degree of grace to another. Add faith to faith, virtue to virtue, knowledge to knowledge, etc.

3. Completion. *Every one of them,* etc. G. R.

Verse 8.

1. Prayer is not confined to the Sanctuary. David, in his banishment, says, *Hear my prayer.*

2. Help is not confined to the Sanctuary. The Lord of hosts is "here, "as well as in his tabernacle. See Ps 84:1.

3. Grace is not confined to the Sanctuary. Here, too, in the wilderness is the covenanting God, the God of Jacob. G. R.

Verse 8. Pleas for answers to prayer in the titles here used.

1. He is JEHOVAH, the living, all wise, all powerful, faithful, gracious, and immutable God.

2. He is God of hosts, having abundant agencies under his control; he can send angels, restrain devils, actuate good men, overrule bad men, and govern all other agents.

3. He is the God of Jacob, of chosen Jacob, as seen in Jacob's dream; God of Jacob in his banishment, in his wrestling (and so a God overcome by prayer), God pardoning Jacob's sins, God preserving Jacob and his seed after him.

Verse 9. Observe,

1. The Faith. Our shield is thine anointed—Thine Anointed is our Shield. This is not David, because he says *our* Shield, but David's greater Son. A gleam of Gospel light through the thick clouds.

2. The Prayer. *Behold, O God,* etc. *Look,* etc. Look upon him as our Representative, and look upon us in him.

3. The Plea.

(a) He has engaged to be our defense from thine anger;

(b) he has been anointed to this office by thee. G. R.

Verse 9.

1. What God is to us.

2. What we would have him look at.

3. Where we would be: hidden behind the shield—seen in the person of Christ.

Verse 10. Here is,

1. A comparison of Places. *A day in thy courts,* etc. How much more a day in heaven! What, then, must an eternity in heaven be!

2. A comparison of Persons. *I would rather be a doorkeeper*, etc. Better be the least in the Church than the greatest in the world. If "better reign in hell than serve in heaven" was Satan's first thought after he fell, it was the first thought only. **G.R.**

Verse 10.

1. Days in God's courts. Days of hearing, of repenting, of believing, of adoration, of communion, of revival, etc.

2. Their preciousness. Better than a thousand days of victory, of pleasure, of money making, of harvest, of discussion, of travelling amid beauties of nature.

3. Reasons for this preciousness. They are more pleasurable, more profitable now, and more preparatory for the future and for heaven. The employment, the society, the enjoyment, the result, etc., are all better.

Verse 11.

1. What God is to his people. *A sun and shield.*

    (a) The source of all good;
    (b) a defense from all evil.

2. What he gives.

    (a) Grace here;
    (b) glory hereafter.

3. What he withholds. All that is not good. If he withholds health or wealth, or his own smiles from us, it is because they are not good for us at that particular time. *G. R.*

Verse 12.

1. The one thing that makes man blessed. Trust in God. Blessed, etc.

    (a) For all things;
    (b) at all times;
    (c) in all circumstances.

2. The Blessing contained in that one thing. God himself becomes ours;

    (a) his mercy for our pardon;
    (b) his power for our protection;
    (c) his wisdom for our guidance;
    (d) his faithfulness for our preservation;
    (e) his all sufficiency for our supply.

3. The certainty of the blessing.

    (a) From David's own experience;

    (b) from the solemn appeal to God respecting it. O Lord God of hosts, etc. *G. R.*

Verse 12. The blessedness of the life of faith over that of carnal enjoyment, religious feeling, self confidence, living upon marks and evidences, trusting in man, etc.

PSALM 85

SERMON OUTLINES AND HELPFUL TIPS

Verse 1. There is,

1. Captivity.

   (a) Of the people of God.
   (b) Although they are the people of God.
   (c) Because they are the people of God. *You only have I known,* etc.

2. Restoration from Captivity: *Thou hast brought back,* etc.

   (a) The fact.

   (b) The Author: *Thou:* by thine own power; in thine own manner; at thine own time.

3. The cause of the Restoration; the Favor of God: *Thou hast been Favorable.*

   (a) On account of Favor past: "Thou hast."
   (b) On account of Favor in reserve.

Verse 2.

1. The subjects of forgiveness: *Thy people.*

   (a) By choice.
   (b) By redemption.
   (c) By effectual calling.

2. The time of forgiveness: *Thou hast forgiven,* etc.

3. The method of forgiveness.

   (a) Forgiven. Hebrew, borne, same word as in Le 16:22: "The goat shall bear upon him all their iniquities."

   (b) Covered; as the mercy seat covered the law that had been broken. The extent of forgiveness: *all their sin.*

Verse 3.

1. The language of penitence. It is implied here that the wrath was,

   (a) Great:

   (b) Just *thy wrath.*

2. The language of faith.

   (a) In the grace of pardon: *Thou hast turned away wrath.* We could not, by anything we could do or suffer.

(b) In the method of pardon: *Turned away.* Turned it from us to our Surety.

3. The language of praise: *Thou hast – thou hast.*

Verse 4.

1. In what salvation consists.

    (a) In the removal of God's enmity from us.
    (b) In the removal of our enmity to him.

2. By whom it is accomplished. By the God of salvation.

    (a) He causes his anger toward us to cease, and
    (b) Our anger toward him.

3. How is it obtained? By prayer: "Turn us, "etc.

Verse 6.

1. Revivals imply decline.

    (a) That there is grace to be revived.
    (b) That this grace has declined.

2. Revivals are from God: *Wilt not thou,* etc.: they cannot be got up by men.

3. Revivals are frequently needed: *Wilt not thou revive us again.*

4. Revivals are in answer to prayer: *Wilt thou not,* etc.

5. Revivals are occasions for great joy.

    (a) *To* the saints.
    (b) *In* God.

Verse 7.

1. Salvation is God's work: *Thy salvation.*

    (a) The plan is his.
    (b) The provision is his.
    (c) The condition is his.
    (d) The application is his.
    (e) The consummation is his.

2. Salvation is God's gift.

    (a) Of his mercy: *Show us thy mercy.*
    (b) Of his grace: *Grant us,* etc.

3. Salvation is God's answer to prayer.

(a) It is the first object of prayer.
(b) It includes every other.

Verse 8.

1. We should look for an answer to prayer. Having spoken to God, we should hear what he has to say to us in reply.

    (a) In his word.
    (b) In his providence.
    (c) By his Spirit in our own souls.

2. We should look for an answer of peace: *He will speak peace.*

3. We should avoid whatever might deprive us of that peace: *But let them not turn*, etc. G. R.

Verse 8. *Thomas Goodwin* has three sermons upon this **Verse**, (*First clause*), entitled The Return of Prayers. (*Second clause*).—Tidings of Peace. (*Last clause*)—The Folly of Relapsing after Peace spoken.

Verse 8. (*last clause*). They should not turn again to folly,

1. Because it will be a greater aggravation in sinning. It is made the aggravation of Solomon's sin (1Ki 11:9), that "God had appeared to him twice."

2. The second reason is intimated in the word *folly*: as if the Lord should have said, Set aside the unkindness and wrong you do to me, yet therein you befool yourselves; you will have the worst of it. *T. Goodwin.*

Verse 10.

1. The attributes displayed in man's salvation.

    (a) Mercy in the promise.
    (b) Truth in its fulfillment.
    (c) Righteousness in the manner of its fulfillment.
    (d) Peace in its results.

2. These attributes harmonized in man's salvation.

    (a) How? *Met together – kissed each other.*

    (b) Why? Each on its own account. All on each other's' account.

    (c) Where? Met and kissed—(1.) In the covenant. (2.) At the incarnation. (3.) At the cross. (4.) At the conversion of every sinner. (5.) At the completion of the saints in heaven. G. R.

Verse 10. The Pulpit, vol. 28, 1836, contains a sermon by R. W. Sibthorpe, in which the preacher,

1. Considers the harmony of the divine perfections in the redemption of a sinner.

2. The wisdom of the divine dealings in *the calling* and guidance of the believer; so that mercy, truth, etc., each becomes in turn conspicuous in our experience.

3. The completeness of the divine image *in the sanctified soul*, so that the perfected saint abounds in mercy and truth, is filled with peace, and is conformed to his righteous Lord.

Verse 12.

1. All spiritual good is from God: *The Lord will give*, etc.

    (a) Is repentance a good thing? The Lord will give repentance.
    (b) Is pardon? *The Lord*, etc.
    (c) Is faith?
    (d) Is justification?
    (e) Is regeneration?
    (f) Is growth in grace?
    (g) Is preservation unto the end?
    (h) Is eternal glory? *The Lord will give*, etc.

2. All temporal good is from God. *Our land*, etc.

    (a) In a lawful manner *our* land.

    (b) In the use of appointed means: *Shall yield her increase*, etc.

    (c) In dependence upon the divine blessing. "Who giveth fruitful seasons, "etc. Spiritual good is not less given in the use of appointed means. G. R.

Verse 12. The fertility of our spheres of labor the gift of God.

Verse 13.

1. The righteousness by which we are justified long precedes our justification: this righteousness is gone before, etc.

2. Our justification by that righteousness precedes our sanctification.

3. The righteousness of sanctification invariably follows that of justification. G. R.

PSALM 86

SERMON OUTLINES AND HELPFUL TIPS

Verse 1.

1. A singular request—that the Lord should bow his ear.

2. A singular plea—"*I am poor and needy.*"

3. The singular grace of God will answer the request, because singular grace has made the petitioner feel his need.

Verse 2.

1. The blessing sought is present, spiritual, complete and final preservation.

2. Our reasons for expecting it are—

> (a) Our belonging to God—"*I am holy.*"
> (b) God's belonging to us—"*my God.*"
> (c) Our faith, which has the promise.
> (d) Our fruits, which prove our faith—"*thy servant*"

Verse 3.—Importunity.

1. When she pleads—"*daily.*"
2. How she pleads—"*I cry.*"
3. To whom she pleads—"*unto thee.*"
4. For what she pleads—"*be merciful.*"

Verse 3.—*I will cry daily* for pardoning, sanctifying, assisting, preserving, providing and guiding mercy.—*William Jay.*

Verse 4.

1. The believer's joy is from God—"*Rejoice*", & c.
2. The believer's joy is in God—"*unto thee*", & c.—**G.R.**

Verse 4.

1. The great lift.
2. The heavy weight—"*my soul*".
3. The weak worker—"*I lift*".
4. The great height—"*unto thee*".
5. The appointed machinery—means of grace; and,
6. The expected aid—"*Rejoice*", etc.

Verse 5.—Encouraging thoughts of God.

1. He has goodness in his essence.
2. He has forgiveness in readiness.
3. He has mercy in action, flowing forth from him plenteously.
4. His very discrimination is gracious—"all them that call upon him."

Verse 6. The praying man desires above all things an answer. Objections to such an expectation. Grounds for continuing to expect, and duties incumbent upon those who realise such expectations.

Verse 6. *The voice of supplication.* It is the voice of weakness, of penitence, of faith, of hope, of the new nature, of knowledge, & c.

Verse 7.

1. Help needed.
2. Help sought.
3. Help found.—**G.R.**

Verse 7.

1. A time to be expected—"*day of my trouble.*"
2. A resolve to be practiced—"*I will call upon thee.*"
3. A result to be experienced—"*thou wilt answer me.*"

Verse 7.—Prayer is the design of trouble, the evidence that it is sanctified, its solace, and the medium of deliverance from it.—*William Jay.*

Verse 8.

1. God is one; the only God: characters of false gods inferior far.

2. His works are unique. Nature, providence, grace, all peculiar in many respects. A good theme for a thoughtful preacher.

Verse 9. The certain conversion of the world as opposed to modern theories.

Verse 10.

1. God is "*great*", therefore great things may be expected of him.

2. He is unsearchable, therefore "*wondrous things*" may be expected of him.

3. He is irresistible, therefore impossibihties to others may be expected of him: "*Thou art God alone*".—**G.R.**

Verse 11. In the disposition of mind which is expressed in these words, the believer stands opposed to four descriptions of character.

1. The ignorant and thoughtless sinner, who neither regards his way nor his end.

2. The Antinomian, who is zealous for doctrines, and a**Verse** from the practice of religion.

3. The Pharisee, who disregards religious sentiment, and makes practice all in all.

4. The hypocrite, who appears to be divided between religion and the world.—*John Hyatt*, 1811.

Verse 11. The Christian as a scholar, a man of action, and a man of devotion.

Verse 11. Holiness taught, truth practiced, God adored; and thus the life perfected.

Verse 11. (*middle clause*). We should walk in the belief of the truth, its practice, enjoyment, and profession.—*William Jay*.

Verse 11. (*third clause*). The necessity, benefit, and reasonableness of whole heartedness in religion.

Verse 12.—The art of praising God by heart.

Verse 13.

1. Where I might have been—"*the lowest hell.*"
2. What thou hast done for me—"*hast delivered.*"
3. What thou art doing—"*great is thy mercy.*"

Verse 13. (*first clause*).—God's mercy *great* in election, redemption, calling, pardon, upholding, etc. It is so, at this very moment, in supplying my needs, preserving from danger, consoling in sorrow, etc. Great is thy mercy *towards me*—so great a sinner, with such needs, so provoking, so full of doubts, etc.

Verses 13-15. The three **Verse**s describe salvation, consequent persecution, and all sufficient consolation.

Verse 15. The shades of the light of love. Compassion upon suffering, grace towards unworthiness, long suffering to provocation, mercy towards sin, truth towards the promise.

Verse 16.

1. My pedigree—"*son of thine handmaid.*"
2. My occupation—"*thy servant.*"
3. My character—needing "*mercy.*"
4. My request "*turn unto me.*"

Verse 16. In what respects a servant of God may be girt with divine power.

Verse 17. What inward feelings and outward providences are "*tokens for good.*"

PSALM 87

SERMON OUTLINES AND HELPFUL TIPS

Verses 2-3.

1. The foundation of Zion.

>   (a) It is but one: "*foundation.*"
>   (b) It is the Lord's: "*his.*"
>   (c) It is in conformity with holiness: "*holy mountains.*"
>   (d) It consists of eternal purposes.
>   (e) It is built up on immutable principles.
>   (f) It is situated in a glorious position.

2. The Favor enjoyed by Zion.

>   (a) God "loves the dwellings of Jacob." He led, fed, guarded, lighted, visited them.
>
>   (b) He loves Zion "better"; and gives all those blessings in a richer form.
>
>   (c) There are more to love.
>
>   (d) Their occupations are more spiritual.
>
>   (e) Their songs and worship are more enthusiastic.
>
>   (f) Their testimony is more powerful.
>
>   (g) Their knowledge of truth is more clear.
>
>   (h) Their fellowship is on a scale more heavenly. Let us be in the Church, and love her.

3. The fame of Zion. "Glorious things are spoken",

>   (a) *of* her in history;
>   (b) *in* her by ministry;
>   (c) *for* her by Jesus;
>   (d) *about* her in prophecy.

Here is a fruitful theme.

Verse 3. The idea of the text presents the Church as "the city of God": let us touch upon some of the "glorious things" that are spoken of it.

1. There are glorious things with respect to the *erection* of the city.

>   (a) There is the plan of its erection. There was never a plan so faultless, so complete, so wonderful for its beauty and grandeur. The gates, the walls, the buildings, the streets, the monuments, the fountains, the gardens, unite to proclaim it a master piece of skill. The Architect was he who built the skies.

(b) There is the *site* where the city is erected. See Ps 87:1.

(c) There is the *date* of the city's erection. A halo and a glory attach, in a case like this, to great antiquity. Now it is long since the city was built. It was standing in the days of Paul "Ye are come unto the city of the living God." Heb 12:22. David was well acquainted with it. Ps 46:1-11.

(d) It was standing before the flood. Noah, Enoch, Abel, dwelt in it. It is almost as old as the creation.

2. There are glorious things to tell of the *defenses* of the city. It has been besieged ever since it was a city at all, and it is not taken to this hour. "We have a strong city", etc.

3. There are glorious things in connection with the *stores* and *supplies* on which the city depends;

(a) their excellence;
(b) their abundance;
(c) their source.

4. There are glorious things respecting the *King* of the city; his name, person, character, etc.

5. There are glorious things in connection with the *citizens* of the day. — *Andrew Gray,* 1805-1861.

Verse 3.

1. Observe, that a city is not like a flower, a tree, or a plant — something that grows out of the earth, and is nourished from the earth, and dependent wholly on its juices. It is an artificial thing, constructed by wisdom and raised by power, as it was designed by genius and forethought.

2. A city upon earth is surrounded generally by walls.

3. Jerusalem (the most celebrated of cities, from which this figure is obviously drawn) was built upon the brow of a hill, an extremely conspicuous and beautiful object.

4. In a city there are various buildings, and structures of various shapes, materials and value: illustrate by the different denominations, & c.

5. A city has municipal laws.

6. It has also trade, traffic, & c.

7. The figure, as applied to the Church of Christ, involves the idea of safety or security, Honor, & c.

8. There is also the idea of fewness. — *John Cumming,* 1843.

Verse 3. The things "spoken" of the city of God.

1. It shall be the permanent and the peculiar residence of God.

2. It shall be the scene of delightful privileges and blessings.

3. It shall be invested with absolute and inviolable security.

4. It shall possess renown and empire throughout the whole world.

5. Its institutions and existence shall be perfected in the celestial state. — *James Parsons,* 1839.

Verse 4. (*last clause*).

1. Behold what the "man" was: a native of "Philistia", a heathen, and an enemy to God.

2. Behold what happened to him: he "was born there," *i.e.* new born in Zion.

3. Behold what he became — he became by his new birth a freeman and burgess of Zion, & c.

Verses 4-5.

1. What is not the most Honorable birth place — not Rahab nor Egypt, nor Babylon, nor any earthly palace or kingdom.

2. What is? "Of Zion", & c.

    (a) Because it is a nobler birth; a being born again of the Spirit of God.

    (b) Because it is a nobler place; the residence of the Highest, and established forever.

    (c) Because it brings nobler rank and privileges. — *G.R.*

Verses 4-7.

1. Zion shall produce many good and great men.
2. Zion's interest shall be established by divine power.
3. Zion's sons shall be registered with Honor.
4. Zion's songs shall be sung with joy and triumph. — *Matthew Henry.*

Verses 4-7.

1. The excellence of the church is here stated.

2. Her enlargement is here promised. — *J. Scholefield,* 1825.

Verse 5. The renowned men of the church of God.

1. Great warriors, who have fought with temptation.

2. Great poets, whose lives were Psalms.

3. Great heroes, who have lived and died for Jesus.

4. Great kings, who have ruled themselves, & c. Apostles, martyrs, confessors, reformers, men renowned for virtues such as only grace can produce.

Verse 5. *This and that man.* The individuality of true religion.

1. Each soul sins for itself.

2. Rejects or accepts the Savior for itself.

3. Must be judged, and

4. Saved or lost individually. The consequent need of personal piety; the temptations to neglect it; and the habits which promote it.

Verse 5. (*last clause*). The Established Church of God—her Head, her protection, her power. & c.

Verse 6.

1. "The Lord" will make the Census.
2. He will "count" whether a man be rightly there or no.
3. Every man truly born in Zion shall be admitted on the register.

Verse 6.

1. The time referred to. "When he writeth up", & c.; when all the true Israel is saved.

2. The account to be taken: "When he writeth up", & c., i.e. revises and reenters the names in the Lamb's Book of Life. Compares the called with the chosen.

3. The test to be applied.

    (a) Their being in Zion, or having the means of grace.
    (b) Their being born there.

4. The completion of their number: "The Lord shall count." An exact number of stones in a perfect building and of members in a perfect body. So in Christ's Church. All make one bride.

5. The notice taken of each one: "This man was born there." Men fell as a whole; they are saved individually. — **G.R.**

Verse 7.

1. In God our joy.
2. From God our supplies.
3. To God our praise.

Verse 7. (*last clause*).—All the springs within me, all the springs which flow for me, are in my God. There are "upper and nether springs", springs "shut up", "valley" springs (Ps 104:10), rock springs, & c.; but all these flow from the Lord.

PSALM 88

SERMON OUTLINES AND HELPFUL TIPS

Verse 1.

1. Confidence in prayer,—"God of my salvation."

2. Earnestness in prayer,—"I have cried."

3. Perseverance in prayer,—"Day and night."—*G.R.*

Verse 2.—Prayer as an ambassador.

1. An audience sought, or the benefit of access.

2. Attention entreated, or the blessing of success.

3. The Process explained, or prayer comes and God inclines.

Verse 3.

1. A good man is exposed to inward troubles.

    (a) To soul troubles.
    (b) To the soul full of troubles.

2. To outward troubles. "My life", etc.

    (a) From outward persecutions.
    (b) From inward griefs.

3. To both inward and outward troubles at the same time. "Soul full", etc., "*and* my life", etc.—*G.R.*

Verse 4. (*last clause*).—Conscious weakness, painfully felt, at certain times, in various duties. Intended to keep us humble, to drive us to our knees, and to bring greater glory to God.

Verses 4-5.

1. The resemblance of the righteous man to the wicked.

    (a) In natural death.
    (b) In bodily infirmities.

2. His difference from them. He is "counted with them" but is not of them.

    (a) He experiences natural death only.
    (b) His strength is perfected in weakness.
    (c) For him to die is gain.—*G.R.*

Verses 6-7.

1. What the afflictions of the people of God appear to be to themselves.

> (a) Extreme,—"laid me in the lowest pit."
> (b) Inexplicable,—"in darkness."
> (c) Humiliating,—"in the deeps."
> (d) Severe,—"thy wrath lieth hard."
> (e) Exhaustive,—"afflicted with all thy waves."

2. What they are in reality.

> (a) Not extreme but light.
> (b) Not inexplicable, but according to the will of God.
> (c) Not humiliating, but elevating. "Humble yourselves under", etc.
> (d) Not severe but gentle. Not in anger but in love.
> (e) Not exhaustive but partial. Not all thy waves, but a few ripples only. The slight motion in the harbor when there is a boisterous ocean beyond.—*G.R.*

Verse 8. (*last clause*).—This may describe us when despondency is chronic, when trouble is overwhelming, when sickness detains us at home, when we feel restrained in Christian labor, or hampered in prayer.

Verse 9.

1. Sorrow before God,—"Mine eye", etc.

2. Prayer to God,—"have called", etc.

3. Waiting for God,—"called daily".

4. Dependence on God,—"I have stretched", etc. These hands can do nothing without thee.—*G.R.*

Verses 10-12.

1. The supposition.

> (a) That a child of God should be wholly dead.
> (b) That he should remain forever in the grave.
> (c) That he should be destroyed.
> (d) That he should always remain in darkness.
> (e) That he should be entirely forgotten, as though he had never existed.

2. The consequences involved in this supposition.

> (a) God's wonders to them would cease.
> (b) His praise from them would be lost.
> (c) His loving kindness to them would be unknown.
> (d) His faithfulness destroyed.
> (e) His wonders to them would be lost to others.
> (f) His former righteousness to them would be forgotten.

3. The plea founded upon these consequences,—"Wilt thou", etc. It cannot be that thy praise for grace shown to thy people can be lost, and none can render it but themselves. "Then what wilt thou do unto thy great name?"—*G.R.*

Verse 13.

1. Blessings delayed to prayer,—"Unto thee", etc.

2. Blessings anticipated by prayer,—"in the morning", etc. Daily mercies anticipated by morning prayers.—*G.R.*

Verse 14.

1. Afflictions are mysterious though just.
2. Just though mysterious.—*G.R.*

Verse 14. Solemn enquiries, to be followed by searching examinations, by sorrowful confessions, stern self-denials, and sweet restorations.

Verse 15.

1. The afflictions of the righteous may be long continued though severe. "I am afflicted, etc., from my youth up."

2. Severe though long continued.

> (a) Painful,—"afflicted."
> (b) Threatening,—"ready to die."
> (c) Terrific,—"suffer thy terrors."
> (d) Distracting,—"I am", etc.—*G.R.*

Verse 16.

1. Good men are often tried men.

2. Tried men frequently misjudge the Lord's dealings.

3. The Lord does not take them at their word, he is better than their fears.—*G.R.*

Verse 18. The loss of friends intended to remind us of our own mortality, to wean us from earth, to lead us to more complete trust in the Lord, to chasten us for sin, and to draw us away to the great meeting place.

Verse 18. The words of our text will lead us to remark that,

1. The happiness of life greatly depends on intimate friendships.

2. The trial of parting with intimate friends is exceedingly painful.

3. In this, as indeed in every affliction, the best consolation is drawn from a belief in, and meditation upon, God's governing providence.—*Joseph Lathrop,* 1845.

PSALM 89

SERMON OUTLINES AND HELPFUL TIPS

Verse 1.

1. Mercies celebrated. When?—"forever"

2. By whom?—by those who are the subjects of them.

3. Therefore they must live forever to celebrate them.

4. Faithfulness declared. (a) To our own generation. (b) To succeeding generations by its influence upon others.

Verse 2.—

1. The Testimony.

> (a) To the constancy of Mercy: (1.) builds up its trophies every moment. (2.) It preserves them forever.
>
> (b) To the constancy of Faithfulness. It remains as the ordinances of heaven.

2. Its Confirmation. "I have said", etc., said it,

> (a) Upon the ground of Scripture.
> (b) of experience.
> (c) of reason.
> (d) of observation of others.

Verses 3-4.

1. The Covenant made. With whom?—with David and in him with David's Lord and Son. The true David—the chosen one—the servant of the Father in redemption.

2. For what?—

> (a) for his seed. He should have a seed and that seed should be established.
> (b) for himself, "his throne", etc.

3. The Covenant confirmed.

> (a) By decree. "I have made", etc.
> (b) By promise. "I will establish."
> (c) By oath. "I have sworn."

Verse 6.—We have a comparison between God and the most excellent in heaven and earth—challenge both worlds.

1. The true God, sovereign of heaven and earth is incomparably great in his BEING and EXISTENCE;

(a) because his being is of himself *eternal;*
(b) because he is a *perfect* being;
(c) because he is *independent;*
(d) because he is unchangeable.

2. God is incomparably great in his ATTRIBUTES and PERFECTIONS.

(a) In his *holiness;*
(b) in his *wisdom* and *knowledge;*
(c) in his *power;*
(d) in his *justice;*
(e) in his patience;
(f) in his *love* and *goodness.*

3. God is incomparably great in his WORKS—creation; providence; redemption, and human salvation.—*Theophilus Jones,* 1830.

Verse 6.—The incomparableness of God, in his Being, Attributes, Works, and Word.—*Swinnock.* (Nichol's Edition of Swinnock's Works, Vol. 4, pp. 373-508.)

Verses 6-7.

1. In creation God is far above other beings. Ps 89:6.

2. In Redemption he is far above himself in creation. Ps 89:7.

Verses 9-10. God's present rule in the midst of confusion, and rebellion; and his ultimate overthrow of all ad**Verse** forces.

Verse 11.

1. God's possession of heaven, the model of his possession of earth.

2. God's possession of earth most certain, and its manifestation in the future most sure.

3. The course of action suggested to his people by the two facts.

Verse 12. The joy of creation in its Creator.

Verse 14.

1. The Equity of the divine government—"justice", etc. No creature can eventually be unjustly dealt with under his dominion, and his kingdom ruleth over all.

2. The Sovereignty of the divine government. Truth before mercy. Mercy founded upon truth. "Thou wilt perform the truth to Jacob and the mercy to Abraham." The covenant made in mercy to Abraham is fulfilled in truth to Jacob.

Verse 15.

1. The gospel is a joyful sound. Good tidings, etc.

2. It is a joyful sound to those who know it, hear it, believe it, love it, obey it.

3. They to whom it is a joyful sound are blessed. "They shall walk", etc.

Verse 15.

1. There is a theoretical knowledge of the gospel.
2. An experimental knowledge, and,
3. A practical knowledge
—W. Drasfield, 1859.

Verse 16.—

1. Exultation.

   (a) "In thy name", etc., as rich in mercy as the God of salvation—of all grace—of all consolation.
   (b) At what season—"all the day", morning, noon, and night.

2. Exaltation. "In thy righteousness", etc.

   (a) How not exalted. Not in their own righteousness.
   (b) How exalted. "In *thy*", etc. Procured for them—by a divine person (*thy*)—imputed to them. Ours, though thine. The righteousness of God as God could not exalt us, but his righteousness as God man can. Exalted above hell, above earth, above Paradise, above angels. Exalted to friends of God—children of God—one with God, to heaven.

Verse 16. (*second clause*).—Consider,

1. What the believer is exalted *above* or *from,* by God's righteousness.

   (a) It exalts him above the law.
   (b) Above the world.
   (c) Above the power and malice of Satan.
   (d) Above death.
   (e) Above all accusations (Ro 8:33-34.)

2. *To* what happiness or dignity the believer is exalted by virtue of that righteousness.

   (a) To a state of peace and reconciliation with God.
   (b) To sonship.
   (c) To fellowship and familiarity with God, and access to him.
   (d) And finally, to a state of endless glory.
   —E. Erskine.

Verse 17.

1. The blessedness of the righteous.

   (a) Their internal glory. Reliance upon divine strength.
   (b) Their internal Honor. "In thy Favor", etc.

2. The participation in that blessedness. The *their* of the people of God becomes *our*. Their strength our horn. Happy they, who, with respect to all the privileges of the saints, can thus turn *their* into *our*.

Verse 17.

1. Consider our natural weakness.
2. Consider our strength in God.
3. Give God the glory of it.

Verse 18.

1. Jehovah—his power, self-existence, and majesty—our defense.

2. The Holy One of Israel—his character, covenant character, and unity—our government.

Verse 19.

1. The work required. "Help."

    (a) By whom? By God himself.
    (b) For what? To reconcile God to man, and man to God.

2. The persons selected for this work.

    (a) Human. "Chosen out of the people."
    (b) Divine. "Thy Holy One."

3. His qualifications for the work.

    (a) His own ability for the office. "One that is mighty."
    (b) His appointment to it by God. "I have laid." etc. "I have chosen", etc.

Verse 19. (*last clause*). Election, extraction, exaltation.

Verses 20-21.

1. The Messiah would be of the seed of David. The true David.
2. He would be a servant of the Father. "My servant."
3. He would be consecrated to his office by God. "With my holy oil", etc.
4. He would perfectly fulfil it. "With whom my hand", etc.
5. He would be sustained in it by the Father. "Mine arm", etc.

Verse 22-23.

1. A prophecy of the conflict of the Messiah with Satan. Satan could not exact any debt or homage for him.

2. Of his refutation of his enemies. "I will beat down", etc. The Scribes and Pharisees were beaten down before his face.

3. Of the destruction of their city and nation. "And plague them", etc.

Verse 26. Our Lord's filial spirit, and how it was displayed.

Verse 29.

1. The subjects of Messiah's reign. "His seed."

    (a) For union—his seed.
    (b) For resemblance.
    (c) For multitude.

2. The duration of his reign.

    (a) They forever one with him.
    (b) He forever on the throne.

Verses 30-34.

1. The persons referred to. "His children." "Ye are all the children", etc.

2. The supposition concerning them. "If his children forsake", etc.

    (a) They may possibly—may fall, though not fall away.
    (b) They will probably, because they are far from being perfect.
    (c) They have actually: as David himself and others.

3. The threatening founded upon that supposition.

    (a) Specified—"the rod—stripes." They shall smart for it sooner or later.
    (b) Certified. "Then will I."

4. The qualification of the threatening. "Nevertheless", etc.

    (a) The nevertheless characterized. Loving kindness not removed, etc.
    (b) Emphasized. The rod may seem to be in anger, nevertheless, etc.

There is,

1. An if.
2. A then.
3. A nevertheless.

Verse 39.

1. Providence may often seem to be at variance with promises.

2. Promises are never at variance with providence. It is the covenant of thy servant and his crown still.

Verse 39. How the throne of King Jesus may be profaned.

Verse 40.

1. What God had done. "Broken down", etc.

2. What he had not done. Not taken away sorrow for his departure and desire for his return.

Verse 43. Cases in which the sword of the gospel appears to have its edge turned.

Verse 44-45.

1. A prophecy that the Messiah would be meek and lowly. "Made his glory to cease."

2. Would become a servant to the Father. "Cast his throne down", etc.

3. Would be cut off in the midst of his days. "The days of his youth", etc.

4. That he would die an ignominious death. "Hast covered him", etc.

Verse 45. The excellence of the first days of Christianity, and in what respect their glory has departed from us.

Verse 46. The hand of God is to be acknowledged.

1. In the nature of affliction. "Wilt thou hide thyself", etc.

2. In the duration of affliction. "How long, Lord?"

3. In the severity of affliction. Wrath burning like fire.

4. In the issue of affliction. How long? forever? In all these respects the words are applicable both to Christ and to his people.

Verse 46. *Remember.* The prayer of the dying thief, the troubled believer, the persecuted Christian.

Verse 47.

1. An appeal to divine goodness. "Remember", etc. Let not my life be all trouble and sorrow.

2. To divine wisdom. "Wherefore", etc. Was man made only to be miserable? Will not man have been made in vain if his life be but short, and that short life be nothing but sorrow?

Verse 52.

1. The voice. "Blessed", etc. In himself in all his works and ways—in his judgments as well as in his mercies—as the God and Father of our Lord Jesus Christ—"for evermore."

2. The echo, "Amen and amen." Amen, says the church on earth—says the church in heaven—say the angels of God—says the whole holy and happy universe—says eternity past and eternity to come.

PSALM 90

SERMON OUTLINES AND HELPFUL TIPS

Verse 1. The near and dear relation between God and his people, so that they mutually dwell in each other.

Verse 1. The abode of the church the same in all ages; her relation to God never changes.

Verse 1.

1. The soul is at home in God. (a) Originally. Its birth place—its native air—home of its thoughts, will, conscience, affections, desires. (b) Experimentally. When it returns here it feels itself at home: "Return unto thy rest", etc. (c) Eternally. The soul, once returned to this home, never leaves it: "it shall go no more out forever."

2. The soul is not at home elsewhere. "Our dwelling place", etc. (a) For all men. (b) At all times. He is ever the same, and the wants of the soul substantially are over the same.—*G.R.*

Verse 2. A Discourse upon the Eternity of God. S. Charnock. Works pg 344-373, Nichol's Edition.

Verse 2. (*last clause*).—The consideration of God's eternity may serve,

1. For the support of our faith; in reference to our own condition for the future; in reference to our posterity; and to the condition of God's church to the end of the world.

2. For the encouragement of our obedience. We serve the God who can give us an everlasting reward.

3. For the terror of wicked men.

—*Tillotson's Sermon on the Eternity of God.*

Verse 3.

1. The cause of death—"thou turnest."

2. The nature of death—"return."

3. The necessities of death—reconciliation with God, and preparation to return.

Verse 4.

1. Contemplate the lengthened period with all its events.
2. Consider what He must be to whom all this is as nothing.
3. Consider how we stand towards Him.

Verse 5. Comparison of mortal life to sleep. See William Bradshaw's remarks in our Notes on this **Verse**.

Verses 5-6. The lesson of the Meadows.

1. Grass growing the emblem of youth.
2. Grass flowering—or man in his prime.
3. The scythe.
4. Grass mown—or man at death.

Verse 7.

1. Man's chief troubles are the effect of death. (a) His own death. (b) The death of others.

2. Death is the effect of Divine anger: "We are consumed by", etc.

3. Divine anger is the effect of sin. Death by sin.—**G.R.**

Verse 8.

1. The notice which God takes of sin. (a) Individual. "*Our* iniquities." (b) Universal notice—"iniquities"—not one only, but all. (c) Minute, even the most secret sins. (d) Constant: "Set them before" him—"in the light", etc.

2. The notice which we should take of them on that account. (a) In our thoughts. Set them before us. (b) In our consciences. Condemn ourselves on account of them. (c) In our wills. Turn from them by repentance—turn to a pardoning God by faith.—**G.R.**

Verse 9.

1. Every man has a history. His life is as a tale—a separate tale—to be told.

2. Every man's history has some display of God in it. All our days, some may say, are passed away in thy wrath—all, others may say, in thy love—and others, some of our days in anger and some in love.

3. Every man's history will be told. In death, at judgment, through eternity.—**G.R.**

Verse 10.

1. What life is *to* most. It seldom reaches its natural limits. One half die in childhood; more than half of the other half die in manhood; few attain to old age.

2. What life is *at* most. "Threescore years", etc.

3. What it is to most beyond that limit. "If by reason", etc.

4. What it is to all. "It is soon cut off", etc.—**G.R.**

Verse 11.

1. The anger of God against sin is not fully known by its effects in this life. "Who knoweth the power", etc. Here we see the hiding of its power.

2. The anger of God against sin hereafter is equal to our greatest fears. "According to thy fear", etc.; or, "the fear of thee", etc.—**G.R.**

Verse 12.

1. The Reckoning. (a) What their usual number. (b) How many of them are already spent. (c) How uncertain the number that remains. (d) How much of them must be occupied with the necessary duties of this life. (e) What afflictions and helplessness may attend them.

2. The use to be made of it. (a) To "seek wisdom"—not riches, worldly Honors, or pleasures—but wisdom; not the wisdom of the world, but of God. (b) To "apply the heart" to it. Not mental merely, but moral wisdom; not speculative merely, but experimental; not theoretical merely, but practical. (c) To seek it at once—immediately. (d) To seek it constantly—"*apply* our hearts", etc.

3. The help to be sought in it. "So teach us", etc. (a) Our own ability is insufficient through the perversion both of the mind and heart by sin. (b) Divine help may be obtained. "If any man lack wisdom." etc.—***G.R.***

Verse 12.—The Sense of Mortality. Show the variety of blessings dispensed to different classes by the right use of the sense of mortality.

1. It may be an antidote for the sorrowful. Reflect, "there is an end."

2. It should be a restorative to the laboring.

3. It should be a remedy for the impatient.

4. As a balm to the wounded in heart.

5. As a corrective for the worldly.

6. As a sedative to the frivolous.

—*R. Andrew Griffin, in "Stems and Twigs", 1872.*

Verse 13. In what manner the Lord may be said to repent.

Verse 14. (*first clause*). See "Spurgeon's Sermons", No. 513: "The Young Man's Prayer."

Verse 14.

1. The deepest yearning of man is for satisfaction.

2. Satisfaction can only be found in the realization of Divine Mercy.

—*C.M. Merry, 1864.*

Verse 14. *O satisfy us early with thy mercy*, etc. Learn,

1. That our souls can have no solid satisfaction in earthly things.

2. That the mercy of God alone can satisfy our souls.

3. That nothing but satisfaction in God can fill our days with joy and gladness.

—*John Cawood,* 1842.

Verse 14.

1. The most cheerful days of earth are made more cheerful by thoughts of Divine mercy.

2. The most sorrowful days of earth are made glad by the consciousness of Divine love.

—*G.R.*

Verse 15.

1. The joy of faith is in proportion to the sorrow of repentance.

2. The joy of consolation is in proportion to suffering in affliction.

3. The joy of the returning smiles of God is in proportion to the terror of his frowns.—*G.R.*

Verse 15. The Balance of life, or the manner in which our joys are set over against our sorrows.

Verse 16.

1. Our duty—"work", and our desire about it.

2. Our children's portion—"glory", and our prayer in reference to it.

Verse 17. The Right Establishment, or the work which will endure—why it will endure and should endure. Why we wish our work to be of such a nature, and whether there are enduring elements in it.

PSALM 91

SERMON OUTLINES AND HELPFUL TIPS

Verse 1.

1. The secret dwelling place. There is the dweller in the dark world, in the favored land, in the holy city, in the outer court; but the holy of holies is the "secret place"—communion, acceptance, etc.

2. The protecting shadow—security, peace, etc.; like hamlets of olden time clustered beneath castle walls. *Charles A. Davis.*

Verse 1.

1. *The person.* One who is in intimate, personal, secret, abiding communion with God, dwelling near the mercy seat, within the veil.

2. The Privilege. He is the guest of God, protected, refreshed, and comforted by him, and that to all eternity.

Verses 1-2. Four names of God.

1. We commune with him reverently, for he is the Most High.
2. We rest in him as the Almighty.
3. We rejoice in him as Jehovah or Lord.
4. We trust him as EL, the mighty God.

Verse 2.

1. Observe the nouns applied to God—refuge from trouble, fortress in trouble, God at all times.

2. Observe the pronouns applied by man—"*I*" will say, "*my* refuge, my fortress, "etc. *G. R.*

Verse 2. The power, excellence, fruit, reasonableness, and open avowal of personal faith.

Verse 3. Invisible protection from invisible dangers; wisdom to meet cunning, love to war with cruelty, omnipresence to match mystery, life to baffle death.

Verse 3. SURELY, or reasons for assured confidence in God's protection.

Verses 3-7. Pestilence, panic, and peace; (for times of widespread disease). *Charles A. Davis.*

Verses 3, 8-9.

1. Saints are safe—"*surely,* "(Ps 91:3).

2. The evil is bounded—"*only,* "(Ps 91:8).

3. The Lord has reasons for preserving his own—*because,* "(Ps 91:9).

Verse 4.

1. The compassion of God.
2. The confidence of saints.
3. The panoply of truth.

Verses 5-6.

1. The exposure of all men to fear. (a) Continually, day and night. (b) Deservedly: "conscience doth make cowards of us all."

2. The exemption of some men from fear. (a) Because of their trust. (b) Because of the divine protection.

Verse 7. How an evil may be near but not nigh.

Verse 8. What we have actually seen of the reward of the wicked.

Verses 9-10.

1. God our spiritual habitation.
2. God the keeper of our earthly habitation.
3. General truth that the spiritual blesses the temporal.

Verse 10.

1. The Personal Blessing.
2. The Domestic Blessing.
3. The connection between the two.

Verses 11-12. A "wrested" Scripture righted.

1. Satan's version—presumptuousness.

2. The Holy Spirit's version—trustfulness. *Charles A. Davis.*

Verses 11-12.

1. The Ministry of Angels as employed by God. (a) Official: "he shall give, "etc. (b) Personal: "over thee." (c) Constant: "in all thy ways."

2. As enjoyed by man. (a) For preservation: "shall bear thee, "etc.; tenderly but effectually. (b) Under limitation. They cannot do the work of God, or of Christ, or of the Spirit, or of the word, or of ministers, for salvation; "are they not all ministering spirits, "etc. *G. R.*

Verse 12. Preservation from minor evils most precious because they are often most grievous, lead to greater evils, and involve much damage.

Verse 13. The believer's love set upon God.

Verse 13.

1. Every child of God has his enemies. (a) They are numerous: "the lion, adder, young lion, dragon." (b) Diversified: subtle and powerful—"lion and adder; " new and old—"young lion" and the" old dragon."

2. He will finally obtain a complete victory over them—"Thou shalt tread, "etc.; "shall put thy foot, "etc.; "the Lord shall bruise Satan, "etc. *G. R.*

Verses 14-16. The six "I wills."

Verse 14. Here we have,

1. Love for love: "Because, "etc. (a) The fact of the saints' love to God. There is, first, love in God without their love, then love for their love. (b) The evidence of his love to them: "I will deliver him"—from sin, from danger, from temptation, from every evil.

2. Honor for Honor. (a) His Honoring God. "He hath known my name" and made it known; God Honoring him; "I will set him on high"—high in Honor, in happiness, in glory. *G. R.*

Verse 15-16. Observe,

1. The exceeding great and precious promises. (a) Answer to prayer: "he shall call, "etc. (b) Comfort in trouble: "I will be with him." (c) Deliverance from trouble: "I will deliver him." (d) Greater Honor after trouble: deliver "and Honor him." (e) Length of days; life long enough to satisfy him. (f) God's salvation; "show him my salvation; "far beyond what man could think or desire.

2. To whom these promises belong; who is the *he* and the *him* to whom these promises are made. He "calls upon God, "says Ps 91:15; he "hath known my name, "says Ps 91:14; he "hath set his love upon me, "says the former part of the same verse; he "has made the Lord his habitation, "says Ps 91:9; he "dwelleth in the secret place of the Most High, "says Ps 91:1. Hannah More says, "To preach privileges without specifying to whom they belong is like putting a letter in the post office without a direction." It may be very good and contain a valuable remittance, but no one can tell for whom it is intended. All the promises of Scripture are plainly directed to those to whom they belong. The direction put upon the promises of this Psalm is unmistakably clear and often repeated. *G. R.*

PSALM 92

SERMON OUTLINES AND HELPFUL TIPS

Verse 1.

1. It is a good thing to have cause for gratitude. Everyone has this.

2. It is a good thing to have the principle of gratitude. This is the gift of God.

3. It is a good thing to give expression to gratitude. This may excite gratitude in others.

—*G.R.*

Verses 1-3. The blessedness of praise,

Ps 92:1. The theme of praise,

Ps 92:2. The ingenuity of praise,

Ps 92:3. Inanimate nature enlisted in the holy work.

—*C.A. Davis.*

Verse 2.

1. Our praises of God should be *intelligent,* declaring his varied attributes.

2. *Seasonable,* declaring each attribute in appropriate time.

3. *Continual,* every night, and every day.

Verse 3.

1. All the powers of the soul shall be praise. "Upon an instrument of ten strings", all the chords of the mind, affections, will, etc.

2. All the utterances of the lips should be praise.

2. All the actions of the life should be praise.

Verse 3. In our praise of God there should be,

1. *Preparation*—for instruments should be tuned.
2. *Breadth of thought*—"upon an instrument of ten strings."
3. *Absorption of the whole nature*—"ten strings."
4. *Variety*—psaltery, harp, etc.
5. *Deep reverence*—"solemn sound."

Verse 4. (*first sentence*).

1. My state—"glad."

2. How I arrived at it—"thou hast made me glad."

3. What is the ground of it?—"through thy work."

4. What, then, shall I do?—ascribe it all to God, and bless him for it.

Verse 4.

1. The most divine gladness—of God's creation, having God's work for its argument.

2. The most divine triumph—caused by the varied works of God in creation, providence, redemption, & c. The first is for our own hearts, the second is for the convincing of those around us.

Verse 5. The unscalable mountains and the fathomless sea: or the divine works and the divine thoughts (God revealed and hidden) equally beyond human apprehension.—*C.A. Davis.*

Verse 7. Great prosperity the frequent forerunner of destruction to wicked men, for it leads them to provoke divine wrath—

1. By hardness of heart, as Pharaoh.
2. By pride, as Nebuchadnezzar.
3. By haughty hatred of the saints, as Haman.
4. By carnal security, as the rich fool.
5. By self-exaltation, as Herod.

Verses 7-10. Contrasts. Between the wicked and God, Ps 92:7-8. Between God's enemies and his friends, Ps 92:9-10.—*C.A. Davis.*

Verses 7, 12-14. The wicked and the righteous portrayed.—*C.A. Davis.*

Verse 10. (*last clause*). Christian illumination, consecration, gladness, and graces, are all of them the anointing of the Spirit.—*William Garrett Lewis,* 1872.

Verse 10. (*last clause*). The subject of David's confidence was—

1. Very comprehensive, including renewed strength, fresh tokens of Favor, confirmation in office, qualification for it, and new joys.

2. Well grounded, since it rested in God, and his promises.

3. Calming all fears.

4. Exciting hopes.

5. Causing pity for those who have no such confidence.

Verse 12.

1. The righteous flourish in all places. Palm in the valley, cedar on the mountain.

2. In all seasons. Both trees are evergreen.

3. Under all circumstances. Palm in drought, cedar in storm and frost. — *G.R.*

Verses 14-16.

1. Regeneration — "planted."
2. Growth in grace — "flourish."
3. Usefulness — "fruit."
4. Perseverance — "old age."
5. The reason of it all — "to shew that the Lord", etc.

Verse 15-16. The reason and the pledge of final perseverance. — *C.A. Davis.*

PSALM 93

SERMON OUTLINES AND HELPFUL TIPS

Whole Psalm. Revivals of religion described.

1. God reigns.
2. His power is felt.
3. His kingdom is established.
4. Opposition is overcome.
5. The word is valued.
6. Holiness is cultivated.

Verses 1-2. The prophet in the first **Verse** describes our King:

1. From his office.

   (a) He "reigns." He is the great and chief Monarch; he is no idle spectator of things below; but wisely, and justly, and powerfully administers all things.

   (b) He is a glorious King: "He is clothed with majesty."

   (c) He is a potent King: "The Lord is clothed with strength."

   (d) He is a warlike King: "He hath girded himself, " buckled his sword upon his armor; for offence towards his enemies, for defense of his kingdom.

2. From his kingdom.

   (a) It is universal: "The world."

   (b) It is fixed, firm, and stable: "The world also is stablished, and cannot be moved."

   (c) It is an everlasting kingdom: "From everlasting to everlasting; thy throne is established of old; thou art from everlasting." *Adam Clarke.*

Verses 1-2. Shew,

1. The royal proclamation.
2. The imperial robe.
3. The stable kingdom.
4. The ancient throne.
5. The Eternal King. ***C.A.D.***

Verses 1-2.

1. Make the great proclamation. The right, stability, antiquity, extent, perpetuity of the Lord's dominion.

2. Note the different emotions it inspires. In the rebellious, condemned, loyal, &c.

3. Negotiate for submission to the King. *C. A. D.*

Verse 3. The voice of the floods.

1. The voice of Nature is the voice of God.

2. It is a voice from God.

3. It is a voice for God. "God hath a voice that ever is heard, In the peal of the thunder, the chirp of the bird: It comes in the torrent, all rapid and strong, In the streamlet's soft gush, as it ripples along; In the waves of the ocean, the furrows of land, In the mountain of granite, the atom of sand; Turn where ye may, from the sky to the sod, Where can ye gaze that ye see not a God?" *G. R. Poetry by Eliza Cook.*

Verse 4.

1. God is mighty in creation.
2. He is mightier in providence.
3. He is mightiest in redemption. *G. R.*

Verse 5.

1. Faithfulness becometh the word of God.
2. Holiness becometh the house of God. *G. R.*

Verse 5 (last clause).

1. Holiness becometh God's typical house, the temple.
2. His greater spiritual house, the church.
3. His smaller spiritual house, the believer.
4. His eternal house, heaven. *C. A. D.*

PSALM 94

SERMON OUTLINES AND HELPFUL TIPS

Verse 1.

1. Retribution the prerogative of God alone.
2. Under what aspects may we desire his rendering it.
3. How, and when he will surely fulfil this righteous wish.

Verse 1.

1. Vengeance belongs to God and not to man.

2. Vengeance is better in the hands of God than of man. *Let us fall into the hands of God,* etc. G. R.

Verse 2. The peculiar provocation of the sin of pride and its kindred vices. Its influence on the proud, on their follow men, and upon God himself.

Verse 3.

I. The sweet potion of the wicked—present triumph.

2. The gall which embitters it—it is but temporary, and is prayed against. *C. A. Davis.*

Verses 5-10.

1. High handed oppression by the wicked (Ps 94:5-6).

2. Hard hearted indifference to Divine supervision (Ps 94:7).

3. Clear headed demonstration of the Divine cognizance and vengeance (Ps 94:8-10). **C.A.D.**

Verses 6-9.

1. Conspicuous sin.
2. Absurd supposition.
3. Overwhelming argument.

Verse 8. The duration of the reign of evil.

1. Till it has filled up its measure of guilt.

2. Till it has proved its own folly.

3. Till it has developed the graces and prayers of saints.

4. Till it has emptied man of all human trust and driven us to look to the Lord alone, his Spirit, and his advent.

Verse 8. Practical Atheists.

1. Truly described.
2. Wisely counseled. *C.A.D.*

Verses 8-11.

1. The Exhortation (Ps 94:8).
2. The Expostulation (Ps 94:9-10).
3. The Affirmation (Ps 94:11). *G. R.*

Verses 9-10. True Rationalism; or, Reason's Revelation of God. *U.A.D.*

Verse 11.

1. With respect to the present world, consider what multitudes of thoughts are employed in vain.

    (a) In seeking satisfaction where it is not to be found.

    (b) In poring on events which cannot be recalled.

    (c) In anticipating evils which never befall us.

    (d) To these may be added the valuing ourselves on things of little or no account.

    (e) In laying plans which must be disconcerted.

2. Let us see what are man's thoughts with regard to religion, and the concerns of a future life.

    (a) What are the thoughts of the heathen world about religion?

    (b) What are all the thoughts of the Christian world, where God's thoughts are neglected?

    (c) What is all that practical atheism which induces multitudes to act as if there were no God?

    (d) What are all the unbelieving, self-flattering imaginations of wicked men, as though God were not in earnest in his declarations and threatenings?

    (e) What are the conceits of the self-righteous, by which they buoy up their minds with vain hopes, and refuse to submit to the righteousness of God? *Andrew Fuller.*

Verse 11. God's intimate knowledge of man. A startling truth. A humiliating truth.

Verses 12-13. Christ's College. The Master, the Book, the Rod, the blessed Scholar, and the result of his education.

Verses 12-13.

1. The Blessed. (a) Divinely taught. (b) Divinely chastised.

2. The Blessing. (a) Rest in Affliction. (b) Rest from Affliction. *G. R.*

Verse 14.

1. Fear implied. That God will cast off, forsake, etc.
2. Fear denied. God will not cast off—will not forsake. *G. R.*

Verse 14.

1. Display his bright doctrine on a dark background. What if the con**Verse** were true? Considerations that might lead us to apprehend it true.

2. Joyfully regard the glowing truth itself. The doctrine declared. The reasons hinted (His people. His inheritance). The confidence expressed. **C.A.D.**

Verse 15.

1. Judgment suspended.
2. Judgment returned.
3. Judgment acknowledged. *G. R.*

Verse 16.

1. The question asked by the church of her champions.
2. The answer of every true hearted man.
3. The yet more encouraging answer of her Lord.

Verses 16-17. The sole source of succor.

1. A loud cry for help. As from a champion, or advocate.
2. Earth's answer. A dead silence, disturbed only by echo (Ps 94:17).
3. The succoring voice that breaks the silence—the Lord's (Ps 94:17). **C.A.D.**

Verse 18. The blessedness of the confession of weakness.

1. The confession.
2. The succor.
3. The time.
4. The acknowledgment. **C.A.D.**

Verse 19.

1. In the multitude of my unbelieving thoughts thy comforts delight my soul.

2. In the multitude of my penitential thoughts thy comforts, etc.

3. In the multitude of my worldly thoughts, etc.

4. In the multitude of my family or social thoughts, etc.

5. Of my desponding thoughts, etc.

6. Of my prospective thoughts, etc.

Or

1. There is no consolation for man in himself.

2. There is no consolation for him in other creatures.

3. His only consolation is in God. **G.R.**

Verse 19.

1. The soul jostled in the thoroughfare of anxious thoughts.
2. The delectable company nevertheless enjoyed. **C.A.D.**

Verse 20. "It is the law of the land, you know, "—the limit of this authority both in temporal and spiritual matters.

Verse 20.

1. God can have no fellowship with the wicked.
2. The wicked can have no fellowship with God. *G. R.*

Verse 20. Divine politics.

1. There are thrones erected in opposition to the throne of God, "thrones of iniquity, "*e.g.* which trespass on civil liberty, which infringe religious equality, which derive revenue from evil commerce, etc.

2. Such thrones, whatever their pretensions, are excluded from divine fellowship; between them and God a great gulf is fixed. **C.A.D.**

Verses 21-22.

1. The Danger of the righteous (Ps 94:21).
2. Their Defense (Ps 94:22). *G. R.*

Verse 21-23.

1. Sentence passed in the court of injustice (Ps 94:21).

2. An element in the case not considered by the court (Ps 94:22).

3. The sentence consequently alighting on the right heads (Ps 94:23). (This passage, under a very thin veil, exhibits Christ. Mt 27:1) **C.A.D.**

Verse 23.

1. None may punish God's enemies but himself. "He shall bring, "etc.

2. None need punish them but himself. (a) It will be complete,—"shall cut them off." (b) Certain. "Yea, "etc. **G.R.**

PSALM 95

SERMON OUTLINES AND HELPFUL TIPS

Verse 1. An invitation to praise the Lord.

1. A favorite method of worship—"let us sing."

2. A fitting state of mind for singing—joyful gratitude.

3. A fitting subject to excite both gladness and thankfulness—the rock of our salvation.

Verse 1. *The rock of our salvation.* Expressive imagery. Rock of shelter, support, indwelling, and supply—illustrate this last by the water flowing from the rock in the wilderness.

Verse 2.

1. What is meant by coming before his presence? Certainly not the holiness of places, etc.

2. What offering is most appropriate when we come into his presence?

Verse 3.

1. The greatness of God as god. He is to be conceived of as great in goodness, power, glory, etc.

2. His dominion over all other powers in heaven or earth.

3. The worship which is consequently due to him.

Verses 4-5. The universality of the divine government.

1. In all parts of the globe.

2. In all providences.

3. In every phase of moral condition. Or, Things deep, or high, dark or perilous are in his hand; circumstances shifting, terrible, overwhelming as the sea, are under his control as much as the comfortable terra firma of peace and prosperity.

Verse 6. A true conception of God begets

1. A disposition to worship.
2. Mutual incitement to worship.
3. Profound reverence in worship.
4. Overwhelming sense of God's presence in worship.
—*C.A. Davis.*

Verses 6-7. God is to be worshipped—

1. As our Creator—"our maker."
2. As our Redeemer, "the people," etc.

3. As our Preserver, "the sheep," etc.
—*George Rogers.*

Verse 7. The entreaty of the Holy Ghost.

1. The special voice—"the Holy Ghost saith"—

    (a) In Scripture.
    (b) In the hearts of his people.
    (c) In the awakened.
    (d) By his deeds of grace.

2. A special duty, "hear his voice", instructing, commanding, inviting, promising, threatening.

3. A special time—"today." While God speaks, after so long a time, in the day of grace, now, in your present state.

4. The special danger—"harden not your hearts", by indifference, unbelief, asking for signs, presumption, worldly pleasures, etc.

Verse 7. Sinners entreated to hear God's voice. "Hear his voice", because—

1. Life is short and uncertain;

2. You cannot properly or lawfully promise to give what is not your own;

3. If you defer, though but till tomorrow, you must harden your hearts;

4. There is great reason to fear that, if you defer it today, you will never commence;

5. After a time God ceases to strive with sinners;

6. There is nothing irksome or disagreeable in a religious life, that you should wish to defer its commencement.

—*Edward Payson.*

Verse 7. The Difference of Times with respect to Religion.—Upon a spiritual account there is great difference of time. To make this out, I will shew you,

1. That *sooner* and *later* are not alike, in respect of eternity.

2. That *times of ignorance* and of *knowledge* are not alike.

3. That *before* and *after voluntary commission of known iniquity,* are not alike.

4. That *before* and *after contracted naughty habits,* are not alike.

5. That the time of *God's gracious and particular visitation* and the time when God *withdraws* his gracious presence and assistance, are not alike.

6. The flourishing time of our *health and strength,* and the hour of *sickness, weakness,* and approach of *death,* are not alike.

7. Now and hereafter, present and future, *this world* and *the world to come,* are not alike.

—*Benjamin Whichcot.*

Verse 7. This supposition, *If ye will hear*, and the consequence inferred thereupon, *harden not your hearts*, doth evidently demonstrate that a right hearing will prevent hardness of heart; especially hearing of Christ's voice, that is, the gospel. It is the gospel that maketh and keepeth a soft heart.—*William Gouge.*

Verses 8-11.

1. Israel's fearful experiment in tempting God.
2. The awful result.
3. Let it not be tried again.
—*C.A. Davis.*

Verse 10. The error and the ignorance which are fatal.

Verse 11. The fatal moment of the giving up of a soul, how it may be hastened, what are the signs of it, and what are the terrible results.

Verses 10-11. The kindling, increasing, and full force of divine anger, and its dreadful results.

PSALM 96

SERMON OUTLINES AND HELPFUL TIPS

Verse 1. The novelties of grace.

1. A new salvation.
2. Creates a new heart.
3. Suggests a new song.
4. Secures new testimonies, and these,
5. Produce new converts.

Verses 1-3.

1. The end desired—to see the earth singing unto the Lord, and blessing his name.

2. The means suggested—the showing forth his salvation from day to day; declaring his glory, etc.

3. The certainly of its accomplishment. The Lord hath said it. "O sing, "etc. When he commands earth must obey. *G. R.*

Verses 1-3. The progress of zeal.

1. The spring of expansive desire, Ps 96:1.
2. The streamlet of practical daily effort, Ps 96:2.
3. The broad river of foreign missions, Ps 96:3. *C. D.*

Verses 1-9. We are to Honor God.

1. With songs, Ps 96:1-2.
2. With sermons, Ps 96:3.
3. With religious services, Ps 96:7-9.
—*Matthew Henry.*

Verses 3 (*first clause*).

1. Declare among the heathen the glory of God's perfections, that they may acknowledge him as the true God.

2. Declare the glory of his salvation, that they may accept him as their only Redeemer.

3. Declare the glory of his providence, that they may confide in him as their faithful guardian.

4. Declare the glory of his word, that they may prize it as their chief treasure.

3. Declare the glory of his service, that they may choose it as their noblest occupation.

4. Declare the glory of his residence, that they may seek it as their best home. *William Jackson.*

Verse 3.

1. What the gospel is, "God's glory," "his wonders."
2. What shall we do with it—declare it.
3. To whom. "Among the heathen, "all people.

Verse 3 (*last clause*). *His wonders among the people.*

1. The wonders of his Being, to inspire them with awe.
2. The wonders of his creation, to fill them with amazement.
3. The wonders of his judgments, to restrain them with fear.
4. The wonders of his grace, to allure them with love. *W. Jackson.*

Verses 4-6. Missionary sermon.

1. Contrast Jehovah of the Bible with gods of human device.
2. Decide between divine worship and idolatry.
3. Appeal for effort on behalf of idolaters. *C. D.*

Verse 6. *Honor and majesty are before him.*

1. As emanations from him.
2. As excellencies ascribed to him.
3. As characteristics of what is done by him.
4. As marks of all that dwell near him. *W. Jackson.*

Verse 6 (latter clause).—What we may see in God's sanctuary (strength, and beauty). What we may obtain there, Ps 90:17 (strength and beauty). *C. D.*

Verse 8. Jehovah possesses a nature and character peculiar to himself; he sustains various offices and relations, and he has performed many works which he alone could perform. On all these accounts something is due to him from his creatures. And when we regard him with such affections, and yield him such services, as his nature, character, offices, and works deserve, then we give unto him the glory which is due to his name.

1. Let us inquire what is due to Jehovah on account of his nature.

2. What is due to Jehovah on account of the character he possesses.

3. What is due to God on account of the relations and offices which he sustains—that of a creator, preserver.

4. What is due to Jehovah on account of the works which he has performed, in nature, providence and redemption. *E. Payson.*

Verse 8. The object of worship. The nature of worship. The accompaniment of worship (an offering). The place of worship. *C. D..*

Verse 9. (first clause). An examination of true and false worship.

1. False worship, in the obscurity of ignorance, in the dulness of formalism, in the offensiveness of indulged sin, in the hideousness of hypocrisy.

2. True worship, in the beauty of holiness. *C. D.*

Verse 9. Holy fear an essential ingredient in true religion.

Verses 10-13. The reign of righteousness.

1. The announcement of a righteous king and judge.
2. The joyful reception prepared for him.
3. His glorious coming. *C. D.*

Verses 11-12. The sympathy of nature with the work of grace; especially dwelling upon its fuller display in the millennial period.

PSALM 97

SERMON OUTLINES AND HELPFUL TIPS

Verse 1. The sovereignty of God a theme for joy in many respects and to many persons, especially when exhibited in a reign of grace.

Verses 3-6. The accompaniments of Christ's gospel advent.

1. The fire of his Spirit.
2. The light of the word.
3. The commotion in the world.
4. The removal of obstacles.
5. The display of the divine glory.

Verses 4-5.

1. The terrors which accompanied the giving of the law: "his lightnings", etc.

2. The reasons for those terrors. (a) To show the guilt of man. (b) His inability to keep the law. (c) To show his need of a law fulfiller on his behalf.—*G.R.*

Verses 4-6. A description of the giving of the law.

1. The lawgiver's heralds, or, *conviction,* Ps 97:4.

2. The effect of his presence, or, *contrition,* Ps 97:5.

3. The proclamation of the law, or, *instruction* (as by a voice from heaven, Ps 97:6).

4. The effect of the law giving, or, divine *manifestation* (Ps 97:6, latter clause).—*C.D.*

Verse 5. The presence of God in the church her invincible power.

Verse 6. The confusion of heart which will ensue from idolatrous worship, even if it be only spiritual. Breaking of the idol, disappointment in it, injury by it, removal from it, etc.

Verse 8.

1. The world is terrified at the divine judgments.
2. The church rejoices in them, "Zion heard", etc.;

or,

1. When the world is glad the church is sad.
2. When the world is sad the church is glad.—*G.R.*

Verse 10.

1. What you do now: "Love the Lord." Reciprocally, personally, supremely, habitually, progressively.

2. What you must do: "Hate evil." Evil working, evil writing, evil speaking, evil thinking; renounce evil, master it, supplant it. —*W.J.*

Verse 10.

1. The distinguishing peculiarity of the people of God: "Ye that love the Lord."

2. Its manifestation: "Hate evil."

3. Its reward: "The Lord preserveth", etc.; "He delivereth", etc. —**G.R.**

Verses 10-11. David notes in God three characteristics of a true friend: First with fidelity and good will He keepeth the souls of the pious. Secondly, with his power and majesty He delivereth them from their enemies. Thirdly, with his wisdom and holiness He enlightens and refreshes them. —*Le Blanc.*

Verse 11.

1. *Where is it sown?* The answer to this will come under the following heads, viz. In the purpose of God, In the purchase of Christ, In the office of the Spirit, In the promises of the Word, In the work of Grace wrought in the heart, and, In the preparations made above in glory.

2. *When is the season of reaping?* And to this, the answer is, The season of reaping the first fruits, of reaping in part, is at certain times in the present life; the season of reaping more fully is at death; and of reaping most fully and perfectly commences at the day of judgment and is continued throughout eternity.

> (a) The season of reaping in part falls out at some times within the course of this present life. Particularly
>
>> (1) Times of affliction have been to the upright, seasons of reaping the joy sown. By this they have been prepared for sufferings, supported under them, and made afterwards to forget their sorrows, by reason of the gladness breaking in from the affecting discovery of what God has done for them, and wrought in them. Thus God causeth light to arise in darkness, and in a rainy day refresheth them with a beam from heaven, brightening the drops that fall; brings his people into the wilderness, and there speaks comfortably unto them.
>>
>> (2) Seasons of suffering for the sake of Christ and the gospel, have been seasons wherein the upright have begun to reap the joy sown. When called to resist unto blood, striving against sin, they have need of more than ordinary comfort, to enable them to meet, and hold firm through the fiery trial: and they have found that then encouragement hath been yielded them in a degree they never before experienced (Joh 16:33).
>>
>> (3) Seasons wherein God has called the righteous to great and difficult service, have been seasons of reaping the beginnings of joys sown. When their heavenly Father has lifted up the light of his countenance upon them, and shed abroad the

sense of his love within them, they are prepared to go whither he sends them, and to do whatever he bids them.

(4) After sore conflicts with Satan, the upright have been revived by the springing of the joy sown. After Christ was tempted came an angel to comfort him. And for the encouragement of his followers he declares, Re 2:17, "To him that overcometh will I give to eat of the hidden manna, and I will give him a white stone, and in the stone a new name written, which no man knoweth saving he that receiveth it."

(5) In waiting upon God in the sanctuary the upright have met with him, and so have had the beginnings of joy sown.

(b) A fuller reaping time will be at death; with some as the soul is going; but with all immediately after its release from the body.

(c) The season in which the righteous shall reap their joy sown, to the full, and in perfection, shall be at the last day. Then Christ shall come to be glorified in his saints, and admired in all them that believe, and lead them all in a body, and all of them perfected, into that presence of God, where there is fulness of joy, and where there are pleasures for evermore. —*Daniel Wilcox.*

Verse 12. *Give thanks at the remembrance of his holiness.* Be thankful for—

1. Its unsullied perfection.
2. Its wondrous forbearance.
3. Its place in our salvation.
4. Its approachableness through Christ.
5. Its predicted triumphs. —*W.J.*

Verse 12.

1. A remembrance at which the world does not give thanks.

2. Reasons which make it a matter of thanksgiving with the righteous. Its bearing on the way of salvation; on the doctrines of the gospel; on the law of the Christian life. —*C.D.*

PSALM 98

SERMON OUTLINES AND HELPFUL TIPS

Verse 1. *A new song.* The duty, beauty, and benefit of maintaining freshness in piety, service, and worship.

Verse 1. *He hath done marvelous things.*

1. He hath created a marvelous universe.
2. He has established a marvelous government.
3. He hath bestowed a marvelous gift.
4. He hath provided a marvelous redemption.
5. He hath inspired a marvelous book.
6. He hath opened a marvelous fullness.
7. He hath effected a marvelous transformation.
—*W. Jackson.*

Verse 1. *The victory.* The victories of God in judgment, and in mercy: especially the triumphs of Christ on the cross, and by his Spirit in the heart, and in and by the church at large.

Verse 2. *The Lord hath made known his salvation.*

1. The contents of which it is composed.
2. The reasons for which it has been provided.
3. The price at which it has been procured.
4. The terms on which it shall be imparted.
5. The way in which it must be propagated.
6. The manner in which its neglect will be punished. *W. J.*

Verse 2. (*first clause*).

1. What is salvation?
2. Why it is called the Lord's: "Salvation is of the Lord."
3. How he has made it known.
4. For what purpose.
5. With what results. *E.G. Gange.*

Verse 2. The great privilege of knowing the gospel.

1. *In what it consists.* (a) Revelation by the Bible. (b) Declaration by the minister. (c) Illumination by the Spirit. (d) Illustration in daily providence.

2. *To what it has led.* (a) We have believed it. (b) We have so far understood it as to growingly rejoice in it. (c) We are able to tell it to others. (d) We abhor those who mystify it.

Verse 2. Salvation's glory.

1. It is divine—"his salvation."
2. It is consistent with justice—"his righteousness."

3. It is plain and simple—"openly showed."

4. It is meant for all sorts of men—"heathen."

Verse 3. (*first clause*). The Lord's memory of his covenant. Times in which he seems to forget it; ways in which even in those times he proves his faithfulness; great deeds of grace by which at other times he shows his memory of his promises; and reasons why he must ever be mindful of his covenant.

Verse 3. (*last clause*). *All the ends of the earth.*

1. Literally. Missionaries have visited every land.

2. Spiritually. Men ready to despair, to perish.

3. Prophetically. Dwell on the grand promises concerning the future, and the triumphs of the church. *E.G.G.*

Verse 3. *All the ends of the earth have seen, &c.*

1. The greatest foreigners have seen it; many have "come from the east and the west; "Greeks, Peter's hearers, the Eunuch, Greenlanders, South Sea Islanders, Negroes, Red Indians, &c., &c.

2. The ripest saints have seen it; they are at the light end of the earth, stepping out of the wilderness into Canaan, &c.

3. The vilest sinners have seen it; those who have wandered so far that they could get no farther without stepping into hell. The dying thief. The woman who was a sinner. Those whom Whitefield called "the devil's castaways." *W. J.*

Verse 4. The right use of noise.

1. "Make a noise." Awake, O sleeper. Speak, O dumb.

2. "Make a joyful noise." The shout of deliverance, of gratitude, of gladness.

3. "Make a loud noise, all the earth." Nature with her ten thousand voices. The church with myriad saints.

4. "Make a joyful noise unto God." Praise him alone. Praise him forever. *E.G.G.*

Verse 6. Joy a needful ingredient of praise. The Lord as King, an essential idea in adoration. Expression in various ways incumbent upon us, when praising joyfully such a King.

Verses 7-8. Nature at worship. The congregation is

1. Vast. Sea, earth, rivers, hills.

2. Varied. Diverse in character, word, aspect, each from each other, constant and alike in this alone, that *all, always* worship God.

3. Happy. In this like the worshippers in heaven, and for the same reason—sin is absent. *E.G.G.*

Verse 8. The song of the sea, and the hallelujah of the hills.

Verse 9. The last judgment as a theme for thankfulness.

Verse 9. *Before the Lord.* Where we are, where our joy should be, where all our actions should be felt to be, where we shall be—"*before the Lord.*" Enquire—What are we before the Lord? What shall we be when he cometh?

PSALM 99

SERMON OUTLINES AND HELPFUL TIPS

Verse 1.

1. The doctrine of divine sovereignty enunciated.

2. The apprehension of divine sovereignty demanded. It ought to be spiritually apprehended. God wants to be King in the hearts of men. All mortals must tremble before the Immortal; especially the wicked.

3. The accessories of divine sovereignty hinted at. Sovereignty never forsakes the mercy seat. Angels are represented on the mercy seat, the ministers of sovereignty,

4. The effect of divine sovereignty described. Men should be "moved" to fear and obey the King before whom angels bow. Men should be moved to seek the mercy which angels study. *William Durban.*

Verse 1. *He sitteth between the cherubims,* etc.

1. Statement made; where God dwells, on the mercy seat. To hear prayer, and confession, and to grant salvation.

2. Effect produced—"Earth moved; "to admiration, to prayer, to sorrowful contrition, to draw near, etc. *E. G. Gange.*

Verse 2.

1. God is great in Zion in Himself, all his perfections are here, which cannot be said of creation, or of his Law, or of the heaven of angels.

2. Great in his works of saving sinners, which he cannot do elsewhere.

3. Great in his glory as displayed in redemption through his Son.

4. Great in his love to his redeemed. *G. R.*

Verse 2. *The Lord is great in Zion.*

1. In the condescension he displays—Zion is his "habitation, "his "rest."

2. In the glory he manifests—power and glory are in the sanctuary, Ps 68:2.

3. In the assemblage he draws. "Every one in Zion appeareth before God, "Ps 84:7.

4. In the blessings he imparts.

5. In the authority he exerts. *W. Jackson.*

Verse 3. The terrors of the Lord, connected with holiness, and worthy of praise.

Verse 4.

1. Trace the process of the working of right principles through three stages—Love, Establishment, Execution.

2. Illustrate from God's character and action.

3. Apply to national, and to daily, life. *C. D.*

Verse 5. *Exalt the Lord your God.*

1. Why? For what he is to you. For what he has done for you. For what he has told you.

2. How? In your affection. In your meditation. In your supplication. In your conversation. In your profession. In your consecration. In your co-operation. In your expectation. *W. J.*

Verse 5.

1. The loyal enthusiasm of worship, it exalts the Lord.

2. The humble diffidence of worship, not aspiring to his exaltation it kneels at his footstool.

3. The good reason for worship.—"He is holy." *C. D.*

Verses 6-7.

1. Prayer offered. Moses the prophet, Aaron the priest, Samuel the ruler, "They called, "&c.

2. Prayer answered. "He answered them, ""he spake, "&c.

3. Prayer vindicated. They kept the other testimonies, &c. *G. R.*

Verse 7. (first clause). The revelation of the cloud, or what God foreshadowed to Israel in the cloudy pillar.

1. That God was willing to commune with man.

2. That sinful man could not see God and live.

3. That God should become incarnate, veiled in flesh as in the cloud.

4. That he should be their shelter, protector, guide.

5. That God manifest in the flesh should lead them to the Promised Land—Heaven. *C. D.*

Verse 8. Mercy and judgment, or the sea of glass mingled with fire. *C. D.*

Verse 8. Observe,

1. That God's vengeance for sin does not prevent his forgiveness of sin; and,

2. That God's forgiveness of sin does not prevent his taking vengeance. *Stephen Bridge*

Verse 9. *The Lord our God.* A very sweet topic will be found in the consideration of the questions, "In what respect is Jehovah ours? and in what relations does he stand to his people?"

PSALM 100

SERMON OUTLINES AND HELPFUL TIPS

Whole Psalm. This is a bunch of the grapes of Eshcol. It is a taste of what is still the promised land. The Jewish church came to its perfection in the reign of Solomon, but a greater than Solomon is here. The perfection of the New Testament church is here anticipated. This psalm teaches,

1. *That there will be a joyful state of the whole world* (Ps 100:1). (a) To whom the address is given—to "all lands, "and all in those lands. (b) The subject of the address—"Make a joyful noise." What a doleful noise it has made! (c) By whom the address is given, by him who secures what he commands.

2. *That this joyful state of the whole world will arise from the enjoyment of the Divine Being* (Ps 100:2). (a) Men have long tried to be happy without God. (b) They will find at last that their happiness is in God. The conversion of an individual in this respect is a type of the conversion of the world.

3. *That this enjoyment of God will arise from a new relation to him* (Ps 100:3). (a) Of knowledge on our part: he will be known as the Triune God, as a covenant God, as the God of salvation—as God. (b) Of rightful claim on his part; (1.) by right of creation—"He hath made us; " (2.) By light of redemption—"Ye were not a people, but are now the people of God, "&c.; "I have redeemed thee: thou art mine"; (3.) by right of preservation—"We are the sheep, "&c.

4. *That this new relation to God will endear to us the ordinances of his house* (Ps 100:4). (a) Of what the service will consist—"thanksgiving" and praise. (b) To whom it will be rendered. Enter into *his* gates—*his* courts—be thankful unto *him*—bless *his* name. That this service will be perpetual; begin on earth, continued in heaven. This fact is founded—

5. *That this service will be perpetual;* begun on earth, continued in heaven. This face is founded— (a) Upon essential goodness. "For the Lord is good." (b) Upon everlasting mercy. "His mercy, "etc. (c) Upon immutable truth. "His truth, "etc. *G. R.*

Verse 2. *Serve the LORD with gladness.*

1. For he is the best of beings.

2. For his commandments are not grievous.

3. For he is your Savior, as well as Creator; your friend, as well as Lord.

4. The angels, so much greater than yourself, know no reason why they should not serve him with gladness.

5. In serving him you serve yourself.

6. You make religion attractive.

7. You get fitness for heaven. *George Bowen.*

Verse 2 (*first clause*) A true heart,

1. Is humble—*serves*.
2. Is pious—"serve the Lord."
3. Is active—*serves*.
4. Is consequently joyful—"with gladness."

Verse 2. (*first clause*). "Serving the Lord with gladness." See "Spurgeon's Sermons, "No. 769.

Verse 3. *Know ye that the LORD he is God.* That you may be true amid superstition, hopeful in contrition, persistent in supplication, unwearied in exertion, calm in affliction, firm in temptation, bold in persecution, and happy in dissolution. *W. J.*

Verse 3. *We are his people.* We have been twice born, as all his people are. We love the society of his people. We are looking unto Jesus like his people. We are separated from the world as his people. We experience the trials of his people. We prefer the employment of his people. We enjoy the privileges of his people. *W. J.*

Verse 4. A Discourse of Thankfulness which is due to God for his benefits and blessings. A Sermon by Thomas Goodwin. Works, vol. 9 pp. 499-514. Nichol's *edition.*

Verse 4.

1. The privileges of access.
2. The duty of thankfulness.
3. The reasons for enjoying both.

Verse 5.

1. The inexhaustible fount—the goodness of God.
2. The ever-flowing stream—the mercy of God.
3. The fathomless oceans – the truth of God. "O the depths!" *W. Durban.*

PSALM 101

SERMON OUTLINES AND HELPFUL TIPS

Whole Psalm. This is a psalm of wills and shalls. There are nine wills and five shalls. Resolutions should be made,

1. With deliberation; not, therefore, upon trifling matters.
2. With reservation. "If the Lord will, "etc.
3. With dependence upon divine strength for their fulfillment.
—*G.R.*

Verse 1.—

1. The sweet work that is resolved upon is to "sing."

2. The sweet singer that thus resolves, namely, David, "l will sing."

3. The sweet subject of the song, "mercy and judgment."

4. The sweet object of this praise, and the manner in which he would sing it—"Unto three, 0 Lord, will I sing."

—*Ralph Ershikine.*

Verse 1. What there is in mercy that affords ground of singing.

1. The freeness and unreservedness of mercy.

2. The unexpectedness of mercy. When I was expecting a frown I got a smile; when I was expecting nothing but wrath, I got a glance of love; instead of a stroke of vengeance, I got a view of glory.

3. The seasonableness of mercy is a ground of singing—grace to help in time of need.

4. The greatness and riches of mercy make the recipients there of sing.

5. The sweetness of mercy makes them sing.

6. The sureness and firmness of mercy make them sing—"The sure mercies of David."

—From *Ralph Erskine's* Sermon, entitled "*The Militant's Song*".

Verse 1.—

1. The different conditions of the righteous man in this life. Not all mercy, nor all judgment, but mercy and judgment.

2. His one duty and privilege in reference to them: "I will sing, "etc.

(a) Because they are both from God.
(b) Because they are both from love.

(c) Because they are both for present good.
(d) Because they are both preparative for the heavenly rest.
—G.R.

Verse 1. The blending of song with holy living. The bell of praise and the pomegranate of holy fruitfulness should both adorn the Lord's priests.

Verse 2.

1. The end desired: "To behave wisely, "etc.; consistency of conduct.

2. The means employed: "When wilt thou come, "etc.; only when God is with us we walk in a perfect way.

3. The test proposed: "Within my house, "where I am most myself and am best known.

—G.R.

Verse 2.—The wisdom of holiness.

1. In selecting our sphere of duty.

2. In timing, :arranging, and balancing duties.

3. In managing others according to their tempers.

4. In avoiding disputes with adversaries.

5. In administering rebuke, giving alms, rendering advice, etc.; the blending of the serpent with the dove.

Verse 2. — *O when wilt thou come unto me?* A devout ejaculation.

1. Revealing the psalmist's need of the divine presence in order to holiness.

2. His intense longing.

3. His full expectation.

4. His the rough appreciation of the condescending visit.

Verse 2 (last clause). Home piety. Its duty, excellence, influence, sphere, and reward. Note also the change of heart and firmness of purpose necessary to it.

Verse 3.

1. The sight of wickedness is to be avoided: "I will set no wicked thing, "etc.

2. When seen it is to be loathed: "I Hate, "etc.

3. When felt it is to be repudiated. It may touch me, but "it shall not cleave to me."

Verse 4. The need of extreme care in the choice of our intimates.

Verse 5. The detestable nature of slander, hurting three persons at once—the speaker, hearer, and person slandered.

Verse 6. The duty of believers who are wealthy to encourage and employ persons of pious character.

Verse 8. The work of the great King when he comes in judgment.

PSALM 102

SERMON OUTLINES AND HELPFUL TIPS

TITLE.

1. Afflicted men may pray.

2. Afflicted men should pray even when overwhelmed.

3. Afflicted men can pray—for what is wanted is a pouring out of their complaint, not an oratorical display.

4. Afflicted men are accepted in prayer—for this prayer is placed on record.

Verses 1-2. Five steps to the mercy-seat. The Psalmist prays for,

1. Audience: "Hear my prayer."
2. Access: "Let my cry come before thee."
3. Unveiling: "Hide not thy face."
4. An intent ear: "Incline thine ear."
5. Answer. *C. Davis.*

Verses 1, 17, 19-20. An interesting discourse may be founded upon these passages.

1. The Lord entreated to hear—Ps 102:1.
2. The Promise given that he will hear—Ps 102:17.
3. The Record that the Lord has heard—Ps 102:19-20.

Verse 2.

1. Prayer in trouble is most needed.
2. Prayer in trouble is most heeded.
3. Prayer in trouble is most speeded: "Answer me speedily."

Or,

1. Prayer in trouble: "In the day, "etc.

2. The prayer of trouble: "Hide not thy face; "not remove the trial, but be with me in it. A fiery furnace is a paradise when God is with us there. *G. R.*

Verse 2 (*first clause*). He deprecates the loss of the divine countenance when under trouble.

1. That would intensify it a thousand fold.
2. That would deprive him of strength to bear the trouble.
3. That would prevent his acting so as to glorify God in the trouble.
4. That might injure the result of the trouble.

Verse 2 (*last clause*).

1. We often need to be answered speedily.
2. God can so answer.
3. God has so answered.
4. God has promised so to answer.

Verses 3-11.

1. The causes of grief. (a) The brevity of life. Ps 102:3. (b) Bodily pain. Ps 102:3. (c) Dejection of spirit. Ps 102:4- 5. (d) Solitariness. Ps 102:6-7. (e) Reproach. Ps 102:8. (f) Humiliation. Ps 102:9. (g) The hidings of God's countenance. Ps 102:10. (h) Wasting away. Ps 102:11.

2. The eloquence of grief. (a) The brevit of life is as vanishing "smoke." (b) Bodily pain is fire in the bones. (c) Dejection of spirit is "withered grass." Who can eat when the heart is sad? (d) Solitariness is like "The pelican in the wilderness, the owl in the desert, and the sparrow upon the housetop." (e) Reproach is being surrounded by madmen—"they that are mad." (f) Humiliation is "eating ashes like bread, "and "drinking tears." (g) The hidings of God's countenance is lifting up in order to be cast down. (h) Wasting away is a shadow declining and grass withering. *G. R.*

Verse 4. Unbelieving sorrow makes us forget to use proper means for our support.

1. We forget the promises.

2. Forget the past and its experiences.

3. Forget the Lord Jesus, our life.

4. Forget the everlasting love of God. This leads to weakness, faintness, etc., and is to be avoided.

Verse 6. This as a text, together with Ps 103:5, makes an interesting contrast, and gives scope for much experimental teaching.

Verse 7. The evils and benefits of solitude; when it may be sought, and when it becomes a folly. Or, the mournful watcher—alone, outside the pale of communion, insignificant, wishful for fellowship, set apart to watch.

Verse 9. The sorrows of the saints—their number, bitterness, sources, correctives, influences, and consolations.

Verse 10.

1. The trial of trials—*thine* indignation and *thy* wrath.

2. The aggravation of that trial—former Favor, "thou hast lifted me up, "etc.

3. The best behavior under it: see Ps 102:9, 12-13.

Verse 10 (*last cause*). The prosperity of a church or an individual often followed by declension; worldly aggrandizement frequently succeeded by affliction; great joy in the Lord very generally succeeded by trial.

Verses 11-12. *I* and *Thou*, or the notable contrast.

1. *I:* my days are like a shadow, (a) Because it is unsubstantial; because it partakes of the nature of the darkness which is to absorb it; because the longer it becomes the briefer its continuance. (b) I am like grass cut down by the scythe; scorched by drought.

2. *Thou.* Lord. Ever enduring. Ever memorable. Ever the study of passing generations of men. C. D.

Verse 13.

1. Zion often needs restoration. It needs "mercy."

2. Its restoration is certain: "Thou shalt arise," etc.

3. The seasons of its restoration are determined. There is a "time" to Favor her; a "set" time.

4. Intimations of those coming seasons are often given "The time, the set time, is come." G. R.

Verses 13-14.

1. Visitation expected.

2. Predestination relied upon.

3. Evidence observed.

4. Enquiry suggested—Do we take pleasure in her stones? etc.

Verses 13-14. The interest of the Lord's people in the concerns of Zion one of the surest signs of her returning prosperity.

Verse 15. The inward prosperity of the church essential to her power in the world.

Verse 16. God is Zion's purchaser, architect, builder, inhabitant, Lord.

1. Zion built up. Conversions frequent; confessions numerous; union firm; edification solid; missions extended.

2. God glorified. In its very foundation; by its ministry; by difficulties and enemies; by poor workers, and poor materials; and even by our failures.

3. Hope excited. Because we may expect the Lord to glorify himself.

4. Inquiry suggested. Am I concerned, as built, or building? not merely doctrinally, but experimentally?

Verse 17.

1. The destitute pray.

2. They pray most.

4. They pray best.

4. They pray most effectually. Or the surest way to succeed in prayer is to pray as the destitute; show the reason of this.

Verse 18.

1. A memorial.
2. A magnificat. *W. Durban.*

Verses 18-21.

1. Misery in extremis.
2. Divinity observant.
3. Deity actively assisting.
4. Glory consequently published.

Verses 19-22.

1. The notice which God takes of the world, Ps 102:19. (a) The place from which he beholds it: "from heaven, " not from an earthly point of view. (b) The character in which he beholds it; "from the height of his sanctuary, "from the mercy-seat.

2. What attracts his notice most in the world. The groaning of the prisoner and of those appointed to death.

3. The purpose for which he notices them. "To loose, " etc.;" to declare," etc. (a) For human comfort. (b) For his own glory.

4. When his notice is thus fixed upon the earth. "When, " etc., Ps 102:22. *G. R.*

Verse 23. For the sick.

1. Submission—The Lord sent the trial—"*He* weakeneth," etc.

2. Service—exonerated from some work, he now requires of me patience, earnestness, etc.

3. Preparation—for going home.

4. Prayer—for others to occupy my place.

5. Expectation—I shall soon be in heaven, now that my days are shortened.

Verse 24.

1. *The prayer.* "Take me not away, "etc. (a) Not in the midst of life, is the prayer of some. (b) Not in the midst of worldly prosperity is the prayer of many, for the sake of those dependent upon them. (c) Not in the midst of spiritual growth, is the prayer of not a few: "Oh spare me, that I

may recover strength, "etc. (d) Not in the midst of Christian work and usefulness, is the prayer of others.

2. *The plea.* "Thy years, "etc.; years are plentiful with thee, therefore to give me longer days will be an easy gift—and thine own are throughout all generations. *G. R.*

Verse 25-27.

1. The unchangeableness of God amidst past changes: "of old," etc. (a) He was the same before as after he had laid the foundations of the earth. (b) He was the same after as before.

2. The unchangeableness of God amidst future changes. "They shall perish," etc. (a) The same before they perish as after. (b) After as before.

3. The unchangeableness of God in the past and the future. "Thou art the same," etc. *G. R.*

Verse 26-27.

1. How far God may change—only in his garments, or outward manifestations of creation and providence.

2. Wherein he cannot change—his nature, attributes, covenant, love, etc.

3. The comfortable truths which may be safely inferred, or which gather support from this fact.

Verse 26-27.

1. The material universe of God. (a) No more to him than a garment to the wearer. (b) Ever waxing old, but he the same. (c) Soon to be changed and left to perish, but of his years no end.

2. Our relation to each (a) Let us never love the dress more than the wearer. (b) Nor trust more in the changeful than in the abiding. (c) Nor live for that which will die out.

Verse 28. The true apostolical succession.

1. There always will be saints.

2. They will frequently be the seed of the saints after the flesh.

3. They will always be the spiritual seed of the godly, for God converts one by means of another.

4. We should order our efforts with an eye to the church's future.

PSALM 103

SERMON OUTLINES AND HELPFUL TIPS

Verse 1. "The Saints blessing the Lord." See "Spurgeon's Sermons, " No. 1,078.

Verse 1.

1. We should bless the Most High himself. It is possible to fail to bless *him*, while we praise his gifts, his word, his works, his ways.

2. We should bless him individually: "*My* soul." Not merely the family through the father, nor the people through the pastor; nor the congregation through the choir; but personally.

3. We should bless him spiritually: "soul." Not only with organ, voice, offering, works, &c.

4. We should bless him unreservedly: "All that is within me."

5. We should bless him resolutely. David preached self-communion, self-encouragement, and self-command. *W. Jackson.*

Verse 1. Here is,

1. Self-converse: "Oh my soul." Many talk freely enough to others, but never talk to themselves. They are strangers to themselves—not on speaking terms with themselves—take no interest in their own souls—are dull and melancholy when alone.

2. Self-exhortation: "Bless the Lord, O my soul." Thy Creator, thy Benefactor, thy Redeemer.

3. Self-encouragement: "All that is within me"—every faculty of my mental, moral and spiritual being: with ten strings—every chord in motion. No need for one faculty of the soul to say to another, "know the Lord, for all shall know him from the least even unto the greatest." *G. R.*

Verse 1 (*First clause*, and Ps 103:22, *last clause*). Personal worship the Alpha and Omega of religion. *C. Davis.*

Verse 2. Inquire into the causes of our frequent forgetfulness of the Lord's mercies, show the evil of it, and advise remedies.

Verse 3.

1. Forgiveness is *in* God: "There is forgiveness with thee." It is his nature to forgive as well as to punish sin.

2. It is *from* God. None can forgive sin but God. None can reveal forgiveness but God.

3. It is like God, full, free, and everlasting—"all thine iniquities." *G. R.*

Verse 3. *Who healeth all thy diseases.*

1. Why is sin called a disease? (a) As it destroys the moral beauty of the creature. (b) As it excites pain. (c) As it disables from duty. (d) As it leads to death.

2. The variety of sinful diseases to which we are subject. Mr 7:21-23; Gal 5:19, &c.

3. The remedy by which God heals these diseases. (a) His pardoning mercy through the redemption of Christ. (b) The sanctifying influences of grace. (c) The means of grace. (d) The resurrection of the body. *From "The Study,"* 1873.

Verse 3 (*last clause*). — Our diseases by nature, our great Physician, the perfect soundness which he works in us, results of that soundness.

Verses 3-5. Mercy's Hexapla.

1. Three curses removed. (a) Guilt put away. (b) Corruption cured. (c) Destruction averted.

2. Three blessings, bestowed. (a) Favors that can gratify. (b) Pleasures that can satisfy. (c) Life that can never die.

Or

1. Pardon. (Ps 103:3)
2. Purification. (Ps 103:4)
3. Redemption.
4. Coronation. (Ps 103:5)
5. Plenty bestowed.
6. Power renewed. *W. Durban.*

Verse 4. (*first clause*). The Redemption of David's life from destruction.

1. His shepherd life.
2. His military life.
3. His persecuted life.
4. His regal life.
5. His spiritual life. *W. J.*

Verse 4. What is redeemed, and from what? Who are redeemed, and by whom?

Verse 5.

1. A singular condition — satisfaction.
2. A singular provision — good things.
3. A singular result — youth renewed.

Verse 5. — "Rejuvenescence." See Macmillan's "Ministry of Nature," pp. 321-347.

Verse 7.

1. God would have men know him.
2. He is his own revealer.
3. There are degrees in the revelation.
4. We may pray for increased knowledge of him.

Verse 8.

1. Mercy specified: "Merciful and gracious."

2. Mercy qualified: "Slow to anger." Mercy itself may be angered, and then how terrible is the anger.

3. Mercy amplified: "Plenteous in mercy." "He will abundantly pardon; "and he only knows what abundant pardon means. *G. R.*

Verse 9.

1. What God will do to his people. He will sometimes chide—contend with them. (a) Providentially, by outward trials. (b) Experimentally, by inward conflicts.

2. What he will not do to them. (a) Not chide continually in this life. (b) Not chide in the least hereafter. (c) "The days of their mourning shall be ended." *G. R.*

Verses 11-13. The height, length and depth of divine love.

Verse 12. "Plenary Absolution." See "Spurgeon's Sermons, " No. 1,108.

Verse 12.

1. The union implied. Between man and his transgressions.

    (a) Legally.
    (b) Actually.
    (c) Experimentally.
    (d) Eternally, in themselves considered.

2. The separation effected.

    (a) By whom? "He hath, "etc.

    (b) How? By his own Son coming between the sinner and his sins.

3. The Re-union prevented. "As far, "etc. When east and west meet, then, and not till then, will the reunion take place. As the two extremities of a straight line can never meet, and cannot be lengthened without receding further from each other, so it will ever be with a pardoned sinner and his sins. *G. R.*

Verses 13-14. "The Tender Pity of the Lord." See "Spurgeon's Sermons, "No. 941.

Verses 13-14.

1. Whom God pities; "them that fear him."

2. How he pities "as a father pitieth his children."

3. Why he pities; "for he knoweth our frame." He hath reason to know out frame, for he framed us, and having himself made man of the dust, "he remembers that we are dust." *Matthew Henry.*

Verse 14.

1. Man's Constitution.
2. God's Consideration. *W. D.*

Verse 15. Man's earthly career. His rise, progress, glory, fall, and oblivion.

Verses 15-18.

1. What man is when left to himself. "As for man, "etc. (a) What here? His days are as grass, his glory as the flower of grass. (b) What hereafter? swept away by a blighting wind, by a blast of divine anger—known no more on the earth, known only in perdition.

2. What the mercy of God does for him. (a) Makes a covenant of grace on his behalf flora everlasting. (b) Makes a covenant of peace with hint in this life. (c) Makes a covenant of promise to him for an eternity to come.

3. Who are the objects of this mercy? (a) Those who fear God. (b) Who walk in the footsteps of pious ancestors. (c) Who rely upon covenant mercy. (d) Who are faithful to their covenant engagements. *G. R.*

Verse 18. The covenant, in what respects we can keep it, in what frame of mind it must be kept, and what is the practical proof of so doing.

Verse 19. "A Discourse upon God's Dominion." See Charnock's Works *Nicol's Edition, Vol. II., pp. 400-499.*

Verse 19.

1. The nature of the throne.
2. The extent of the dominion.
3. The character of the monarch.
4. The consequent joy of the subjects: "Bless the Lord."

Verse 20. The angels' service instructive to us.

1. Their personal strength is excellent. As servants of God we also should see to our own spiritual health and rigour.

2. They are practical in their obedience, not theorists.

3. They are attentive while at work, ready to learn more, and holding fellowship with God, who speaks personally to them.

4. They do all in the spirit of joyful praise, blessing the Lord.

Verses 20-21.

1. The center of praise: "Bless the Lord." All praise centers in him.

2. The concert of praise. (a) Angels. (b) The hosts of the redeemed. (c) Ministers in particular. (d) The surrounding creation.

3. The climax of praise: "Bless the Lord, O my soul." This has the highest claim upon me for gratitude and praise. Vast as the chorus may be, it will not be perfect without my note of praise. This is the culminating note: "Bless the Lord, O my soul." **G.R.**

Verse 21. Who are God's ministers? What is their business? To do his pleasure. What is their delight? To bless the Lord.

Verses 21-22. Henry Melvill has a notable sermon upon "The Peril of the Spiritual Guide." The drift of it may be gathered from the extract which we have placed as a note upon the passage.

Verse 22.

1. The Chorus.
2. The Echo. **W.D.**

PSALM 104

SERMON OUTLINES AND HELPFUL TIPS

Verse 1. *(first clause)* — An exhortation to one's own heart.

1. To remember the Lord as the first cause of all good. Bless not man, or fate, but the Lord.

2. To do this in a loving, grateful, hearty, praising manner. Bless the Lord.

3. To do it truly and intensely. O my soul.

4. To do it now — for various reasons and in all possible ways.

Verse 1 (second clause). He is all this essentially, and in nature, providence, grace, and judgment.

Verse 2 (first clause). The clearest revelation of God is still a concealment; even light is but a covering to him. God is clothed with light as we see him in his omniscience, his holiness, his revelation, his glory, in heaven and his grace on earth.

Verse 3 (last clause).

1. God is leisurely in his haste: "he walketh, "etc.

2. God is swift even in his slackness: "he walketh on the wings of the wind."

3. The practical conclusions are that there is time enough for the divine purposes but none for our trifling; and that we should both wait with patience for the victory of his cause and hasten it by holy activity.

Verse 4.

1. The Nature of Angels Spirits.

2. The Lord of Angels. "Who maketh, "etc. What must Iris own spirituality be who maketh spirits?

3. The ministry of Angels.

    (a) Their office: "ministers."
    (b) Their activity or zeal: "a flaming fire."
    (c) Their dependence: made ministers.
    — *G. Rogers.*

Verse 7. The power of the divine word in nature shows its power in other spheres.

Verse 9.

1. All things have their appointed bounds.

2. To pass those bounds without special permission by God is transgression. "Thou hast set a bound that they may not pass."

3. Extraordinary cases should be followed by a return to ordinary duties. "That they turn not again, "etc. **G.R.**

Verse 10. The thoughtfulness of God for those who, like the valleys, are lowly, hidden, and needy: the abiding character of his supplies: and the joyous results of his care.

Verse 10. God's care for wild creatures, reflections from it.

1. Shall he not much more care for his people?
2. Will he not look after wild, wandering men?
3. Ought we not also to care for all that live?

Verse 10. From the fertility, life and music which mark the course of a stream, illustrate the beneficial influences of the Gospel. *C.A. Davis.*

Verse 14. *In the Hayfield.* (See "Spurgeon's Sermons, "No. 757.) "He causeth the grass to grow for the cattle."

1. Grass is in itself instructive.

   (a) As a symbol of our mortality: "All flesh is grass."

   (b) As an emblem of the wicked.

   (c) As a picture of the elect of God. Isa 35:7 44:4 Ps 72:6,16

   (d) Grass is comparable to the food wherewith the Lord supplies the necessities of his chosen ones. Ps 23:2 So 1:7

2. God is seen in the growing of the grass.

   (a) As a worker: "He causeth, "etc. See God in common things—in solitary things.

   (b) See God as a caretaker: "He causeth the grass to grow for the cattle." God cares for the beasts—the helpless—dumb and speechless things—providing suitable food for them: "grass". Let us, then, see his hand in providence at all times.

3. God's working in the grass for the cattle gives us illustrations concerning grace.

   (a) God "cares for oxen" and satisfies their wants: there must then be something somewhere to satisfy the needs of the nobler creature man, and his immortal soul.

   (b) Though God provides the grass for the cattle, the cattle must eat it themselves. The Lord Jesus Christ is provided as the food of the soul. We must, by faith, receive and feed upon Christ.

(c) Preventing grace may here be seen in a symbol: before the cattle were made, in this world there was grass. There were covenant supplies for God's people before they were in the world.

(d) Here is an illustration of free grace: the cattle bring nothing to purchase the food. Why is this?

(1) Because they belong to him, Ps 1:10.

(2) Because he has entered into a covenant with them to feed them, Ge 9:9,10.

In the text there is a mighty blow to free will: "He causeth the grass to grow." Grace does not grow in the heart without a divine cause. If God cares to make grass grow he will also make us grow in grace. Again; the grass does not grow without an object; it is "for the cattle": but the cattle grow for man. What then, does man grow for? Observe, further, that the existence of the grass is necessary to complete the chain of nature. So the meanest child of God is necessary to the family.

Verse 16. "The Cedars of Lebanon." (See "Spurgeon's Sermons," No. 529.)

1. The absence of all human culture. These trees are peculiarly the Lord's trees, because,

(a) They owe their planting entirely to him: "He hath planted."

(b) They are not dependent upon man for their watering.

(c) No mortal might protects them.

(d) As to their inspection—they preserve a sublime indifference to human gaze.

(e) Their exultation is all for God.

(f) There is not a cedar upon Lebanon which is not independent of man in its expectations.

2. The glorious display of divine care.

(a) In the abundance of their supply.
(b) They are always green.
(c) Observe the grandeur and size of these trees.
(d) Their fragrance.
(e) Their perpetuity.
(f) They are very venerable.

3. The fullness of living principle: "The trees of the Lord are full of sap."

(a) This is vitally necessary.
(b) It is essentially mysterious.
(c) It is radically secret.
(d) It is permanently active.

(e) It is externally operative.
(f) It is abundantly to be desired.

Verses 17-18. "Lessons from Nature." (See "Spurgeon's Sermons, " No. 1,005.)

1. For each place God has prepared a suitable form of life: for "the fir trees, ""the stork"; for "the high hills" "the wild goat, "etc. So, for all parts of the spiritual universe God has provided suitable forms of divine life.

    (a) Each age has its saints.

    (b) In every rank they are to be found. The Christian religion is equally well adapted for all conditions.

    (c) In every church spiritual life is to be found.

    (d) God's people are to be found in every city.

2. Each creature has its appropriate place.

    (a) Each man has by God a providential position appointed to him.
    (b) This is also true of our spiritual experience.
    (c) The same holds good as to individuality of character.

3. Every creature that God has made is provided with shelter.

4. For each creature the shelter is appropriate.

5. Each creature uses its shelter.

Verse 19.

1. The wisdom of God as displayed in the material heavens. In the changes of the moon and the variety of the seasons.

2. The goodness of God as there displayed in the adaptation of these changes to the wants and enjoyments of men.

3. The faithfulness of God as there displayed. Inspiring confidence in his creatures by their regularity.

"So like the sun may I fulfill
The appointed duties of the day;
With ready mind and active will
March on and keep my heavenly way."

Verse 20. Darkness and the beasts that creep forth therein.

1. Ignorance of God, and unrestrained lusts. Ro 1:2 Sins discovered. Beasts there before, but not noticed, now terrify man.

3. Spiritual despondency, dismay, despair, etc.

4. Church lethargy. All sorts of heresies, etc., begin to creep forth.

5. Papal influence. Monks, friars, priests, etc., creep about in this dark age. *A.G. Brown.*

Verse 20.

1. Night work is for wild beasts: "Thou makest darkness, " etc.

2. Day work is for men: "Man goeth forth, "etc. Good men do their work by day; bad men by night: their work is in the dark. Ministers who creep into their studies by night, and "roar after their prey, "and "seek their meat from God", are more like wild beasts than rational men.—*G.R.*

Verse 21. Inarticulate prayers, or how faulty the expression may be and yet how real the prayer in the esteem of God. **Verse 22.** From the effect of sunrise on the beasts of prey, exhibit the influence of Divine Grace on our evil passions. **C.A.D.**

Verse 23. "*Early Closing.*" A sermon preached on behalf of the "Early Closing Association, "by James Hamilton, D.D., 1850. In the "Pulpit," Vol. 57.

Verse 24.

1. The language of wonder: "O Lord, how manifold, "etc. Their number, variety, cooperation, harmony.

2. Of admiration: "In wisdom, "etc. Everywhere the same wisdom displayed. God, says Dr. Chalmers, is as great in minutia as in magnitude.

3. Of gratitude: "The earth is full," etc. **G.R.**

Verse 24.

1. The works of the Lord are multitudinous and varied.

2. They are so constructed as to show the most consummate wisdom in their design, and in the end for which they are formed.

3. They are all God's property, and should be used only in reference to the end for which they were created. All abuse and waste of God's creatures are spoil and robbery on the property of the Creator. *Adam Clarke.*

Verse 26. *There go the ships.* (See" Spurgeon's Sermons, "No. 1,259.)

1. We see that the ships go.

    (a) The ships are intended for going.
    (b) The ships in going at last disappear from view.
    (c) The ships as they go are going upon business.
    (d) The ships sail upon a changeful sea.

2. How go the ships?

    (a) They must go according to the wind.

    (b) But still the mariner does not go by the wind without exertion on his own part.

    (c) They have to be guided and steered by the helm.

    (d) He who manages the helm seeks direction from charts and lights.

    (e) They go according to their build.

3. Let us signal them.

    (a) Who is your owner?
    (b) What is your cargo?
    (c) Where are you going?

Verse 27. Trace the analogy in the spiritual world. The saints waiting, Ps 5:27; their sustenance from the opened hand, Ps 5:28; their trouble under the hidden face; their death if the Spirit were gone, Ps 5:29; their revival when the Spirit returns, Ps 5:30.

Verse 29.

1. The commencement of life is from God: "Thou sendest forth thy Spirit, "etc.

2. The continuance of life is from God: "Thou renewest, " etc.

3. The decline of life is from God: "Thou hidest thy face, " etc.

4. The cessation of life is from God: "Thou takest away their breath, "etc.

5. The resurrection of life is from God: "Thou renewest, " etc. **G.R.**

Verse 30. The season of Spring and its moral analogies. See John Foster's "Lectures, "1844.

Verse 32.

1. What there is in a Look of God. "He looketh, "etc.

    (a) What in a look of anger.

    (b) What in a look of love. He looked out of the fiery pillar upon the Egyptians." The Lord hath looked out from his pillar of glory," etc. He gave another look from the same pillar to Israel.

2. What there is in a Touch of God: "He toucheth," etc. A touch of his may raise a soul to heaven, or sink a soul to hell. **G.R.**

Verse 33.

1. The singer—"I."

2. The song—"praises."

3. The audience—"The Lord," "My God."

4. The length of the song—"long as I live; while I have my being."—*A.G.B.*

Verse 33. Two "I wills."

1. Because he made me live.
2. Because he has made me to live in him.
3. Because he is Jehovah and "my God."
4. Because I shall live forever, in the best sense.

Verse 34.

1. David's contemplation.
2. David's exultation. *Thomas Horton.*

Verse 35.

1. They who praise not God are not fit to be on the earth: "Let the sinners be consumed, "etc.

2. Much less are they fit to be in heaven.

3. They who praise God are fit both for earth and heaven. Though others do not praise him here, the saints will. "Bless thou the Lord," etc.

> (a) In opposition to others, they praise him on earth.

> (b) In harmony with others, they praise him in heaven, etc. Everywhere it is with them, "Praise ye the Lord."—*G. R.*

PSALM 105

SERMON OUTLINES AND HELPFUL TIPS

Verse 1.

1. Praise God for former mercies.
2. Pray for further mercies.
3. Publish his famous mercies.

Verse 1. A series of holy exercises.

"Give thanks"—
"call upon his name"—
"make known"—
"sing"—
"talk"—
"glory"—
"rejoice"—
"seek"—
"remember".

Verse 2.

1. The pleasure of talking to God. "Sing, "etc.; making melody in the heart.
2. The duty of talking of God. "Talk ye, "etc. **G.R.**

Verse 2. The Christian's table talk.

Verse 3.

1. Those who find: or—"glory ye, "etc.
2. Those who seek: or—"rejoice."

Verse 3 (second clause). Let the seeker rejoice that there is such a God to seek, that he invites us to seek, that he moves us to seek, enables us to seek, and promises to be found of us. The tendency of the seeker is to despond, but there are many grounds of comfort.

Verse 4. How can we seek the Lord's strength?

1. By desiring to be subject to it.
2. By being supported by it.
3. By being equipped with it for service.
4. By seeing its results upon others.

Verse 4. Threefold seeking.

1. The Lord for mercy.
2. His strength for service.
3. His face for happiness. *A.G. Brown.*

Verse 4 (last clause). Seeking the Lord the perpetual occupation of a believer.

Verse 5. Themes for memory.

1. What God has done.
2. What he has said.

Verse 5. Our memory and God's memory. "Remember." "He hath remembered."

Verse 7. God's relation to his elect and to all mankind.

Verse 9. The making, swearing, and confirming of the covenant. See our comment on these **Verse**s with the passages referred to.

Verse 12. Comfort to the few. The typical and spiritual Israel few at first. A few in the ark peopled the world. Small companies have done wonders. Christ's presence is promised to two or three. God saith not by many or by few, etc.

Verse 13.

1. God's people may be often removed.
2. They can never be injured.
3. God's property in them will not be renounced.

Verse 14. Dr. T. Goodwin has an excellent sermon on these **Verse**s, entitled "The Interest of England, "in which he condenses the history of the world, to show, that those nations which have persecuted and afflicted the people of God have invariably been broken in pieces. (*Goodwin's Works*, volume 12 pg 34-60, Nichol's edition).

Verse 15. In what respect Abraham was a prophet, and how far believers are the same.

Verse 16.

1. All things come at the call of God. He called for plenty, and it came, for famine, and it came; for captivity, and it came; for deliverance, and it came.

2. The most unlikely means of accomplishing an end with man is often the direct way with God. He fulfilled the promise of Canaan to Abraham by banishing him from it; of plenty, by sending a famine; of freedom, by bringing into captivity. *G.R.*

Verse 19. The duration of our troubles, the testing power of the promise, the comfortable issue which is secured to us.

Verse 24 (second clause). In what respects grace can make believers stronger than their enemies.

Verse 25.

1. The natural hatred of the world to the church.
2. God's permitting it to be shown. When? Why?
3. The subtle manner in which this enmity seeks its object.

Verse 32. *He gave them hail for rain.* Judgment substituted for mercy.

Verse 37 (first clause). Wealth found upon us after affliction.

Verse 37 (second clause). A consummation to be desired. This was the direct result of the divine presence. The circumstances out of which it grew were hard labor, and persecution. It enabled them to leave Egypt, to journey far, to carry burdens, to fight enemies, etc.

Verse 39.

1. A dark cloud of providence is the guide of the people of God by day.

2. A bright cloud of promises is their guide by night. **G.R.**

Verse 39. The Lord's goodness exemplified in our varying conditions.

1. For prosperity—a cloud.

2. For adversity—a light. A good text would be found in "light in the night."

Verse 40.

1. God often gives in love what is not asked. So the bread from heaven which was beyond all they could ask or think.

2. He sometimes gives in anger what is asked. They asked for flesh to eat—"and he brought quails."—**G.R.**

Verse 41. We have,

1. A type of the person of Christ, in the rock.

    (a) Unsightly as Horeb—"When we shall see him, there is no beauty, "etc. (Isa 43:2).

    (b) Firm and immovable "Who is a rock, save our God?" (2Sa 22:32).

2. A type of the sufferings of Christ, in the smitten rock.

    (a) Smitten by the rod of the Law.

    (b) Smitten to the heart.

3. A type of the benefits of Christ, in the water flowing from the rock—pure, refreshing, perpetual, abundant. *James Bennett*, 1828.

Verse 41.

1. The miraculous energy of God's grace in the conversion of a sinner: "He opened the rock, and the waters gushed out."

2. The effect in relation to others, which demonstrates at once the excellence and the reality of the miracle in ourselves: "They ran in the dry places like a ri**Verse**"—*Thomas Dale*, 1836.

Verse 41.

1. The grand source—the rock opened.
2. The liberal stream—"gushed out".
3. The continued flow—"in dry places".

Verse 42.

1. The grand source—the rock opened.
2. The liberal stream—"gushed out".
3. The continued law—"in dry places".

Verse 45. Obedience to God the design of his mercies to us.

PSALM 106

SERMON OUTLINES AND HELPFUL TIPS

Verse 1. Take this **Verse** as the theme of the Psalm, and we shall then see that its exhortation to praise,

1. Is directed to a special people: chosen, redeemed, but sinful, borne with, and forgiven.

2. Is supported by abundant arguments. Man not to be praised, for he sins. God gives in his goodness, and forgives in his mercy, and is therefore to be thanked.

3. Is as applicable now as ever: for our story is a transcript of Israel's.

Verse 2.

1. A challenge.

2. A suggestion: at least let us do what we can.

3. An ambition: in the ages to come we will make known with the church to angels, and all intelligent beings, the mighty acts of divine grace.

4. A question—shall I be there?

Verse 3. The blessedness of a godly life.

Verse 4.

1. The language of Humility: "Remember me, O Lord." Let me not escape thy notice amongst the many millions of creatures under thy care.

2. The language of Faith.

    (a) That God has a people to whom he shows special Favor.

    (b) That he himself has provided salvation for them.

3. The language of prayer.

    (a) For the free gift of salvation.

    (b) For the common salvation—not wishing to be peculiar, but to be as "Thy people", taking them for all in all, both here and hereafter. Walking in the footsteps of the flock.

"Be this my glory, Lord, to be
Joined to thy saints, and near to thee."—*G.R.*

Verses 4, 7, 45. In Ps 106:4, a remembrance desired. In Ps 106:7, a failure of remembrance deplored. In Ps 106:45, a divine remembrance extolled.

Verse 5.

1. The Persons: "Thy chosen"; "Thy nation"; "Thine inheritance."

2. The Privileges: "The good of thy chosen"; "The gladness of thy nation"; "The glory of thine inheritance."

3. The Pleas: "That I may see", etc. They were once as I am: make me what they are now.

   (a) My salvation is everything to me. "That I may see," etc. "That I may rejoice", etc. They are many, I am but one. "That I may glory", etc. — *G.R.*

Verse 6. In what respects men may be partakers in the sins of their ancestors.

Verses 7-8.

1. On man's part a darkened understanding, ungrateful forgetfulness, and provocation.

2. On God's part: understanding discovering a reason for mercy; memory mindful of the covenant; patience revealing its power.

Verses 7-8.

1. A special provocation; they murmured at the Red Sea.

2. A special deliverance; "Nevertheless", etc.

3. A special Design; "For his own sake"; "That he might make his power known." — *G.R.*

Verse 8. Salvation by grace a grand display of power.

Verse 8.

"Why are men saved?" See "Spurgeon's Sermons", No. 115.

1. The glorious Savior, "He."

2. The favored persons, who are they?

   (a) They were a stupid people: "Our fathers understood not", etc., Ps 106:7.

   (b) An ungrateful people: "They remembered not", etc., Ps 106:7,13,24, etc.

   (c) A provoking people.

3. The reason of salvation: "He saved them for his name's sake." The name of God is his person, his attributes, and his nature. We might, perhaps, include this also: "My name is in him" — that is, in Christ; he saves us for the sake of Christ, who is the name of God. He saved them that he might manifest his nature: "God is love." He saved them to vindicate his name.

4. The obstacles removed: "Nevertheless."

Verse 9. *Israel at the Red Sea.* See "Spurgeon's Sermons", No. 72.

1. Israel's three difficulties.

(a) The Red Sea in front of them. This was not put there by an enemy; but by God himself. The Red Sea represents some great and trying providence placed in the path of every newborn child of God, to try his faith, and the sincerity of his trust in God.

b) The Egyptians behind them,—the representatives of the sins which we thought were dead and gone.

(c) The third difficulty was faint hearts within them.

2. Israel's three helps.

(a) Providence.

(b) Their knowledge that they were the covenant people of God.

(c) The man,—Moses. So the believer's hope and help is in the God man Christ Jesus.

3. God's grand design in it. To give them a thorough baptism into his service, consecrating them forever to himself (1Co 1-2).

Verse 9. (*second clause*). Dangerous and difficult paths rendered safe and easy by God's leadership.

Verse 11. (*second clause*). Song over sins forgiven.

Verses 12-14. The faith of nature, based on sight, causes transient joy, soon evaporates, dies in utter unbelief, and conducts to greater sin.

Verses 13-15.

1. Mercies are sooner forgotten than trials: "They soon forgot", etc. We write our afflictions on marble, our mercies upon sand.

2. We should wait for God, as well as upon God: "They waited not," etc.

3. Immoderate desire for what we have not of worldly goods, tempts God to deprive us of what we have: Ps 106:14.

4. Prayer may be answered for evil as well as for good: "He gave them their request", then smote them with a plague.

5. Carnal indulgence is inimical to spiritual mindedness: Ps 106:15. Better have a lean body and healthy soul, than a healthy body and leanness of soul. "Poor in this world, rich in faith." There are few of whom it can be said, "I wish thou mayest prosper and be in health," etc. (3Jo 2). **G.R.**

Verse 14. The wickedness of inordinate desires.

1. They are out of place—"in the wilderness."
2. They are assaults upon God—"and tempted God."
3. They are despisers of former mercies—see preceding Verses.
4. They involve solemn danger—see following Verse.

Verse 16. The sin of envy. Its base nature, its cruel actions its unscrupulous ingratitude, its daring assaults, its abomination before God.

Verse 19. The sinner as an inventor.

Verses 19-22.

1. The Sin remembered.

> (a) Idolatry: not forgetting God merely, or disowning him, but setting up an idol in his place.
>
> (b) Idolatry of the worst kind: changing be glory of God into the similitude of an ox, etc.
>
> (c) The idolatry of Egypt under which they had suffered, and from which they had been delivered.
>
> (d) Idolatry after many wonderful interpositions of the true God in their behalf.

2. The Remembrance of Sin.

> (a) For Humiliation. It was the sin of their fathers.
>
> (b) For self-condemnation. "We have sinned with our fathers." It was our nature in them, and it is their nature in us that has committed this great sin.

Verse 23. Moses, the intercessor, a type of our Lord. Carefully study his pleading as recorded in Ex 32:1-35.

Verse 23.

1. Mediation required: "He said that he would destroy them," etc.

2. Mediation offered: "Moses stood before him in the breach."

3. Mediation accepted: "To turn away his wrath", etc. Ex 32:1-35. **G.R.**

Verse 24-26. Murmuring.

1. Arises from despising our mercies.
2. Is fostered by unbelief.
3. Is indulged in all sorts of places.
4. Makes men deaf to the Lord's voice.
5. Provokes great judgments from the Lord.

Verse 24-27.

1. The Rest promised: "The pleasant land."

2. The Refusal of the Rest: "They despised", etc.

3. The Reason of the Refusal: unbelief. "They could not enter in because of unbelief." — **G.R.**

Verse 30-31. The effects of one decisive act for God; immediate, personal, and for posterity.

Verses 32-33.

1. The afflictions of God's people are for the trial of their faith.

2. The trial of their faith is to bring them from dependence upon circumstances to depend upon God himself.

3. The forbearance of God with his people is greater than that of the best of men. **G.R.**

Verse 33.

1. What it is so to speak unadvisedly.
2. What is the great cause of it—"they provoked his spirit."
3. What the results may be.

Verse 34-42.

1. What Israel did not do. They began well, but did not complete the conquest of their foes: Ps 106:34.

2. What they did do: Ps 106:35-39.

    (a) They became friendly with them.

    (b) They adopted their habits: "learned their works."

    (c) They embraced their religion: "served their idols."

    (d) They imitated their cruelties; Ps 106:37-38.

    (e) They did worse than the heathen (Ps 106:39), they added wicked inventions of their own.

3. What God did to them: Ps 106:40-42. He gave them into the hands of their enemies, and suffered them to be severely oppressed by them. We must either conquer all our foes or be conquered by them. Bring your shield from the battle or be brought home upon it.—**G.R.**

Verse 37. Moloch worship in modern times. Children sacrificed to fashion, wealth, and loveless marriage among the higher classes. Bad example, drinking customs, etc., among the poorer sort. A needful subject.

Verse 44-45. Sin in God's people.

1. Is very provoking to God.

2. Ensures chastisement.

3. Is to be sincerely mourned—"their cry."

4. Will be graciously forgiven, and its effect removed. So the covenant promises.

Verse 47.

1. An earnest Prayer: "Save us, O Lord", etc.

2. A Believing Prayer: "O Lord *our* God."

3. A humble Prayer: "Gather us from among the heathen."

4. A sincere Prayer: "To give thanks unto thy holy name"; to own thy justice and holiness in all thy ways.

5. A confident Prayer: "To triumph in thy praise." None but bruised spices give forth such odors.—*G.R.*

Verse 48.

1. God is to be praised as the "God of Israel."

> (a) Of typical Israel.
> (b) Of the true Israel.

2. He is to be praised as the God of Israel under all circumstances: for his judgments as well as for his mercies.

3. At all times: "From everlasting to everlasting."

4. By all people: "Let all the people say, Amen."

5. As the beginning and end of every song: "Praise ye the Lord."—*G.R.*

Verse 48. *Let all the people say, Amen.* The exhortation to universal praise. All men are indebted to the Lord, all have sinned, all hear the gospel, all his people are saved. Unanimity in praise is pleasant, and promotes unity in other matters.

PSALM 107

SERMON OUTLINES AND HELPFUL TIPS

Whole Psalm. This psalm is like the Interpreter's house in Bunyan's "Pilgrim's Progress." Pilgrim is told that he will there see excellent and profitable things. The same promise is given in the introduction to this psalm, where we have,

1. The source of these excellent things—the goodness and all enduring mercy of God; mercy not exhausted by the unworthiness of its objects.

2. Their acknowledgment, "Let the redeemed of the Lord say so." Men will not own it, but the redeemed of the Lord will. It is the experience of such that is pictorially represented in this psalm. Let everyone speak of God as he finds. Is he good when he takes away as well as when he gives "The redeemed of the Lord will say so." Is he merciful when he frowns as well as when he smiles? "The redeemed of the Lord say so." Does he make all things work together for good to them that love him? "Let the redeemed of the Lord say so."

3. Their end. Praise and thanksgiving: "Oh give", etc.

(a) For general mercies;
(b) For redemption;
(c) For special deliverances.—*G.R.*

Verses 1-2. The duty of praise is universal, the real presentation of it remains with the redeemed. Particular redemption should lead to specific praise, special testimony to truth and special faith in God: "Let the redeemed of the Lord say so."

Verse 3. The ingathering of the chosen.

1. All wandered.

2. Their ways different.

3. All observed of the Lord.

4. All brought to Jesus as to one centre. Note ways, and times of gathering.

Verse 4. Wandering Jews. Illustrate the roaming of a mind in search of truth, peace, love, purity, etc.

Verse 4. The words contain a brief history of man's fall and misery and of his restoration by Jesus Christ; which are described under these particulars.

1. The lost state of men by nature.

2. They are brought to a right sense of it, and cry to the Lord Jesus for deliverance.

3. He hears them and delivers them out of all their distresses.

4. The tribute of thanks due to him for this great deliverance.

—*W. Romaine.*

Verse 5. Spiritual hunger the cause of faintness. Necessity of feeding the soul.

Verse 7. Divine grace stimulating our exertions. "He led them forth ...that they might go."

Verse 8. He who has enjoyed God's help should mark,

1. In what distress he has been;
2. How he has called to God;
3. How God has helped him;
4. What thanks he has returned; and,
5. What thanks he is yet bound to render.
—*Lange's Commentary.*

Verse 9. A great general fact. The condition, the benefactor, the blessing "goodness", the result—"satisfieth." Then the further result of praise as seen in Ps 107:8.

Verses 12-13.

1. The convicted soul's abject condition—humbled, exhausted, prostrate, deserted.

2. His speedy deliverance. Cried, cried while in trouble, unto the Lord, he saved, out of their distresses.

Verse 13. Man's work and God's work. *They* cried and *He* saved.

Verse 14. God gives light, life, liberty.

Verse 20. Recovery from sickness must be ascribed to the Lord, and gratitude should flow forth because of it. But the text describes spiritual and mental sickness. Notice,

1. The Patient in his extremity.

    (a) He is a fool: by nature inclined to evil.

    (b) He has played the fool (see Ps 107:17), "transgression", "iniquities."

    (c) He now has lost all appetite and is past all cure.

    (d) He is at death's door.

    (e) But he has begun to pray.

2. The Cure in its simplicity.

    (a) Christ the Word is the essential cure. He heals the guilt, habit, depression, and evil results of sin. For every form of malady Christ has healing; hence preachers should preach him much, and all meditate much upon him.

    (b) The word in the Book is the instrumental cure: its teachings, doctrines, precepts, promises, encouragements, invitations, examples.

(c) The word of the Lord by the Holy Spirit is the applying cure. He leads us to believe. He is to be sought by the sick soul. He is to be relied upon by those who would bring others to the Great Physician.

Verse 26. The ups and downs of a convicted sinner's experience.

Verse 27. The awakened sinner staggered and nonplussed.

Verses 33-34. The scene which here opens with a landscape of beauty and fertility is suddenly changed into a dry and barren wilderness. The rivers are dried up, the springs cease to flow among the hills, and the verdant fields are scorched and bare. The reason assigned for this is "the wickedness of them that dwell therein." This picture needs no interpretation to the people of God. It is precisely what happens within them when they have fallen into sin.—*G.R.*

Verse 34. The curse, cause, and cure of barrenness in a church.

Verse 35. Hope for decayed churches lies in God; he can work a marvelous change, he does do it—"turneth": he will do it when the cause of barrenness is removed by repentance.

Verses 35-38. Here the scene again changes. The springs again gush forth, calm lakes again repose in the midst of foliage and flowers, the hills are clothed with luxuriant vines, and the fields are covered with corn; plenty abounds both in town and country, and men and cattle increase. This picture, too, has its counterpart in experimental godliness. "Instead of the thorn shall come up", etc., "The wilderness and the solitary place shall be glad for them", etc. The one scene precedes prayer, the other follows it. A desolate wilderness before, the garden of Eden behind.—*G.R.*

Verses 39-41. The scene again is reVersed. There is a change again from freedom to oppression; from plenty to want; from Honor to contempt. Then a revival again as suddenly appears. The poor and afflicted are lifted up, and the bereaved have "families like a flock." Such are the changeful scenes through which the people of God are led; and such the experience by which they are made meet for the pure, perfect, and perpetual joys of heaven.—*G.R.*

Verses 42-43. Such surprising turns are of use,

1. For the solacing of saints; they observe these dispensations with pleasure: "The righteous shall see it, and rejoice", in the glorifying of God's attributes, and the manifestation of his dominion over the children of men.

2. For the silencing of sinners: "all iniquity shall stop her mouth"; *i.e.* it shall be a full conviction of the folly of those that deny the divine presence.

3. For the satisfying of all concerning the divine goodness: "Whoso is wise, and will observe these things"—these various dispensations of divine providence, "even they shall understand the lovingkindness of the Lord."—*M. Henry.*

Verse 43. The best observation and the noblest understanding.

PSALM 108

SERMON OUTLINES AND HELPFUL TIPS

Whole Psalm. Parts of two former psalms are here united in one.

1. Repetition is here sanctioned by inspiration.

   (a) Of what? Of hymns, of prayers, of sermons.

   (b) For what? For impression. "As we said before so say I now again, if any man preach", etc. For confirmation: "Rejoice in the Lord, and again I say rejoice": they went through Syria and Cilicia again confirming the churches. For preservation: quotations authenticate originals, a writing in two copies is safer than in one.

2. Rearrangement is here sanctioned by inspiration.

   (a) Different experiences may require it. Sometimes the heart is most fixed at the commencement of a spiritual exercise: sometimes at its close. Hence the commencement of one psalm is the close of another.

   (b) Different occasions may require it. As of sorrow and joy. Two parts of two different hymns may better harmonise with a particular occasion than either one separately considered. — *G.R.*

Verse 1.

1. The best occupation: praise. Worthy—

   (a) Of the heart in its best condition.
   (b) Of the best faculties of the best educated man.

2. The best resolution.

   (a) Arising from a fixed heart.
   (b) Deliberately formed.
   (c) Solemnly expressed.
   (d) Joyfully executed.

3. The best results. To praise God makes a man both happier and holier, stronger and bolder — as the succeeding verses show.

Verse 2. The benefit of early rising. The sweetness of the Sabbath morning early prayer meeting.

Verse 3. We must not restrain praise because we are overheard by strangers, nor because the listeners are heathen, or ungodly, or are numerous, or are likely to oppose. There may be all the more reason for our outspoken praise of God when we are in such circumstances.

Verses 4-5. The greatness of mercy, the height of truth, and the immensity of the Divine praise.

Verse 6. The prayer of a representative man. There are times when to answer *me* is to deliver the church—at such times I have a powerful plea.

Verse 7. God's voice the cause of joy, the reason for action, the guarantee of success.

Verse 8. *Judah is my lawgiver* Jesus the sole and only lawmaker in the church.

Verse 11. (*first clause*).—Confidence in a frowning God.

Verse 11. (*second clause*). Whether God will go forth with our hosts depends upon—Who they are? What is their object? What is their motive and spirit? What weapons do they use? etc.

Verse 12. The failure of human help is often

1. The direct cause of our prayer.
2. The source of urgency in pleading.
3. A powerful argument for the pleader.
4. A distinct reason for hope to light upon.

Verse 13. How, when, and why a believer should do valiantly.

PSALM 109

SERMON OUTLINES AND HELPFUL TIPS

Verse 1. The silence of God. What it may mean: what it involves: how we may endeavor to break it.

Verse 1. *God of my praise.* A text which may be expounded in its double meaning.

Verses 1-3.

1. God is for his people when the wicked are against them (Ps 109:1);

>(a) for his people's sake;
>(b) for his own sake.

2. The wicked are against his people when he is for them (Ps 109:2-3);

>(a) from hatred to God;
>(b) from hatred to his people. — *G.R.*

Verse 2. Slander. Its cause — wickedness and malice. Its instruments — deceit and lies. Its frequency — Jesus and the saints slandered. Its punishment. Our resort when tried by it — prayer to God.

Verse 4. On the excellency of prayer. See Expository Notes.

Verse 4. Our Lord's adversaries, and his resort.

Verses 4-5.

1. David's spirit and conduct towards his enemies.

>(a) His spirit is love — love for hatred; hence his denunciations are against their sins, rather than against them.
>(b) His conduct. He returned good for evil; he interceded for them.

2. Their spirit and conduct towards him.

>(a) Hatred for love.
>(b) Evil for good. — *G.R.*

Verse 5. *Evil for good.* This is devil like. Have not men been guilty of this to parents, to those who have warned them, to saints and ministers, and especially to the Lord himself?

Verse 5. How has the Redeemer been recompensed? Show what he deserves and what he receives from various individuals. He feels the unkindness of those who are ungrateful.

Verse 6. It is the law of retribution to punish the wicked by means of the wicked. — *Starke.*

Verse 7. When may prayer become sin? From what is sought, how sought, by whom sought, and wherefore sought.

Verse 8. *Let his days be few.* Sin the great shortener of human life. After the flood the whole race lived a shorter time; passion and avaricious care shorten life, and some sins have a peculiar power to do this, lust, drunkenness, & c.

Verse 20-21.

1. David leaves his enemies in the hand of God (Ps 109:20).
2. He puts himself into the same hands (Ps 109:21). — *G.R.*

Verse 21. The plea of a believer must be drawn from his God, his "name" and "mercy." The opposite habit of searching for arguments in self very common and very disappointing.

Verse 21. The peculiar goodness of divine mercy.

Verse 22. The inward sorrows of a saint. Their cause, effects, consolations and cure.

Verses 26-27.

1. The Prayer.
2. The Believing Title: "O Lord my God."
3. The attribute relied upon.
4. The motive for the petition.

Verse 28. The divine cure for human ill will; and the saint's temper when he trusts therein — "let thy servant rejoice."

Verse 29.

1. A prayer for the repentance of David's adversaries.

2. A prophecy for their confusion if they remain impenitent. — *G.R.*

Verse 30. Vocal praise. Should be personal, resolute, intelligent, abundant, hearty. It should attract others, join with others, stimulate others, but never lose its personality.

Verses 30-31.

1. David's *will* with respect to himself: "I will... yea, I will" etc. (Ps 109:30).

2. His *shall* with respect to God: "he shall", etc. (Ps 109:31). — *G.R.*

Verses 30-31. He promises God that he will praise him, Ps 109:30. He promises himself that he shall have cause to praise God, Ps 109:31. — *Matthew Henry.*

Verse 31.

1. The character to whom the promise is made — the poor.

2. The danger to which he is exposed — those that condemn his soul.

3. The deliverance which is promised to him — divine, opportune, efficient, complete, everlasting.

PSALM 110

SERMON OUTLINES AND HELPFUL TIPS

Verse 1. Here the Holy Ghost begins with the kingdom of Christ, which he describeth and magnifieth,—

1. By his unction, and ordination, thereunto, by the word or decree of his Father: "The Lord said".

2. By the greatness of his person in himself, while yet he is nearly allied in blood and nature unto us; "My Lord".

3. By the glory, power, and heavenliness of his kingdom, for in the administration thereof he sitteth at the right hand of his Father: "Sit thou at my right hand".

4. By the continuance and victories thereof: "Until I make thy foes thy footstool."—*Edward Reynolds.*

Verse 1. *My Lord.*

1. Christ's condescending nearness to us does not destroy our reverence: he was David's son, and yet he calls him Lord; he is our brother, bridegroom, and so on, and yet our Lord.

2. Christ's glory does not diminish his nearness to us, or familiarity with us. Sitting on the throne as Lord, he is yet "my Lord."

3. It is under the double aspect as Lord, and yet ours, that Jehovah regards him and speaks with him, and ordains him to the priesthood. Ever in these two lights let us regard him.

Verse 1. *Sit,* etc.

1. Our Lord's quiet amid passing events.

2. The abundance of his present power.

3. The working of all history towards the ultimate end, which will be—

4. His easy victory: putting his foot on his foes as readily as we tread on a footstool.

Verse 2.

1. What is that rod? The gospel (Illustrated by Moses' rod).
2. Who sends it? "The Lord."
3. Whence it comes? Out of the church of God.
4. What is the result? Jesus reigns.

Verse 3. A willing people and an immutable Leader.

1. The promise made to Christ concerning his people: "Thy people shall be willing, "etc.

　　(a) A promise of time: "In the day," etc.

(b) Of persons: "Thy people."

(c) Of disposition: "Shall be willing."

(d) Of character: "In the beauties of holiness."

(e) The majestic figure employed: "From the womb of the morning: thou hast the dew of thy youth."

2. The promise made to Christ concerning himself: "Thou hast the dew of thy youth." Jesus Christ has the dew of his youth personally, doctrinally, and mystically, being surrounded by new converts, who are as the early dew. *Spurgeon's Sermons*, No. 74.

Verse 3. This is a prophecy of the subjects of Christ's kingdom.

1. Who they are; "Thy people."

(a) A people. This denotes distinction, separation, similarity, organization. They are not a confused rabble, but a united community.

(b) His people. By gift, by purchase, by effectual calling.

2. What they are.

(a) A loyal people: "willing."

(b) A conquered people: "in the day of thy power."

(c) A holy people: "in the beauties of holiness."

(d) A numerous people: "from the womb of the morning," etc. The number of converts at the first proclamation of Christ's gospel was but the dew of his youth. **G.R.**

Verse 3. First, the internal evidence of Christ's kingdom is in his people's willingness: "Thy people shall be willingness—thy people shall bc a people all willing"—all volunteers, not pressed men. Secondly, the external evidence of it lies in his people's holiness; "the beauties of holiness; "or as it may be rendered—"in the magnificence of his sanctuary, "for the ornaments of the sanctuary and the dress of the priests were very splendid. When you once give yourselves to God, you become temples of God; and sanctity must adorn that heart which is a living temple of the Holy Ghost. *J. Bennett*, in a Sermon, 1829.

Verse 3. All true followers of Jesus are

(1) priests—beauties of holiness are their sacerdotal robes;
(2) soldiers—"in the day of thine armies";
(3) volunteers;
(4) benefactors—as the dew.
—Suggested by a paper in *The Baptist Magazine*.

Verse 3. Here we have a cluster of subjects:—the willingness of the Lord's people, the beauty of holiness, young converts the life and glory of the church, the mystery of conversion, and so on.

Verse 4. The eternal priesthood of Christ. On what its perpetuity is founded and the blessed results flowing therefrom.

Verse 4. These words offer three points of special observation.

1. The ceremony used at the consecration of our Lord: "The Lord sware."

2. The office conferred upon him by this rite or ceremony: "Thou art a priest."

3. The prerogatives of his office; which office is here declared to be,

>   (a) Perpetual, "forever."
>   (b) Regular, "after the order."
>   (c) Royal, "of Melchizedek."
>   —*Daniel Featley.*

Verse 4. Melchizedek: a fruitful subject. See notes.

Verse 5. The certain overthrow of every power which opposes the gospel.

Verse 6. The fearful calamities which have happened to nations through their sinful rejection of the Lord Jesus.

Verse 7. Christ's alacrity, self-denial, and simplicity, the causes of his success. Example to be imitated.

Verse 7. Christ's humiliation and exaltation.

PSALM 111

SERMON OUTLINES AND HELPFUL TIPS

Verse 1. *Praise ye the Lord*; there is an exhortation. "*I will praise the Lord;*" there is a vow. It shall be "*with my whole heart*"; there is experimental godliness. It shall be "*in the assembly of the upright*"; there is a relative position occupied along with the family of God.—*Joseph Irons.*

Verse 1. *With my whole heart.* This includes spirituality, simplicity, and earnestness.—*Joseph Irons.*

Verse 1.

1. Who are the upright?

2. What are they doing? Praising God.

3. What shall I do if I am Favored to stand among them? "I will praise the Lord."

Verse 1. Where I love to be, and what I love to do.

Verse 2. The Christian philosopher.

1. His sphere: "The works of the Lord."
2. His work: "Sought out."
3. His qualification: "Pleasure therein."
4. His conclusion: "Praise, "as in Ps 111:1.

Verses 2-9. The psalmist furnishes us with matter for praise from the works of God.

1. The greatness of his works and the glory of them.
2. The righteousness of them.
3. The goodness of them.
4. The power of them.
5. The conformity of them to his word of promise.
6. The perpetuity of them.—*Matthew Henry.*

Verse 3 (last clause). As an essential attribute, as revealed in providence, as vindicated in redemption, as demonstrated in punishment, as appropriated by believers.

Verse 4. The compassion of the Lord as seen in aiding the memories of his people.

Verses 4-5. God's marvels ought not to be nine day wonders.

1. *It is God's design that his wonders should be remembered,* therefore,

   (a) He made them great.
   (b) He wrought them for an undeserving people.
   (c) He wrought them at memorable times.
   (d) He put them on record.
   (e) He instituted memorials.

    (f) He bade them tell their children.
    (g) He so dealt with them as to refresh their memories.

2. It is our wisdom to remember the Lord's wonders.

    (a) To assure us of his compassion: "The Lord is gracious."
    (b) To make us consider his bounty: "he hath given meat."
    (c) To certify us of his faithfulness: "he will ever be mindful of his covenant."
    (d) To arouse our praise: "Praise ye the Lord."

Verse 5. There is,

1. Encouragement from the past: "He hath given meat," etc.
2. Confidence for the future: "He will ever be mindful," etc. —*G. R.*

Verse 6. The power of God an encouragement for the evangelization of the heathen.

Verse 9. *Redemption.* Praise our Triune Jehovah for his redemption. Write it down where you may read it. Affix it where you may see it. Engrave it on your heart that you may understand it. It is a word big with importance. In it is enfolded your destinies and those of the Church, to all future ages. There are heights in it you never can have scaled, and depths you never can have fathomed. You have never taken the wings of the morning, and gained the utmost parts of earth, to measure the length and breadth of it. Wear it as a seal on your arm, as a signet on your right hand, for Jesus is the author of it. O! prize it as a precious stone, more precious than rubies...Let it express your best hopes while living, and dwell on your trembling lips in the moment of dissolution; for it shall form the chorus of the song of the redeemed throughout eternity. —*Isaac Saunders,* 1818.

Verse 9. *He hath commanded his covenant forever.* As he covenanted, so he looketh that his covenants should be respected, which are as binding to us, as his covenant is to him; and, through grace, his covenant is as binding to him, as those are to us. —*John Trapp.*

Verse 9. *Holy and reverend,* or, *terrible, is his name.* "*Holy is his name,* "and therefore "*terrible*" to those who, under all the means of grace, continue unholy. —*George Horne.*

Verse 9. *Holy and reverend is his name.* Which therefore we should not presume on a sudden to blurt out. The Jews would not pronounce it. The Grecians (as Suidas observeth), when they would swear by their Jupiter, forbare to mention him. This should act as a check to the profaneness common amongst us. Let those that would have their *name reverend,* labor to be *holy* as God is holy. —*John Trapp.*

Verse 9. *Redemption.* Conceived, arranged, executed, and applied by God. By price and by power. From sin and death. That we may be free, the Lord's own, the Lord's glory.

Verse 9. Redemption.

1. Its author: "He sent."
2. Its objects: "Unto his people."

3. The pledge it gives us: "He hath commanded his covenant, "etc.
4. The praise it creates in us.

Verse 9. *Holy and reverend.*

1. The holiness of God the object of our reverence.

2. Such reverence has much useful influence over us.

3. It should always accompany our faith in redemption and covenant. See preceding clauses of **Verse**.

Verse 10.

1. The beginner in Christ's school.
2. The man who has taken a degree: "a good understanding, " etc.
3. The Master who receives the praise.

Verse 10.

1. The beginning of wisdom: "The fear of the Lord"—God is feared.
2. Its continuance: "a good understanding have all they that do his commandments"—when the fear of the Lord in the heart is developed in the life.
3. Its end, praising God forever: "his praise, "etc.—G. R.

PSALM 112

SERMON OUTLINES AND HELPFUL TIPS

Verse 1. "Praise ye the LORD."

1. Who should be praised? Not man, self, wealth, etc., but God only.

2. Who should praise him? All men, but specially his people, the blessed ones described in this psalm.

3. Why should they do it? For all the reasons mentioned in succeeding **Verse**s.

4. How should they do it? Chiefly by leading such a life as is here described.

Verse 1 (second clause).

1. Fear of the Lord; what it is.

2. Its connection with the delight mentioned.

3. The qualities in the commandments which excite delight in God fearing minds.

Verse 2. The real might of the holy seed and their true blessedness.

Verse 3. The riches of a Christian: content, peace, security, power in prayer, promises, providence, yea, God himself.

Verse 3. The enduring character of true righteousness.

1. Based on eternal principles.
2. Growing out of an incorruptible seed.
3. Sustained by a faithful God.
4. United to the ever living Christ.

Verse 3. Connection of the two clauses—How to be wealthy and righteous. Note the following **Verse**s, and show how liberality is needful if rich men would be righteous men.

Verse 4 (whole **Verse**).

1. The upright have their dark times.
2. They shall receive comfort.
3. Their own character will secure this.

Verse 4 (first clause).

1. The character of the righteous: "upright, " "gracious, "etc.

2. His privilege.

    (a) Light as well as darkness.

(b) More light than darkness.

(c) Light in darkness: inward light in the midst of surrounding darkness. Light seen above, when all is dark below. Even darkness itself becomes the harbinger of day.—G. R.

Verse 4 (last clause). A Trinity of excellencies found in true Christians, in Christ, and in God: their union forms a perfect character when they are well balanced. Show how they are exemplified in daily life.

Verse 5.

1. A good man is benevolent, but a benevolent man is not always good.

2. A good man is prudent, but a prudent man is not always a good man. There must first be goodness and then its fruits. "Make the tree good, "etc.—*G.R.*

Verse 5. "Lending."

1. It is to be done.

2. It is to be done as a Favor; borrowing is seeking alms.

3. It should be done very discreetly. Add to this a homily on borrowing and repaying.

Verse 6.

1. In this life the Christian is,

    (a) Steadfast;
    (b) Calm;
    (c) Unconquerable: and

2. When this life is over his memory is,

    (a) Beloved;
    (b) Influential;
    (c) Perpetual.

Verse 6.

1. The character of the righteous is eternal: "surely," etc.
2. His influence upon others is eternal: "shall be had," etc.—*G.R.*

Verse 7.

1. "He shall not be afraid, "etc.: peaceful.
2. "His heart is fixed": restful.
3. "Trusting in the Lord": trustful; the cause of the former.

Verse 7.

1. The waves: "evil tidings."
2. The steady ship: "he shall not be afraid."
3. The anchor: "his heart is fixed, trusting."
4. The anchorage: "in the Lord."

Verse 8. Heart establishment, the confidence which flows from it, the sight which shall be seen by him who possesses it.

Verse 8.

1. The security of the righteous: "his heart is established."
2. His tranquility: "he shall not be afraid; "and,
3. His expectancy: "until, "etc. — *G.R.*

Verse 9. Benevolence: its exercise in alms giving, its preserving influence upon character, and the Honor which it wins.

Verse 10.

1. What the wicked must see, and its effect upon them.
2. What they shall never see (their desire), and the result of their disappointment.

PSALM 113

SERMON OUTLINES AND HELPFUL TIPS

Whole Psalm. The psalm contains three parts:

1. An exhortation to God's servants to praise him.

2. A form set down how and where to praise him, **Verse** 2, 3.

3. The reasons to persuade us to it.

    (a) By his infinite power, **Verse** 4, 5.

    (b) His providence, as displayed in heaven and earth, **Verse 6.**—*Adam Clarke.*

Verse 1. The repetitions show,

1. The importance of praise.
2. Our many obligations to render it.
3. Our backwardness in the duty.
4. The heartiness and frequency with which it should be rendered.
5. The need of calling upon others to join with us.

Verse 1.

1. To whom praise is due: "the Lord."

2. From whom it is due: "ye servants of the Lord."

3. For what is it due: his "name."

a. For all names descriptive of what he is in himself.
b. For all names descriptive of what he is to his servants.—*G. R.*

Verses 1, 9. Praise ye the Lord.

1. Begin and end life with it, and do the same with holy service, patient suffering, and everything else.

2. Fill up the interval with praise. Run over the intervening **Verse**s.

Verse 2.

1. The work of heaven begun on earth: to praise the name of the Lord.

2. The work of earth continued in heaven: "and for evermore." If the praise begun on earth be continued in heaven, we must be in heaven to continue the praise.—*G. R.*

Verse 2.

1. It is time to begin to praise: "from this time." Is there not special reason, from long arrears, from present duty, etc.?

2. There is no time for leaving off praise: "and for evermore." None supposable or excusable.

Verse 3. God is to be praised.

1. All the day.
2. All the world over.
3. Publicly in the light.
4. Amidst daily duties.
5. Always—because it is always day somewhere.

Verse 3.

1. Canonical hours abolished.
2. Holy places abolished—since we cannot be always in them.
3. Every time and place consecrated.

Verses 5-6.

1. The greatness of God as viewed from below, **Verse 5.**

2. The condescension of God as viewed from above, **Verse 6.**

>   (a) In creation.
>   (b) In the Incarnation.
>   (c) In redemption.—G. R.

Verses 5-6. The unparalleled condescension of God.

1. None are so great, and therefore able to stoop so low.

2. None are so good, and therefore so willing to stoop.

3. None are so wise, and therefore so able to "behold" or know the needs of little things.

4. None are infinite, and therefore able to enter into minutiae and sympathize with the smallest grief: Infinity is seen in the minute as truly as in the immense.

Verse 6.

1. The same God rules in heaven and earth.
2. Both spheres are dependent for happiness upon his beholding them.
3. They both enjoy his consideration.
4. All things done in them are equally under his inspection.

Verse 7. The gospel and its special eye to the poor.

Verses 7-8.

1. Where men are? In the dust of sorrow and on the dunghill of sin.

2. Who interferes to help them? He who dwelleth on high.

3. What does he effect for them? "Raiseth, lifteth, setteth among princes, among princes of his people."

Verse 8. Elevation to the peerage of heaven; or, the Royal Family increased.

Verse 9. For mothers' meetings. "A joyful mother of children."

1. It is a joy to be a mother.

2. It is specially so to have living, healthy, obedient children.

3. But best of all to have Christian children. . . . Praise is due to the Lord who gives such blessings.

Verse 9.

1. A household God, or, God in the Household: "He maketh, "etc. Have you children? It is of God. Have you lost children? It is of God. Have you been without children? It is of God.

2. Household worship, or, the God of the Household: "Praise ye the Lord."

>   (a) In the family.
>   (b) For family mercies. — G. R.

PSALM 114

SERMON OUTLINES AND HELPFUL TIPS

Verses 1-2. The time of first delivery from sin a season notable for the peculiar presence of God.

Verses 1-2. The Lord was to his people—

1. A deliverer.
2. A priest—"his sanctuary."
3. A king—"his dominion."

Verses 1, 7. "The house of Jacob" and "the God of Jacob," the relation between the two.

Verse 2. The church the temple of sanctity and the domain of obedience.

Verse 3. *The sea saw it, and fled;* or rather, "The sea saw and fled"—it saw God and all his people following his lead, and it was struck with awe and fled away. A bold figure! The Red Sea mirrored the hosts which had come down to its shore, and reflected the cloud which towered high over all, as the symbol of the presence of the Lord: never had such a scene been imaged upon the surface of the Red Sea, or any other sea, before. It could not endure the unusual and astounding sight, and fleeing to the right and to the left, opened a passage for the elect people. A like miracle happened at the end of the great march of Israel, for "*Jordan, was driven back.*" This was a swiftly flowing river, pouring itself down a steep decline, and it was not merely divided, but its current was driven back so that the rapid torrent, contrary to nature, flowed uphill. This was God's work: the poet does not sing of the suspension of natural laws, or of a singular phenomenon not readily to be explained; but to him the presence of God with his people is everything, and in his lofty song he tells how the river was driven back because the Lord was there. In this case poetry is nothing but the literal fact, and the fiction lies on the side of the atheistic critics who will suggest any explanation of the miracle rather than admit that the Lord made bare his holy arm in the eyes of all his people. The division of the sea and the drying up of the river are placed together though forty years intervened, because they were the opening and closing scenes of one great event. We may thus unite by faith our new birth and our departure out of the world into the promised inheritance, for the God who led us out of the Egypt of our bondage under sin will also conduct us through the Jordan of death out of our wilderness wanderings in the desert of this tried and changeful life. It is all one and the same deliverance, and the beginning ensures the end.

Verse 3. The impenitence of sinners rebuked by the inanimate creation.

Verse 3. *Jordan was driven back,* or death overcome.

Verse 4. The movableness of things which appear to be fixed and settled. God's power of creating a stir in lethargic minds, among ancient systems, and prejudiced persons of the highest rank.

Verses 7-8. Holy awe.

1. Should be caused by the fact of the divine presence.

2. Should be increased by his covenant character—"the God of Jacob."

3. Should culminate when we see displays of his grace towards his people—"which turned, "etc.

4. Should become universal.

Verse 8. Wonders akin to the miracle at the rock.

1. Christ's death the source of life.
2. Adversity a means of prosperity.
3. Hard hearts made penitent.
4. Barrenness of soul turned into abundance.

Verse 8. Divine supplies.

1. Sure—for he will fetch them even from a rock.
2. Plentiful—"a mere or standing water."
3. Continual "fountain of waters."
4. Instructive. Should create in us holy awe at the power, etc., of the Lord.

PSALM 115

SERMON OUTLINES AND HELPFUL TIPS

Verse 1. The passage may be used as,

1. A powerful plea in prayer.
2. An expression of the true spirit of piety.
3. A safe guide in theology.
4. A practical direction in choosing our way of life.
5. An acceptable spirit when surveying past or present success.

Verse 1.

1. No praise is due to man. Have we a being? Not unto us, etc. Have we health? Not unto us, etc. Have we outward comforts? Not unto us, etc. Friends? Not unto us, etc. The means of grace? Not unto us, etc. Saving faith in Christ? Not unto us, etc. Gifts and graces? Not unto us, etc. The hope of glory? Not unto us, etc. Usefulness to others? Not unto us, etc.

2. All praise is due to God. (a) Because all we have is from mercy. (b) Because all we expect is from faithfulness. *G. R.*

Verse 2. A taunting question, to which we can give many satisfactory replies.

Verse 2. Why do they say so? Why doth God permit them to say so? *Matthew Henry.*

Verses 2-3.

1. The inquiry of heathens: Ps 115:2. (a) Of ignorance. They see a temple but no god. (b) Of reproach to the people of God when their God has forsaken them for a time: "While they say daily unto me, where, "etc.

2. The reply to their inquiry: Ps 115:3. Do you ask where is our God? Ask rather where he is not? Do you ask what he has done? "He has done whatsoever he hath pleased." *G. R.*

Verse 3.

1. His position betokens absolute dominion.
2. His actions prove it.
3. Yet he condescends to be "our God."

Verse 3 (*second clause*). The sovereignty of God. Establish and improve the great scriptural doctrine, that the glorious God has a right to exercise dominion over all his creatures; and to do, in all respects, as he pleases. This right naturally results from his being the *Former* and the *Possessor* of heaven and earth. Consider

1. He is infinitely wise; he perfectly knows all his creatures, all their actions, and all their tendencies.

2. He is infinitely righteous.

3. He is infinitely good. *George Burder.*

Verses 4-8.

1. The character of idol gods. Whether our gods are natural objects or riches or worldly pleasures, they have no eye to pity, no ear to hear petitions, no tongue to counsel, no hand to help.

2. The character of the true God. He is all eye, all ear, all tongue, all hand, all feet, all mind, all heart.

3. The character of the idol worshippers. All become naturally assimilated to the objects of their worship.

Verse 8. The likeness between idolaters and their idols. Work it out in the particulars mentioned.

Verse 9. The living God claims spiritual worship; the life of such worship is faith; faith proves God to be a living reality—"He is their help, "etc. Only elect Israel will ever render this living worship.

Verses 9-11.

1. The reproof. "O Israel!" "O house of Aaron!" "Ye who fear the Lord." Have you been unbelieving towards your God?

2. The correction or admonition. "Trust in the Lord, "Have you trusted in the true God as others have in their false gods?

3. The instruction. "He is their help, "etc. Let churches, ministers, and all who fear God know that at all times and under all circumstances he is their help and their shield. *G. R.*

Verse 10.

1. Those who publicly serve should specially trust. "O house of Aaron, trust."

2. Those who are specially called shall be specially helped. "He is their help."

3. Those who are specially helped in service may be sure of special protection in danger...and their shield.

Verse 11. Filial fear the foundation of fuller faith.

Verse 12. What we have experienced. What we may expect. *Matthew Henry.*

Verses 12-13.

1. **What God *has done* for his people**: "He hath been mindful of us." (a) Our preservation proves this. (b) Our mercies. (c) Our trials. (d) Our guidance. (e) Our consolations. Everything, even the minutest blessing, represents a thought in the mind of God respecting us. "How precious are thy thoughts concerning me, O God, how great, "etc., and those thoughts go back to an eternity

before we came into being. "The Lord hath been mindful of us"; then should we not be more mindful of him?

2. **What he *will do* for his people**—"He will bless us." (a) Greatly. His blessings are like himself, great. They are blessed whom he blesses. (b) Suitably. The house of Israel, the house of Aaron, all who fear him, according to their need, both small and great. (c) Assuredly. "He will," ""he will," ""he will," ""he will." With one" will" he curses, with four "wills" he blesses. *G. R.*

Verse 13.

1. The general character—"fear the Lord."
2. The degrees of development—"small and great."
3. The common blessing.

Verse 14.

1. Gracious increase—in knowledge, love, power, holiness, usefulness, etc.

2. Growing increase—we grow faster, and advance not only more, but more and more.

3. Relative increase—our children grow in grace through our example, etc.

Verse 14. The blessings of God are,

1. *Ever flowing* "more and more."

2. *Over flowing*—"you and your children." Let parents seek more grace for themselves for the sake of their children. (a) That they may be more influenced by their example. (b) That their prayers may be more prevalent on their behalf. (c) That their children may be more blessed for their sakes. *G. R.*

Verse 15. A blessing.

1. Belonging to a peculiar people—"ye."
2. Coming from a peculiar quarter—"of the Lord, "etc.
3. Bearing a peculiar date—"are."
4. Stamped with peculiar certainty—"Ye are blessed."
5. Involving a peculiar duty—"Bless the Lord now and evermore."

Verse 15. The Creator's blessing—its greatness, fulness, variety, etc.

Verse 16. Man's lordship over the world, its limit, its abuse, its legitimate bound, its grand design.

Verses 17-18.

1. Missing voices—"The dead praise not."
2. Their stimulus upon ourselves—"But we."
3. Their cry to others—"Praise ye the Lord." Let us make up for the silent voices.

Verses 17-18.

1. They who do not praise God here will not praise him hereafter. No reprieve therefore from punishment.

2. They who praise God in this life will praise him for evermore. Hallelujah for this. "Praise the Lord." **G.R.**

Verses 17-18. A new year's sermon.

1. A mournful memory—"the dead."
2. A happy resolve—"but we will bless the Lord."
3. An appropriate commencement—"from this time forth."
4. An everlasting continuance—"and for evermore."

PSALM 116

SERMON OUTLINES AND HELPFUL TIPS

Verses 1-2.

1. Present—"I love."
2. Past—"He hath."
3. Future—"I will."

Verses 1-2. Personal experience in reference to prayer.

1. We have prayed, often, constantly, in different ways, etc.
2. We have been heard. A grateful retrospect of usual answers and of special answers.
3. Love to God has thus been promoted.
4. Our sense of the value of prayer has become so intense that we cannot cease praying.

Verses 1, 2, 9. If you cast your eyes on the first **Verse** of the Psalm, you find a *profession of love—I love the Lord*; if on the second, a *promise of prayer—I will call on the Lord*; if on the ninth, a *resolve of walking—I will walk before the LORD*. There are three things should be the object of a saint's care, the devotion of the soul, profession of the mouth, and conversation of the life: that is the sweetest melody in God's ears, when not only the voice sings, but the heartstrings keep tune, and the hand keepeth time. *Nathanael Hardy.*

Verse 2. "He hath, "and therefore "I will." Grace moving to action.

Verses 2, 4, 13, 17. Calling upon God mentioned four times very suggestively—I will do it (Ps 116:2), I have tried it (Ps 116:4), I will do it when I take (Ps 116:13), and when I offer (Ps 116:17).

Verses 2, 9, 13-14, 17. The "I wills" of the Psalm. I will call (Ps 116:2), I will walk (Ps 116:9), I will take (Ps 116:13), I will pay (Ps 116:14), I will offer (Ps 116:17).

Verses 3-4, 8. See Spurgeon's Sermon, "To Souls in Agony, " Metropolitan Tabernacle Pulpit, No 1216.

Verses 3-5. The story of a tried soul.

1. Where I was. Ps 116:3.
2. What I did. Ps 116:4.
3. What I learned. Ps 116:5.

Verses 3-6.

1. The *occasion*. (a) Bodily affliction. (b) Terrors of conscience. (c) Sorrow of heart. (d) Self accusation: "I found, "etc.

2. The *petition*. (a) Direct: "I called, "etc. (b) Immediate: "then, "when the trouble came; prayer was the first remedy sought, not the last, as with many. (c) Brief—limited to the due thing needed: "deliver my soul." (d) Importunate: "O Lord, I beseech thee."

3. The *restoration*. (a) Implied: "gracious, "etc., Ps 116:5. (b) Expressed, Ps 116:6, generally: "The Lord preserveth, "etc.; particularly; "I was brought low, " etc.: helped me to pray, helped me out of trouble in answer to prayer, and helped me to praise him for the mercy, the faithfulness, the grace, shown in my deliverance. God is glorified through the afflictions of his people: the submissive are preserved in them, and the lowly are exalted by them. *G. R.*

Verse 5.

1. Eternal grace, or the purpose of love.
2. Infinite justice, or the difficulty of holiness.
3. Boundless mercy, or the outcome of atonement.

Verse 6.

1. A singular class—"simple."
2. A singular fact—"the Lord preserveth the simple."
3. A singular proof of the fact—"I was, "etc.

Verse 7. *Return unto thy rest, O my soul.* Rest in God may be said to belong to the people of God on a fourfold account.

1. By designation. The rest which the people of God have in him is the result of his own purpose and design, taken up from his mere good pleasure and love.

2. By purchase. The rest which they wanted as *creatures* they had forfeited as *sinners*. This, therefore, Christ laid down his life to procure.

3. By promise. This is God's kind engagement. He has said, "My presence shall go with thee, and I will give thee rest, "Ex 33:14.

4. By their own choice gracious souls have a rest in God. *D. Wilcox.*

Verse 7. *Return unto thy rest, O my soul.* When, or upon what occasion a child of God should use the Psalmist's language.

1. After converse with the world in the business of his calling every day.
2. When going to the sanctuary on the Lord's day.
3. In and under any trouble he may meet with.
4. When departing from this world at death. *D. Wilcox.*

Verse 7.

1. The rest of the soul: "My rest, "this is in God. (a) The soul was created to find its rest in God. (b) On that account it cannot find rest elsewhere.

2. Its departure from that rest. This is implied in the word "Return."

3. Its return. (a) By repentance. (b) By faith, in the way provided for its return. (c) By prayer.

4. Its encouragement to return. (a) Not in itself, but in God. (b) Not in the justice, but in the goodness of God: "for the Lord, "etc. "The goodness of God leadeth thee to repentance." **G.R.**

Verse 8. The trinity of experimental godliness.

1. It is a unity—"Thou hast delivered"; all the mercies come from one source.

2. It is a trinity of deliverance, *of* soul, eyes, feet; *from* punishment, sorrow, and sinning; *to* life, joy, and stability.

3. It is a trinity in unity: all this was done for me and in me—"my soul, mine eyes, my feet."

Verse 9. The effect of deliverance upon ourselves: "I will walk, " etc.

1. Walk by faith in him.
2. Walk in love with him.
3. Walk by obedience to him. *G. R.*

Verses 10-11.

1. The rule: "I believed, "etc. In general the Psalmist spoke what he had well considered and tested by his own experience, as when he said, "I was brought low and he helped me." "The Lord hath dealt bountifully with me."

2. The exception; "I was greatly afflicted, I said, "etc. (a) He spoke wrongfully: he said "All men are liars, " which had some truth in it, but was not the whole truth. (b) Hastily: "I said in my haste, "without due reflection. (c) Angrily, under the influence of affliction, probably from the unfaithfulness of others. Nature acts before grace—the one by instinct, the other from consideration. *G. R.*

Verse 11. A hasty speech.

1. There was much truth in it.

2. It erred on the right side, for it showed faith in God rather than in the creature.

3. It did err in being too sweeping, too severe, too suspicious.

4. It was soon cured. The remedy for all such hasty speeches is—Get to work in the spirit of Ps 116:12.

Verse 12. Overwhelming obligations.

1. A sum in arithmetic—"all his benefits."
2. A calculation of indebtedness—"What shall I render?"
3. A problem for personal solution—"What shall *I*?" See Spurgeon's Sermon, No. 910.

Verses 12, 14. Whether well composed religious vows do not exceedingly promote religion. Sermon by Henry Hurst, A.M., in "The Morning Exercises."

Verse 13. Sermon on the Lord's supper. We take the cup of the Lord

1. In memory of him who is our salvation.
2. In token of our trust in him.
3. In evidence of our obedience to him.
4. In type of communion with him.
5. In hope of drinking it new with him ere long.

Verse 13. The various cups mentioned in Scripture would make an interesting subject.

Verse 14. *Vow.* Or the excellence of time present.

Verse 15.

1. *The declaration.* Not the death of the wicked, nor even the death of the righteous is in itself precious; but, (a) Because their persons are precious to him. (b) Because their experience in death is precious to him. (c) Because of their conformity in death to their Covenant Head; and (d) Because it puts an end to their sorrows, and translates them to their rest.

2. *Its manifestation.* (a) In preserving them from death. (b) In supporting them in death. (c) In giving them victory over death. (d) In glorifying them after death.

Verse 15. See Spurgeon's Sermons "Precious Deaths, "No. 1036.

Verse 16. *Holy Service.*

1. Emphatically avowed.
2. Honestly rendered—"truly."
3. Logically defended—"son of thine handmaid."
4. Consistent with conscious liberty.

Verse 17. This is due to our God, good for ourselves, and encouraging to others.

Verse 17. *The sacrifice of thanksgiving.*

1. How it may be rendered. In secret love, in conversation, in sacred song, in public testimony, in special gifts and works.

2. Why we should render it. For answered prayers (Ps 116:1-2), memorable deliverances (Ps 116:3), choice preservation (Ps 116:6); remarkable restoration (Ps 116:7-8), and for the fact of our being his servants (Ps 116:16).

3. When should we render it. *Now*, while the mercy is on the memory, and as often as fresh mercies come to us.

Verse 18.

1. How vows may be paid in public. By going to public worship as the first thing we do when health is restored. By uniting heartily in the song. By coming to the communion. By special thank offering. By using fit opportunities for open testimony to the Lord's goodness.

2. The special difficulty in the matter. To pay them *to the Lord*, and not in ostentation or as an empty form.

3. The peculiar usefulness of the public act. It interests others, touches their hearts, reproves, encourages, etc.

Verse 19. The Christian at home.

1. In God's house.
2. Among the saints.
3. At his Favorite work, "Praise."

PSALM 117

SERMON OUTLINES AND HELPFUL TIPS

Whole Psalm. The universal kingdom.

1. The same God.
2. The same worship.
3. The same reason for it.

Verse 2. *Merciful kindness.* In God's kindness there is mercy, because,

1. Our sin deserves the reverse of kindness.
2. Our weakness requires great tenderness.
3. Our fears can only be so removed.

Verse 2 (*last clause*)

1. In his attribute—he is always faithful.
2. In his revelation—always infallible.
3. In his action—always according to promise.

PSALM 118

SERMON OUTLINES AND HELPFUL TIPS

Verses 1-4.

1. The subject of songs "O give thanks unto the Lord, for he is good."

2. The chorus—"His mercy endureth forever"

3. The choir—"Let Israel now say, "etc.; "Let the house of Aaron, "etc.; "Let them that fear the Lord, "etc.

4. The rehearsal—"Let them *now* say, "that they may be better prepared for universal praise hereafter.

Verse 5.

1. The season for prayer—"in distress."
2. The answer in season—"The Lord answered me."
3. The answer beyond the request—"And set me, "etc.

Verse 6.

1. When may a man know that God is on his side?
2. What confidence may that man enjoy who is assured of divine aid?

Verse 7.

1. The value of true friends.
2. The greater value of help from above.

Verses 8-9. Better. It is wiser, surer, morally more right, more ennobling, more happy in result.

Verse 10. Take a wide range and consider what has been done, should be done, and may be done "in the name of the Lord."

Verse 12.

1. Faith's innumerable annoyances.
2. Their speedy end.
3. Faith's complete victory.

Verse 13.

1. Our great antagonist.
2. His fierce attacks.
3. His evident object: "that I might fall."
4. His failure: "but the Lord helped me."

Verse 14.

1. Strength under affliction.
2. Song in hope of deliverance.
3. Salvation, or actual escape out of trial.

Verse 15. The joy of Christian households. It is joy in salvation: it is expressed,—"The voice": it abides: "the voice *is*":it is joy in the protection and Honor given by the Lord's right hand.

Verse 15-16.

1. True joy is peculiar *to* the righteous.

2. *In* their tabernacles: in their pilgrimage state.

3. *For* salvation: rejoicing and salvation go together.

4. *From* God: "the right hand, "etc.: three right hands; both the salvation and the joy are from the hand of the Father and the Son and the Holy Ghost; the right hand of each doeth valiantly. *G. R.*

Verse 17.

1. Good men are often in special danger: Joseph in the pit; Moses in the ark of bulrushes; Job on the dunghill; David's narrow escapes from the hand of Saul; Paul let down in a basket; what a fruit basket was that! How much was suspended upon that cord! The salvation of how many!

2. Good men have often a presentiment of their recovery from special danger: "I shall not die, but live."

3. Good men have a special desire for the preservation of their lives: "live and declare the works of the Lord." *G. R.*

Verses 17, 19, 22. The victory of the risen Savior and its far reaching consequences:

(1) Death is vanquished;
(2) the gates of righteousness are opened;
(3) the cornerstone of the church is laid.
—*Deichert, in Lange's Commentary.*

Verse 18.

1. The afflictions of the people of God are chastisements: "The Lord hath chastened me."

2. Those chastisements are often severe: hath chastened me *sore*.

3. The severity is limited: "it is not unto death." *G. R.*

Verse 19.

1. Access to God desired.
2. Humbly requested: "Open to me."
3. Boldly accepted: "I will go into them."
4. Gratefully enjoyed: "And praise the Lord."

Verse 22. In these words we may notice the following particulars.

1. The metaphorical view in which the church is here represented, namely, that of a *house* or *building*.

2. The character that our Immanuel bears with respect to this building; he is *the stone* in a way of eminence, without whom there can be no building, no house for God to dwell in among the children of men.

3. The character of the workmen employed in this spiritual structure; they are called *builders*.

4. A fatal error they are charged with in building the house of God; they *refuse* the stone of God's choosing; they do not allow him a place in his own house.

5. Notice the place that Christ should and shall have in this building, let the builders do their worst: he *is made the head stone of the corner*. The words immediately following declare how this is effected, and how the saints are affected with the news of his exaltation, notwithstanding the malice of hell and earth: "This is the Lord's doing, and it is wonderful in our eyes." *Ebenezer Erskine.*

Verses 22-23.

1. The mystery stated. (a) That which is least esteemed by men as a means of salvation is most esteemed by God. (b) That which is most esteemed by God when made known is least esteemed by man.

2. The mystery explained. The way of salvation is the Lord's doing, therefore marvelous in our eyes.—*G.R.*

Verses 22-25.

1. Christ rejected.
2. Christ exalted.
3. His exaltation is due to God alone.
4. His exaltation commences a new era.
5. His exaltation suggests a new prayer.
—See Spurgeon's Sermon, no. 1,420.

Verse 24.

1. What is spoken of.

   (a) The gospel day.
   (b) The sabbath day.

2. What is said of it.

   (a) It is given by God.
   (b) To be joyfully received by man.—*G.R.*

Verse 25.

1. The object of the prayer.

    (a) Salvation from sin.
    (b) Prosperity in righteousness.

2. The earnestness of the prayer: "I beseech thee, I beseech thee".

3. The urgency of the prayer, "now—now"—now that the gates of righteousness are open, now that the foundation stone is laid, now that the gospel day has come—now, Lord! now!—*G.R.*

Verse 27. *Bind the sacrifice,* etc. Devotion is the mother, and she hath four daughters.

1. Constancy: "Bind the sacrifice."
2. Fervency: Bind it "with cords."
3. Wisdom: Bind it "to the altar."
4. Confidence: Even to the "horns" of the altar. —*Thomas Adams.*

Verse 27. *Bind the sacrifice with cords,* etc.

1. What is the sacrifice? Our whole selves, every talent, all our time, property, position, mind, heart, temper, life to the last.

2. Why does it need binding? It is naturally restive. Long delay, temptations, wealth, rank, discouragement, skepticism, all tend to drive it from the altar.

3. To what is it bound? To the doctrine of atonement. To Jesus and his work. To Jesus and out work.

4. What are the cords? Our own vows. The need of souls. Our joy in the work. The great reward. The love of Christ working upon us by the Holy Spirit.

Verse 28.

1. The gladdest fact in all the world: "Thou art my God."
2. The fittest spirit in which to enjoy it: "Praise thee"

Verse 28.

1. The effect of Christ being sacrificed for us: "Thou art my God."

2. The effect of our being offered as an acceptable sacrifice to him: "I will praise thee, I will exalt thee." Or,

    (a) The covenant blessing: "Thou art my God."
    (b) The covenant obligation: "I will praise thee."—*G.R.*

Verse 29.

1. The beginning and the end of salvation is mercy.

2. The beginning and end of its requirements is thanksgiving.—*G.R.*

PSALM 119 (part 1 vv. 1-56)

SERMON OUTLINES AND HELPFUL TIPS

Verse 2. — Blessed are they that keep his testimonies, and that seek him with the whole heart.

1. **The sacred Quest**: "Seek him." He has been sought among the trees, the hills, the planets, the stars. He has been sought in his own defaced image, man. He has been sought amid the mysterious wheels of Providence. But these quests have often been prompted simply by intellect, or compelled by conscience, and have therefore resulted but in a cold faint light. He has been sought in the word which this psalm so highly extols, when it has led up the smoke covered and gleaming peaks of Sinai. It has been followed, when it has led beneath the olives of Gethsemane to witness a mysterious struggle in blood sweating and anguish; to Calvary, where, in the place of a skull, life and immortality are brought to light. The sacred quest but there begins.

2. **The Conduct of the Quest**. Seekers might be mistakenly dejected by so literal an interpretation of the "whole heart." We do not hesitate to say a stream is in its whole volume flowing towards sea while there are little side creeks in which the water eddies backward; or to say the tide is coming despite receding waves; or that spring is upon us despite hailstorm and biting wind. Indication of,

    (a) Unity

    (b) Intensity.

    (c) Determination.

No one conducts this quest aright who is not prompted to or sustained in it by the gracious Spirit.

3. Blessedness both in the pursuit and issue.

    (a) Blessedness in the bitterness of penitence. The door handle touched by him drops of myrrh. The rising sun sends kindling beams upon the highest peaks.

    (b) Blessedness in the happy findings of salvation and adoption.

    (c) Blessedness in the perpetual pursuit. — William Anderson, of Reading, 1882.

Verse 2. — The double blessing.

1. On keeping the testimonies.

2. On seeking the Lord.

Verse 2. — That seek him with the whole heart.

1. Seek what? God himself. No peace until he is found.

2. Seek where? In his testimonies.

   (a) By studying them.

   (b) By keeping to them.

3. Seek how? With the Whole heart. — George Rogers.

Verse 2. — Seeking for God.

1. The Psalmist's way of seeking God.

   (a) He sought God with the heart. Only the heart can find God. Sight fails.

   "The scientific method" fails. All reason fails. Only love and trust can succeed. Love sees much where all other perception finds nothing. Faith generally goes with discovery, and nowhere so much as in finding God.

   (b) He sought God with all his heart.

   (1) Half heartedness seldom finds anything worth having.

   (2) Half heartedness shows contempt for God.

   (3) God will not reveal himself to half heartedness. It would be putting the highest premium possible upon indifference.

2. The Psalmist's plea in seeking God: "Let me not wander from thy commandments"

   (a) God's commandments lead, presently, into his own presence. If we take even the moral law, every one of the ten commandments leads away from the world, and sin, into that seclusion of holiness in which he hides. It is thus with all the commandments of the Scriptures.

   (b) The earnestness of the souls search for God becomes, in itself, a plea with God that he will be found of us. God, who loves importunity in prayer, loves it no less when it takes the form of searching with all the heart. He who seeks with all the heart finds special encouragement to pray: "Let me not wander from thy commandments." — F.G. Marchant.

Verse 2. — That seek him. We must remember six conditions required in them who would seek the Lord rightly.

1. We must seek him in Christ the Mediator. Joh 14:6.

2. We must seek him in truth. Jer 10:10 Joh 4:24 Ps 7:6.

3. We must seek him in holiness. 2Ti 2:19 Heb 12:14 1Jo 1:3.

4. We must seek him above all things and for himself.

5. We must seek him by the light of his own word.

6. We must seek him diligently and with perseverance, never resting till we find him, with the spouse in the Canticles. — William Cowper.

Verse 2,4-5,8. — Blessed are they that keep. "Thou hast commanded; us to keep." "O that my ways were directed to keep." "I will keep." Blessedness of keeping God's precepts — displayed (Ps 119:2), commanded (Ps 119:4), for (Ps 119:5), resolved upon (Ps 119:8). — **C.A.D.**

Verse 3. — They also do no iniquity. They work no iniquity

1. Purpose of heart;

2. Delight;

3. Perseverance;

4. Nor at all when heart is fully sanctified unto God; Christ dwelling in it by faith casting out sin. — Adam Clarke.

Verse 3. — The relation between negative and positive virtue. Or with God the best preventive of iniquity.

Verse 4. —

1. Take notice of the law giver: "Thou." :Not thy equal one that will be baffled, but the great God.

2. He hath interposed authority: "hast commanded."

3. The nature of this obedience, or thing commanded: "To keep thy precepts." — T. Manton.

Verse 4. — The supplementary commandment. God having ordained moral law, supplements it with a commandment prescribing the manner keeping it. Hence:

1. God is not indifferent to men's treatment of his — whether they observe, neglect, or defy it.

2. When observed, discriminates the spirit of its observance, whether slavish, partial, or diligent.

3. There is but one spirit of obedience which satisfies requirement. "Diligently" implies an obedience which is, — careful ascertan the law — prompt to fulfil it (Ps 119:60) — unreserved — love inspired ("diligently, "old meaning, through the Latin, "lovingly, " Ps 119:47,113).

4. Does our obedience come up to this standard? — C A.D.

Verse 4. — Not only is service commanded, but the manner of it. Heartiess, care, perseverance required, because without these it will not be uniform, or victorious over difficulty.

Verse 4. — How to obey: "Diligently."

1. Not, partially, but fully.

2. Not doubtfully, but confidently.

3. Not reluctantly, but readily.

4. Slovenly, but carefully.

5. Not coldly, but earnestly.

6. Not fitfully, but regularly. — W. J.

Verses 4-6. — A willing recognition (Ps 119:4). An ardent as (Ps 119:5). A happy consequence (Ps 119:6). — W. D.

Verse 5. — The prayer of the gracious.

1. Suggested by each preceding clause of blessing.

2. By a consciousness of failure.

3. By a loving clinging to the Lord.

Verse 5. —

1. The end desired: "To keep thy statutes." Not to be safe merely, or happy, but holy.

2. The help implored.

    (a) To understand the divine precepts.

    (b) To keep them. — G. R.

Verse 5. — Longing to obey.

1. It is a noble aspiration. There is nothing grander than the desire to do this except the doing of it.

2. It is a spiritual aspiration. Not the offspring of our carnal nature. It is the heart of God in the new creature.

3. It is a practicable aspiration. We sometimes sigh for the impossible. But this may be attained by divine grace.

4. It is an intense aspiration. It is the "Oh!" of a burning wish.

5. It is an influential aspiration. It does not evaporate in sighs. It is a mighty incentive implanted by grace which will not let us rest without holiness. — W. J.

Verse 6. — See "Spurgeon's Sermons, "No. 1443: "A Clear Conscience."

Verse 6. — Holy confidence the offspring of universal obedience.

Verse 6. — The armour of proof.

1. Universal obedience will give unabashed confidence —

(a) Before the criticising world.

(b) In the court of conscience.

(c) At the throne of grace.

(d) In the day of judgment.

2. But our obedience is far from universal, and leaves us open to

(a) The world's shafts.

(b) The rebukes of conscience.

(c) It paralyses our prayers

(d) It dares not appear for us at the bar of God.

3. Then let us by faith wrap ourselves in the perfect righteousness of Christ. Our answer to the world's cavil. We are not faultless, and for salvation we rest wholly on another. This righteousness is —

(a) The salve of our wounded conscience.

(b) Our mighty plea in prayer.

(c) Our triumphant vindication in the judgment day. — C. A.D.

Verse 6. — Topic: — Self respect depends on respect for one greater than self. — W. D.

Verse 7. — The best of praise, the best of learning, the best of blendings, viz., praise and holiness.

Verse 7. —

1. The professor of sacred music: "I will praise."

2. The subject of his song: "Thee."

3. The instrument: "Heart."

4. The instrument tuned: "Uprightness of heart."

5. The musician's training academy: "Judgments." — **W.D.**

Verse 7. — Learning and praising.

1. They are two spiritual exercises. It is possible for learners and singers to be carnal and sensual; but in this case they are employed about the righteous ends, works, and ways of the Lord.

2. They are two appropriate exercises. What can be more seemly than to learn of God and to praise him?

3. They are two profitable exercises. The expectations of the most utilitarian are surpassed. The pleasure and the profit yield abundant reward. Heart, head, life are all benefited.

4. They are two mutually assisting exercises. In the one we are receptive, and in the other communicative. By the one we are fitted to do the other. By the former we are stimulated to do the latter. How wonderfully the lesson is turned into a song, and the learner into a singer. — W.J.

Verse 7. —

1. Deficiency confessed: "When I shall have learned." This is essential to growth. It is an admission all can truly make.

2. Progress anticipated. He gave his heart to the work of learning. He sought divine help.

3. Praise promised. He promised it to God alone. He vowed it should be sincere: "with upright heart." — W. Williams, of Lambeth, 1882.

Verse 8. —

1. A hopeful resolve for life.

2. A dreadful fear.

3. A series of considerations removing the fear.

Verse 8. —

1. The resolution: "I will keep, "etc.

2. The position: "O forsake me not utterly."

    (a) Filial submission. I deserve it occasionally.

    (b) Filial confidence. "Not utterly."

3. The connection between the two. Obedience without prayer and prayer without obedience are equally in vain. To make headway both oars must be applied. God cannot abide lazy beggars, who while they can get anything by asking will not work. — **G.R.**

Verse 8. — O forsake me not utterly. Divine desertion deprecated.

1. The anguished prayer.

    (a) Sovereign forsaking. Sovereignty is not arbitrariness or capriciousness: perhaps its right definition is mysterious kingly love; unknown now, but justified when revealed.

    (b) Vicarious forsaking.

    (c) Forsaking on account of sin. David, Jonah, and Peter. The seven churches of Asia; the Jews. But to know what "utter" both in regard to degree and time means, we must go to hell. Like one trembling on the very verge of hell, he prays. Like belated traveller, in vast wood and surrounded by beasts of prey, sighs at day's departure. Like the watch on the raft seeing the sail that he has shouted himself hoarse to stop fading away in the sky line.

2. Its doctrinal foundation. Where he condescends to dwell, his abode is perpetual. He can only utterly forsake us because he was deceived in us. He can only utterly forsake because baffled. Both imply blasphemy. Thou who hatest putting away thou who hast never yet utterly forsaken any saint, make not me the solitary exception.

3. Historical certainty of answer. The saint and the church in all time delivered. It may tarry till "eventide, "as in Cowper's case. His face bore after death an expression of delighted surprise. — W.A.

Outlines Upon Keywords of The Psalm, by Pastor C. A. Davis

Verse 9-16. — Sanctification by the word, declared generally (Ps 119:9); sought personally (Ps 119:10-12); published to others (Ps 119:13); personally rejoiced in (Ps 119:14-16).

Verse 9. —

1. The young man's question.

2. The wise man's reply.

Verse 9. — In the word of God, when applied to the heart by the Spirit of God, there is,

1. A sufficiency of light to discover to men the need of cleansing their way.

2. Sufficiency of energy for the cleansing their way.

3. A sufficiency of pleasure to encourage them to choose to cleanse their way.

4. A sufficiency of support to sustain them in their cleansed way. — Theophilus Jones, in a "Sermon to the Young, "1829.

Verse 9. The word of God provides for the cleansing of the way.

1. By pointing out to the young man the evil of the way.

2. By discovering an infallible remedy for the disorders of his nature — the salvation that is by Jesus Christ.

3. By becoming a directory in all the paths of duty to which he may be called. — Daniel Wilson, 1828.

Verse 9. — The Psalmist's rules for the attainment of holiness deduced from his own experience.

1. Seek God with thy "whole heart" (Ps 119:2). Be truly sensible of your wants.

2. Keep and remember what God says (Ps 119:11): "Thy word have I hidden, "etc.

3. Reduce all this to practice (Ps 119:11): "That I might not sin against thee."

4. Bless God for what he has given (vet. 12): "Blessed art thou, "etc.

5. Ask more (Ps 119:12): Teach me thy statute, .

6. Be ready to communicate his knowledge to others (Ps 119:13): "With my lips have I declared."

7. Let it have a due effect on thy own heart (Ps 119:14): "I have rejoiced, "etc.

8. Meditate frequently upon them (Ps 119:15): "I will meditate, "etc.

9. Deeply reflect on them (Ps 119:16): "I will have respect, "etc. As food undigested will not nourish the body, so the word of God not considered with deep meditation and reflection will not feed the soul.

10. Having pursued the above course he should continue in it, and then his happiness would be secured (Ps 119:16): "I will not forget thy word: I will (in consequence) delight myself in thy statutes." — Adam Clarke.

Verse 9. — A question and answer for the young. The Bible is a book for young people. Here it intimates,

1. That the young man's way needs to be cleansed. His way of thinking, feeling, speaking, acting.

2. That he must take an active part in the work. The efficient cause in the operation is God. Other good influences are also at work. But the young man must be in hearty and practical sympathy with the work.

3. That he must use the Bible for the purpose. This records facts, presents incitations, enjoins precepts, utters promises, and sets up examples, all which are adapted to make a young man holy. By reading, studying, and imitating the Scriptures in a lowly and prayerful spirit the young shall escape pollution and ornament society. — W.J.

Verse 9. — A word to the young.

1. Show how the young man is in special danger of defiling his way. Through,

    (a) His strong passions.

    (b) His immature judgment.

    (c) His inexperience.

    (d) His rash self sufficiency.

    (e) His light companions, and,

    (f) His general heedlessness.

2. The circumspection he should use to cleanse his way. "Taking heed, "

    (a) Of his evil propensities.

(b) Of his companions.

   (c) Of his pursuits.

   (d) Of the tendencies of all he does.

3. The infallible guide by which his circumspection is to be regulated: "according to thy word" — that is to say,

   (a) Its precepts.

   (b) Its examples.

   (c) Its motives.

   (d) Its warnings.

   (e) Its allurements. — **C.A.D.**

Verse 10. —

1. A grateful review.

2. An anxious forecast.

3. A commendable prayer.

Verse 10. — The believer's two great solicitudes.

1. What he is anxious to find: "I have sought thee."

2. What he is afraid of losing: "Thy commandments." — W. D.

Verse 10. — Sincerity not self sufficiency.

1. The believer must be conscious of wholeheartedness in seeking God.

2. But consciousness of sincerity does not warrant self sufficiency.

3. The most wholehearted seeker must still look to divine grace to keep him from wandering. — **C.A.D.**

Verse 11. — The best thing, in the best place, for the best of purposes.

Verse 12. — The blessedness of God, and the mode of entering into it.

Verse 12. —

1. David gives glory to God: "Blessed art thou, O LORD."

2. He asks grace from God. — Matthew Henry.

Verse 12. —

1. What it is, or how God doth teach us.

    (a) God doth teach us outwardly; by his ordinances, by the ministry of men.

    (b) Inwardly; by the inspiration and work of the Holy Ghost.

2. The necessity of his teaching.

3. The benefit and utility of it. — T. Manton.

Verse 12. — Desire for Divine Teaching excited by the Recognition of Divine Blessedness.

1. Unveil in some inadequate degree the happiness of the ever blessed God, arising from his purity, benevolence, love.

2. Show the way in which man may become partaker of that blessedness by conformity to his precepts.

3. Utter the prayer of the text. — **C.A.D.**

Verse 13. — Speech fitly employed. It is occupied with a choice subject, a full subject, a subject profitable to men, and glorifying to God.

Verse 14. — Practical religion, the source of a comfort surpassing riches. It gives a man ease of mind, independence of carriage, weight of influence, and other matters supposed to arise out of wealth.

Verse 14. —

1. The subject of rejoicing. Not the "testimonies" merely, but their observances, "the way of, "etc.

2.. The rejoicing in that subject.

    (a) In its inward peace.

    (b) In its external consequences.

3. The degree of the rejoicing: "as much as, "etc. — **G.R.**

Verse 14. — The two scales of the balance. Whatever riches are good for, God's testimonies are good for.

1. Riches are desirable as the means of procuring the necessaries of life; but God's testimonies supply the necessities of the soul.

2. Riches are desirable as a means of procuring personal enjoyment; but God's testimonies produce the highest joy.

3. Riches are desirable as a means of attaining personal improvement; but God's testimonies are the highest educators.

4. Riches are desirable as a means of doing good; but God's testimonies work the highest good. — C.A.D.

Verse 15. — The contemplative and active life; their common food, object, and reward.

Verse 16. —

1. What there is to be delighted in.

2. What comes of such delight: "I will never forget."

3. What comes of such memory — more delight.

Outlines Upon Keywords of The Psalm, by Pastor C. A. Davis.

Verse 17-24. — Divine bounties desired. Life, for godly service (Ps 119:17). Illumination (Ps 119:18). Guidance homeward for the stranger ("thy commandments") (Ps 119:19-20), and, glancing at the proud who err from this guidance (Ps 119:21), the Psalmist prays for removal of the "reproach" entailed by fidelity to God (Ps 119:22-24).

Verse 17. —

1. A bountiful master.

2. A needy servant — begging for very life.

3. A suitable recompense: "and keep thy word."

Verse 17. — We are here taught,

1. That we owe our lives to God's mercy.

2. That therefore we ought to spend our lives in God's service. — Matthew Henry.

Verse 18. —

1. The precious casket: "thy law."

2. The invisible treasure: "wondrous things."

3. The miraculous eyesight: "that I may behold."

4. The divine oculist: "Open thou mine eyes."

Verse 18. — The hidden wonders of the gospel. There are many hidden things in nature; many in our fellow men; so there are many in the Bible. The things of the Bible are hidden because of the blindness of Man.

1. The blind man's sorrow: "Open mine eyes." I cannot see. I have eyes and see not. The pain of this conscious blindness when a man really feels it.

2. The blind man's conviction:"That I may behold wondrous, "etc. There are wondrous things there to be seen. I am sure of it. There is a wonderful view,

    (a) of sin;

    (b) of hell, as its desert;

    (c) of One ready to save;

    (d) of perfect pardon;

    (e) of God's love:

    (f) of all sufficient grace;

    (g) of heaven.

3. The blind man's wisdom. The fault is in my eyes, not in thy word. "Open my eyes, "and all will be well. The reason for not seeing is because the eyes are blinded by sin. There is nothing wanting in the Bible.

4. The blind man's prayer:"Open thou mine eyes."

    (a) I cannot open them.

    (b) My dearest friends cannot.

    (c) Only thou canst. "Lord, I pray thee, now open them." Many seek to stop such praying. Be like Bartimaeus who "cried so much the more."

    5. The blind man's anticipation:"That I may behold."

    (a) The joy of a cured blind man when he is about to behold, for the first time, the beauties of nature.

    (b) The joy of the spiritually healed when they begin "looking unto Jesus."

    (c) The personal character of the joy: "Open thou mine eyes, that I may behold." I have hitherto had to see through the eyes of others. I would depend on other eyes no longer.

The glad anticipation of Job: "Whom I shall see for myself, and mine eyes shall behold, and not another." — Frederick G. Marchant, 1882.

Verse 18. — God's word suited to man's sense of wonder.

1. We shall make some remarks on the sense of wonder in man, and what generally excites it. One of the first causes of wonder is the new or unexpected. The second source is to be found in things beautiful and grand. A third source is the mysterious which surrounds man— there are things unknowable.

2. God has made provision for this sense of wonder in his revealed word. The Bible addresses our sense of wonder by constantly presenting the new and unexpected to us; it sets before us

things beautiful and grand. If we come to the third source of wonder, that which raises it to awe, it is the peculiar province of the Bible to deal with this.

3. The means we are to use in order to have God's word thus unfolded — the prayer of the Psalmist may be our guide — "Open thou mine eyes, that I may behold wondrous things out of thy law." — John Ker, of Glasgow, 1877.

Verse 18. — Wondrous sights for opened eyes.

1. The wondrous things in God's law. A wondrous rule of life. A wondrous curse against transgression. A wondrous redemption from the curse shadowed forth in the ceremonial law.

2. Special eyesight needed to behold them. They are spiritual things. Men are spiritually blind. 1Co 2:14.

3. Personal prayer to the Great Opener of eyes. — **C.A.D.**

Verse 20. —

1. The word sought, and sought at all times.

2. The word sought, and sought with intense desire.

3. The word sought, and sought the more intensely the more it is found. It was because he had found so much in the word of the Lord already, that the soul of the Psalmist was breaking to find more. Those who have been once admitted to "the secret of the Lord" find their highest joy in knowing that secret still more fully. It is to those who know that secret that the promise is given: "He will show them his covenant:" Ps 25:14. — F.G.M.

Verse 20. — One of the best tests of character and prophecies of what a man will be, are his longings.

1. The saint's absorbing object: "Thy judgments." The word here is synonymous with the "word" of God.

    (a) The Psalmist greatly reverenced the word.

    (b) He intensely desired to know its contents.

    (c) He wishes to feed upon God's word.

    (d) He longed to obey it.

    (e) He longed to feel the power of God's judgments in his own heart.

2. The saint's ardent longings.

    (a) They constitute a living experience.

    (b) The expression used in the text represents a humble sense of imperfection.

    (c) It indicates an advanced experience.

  (d) It is an experience which we may term a bitter sweet.

  (e) These longings may become very wearying to a man's soul.

3. Cheering reflections.

  (a) God is at work in your soul.

  (b) The result of God's work is very precious.

  (c) It is leading on to something more precious.

  (d) The desire itself is doing you good.

  (e) It makes Christ precious. See "Spurgeon's Sermons, "No. 1586: "Holy Longings."

Verse 21. —

1. The character of the proud.

2. God's dealings with them.

3. Our own relation to them.

Verse 21. —

1. The sin; "Err from the commandments."

  (a) By neglect; or,

  (b) By abuse of them.

2. Its origin — pride: pride of reason, of heart, of life.

3. Its punishment.

  (a) Rebuke.

  (b) Condemnation. — **G.R.**

Verse 23. — Meditation.

1. Our best employment while others slander.

2. Our best comfort under their falsehood.

3. Our best preservative from a spirit of revenge.

4. Our best mode of showing our superiority to their attacks.

Verse 24. —

1. He reverenced them as God's testimonies.

2. He revelled in them as his delight.

3. He referred to them as his counsellors.

Outlines Upon Keywords of The Psalm, by Pastor C. A. Davis.

Verse 25-32. — Quickening. Prayed for with confession (Ps 119:25-26). When obtained shall be talked of (Ps 119:27). Desired for the sake of strength (Ps 119:28), of truthfulness (Ps 119:29-31), and of activity (Ps 119:32).

Verse 25. —

1. Nature and its tendency.

2. Grace and its mode of operation.

3. Both truths in their personal application.

Verse 25. — Quicken thou me, etc.

1. There are many reasons why we should seek quickening.

    (a) Because of the deadening influence of the world. "Thy soul cleaveth, "etc.

    (b) The influence of vanity (see Ps 119:37).

    (c) Because we are surrounded by deceivers (see Ps 119:87-88).

    (d) Because of the effect of seasons of affliction upon us (see Ps 119:7).

2. Some of the motives for seeking quickening.

    (a) Because of what you are— a Christian; life seeks more life.

    (b) Because of what you ought to be.

    (c) Because of what we shall be.

    (d) In order to obedience (see Ps 119:88).

    (e) For your comfort (Ps 119:107,50).

    (f) As the best security against the attacks of enemies (Ps 119:87-88).

    (g) To invigorate our memories (Ps 119:93).

    (h) Consider (as a motive to seek this quickening) the terrible consequences of losing spiritual life; or, in other words, lacking it in its manifest display.

3. Some of the ways in which the quickening may be brought to us.

    (a) It must be by the Lord himself. "Quicken me, O Lord."

(b) By the turning of the eyes (Ps 119:37).

(c) By the word (Ps 119:50).

(d) By the precepts (Ps 119:93).

(e) By affliction (Ps 119:107).

(f) By divine comforts.

4. Enquire where are our pleas when we come before God to ask for quickening.

(a) Our necessity (Ps 119:107, etc.).

(b) Our earnest desire (Ps 119:40).

(c) Appeal to God's righteousness (Ps 119:40).

(d) To his lovingkindness (Ps 119:88,149,156).

(e) The plea in the text: "according to thy word" (Ps 119:28,107). See "Spurgeon's Sermons, "No. 1350: "Enlivening and Invigorating."

Verse 26. — Confession. Absolution. Instruction.

Verse 26. —

1. The duty: "I have declared my ways" — made known my experience of thy word to others.

2. Its notice by God: "Thou heardest me."

3. Its reward. More knowledge will be given: "Teach me, "etc. — **G.R.**

Verse 27. —

1. A student's prayer.

   1. It deals with the main subject of the conversation which is to be that student's occupation— "the way of God's precepts."

   2. A confession is implied: "Make me, "etc.

   3. A great boon is asked— to understand, to know, thy statutes.

   4. The Fountain of all wisdom is applied to.

2. The occupation of the instructed man.

   1. He testifies of God's works— his wondrous works— Christ's work for us; the Holy Spirit's work in us. The wonderful character of these works of God, a wide field for devout study.

   2. He speaks very plainly: "I will talk, "etc.

3. He will speak very frequently: "I will talk."

   4. He will speak to the point: "So" — i.e., according to understanding.

3. The intimate relation between the prayer of the student and the pursuit that he subsequently followed. See "Spurgeon's Sermons, "No. 1344: "The Student's Prayer."

Verse 27. — Education for the ministry.

1. The student at college: "Make me to understand." His lesson. His instructor. His application.

2. The preacher at his work: "So shall I talk, "etc. His qualification. His theme. His manner. — **C.A.D.**

Verse 29. — The way of lying.

1. Describe the way of lying. Various paths, e.g., erroneous views of doctrine: false grounds of faith: looseness of practice: shrinking from the daily cross.

2. Show why it is thus named. It does not furnish its promised pleasures. It does not lead to its professed goal. It lies through the territory of the father of lies.

3. Notice the peculiarity in the prayer against it. Not remove me from, but remove from me: for the way of lying is within us.

4. Our deliverance from the way of lying lies with God. — **C.A.D.**

Verse 29-30. —

1. The way of lying, our wish to have it removed, and the method of answer.

2. The way of truth, our choice, and the method of carrying it out.

Verse 31. — Reasons for sticking to the Divine testimonies.

Verse 31. — A wholesome mixture.

1. Sturdy fidelity.

2. Self distrust,

3. Importunate prayer. — **C.A.D.**

Verse 32. — The Fettered Racer set free.

1. The course that invited him.

2. The shackles that bound him.

3. The impatience that prompted him.

4. The Lord that freed him.

5. Now let him go. — **C.A.D.**

Verse 32.

1. Liberty desired.

2. Liberty rightly used. Or, the effect of the heart upon the feet.

Verse 32. — The text will give us occasion to speak,

1. Of the benefit of an enlarged heart. The necessary precedence of this work on God's part, before there can be any serious bent or motion of heart towards God on our part.

2. The subsequent resolution of the saints to engage their hearts to live to God.

3. With what earnestness, alacrity and rigour of spirit this work is to be carried on: "I will run." — T. Manton.

Verse 32. —

1. The way of obedience: "Thy commandments."

2. The duty of obedience: "I will run" — not stand still — not loiter — not creep — not walk, but run.

3. The life of obedience.

> (a) Where it lies — in the heart.
>
> (b) Whence it comes: "When thou shalt, "etc.
>
> (c) What it does — enlarges the heart. — **G.R.**

Outlines Upon Keywords of The Psalm, by Pastor C. A. Davis.

Verse 33-40. — Faithfulness secured by divine in working. Prayer for divine teaching, understanding, constraint, and control of heart and eyes, to ensure persevering and wholehearted faithfulness (Ps 119:33-37). The Psalmist, thus established in the word, prays for the establishment of the word to himself (Ps 119:38); deprecates the reproach of unfaithfulness (Ps 119:39); and enforces the whole prayer by the vehemence of the desire which prompts it (Ps 119:40).

Verse 33. — In this prayer for grace observe,

1. The person to whom he prays: "0 Lord."

2. The person for whom: "teach me."

3. The grace for which he prayeth: to be taught.

4. The object of this teaching: "The way of thy statutes." The teaching which he begs, is not speculative, but practical, to learn how to walk in the way of God. — T. Manton.

Verse 33. — The superior efficacy of divine teaching: it secures holy practice and insures its perpetuity.

Verse 33-34. — Light from above.

1. The blinding power of sin. "Teach me", i.e., "point out to me." "Give me understanding." Whatever may have been the original amount of light which came item eating from the tree of knowledge of good and evil, that light has long been insufficient.

> (a) Men need light to discern the right way from the wrong.

> (b) Men need light to understand the beauties of the right way. Such beauties line the way of truth on either hand, but only the God taught mind appreciates them. Even Jesus, who is the way, the truth, and the life, is as a root out of a dry ground, till the mind is taught of the Lord. Sin is the cause of this blindness. The farther any man walks in the way of sin, the less can he see of the beauties of holiness.

2. The enlightening grace of the Lord. "Teach me." "Give me understanding." This grace,

> (a) May be boldly asked: "If any man lack wisdom let him ask of God."

> (b) Will be freely given. "Who giveth to all men liberally." "Ask, and it shall be given."

> (c) Will be amply sufficient. "I shall keep it unto the end." "I shall keep Thy law." To see is to follow.

3. The stimulating power of clearly revealed truth. "I shall observe it with my whole heart." To see is not only to follow, but to follow with love and gladness. It is written of the light which will come before the throne, "We shall be like him, for we shall see him as he is." "O thou, that dwellest between the Cherubim, shine forth, "even here, on the way that leads to thy presence. — F.G.M.

Verse 33-35. — Alpha and Omega.

1. God, the giver of spiritual instruction: Ps 119:33.

2. Of spiritual understanding, without which this instruction is in vain: Ps 119:34.

3. Of grace for practical obedience when thus instructed: Ps 119:35.

4. For wholehearted obedience: Ps 119:84.

5. For final perseverance: Ps 119:33. — **C.A.D.**

Verse 33-36. — Human Dependence on Divine help.

1. There can be no steady keeping in the way of the Lord without the Lord's guidance: Ps 119:83.

2. There can be no observing of the way with the heart without Divine light for the mind: Ps 119:34.

3. There can be no diligent pursuit of the way till divine energy be given to the will: Ps 119:35.

4. There can be no true love of the way unless the heart be constrained by the love of God: Ps 119:36. He who said, "Without me ye can do nothing, "is necessary for us to see the way, to understand the way, to walk in the way, and to love the way. — F. G. M.

Verse 34. — The influence of the understanding upon the heart, and the united power of understanding and heart over the life.

Verse 34. — Seeing and loving.

1. When men see they love (the whole **Verse**).

2. When men love they see. Only the loving heart would have seen enough to write such a **Verse**. — F. G. M

Verse 35. — The prayer of a child, and the delight of a child. Or, Our pleasure in holiness a plea for grace.

Verse 35. —

1. Delight avowed.

2. Disinclination implied.

3. Constraint implored. — W. W.

Verse 36. — Holiness a cure for covetousness.

Verse 36,112. — The Cooperation of the Divine and the Human in Salvation.

1. It is God that worketh in you: Ps 119:36.

2. Therefore work out your own salvation with fear and trembling: Ps 119:112. — **C.A.D.**

Verse 37. — Quicken thou me in thy way. This brief prayer —

1. Deals with the believer's frequent need.

2. It directs us to the sole worker of quickening: "Thou."

3. It describes the sphere of renewed rigour: "in thy way."

4. It denotes that there may be special reasons and special seasons for this prayer — times of temptation: Ps 119:37; seasons of affliction: Ps 119:107; when called to some extraordinary service. See "Spurgeon's Sermons, "No. 1073: "A Honeycomb."

Verse 37. — Here is,

1. Conversion from "vanity."

2. Conversion to — "thy way."

3. Conversion by— "Quicken thou me." — G. R.

Verse 37. — David prays,

1. For restraining grace that he might be prevented and kept back from that which would hinder him in the way of his duty: "Turn away mine eyes from beholding vanity."

2. For constraining grace, that he might not only be kept from everything that would obstruct his progress heavenward, but that he might have that grace which was necessary to forward him in that progress: "Quicken thou me in thy way." — **M. Henry.**

Verse 38. — Confirmation. What? "Thy word established." To whom? "Unto thy servant." Why? "Who is devoted, "etc.

Verse 38. — Fear of God evidences itself,

1. By a dread of his displeasure.

2. Desire of his Favor.

3. Regard for his excellencies.

4. Submission to his will.

5. Gratitude for his benefits.

6. Conscientious obedience to his commands. — Charles Buck.

Verse 38. — The four kinds of fear.

1. The fear of man, by which we are led rather to do wrong than to suffer evil.

2. Servile fear, through which we are induced to avoid sin only from the dread of hell.

3. Initial fear, in which we avoid sin partly from the fear of hell, but partly also from the love of God, which is the fear of ordinary Christians.

4. Filial fear, when we are afraid to disobey God only and altogether from the love we bear him. Jer 32:40. — Ayguan, in J. Edward Vaux's "Preacher's Storehouse, "1878

Verse 39. —

1. Man's judgment dreaded.

2. God's judgment approved.

Verse 39. — The reproach of inconsistency.

1. The disHonor caused by it (2Sa 12:14).

2. The danger of incurring it.

3. The prayer against it. — **C.A.D.**

Verse 40. —

1. Gracious longings experienced.

2. Great necessity felt— more life needed.

3. Wise petition offered.

Outlines Upon Keywords of The Psalm, by Pastor C. A. Davis.

Verses 41-48. — Promised mercies. Desired (Ps 119:41), as an answer to "him that reproacheth" (Ps 119:42-43); as a means of faithfulness (Ps 119:44); liberty (Ps 119:45); boldness (Ps 119:46); delight (Ps 119:47), and eager longing (Ps 119:48).

Verse 41. — See "Spurgeon's Sermons, "No. 1524: "Your Personal Salvation."

Verse 41. —

1. God's mercies come to us unsought continually. His sparing mercies, temporal mercies, etc.

2. The chief outcome of God's mercies is his salvation. It is our greatest need; it is his greatest gift.

3. We should have a personal interest in this salvation: "Let thy mercies come also unto me."

4. When we seek God's salvation, we may plead his promise: "according to thy word." — Horatio Wilkins, of Cheltenham, 1882.

Verse 41. — Even me.

1. In me there is need of mercy.

2. To me mercy can come.

3. Thy salvation suits me.

4. Special difficulties would daunt me.

5. Thy word encourages me.

Verse 41. —

1. Salvation is all of mercy.

2. All mercies are in salvation.

3. All men should be anxious for salvation to come to them.

4. It can only come according to God's word. — W.W.

Verse 41-43. — A Comprehensive Prayer.

1. The possession of salvation, Ps 119:41.

2. Is the power for defense: Ps 119:42.

3. And the qualification for usefulness: Ps 119:43. — **C.A.D.**

Verse 42. — Faith's answer to reproach found in the fact that she trusts God's word.

Verse 42-43, 47. — Faith, hope, and love. "I trust." "I have hoped." "I have loved." Faith warring, hope testifying, love obeying.

Verse 43. — How the true preacher could be silenced, and his plea that he may not be so.

Verse 44. — The perpetuity of gracious living. On what it is conditioned: "So." How entirely it is consistent with free agency: "I keep." How continuous it is, and how eternal.

Verse 44. — Heaven begun below.

1. The present life of the believer — keeping God's law.

2. The continual care of the believer — to keep God's law.

3. The eternal prospect of the believer — keeping God's law for ever and e**Verse** — **C.A.D.**

Verse 45-47. — Liberty of walk. Liberty of speech. Liberty of heart.

Verse 45-48. — The true freeman enjoys —

1. Free walk with God.

2. Free talk about God.

3. Free love unto God.

4. Free exercise, of soul, (a) in holy practice; (b) in heavenly meditation. — W. Durban.

Verse 45-48. — Five things the Psalmist promises himself here in the strength of God's grace.

1. That he should be free and easy in his duty: "I will walk at liberty."

2. That he should be bold and courageous in his duty: "I will speak of thy testimonies also before kings."

3. That he should be cheerful and pleasant in his duty: "I will delight myself in thy commandments."

4. That he should be diligent and vigorous in his duty: "I will delight myself in thy commandments."

5. That he should be thoughtful and considerate in his duty: "I will meditate in thy statutes." — **M. Henry.**

Verse 46-48. — Lips, heart, and hands.

1. Public profession of God's word ("I will speak, "Ps 119:46) must be warranted by —

2. Private delight in God's word ("I will delight myself, " Ps 119:47), which must result in—

3. Practical obedience to God's word ("I will lift up my hands, " Ps 119:48).

Verse 46. —

1. The truly earnest must speak.

2. They are at no loss for good subjects: "Thy testimonies." The range is boundless— the variety endless.

3. They never fear any audience: "before kings." — W.W.

Verse 48. —

1. Love renewing its activity.

2. Love refreshing itself with spiritual food.

Verse 48. —

1. Scripture in the hand for reading. Often in the hand.

2. In the mind for meditation: "I will meditate, "etc.

3. In the heart for love: "Which I have loved." — **G.R.**

Verse 48. — Religion engaged the whole manhood of David: hands, heart, head.

1. The uplifted hands.

    (a) Taking an oath of allegiance to God's word. Ge 14:22 Eze 20:28. To receive its doctrines, obey its precepts, regard its warnings, uphold its Honor.

    (b) Imploring a blessing upon God's word. Ge 48:14; Le 9:22 Lu 24:50. That its light might spread: "Fly abroad, thou mighty gospel; "that its influence may become universal.

2. The loyal heart.

    (a) This accounts for uplifted hands. He had loved the word himself. Religion is inward first, then outward. We must love it before we are anxious to spread it.

    (b) But what accounts for the loyal heart? The word had brought him salvation, yielded him sustenance, afforded him guidance. We love the world for its joyous effects upon ourselves.

3. The studious mind.

    (a) Devout meditation the best employment.

    (b) The Word of God affords a grand field for it.

    (c) To meditate in it learn to love it: "have loved, ""will meditate." — H.W.

Verse 48. —

1. God's commandments loved. We love the law when we love the LawgiVerse We love his will only when our hearts are reconciled and renewed. Hence the need of spiritual renewal.

2. God's commandments the subject of prayer: "My hands also will I lift up." Perowne says, "The expression denotes the act of prayer." We may pray for a fuller knowledge, a deeper experience, a readier and more perfect obedience.

3. A theme for meditation. Amidst the hurry of outward activities we must not forget the need of quiet meditation. — H.W.

Outlines Upon Keywords of The Psalm, by Pastor C. A. Davis.

Verse 49-56. — Hope in affliction. It arises from God's word (Ps 119:49). It produces comfort (Ps 119:50), even in trouble caused by the wicked (Ps 119:51-53). It gladdens the believer's pilgrimage and his holy night seasons (Ps 119:54-56).

Verse 49. —

1. The personality of the word: "The word unto thy servant."

2. The application of the word: "upon which thou hast caused me to hope."

3. The pleading of the word: "Remember the word, "etc.

Verse 49. — The word of hope.

1. God's word the foundation of human hope. (The fact of a revelation. The substance of the revelation.)

2. Particular words of God which have been found peculiarly hope enkindling.

3. The pleading of such words at the throne of grace. — **C.A.D.**

Verse 50. — Each man has his own affliction and his own consolation. Quickened piety the best comfort. The word the means of it.

Verse 50. —

1. The need of consolation.

2. The consolation needed. — **G.R.**

Verse 51. — The proud man's contumely, and the gracious man's constancy.

Verse 51. — Fidelity in the face of contempt.

1. The proud deride the believer's subjection to God's law.

2. They ridicule the believer's delight, in God's service.

3. They are met by the believer's resolution to cleave to God. 2Sa 6:20,22. — **C.A.D.**

Verse 52. — Comfort derived from a review of the ancient doings of the Lord towards the wicked and his people.

Verse 52. —

1. The dead speaking to the living.

2. The living listening to the dead. — **G.R.**

Verse 52. — Sweet water from a dark well.

1. God's judgments are calculated to inspire terror.

2. But they prove God's superintending care over the world.

3. They are ever against sin, and for holiness.

4. In all times of judgment God delivers his people. Noah, Lot, etc.

5. Therefore God's judgments are a source of comfort to the believer. — G.A.D.

Verse 53. — The sensations of godly men at the sight of sinners: horror at their crime, their perseverance in it, their rejection of grace, and their end.

Verse 53. — Horror stricken.

1. The guilt and danger of impenitent sinners.

2. The horror and concern of godly spectators.

3. The prayer and labor which such concern should dictate, — G.A.D.

Verse 54. — Here is —

1. Light in darkness.

2. Companionship in solitude.

3. Activity in rest: "house of pilgrimage." — **G.R.**

Verse 54. — The cheerful pilgrim.

1. A good man views his residence in this world as only the house of his pilgrimage.

2. The situation, however disadvantageous, admits of cheerfulness.

3. The sources of his joy are derived from the Scriptures. — W. Jay.

Verse 54. — See "Spurgeon's Sermons, "No. 1652: "The Singing Pilgrim."

Verse 55,49. — "Remember." "I have remembered."

Verse 55. — Night memories. Day duties. How they act and react upon each other.

Verse 55. — Dark nights. Bright memories. Right results. — **C.A.D.**

Verse 55. —

1. Happy though restless night.

2. Happy though busy day. — **W.D.**

Verse 56. — The gains of godliness; or, what a man gets through holy living.

Verse 56. —

1. The duty: "I kept thy precepts."

2. Its reward: "This I had, "etc. Protection: "this I had." Guidance: "this I had." Prosperity: "this I had." Consolation: "this I had." — **G.R.**

PSALM 119 (part 2 vv. 57-120)

Outlines Upon Keywords of The Psalm, by Pastor C. A. Davis.

Verse 57-64. — The believer's portion. The Lord is the believer's portion (Ps 119:57); heartily sought (Ps 119:58-60); remaining though all else be taken away (Ps 119:61); causing joy even at midnight (Ps 119:62), and the selection of congenial company (Ps 119:63-64).

Verse 57. —

1. The infinite possession: "Thou art my portion, O LORD." Notice—

   (a) A clear distinction made by the Psalmist between his portion and that of the ungodly here and hereafter: See Ps 48:2.

   (b) positive claim: "Thou art my portion, O LORD." This "portion" is boundless, abiding, appropriate, satisfying, elevating, all of grace.

2. The appropriate resolution: "I have said that I would keep thy words."

   (a) Notice the preface: "I have said."

   (b) The link between the portion possessed and the resolution made.

   (c) The work of keeping God's words. Keep him who is the Word— Christ Jesus. Keep the word of the gospel— doctrines, precepts, promises (kept in the heart to comfort the believer). This blessed subject suggests a solemn contrast. See the portion of that servant who did not keep his Lord's word: Mt 24:48-51 See "Spurgeon's Sermons, " No. 1372: "God our Portion, and his Word our Treasure."

Verse 57 (first clause). — The believer's portion.

1. Show the validity of his claim: "my."

   (a) A gift by covenant: Heb 8:10-13.

   (b) Involved in joint heirship with Christ: Ro 8:17.

   (c) Confirmed by the experience of faith.

   2. Survey the superlative value of his possession: "The Lord."

   (a) Absolutely good.

   (b) Infinitely precious.

   (c) Inexhaustibly full.

   (d) Everlastingly sure.

 3. Suggest a method of deriving the greatest present advantage from it.

(a) Meditate much upon God, under the conviction that he is your portion.

(b) Carry all cares to him, and cast every burden on him.

(c) Refer every temptation to the word of his law, and every doubt to the word of his promise.

(d) Draw largely upon his riches to meet every need as it arises. — John Field, of Sevenoaks, 1882.

Verse 57-58. — The believer's estate, profession, and petition.

Verse 58. — The soul's sunshine.

1. God's Favor the one thing needful.

2. Wholeheartedness the one mode of entreating it.

3. Covenant mercy the one plea for obtaining it. — **C.A.D.**

Verse 58. — We may learn how a seeker may come to enjoy saving Favor, by a careful study of —

1. The Profession: "I intreated thy Favor with my whole heart."

    (a) What he did: "I intreated." Heb. "I painfully sought thy face." Earnest desire. Importunate supplication. Painful sorrow for sin.

    (b) How he did it: "With my whole heart." The intellect, affections, will, all engaged and concentrating effort. Otherwise, seeking is solemn trifling. This only worthy of our purpose, pleasing to God, and successful.

    (c) The evidence that we are doing it. Frequent prayer, searching the word, often enquiring. The first and main business — Giving up for Christ.

2. The Petition: "Be merciful unto me."

    (a) God's Favor to be expected on the terms of mercy only.

    (b) Happily, this is a prayer every sinner can and should use.

    (c) Blessedly true it is, that it never fails.

3. The Plea: "According to thy word."

    (a) A plea that cannot be gainsaid is a great thing in an entreaty.

    (b) The promise of God is just such a plea.

    (c) Seek it out, lay hold of it, and urge it. — **J.F.**

Verse 59. —

1. Self examination: "I thought on" my private "ways" — my social ways— my sacred ways— my public ways.

2. Its advantages: "And turned my feet, "etc. — **G.R.**

Verse 59. —

1. Unthinking and straying.

2. Thinking and turning. — **C.A.D.**

Verse 59. —

1. Conviction.

2. Conversion. — W. D.

Verse 59. — Thinking on our own ways. Enquire,

1. Why so generally neglected?

    (a) Want of courage.

    (b) Occupied too much.

    (c) Unpleasant, and therefore the chief care of many is to banish it.

2. When is it wisely conducted?

    (a) When honestly engaged in.

    (b) When thoroughly carried out.

    (c) When Scripture is made the referee and standard.

4. When Divine help is sought.

5. What end will it serve?

    (a) Turn us from our own ways with shame and penitence.

    (b) Turn us to God's testimonies with earnestness, reverence, and hopefulness. — **J.F.**

Verse 59. —

1. Right thinking: "I thought on my ways."

    (a) That this thought upon his ways caused the Psalmist dissatisfaction is evident.

    (b) Right thinking upon our ways will suggest a practical change.

    (c) The retrospect we take of our life should suggest that any turn we make should be towards God: "Unto thy testimonies."

(d) Right thinking also suggests that such a turning is possible.

2. Right turning. The turn was—

(a) Complete.

(b) Practical.

(c) Spiritual.

(d) Immediate.

(e) It must be a divine work. See "Spurgeon's Sermons," No.1181: "Thinking and Turning."

Verse 60. — The dangers of delay. The reasons for prompt action.

Verse 60. — A sermon to loiterers.

1. Reflection. Keeping God's commandments is my duty; is my welfare. Commandments delayed may be never kept. Delay is in itself disobedience. Alacrity is the soul of obedience.

2. Resolve. I will make haste and delay not. — **C.A.D.**

Verse 60. —

1. Quick.

2. Sure. — **W.D.**

Verse 60. — Procrastination considered in its most important application; that is, to religion.

1. This procrastination is irrational.

2. It is unpleasant, disagreeable, painful.

3. It is disgraceful.

4. It is sinful, and that is the highest degree.

5. It is dangerous. — John Angell James.

Verse 61. —

1. Spiritual highway robbery.

2. The traveler keeping his road. Or, what enemies can do, and what they cannot do.

Verse 62. —

1. The duty of gratitude: "give thanks."

2. The subject for gratitude: "thy righteous judgments."

3. The season for gratitude: at night as well as in the day. — **G.R.**

Verse 62. — Up in the night. Singing in the night. Reasons for such singular conduct.

Verse 62. — The nightingale.

1. A natural association of thought: "midnight" and "judgments." Exodus 7, etc.

2. An incongruous association of feeling: "thanks" and "judgments."

3. A full justification of this apparent incongruity: "thanks because of thy righteous judgments."

4. A vigorous performance of an incumbent duty: "at midnight I will rise to give thanks." — **C.A.D.**

Verse 63. —

1. True religion is friendly.

2. Our friendliness should be catholic.

3. Our friendliness should be discriminating.

4. Such friendliness is most useful.

Verse 63. — Of good and bad company. How to avoid the one, and improve the other. See W. Bridge's Sermon, in his works, vol. v. p. 90. Tegg's edition, 1845.

Verse 63. — The believer's choice of companions.

1. Ought to be decided by their piety: "Them that fear thee."

2. Is directed by their conduct: "Them that keep thy precepts."

3. Should be extended as far as: possible: "All."

4. Involves reciprocal obligation: "I am a companion." — **J.F.**

Verse 64. — The sum and substance of this **Verse** will be comprised in these five propositions: —

1. That saving knowledge is a benefit that must be asked of God.

2. That this benefit cannot be too often or sufficiently enough asked: it is his continual request.

3. In asking, we are encouraged by the bounty or mercy of God.

4. That God is merciful all his creatures declare.

5. That his goodness to all his creatures should confirm us in: hoping for saving grace or spiritual good things. — T. Manton

Verse 64. —

1. Observations in the school of nature.

2. Supplications enter the school of grace.

Verse 64. — The mercy of God in nature and his mercy as revealed in word.

1. The one excellent; the other super excellent.

2. The one easily given; the other coming through a great sacrifice.

3. The one may enjoyed, and even increase condemnation; the other, if enjoyed, is salvation.

4. The one should lead to repentance; the other is s adapted for the penitent's restoration to holiness. — **J.F.**

Outlines Upon Keywords of The Psalm, by Pastor C. A. Davis.

Verse 65-72. — The Lord's dealings. Gratefully acknowledged (Ps 119:65), and their instructiveness still desired (Ps 119:66), even affliction from him is "good" (Ps 119:67-68), and with its beneficial result is preferred to the prosperity of the wicked (Ps 119:69-72).

Verse 65. — The servant giving his master a character; or, tallying with Scripture: two fruitful themes.

Verse 65. —

1. Experience confirmed by the word.

2. The word by experience. — **G.R.**

Verse 65. — A servant's story.

1. Although he knew my faults he engaged me.

2. Although I am so far beneath him, yet he familiarly teaches me.

3. Although I am always ailing, he is very kind to me in my afflictions.

4. Although I am one of the meanest of his servants, he permits me to feast his own table.

5. Although I do little work, he will pay me good

6. Although I am to have such great wages, I have very many perquisites.

7. Although my Master is all this to me (can you believe it?) I murmur and repine at him if he crosses me in anything. Application: —

> (a) Does the word: servant "sound like a misnomer?" — "not servants...but I have called you friends."
>
> (b) Though he calls me "friend, "I shall never cease to call him "Master." — Richard Andrew Griffin, in "Stems and Twigs."

Verse 66. —

1. Singular faith: "I have believed thy commandments."

2. Special petition based upon it: "Teach me."

Verse 66. — The value of a good judgment to sound knowledge.

1. It carefully discriminates between truth and error.

2. It puts each truth in its proper relation to other truths.

3. It holds every truth firmly, but has the greater care for the more important.

4. It rather avoids the curious and the speculative, but really loves the plain and useful.

5. Knowing that truths are rightly held only, when applied, it turns all to practical account.

6. Knowing also, that good food may, under some circumstances, become poisonous, it is careful in its selection and use of truths. — **J.F.**

Verse 67. —

1. The dangers of prosperity.

2. The benefits of adversity. — **G.R.**

Verse 67. — The restraining power of affliction

Verse 67,71,75. — Affliction thrice viewed and thrice blessed. I

1. Before affliction: straying.

2. In affliction: learning.

3. After affliction: knowing. — **C.A.D.**

Verse 68. — The double plea for a choice blessing. The goodness of God the hope of our ignorance.

Verse 68. — Thou art good and doest good. The nature and work of God are manifest in nature, providence, grace, and glory. They are morally good; beneficially good; perfectly good; immeasurably good; immutably good; experimentally good; satisfactorily good. — **W.J.**

Verse 68 (first clause). — A sermon on God's goodness.

1. The perfectness of it.

2. The proofs of it.

3. The power it should have over us. — **J.F.**

Verse 69. — Wholehearted obedience the best solace under slander; the best answer to it; and the best way of converting the slanderers.

Verse 70. —

1. Fatty degeneration of the heart.

2. Thorough regeneration of the heart.

Verse 70. — A fatty heart.

1. The diagnosis of the disease.

2. Its symptoms. Pride; no delight in God, nor in his law; dislike to his people; readiness to lie: Ps 119:69.

3. Its fatal character.

4. Its only cure. Ps 101:10 Eze 36:26. — **C.A.D.**

Verse 71. —

1. David knew what was good for him.

2. David learned what is good essentially. Active obedience is learned by passive obedience.

Verse 71. — Affliction an instructor.

1. Never welcomed: "Have been."

2. Often impatiently endured.

3. Always gratefully remembered: "It is good, "etc.

4. Efficient for a perverse scholar: "That I might learn."

5. Indispensable in the education of all. — **J.F.**

Verse 71. — The school of affliction.

1. The reluctant scholar sent to school.

2. The scholar's hard lesson.

3. The scholar's blessed learning.

4. The scholar's sweet reflection. — **C.A.D.**

Verse 72. — The advantages of riches far excelled by the blessings of the word.

Verse 72. — A valuation.

1. The saints' high estimate of God's law.

2. Show when it was formed: in affliction: Ps 119:71.

3. Vindicate its truth— by illustrating the hollowness of riches, and the satisfaction found in godliness. — **C.A.D.**

Verse 72. — The word, better than gold and silVerse

1. It gives what gold and silver cannot purchase.

2. Without what it gives, gold and silver may be a curse.

3. Without gold and silver, it may yield its treasure more freely and fully than with them.

4. The word and what it gives shall rejoice the heart when gold and silver shall be useless to their disappointed worshippers. — **J.F.**

Verse 72. — The law of thy mouth is better, etc.

1. It is more refining, and makes me a better man.

2. It is more enriching, and makes me a wealthier man.

3. It is more distinguishing, and makes me a greater man.

4. It is more sustaining, and makes me a stronger man.

5. It is more preserving, and makes me a safer man.

6. It is more satisfying, and makes me a happier man.

7. It is more lasting, and better suited to me as an immortal man. — **W.J.**

Outlines Upon Keywords of The Psalm, by Pastor C. A. Davis.

Verse 73-80. — Natural and spiritual creation. The Psalmist prays to the Creator for spiritual life or "understanding" (Ps 119:73), he will then be welcomed by the spiritual (Ps 119:74). He submissively receives affliction for spiritual training (Ps 119:75-77), deprecates the hostility of the proud (Ps 119:78), craves the company of the spiritual (Ps 119:79), and prays for heart soundness (Ps 119:80).

Verse 73. —

1. Consider the Lord's great care in our creation.

2. See in it a reason for his perfecting the new creation within us.

3. Observe the method of this perfecting.

Verse 74. —

1. The encouraging influence of good men upon others.

2. The instructive influence of others upon them: — **G.R.**

Verse 74. — Con**Verse** with a tried but steadfast believer is a source of gladness to the children of God.

1. He has a thrilling talc of experience to tell.

2. He has valuable counsels and cautions to give.

3. He is a monument of God's faithfulness, confirming the hope of others.

4. He is an epistle of Christ, written expressly to illustrate the preciousness and the power of the gospel. — **J.F.**

Verse 75. — Experimental knowledge: positive, personal, glorifying to God, consoling to the saints.

Verse 76. — Comfort.

1. May be a matter of prayer.

2. Is provided for in the Lord.

3. Is promised in the word.

4. Is of great value to the believer.

Verse 76. —

1. The need of comfort.

2. The source of comfort: "Thy merciful kindness."

3. The rule of comfort: "According to thy word." — **G.R.**

Verse 77. —

1. Visitors invited.

2. Boon expected.

3. Welcome guaranteed: "for thy law, "etc.

Verse 77. — Divine life — it is born, sustained, increased, by God's tender mercies. — **W.W**

Verse 78. —

1. A hard thing— to make the proud ashamed.

2. A cruel thing— "they dealt per**Verse**ly with me, "etc.

3. A wise thing— "but I will meditate, "etc.

Verse 79. — Restoration to church fellowship.

1. Good men may be in such a case as to need to be restored.

2. They should not be ashamed to seek it.

3. They should pray about it.

Verse 79. — Select society.

1. Sociableness is an instinct of human nature.

2. Sociableness is helpful to a wholesome Christian life.

3. The choice of society should be a subject of prayer. — **C.A.D.**

Verse 80. —

1. David's prayer for sincerity — that his heart might be brought to God's statutes, and that it might be sound in them, not rotten or deceitful.

2. His dread of the consequences of hypocrisy: "that I be not ashamed." Shame is the portion of hypocrites, here or hereafter. — **M. Henry.**

Verse 80. —

1. The heart in religion.

2. The necessity of its being sound in it.

3. The result of such sound heartedness.

Outlines Upon Keywords of The Psalm, by Pastor C. A. Davis.

Verse 81-88. — Hope in depression. In the depression arising from mortal frailness (Ps 119:81-81), and from unjust persecution (Ps 119:85-87), the word of God is the source of joy and comfort.

Verse 81. — Text suitable for a missionary sermon.

1. The condition of the heathen world, enough to make the Christian faint for the salvation of God to visit it.

    (a) The grossness of its darkness.

    (b) Its wide area.

    (c) Its long continuance.

    (d) The limited character and effect of mission labor.

    (e) The opposing influences.

2. This condition, though exceedingly sad, is not hopeless. Because —

(a) Of the intention, adaptation, and universal call of the gospel.

(b) Of Christ's commission to his church.

(c) Of the compassionate character of the spiritually enlightened, produced by their faith in the word.

(d) Of the prophecies and promises. Thus, there is hope in the word.

3. If Christians are fainting for the salvation, but hoping in the word, their interest in mission work will be intense, and will show itself,

(a) In earnest prayer for more laborers, and greater results.

(b) In devoting themselves, if possible, to the work.

(c) In free and generous giving, to help on the work. — **J.F.**

Verse 81. — My soul fainteth, etc. Men faint for health, provision, rest, promotion, success, and in some instances for salvation. David fainted.

1. For his own salvation.

(a) From guilt: "Deliver me from all my transgressions; " "from blood guiltiness."

(b) From defilement: "Create in me a clean heart." "Wash me."

(c) From formality: "Let the words of my mouth, "etc.

(d) From darkness: "Why hidest thou thyself?" "Lift up, " etc. "Say unto my soul, "etc.

(e) From unhappiness: "Out of the depths, " etc.

2. For the salvation of others.

(a) He talked about it: "Time for thee to work, Lord."

(b) He prayed for it: "Oh that the salvation, "etc. "Let thy work, "etc. "God be merciful unto us:" "Save now, I beseech thee."

(c) He labored for it: "I will make mention of thy righteousness:" "I will teach transgressors thy ways." — **W.J.**

Verse 81. —

1. Eagerness of expectation.

2. Energy of hope.

3. Establishment of promise: "In thy word."

Verse 81. — Salvation, in Scripture, hath divers acceptations: it is put—

1. For that temporal deliverance which God giveth, or hath promised to give to his people: so it is taken. Ex 14:13.

2. For the exhibition of Christ in the flesh. Ps 98:2-3 Lu 2:29-30.

3. For the benefits which we have by Christ on this side of heaven; as the pardon of sin, and the renovation of our natures. Mt 1:21; Tit 3:5 Ps 51:12.

4. For everlasting life: "Receiving the end of your faith, even the salvation of your souls" (1Pe 1:9); meaning thereby our final reward. — T. Manton.

Verse 81. —

1. Faint.

2. Pursuing. — **W.D.**

Verse 82. — Answer to the enquiry— When wilt thou comfort me?

1. When your grief has answered its purpose.

2. When you believe.

3. When you leave sin.

4. When you obey.

5. When you submit to my will.

6. When you seek my glory.

Verse 82. —

1. How longingly the believer turns to God for comfort in his affliction: "When wilt thou comfort me?"

2. How intently he gazes upon the Divine promises: "My eyes fail for thy word."

3. How the weariness of waiting cannot wear out his patience, while hope increases his importunity: "When wilt thou?" — **J.F.**

Verse 82. — The pleading of the eyes.

1. How the eyes speak. By "expression" of the moods of the soul, as— longing, Isa 8:17; faith, Isa 45:22 Heb 12:2; expectation, Ps 5:3 Php 3:20 Tit 2:13; love, 2Co 3:18 Joh 1:14.

2. What the eyes say. "When wilt thou comfort me? Brushing aside all other comforters, thou art my sun: my life: my love: my all."

3. How the pleading eyes shall meet the responsive Eye of the Lord: Heb 9:18. In the look of the recognition of grief, Ex 2:25; in the look of pardon, Lu 22:61; of strength giving, Jud 6:14; of complacent love, Isa 66:2. — **C.A.D.**

Verse 83. —

1. The outward man in ill case.

2. Character blackened.

3. Constantly exposed to discomfort.

4. Contents maturing.

Verse 83. — A bottle in the smoke.

1. God's people have their trials.

    (a) From the poverty of their condition.

    (b) Our trials frequently result from our comforts.

    (c) The ministry hath much smoke with it.

    (d) The poor bottle in the smoke keeps there for a long time, until it gets black.

2. Christian men feel their troubles; they are like "bottles" in the smoke.

    (a) The trial that we do not feel is no trial at all.

    (b) Trials which are not felt are unprofitable trials. A bottle in the smoke gets very black, becomes very useless, in an empty bottle.

3. Christians do not, in their troubles, forget God's statutes — the statutes of command, the statutes of promise. Why was it that David still held fast by God's statutes?

    (a) He was not a bottle in the fire, or he would have forgotten them.

    (b) Jesus Christ was in the smoke with him, and the statutes were in the smoke with him, too.

    (c) The statutes were in the soul, where the smoke does not enter. — From "Spurgeon's Sermons." No. 71.

Verse 84. — A solemn question pointing to the shortness of life, the severity of sorrow, the necessity of industry, the nearness of the reward.

Verse 85. — Pits; or, the secret schemes of wicked men against the godly.

Verse 86 (last clause). — A prayer for all occasions. See the many cases in which it is used in Scripture.

Verse 87. —

1. What the good man loses by gaining.

2. What he gains by losing. — **G.R.**

Verse 87. —

1. "Almost, "but not altogether.

2. The saving clause: "I forsook not thy precepts."

Verse 87. — Passing through fires, and the asbestos covering.

Verse 88. —

1. New life is the cause of new obedience.

2. New obedience is the effect of new life. — **G.R.**

Verse 88. — Quickening.

1. Our greatest need.

2. God's most gracious boon.

3. The guarantee of our steadfastness; and so,

4. The promoter of God's glory.

Verse 88. —

1. He closes with a frequent petition: "Quicken thou me— make me alive." All true religion consists in the LIFE of God in the SOUL of man.

2. The manner in which he wishes to be quickened: "After thy lovingkindness." He wishes not to be raised from the death of sin by God's thunder, but by the loving voice of a tender Father.

3. The effect it should have upon him: "So shall I keep the testimony of thy mouth." Whatever thou speakest I will hear, receive, love, and obey. — Adam Clarke.

Outlines Upon Keywords of The Psalm, by Pastor C. A. Davis.

Verse 89-96. — The immutable word of God. Is enthroned in heaven (Ps 119:89), and on earth (Ps 119:90-91), is the salvation of the believer in affliction (Ps 119:92,94), His resource in danger (Ps 119:95), and the embodiment of perfection (Ps 119:96).

Verse 89-92. — The Psalmist here tells us the prescription which soothed his pains and sustained his spirits. Here we have strong consolation.

1. In certain facts which he remembered.

    (a) The eternal existence of God.

    (b) The immutability of his word.

    (c) The faithfulness of the fulfilment of that word.

    (d) The perpetuity of the word in nature.

(e) The perpetuity of the word in experience.

2. The delights which tie experienced in the time of his trouble. In bereavements; when everything seemed shifting and inconstant; when his own faith failed him; when all helpers failed him; he fell back upon the eternal settlements: "O Lord, thy word is settled, "etc. See "Spurgeon's Sermons, "No. 1656: "My Solace in my Affliction."

Verse 89. — Eternal settlements, or, heavenly certainties.

Verse 89. — God's eternal calm (in contrast with earth's mutations) imaged in the starry heavens. — William Bickle Haynes, of Stafford, 1882.

Verse 89. — Consider,

1. The term, "thy word."

> (a) A word is a revealed thought. The Scriptures are just this: the thoughts and purposes of God made intelligible to man.
>
> (b) But a "word" also marks specially unity (it is one word) and wholeness or completeness, a word, not a syllable. The Scriptures are one and complete.

2. The statement, "for ever settled in heaven."

> (a) "Settled in heaven" before it came to earth; therefore it could come as a continuous unfolding, through various dispensations, without the shadow of hesitation or contradiction manifest in it.
>
> (b) Abides "settled in heaven, "for its central revelation; the atonement is a completed fact, and Christ is now in heaven a perfected Savior; thus the word is unalterable.
>
> (c) "For ever settled in heaven." Not only because God in heaven is of one mind and cannot be turned; but because righteousness itself, the righteousness of heaven, demands that an atonement by suffering shall be fully and everlastingly answered by its due reward.

3. The lessons.

> (a) If settled in heaven, men on earth can never unsettle it.
>
> (b) The wicked may not indulge a future hope arising from any new dispensation beyond the grave; God's present word to us cannot then be unsettled.
>
> (c) The godly may rely on a settled word amidst the unsettled experiences and feelings incident to earth. — **J.F.**

Verse 90. — The stability of the earth a present picture of everlasting faithfulness.

Verse 90-91. — Consider,

1. The steadfastness of nature as dependent upon the divine decree: "according to thy ordinances."

2. The subserviency of nature to the divine will: "for all are thy servants."

3. The fixedness of nature's laws, together with their subserviency to God's purposes, as a confirmation of the Christian's faith in the written word, in the care of a divine providence, and in the sureness of spiritual and heavenly things. "Thy faithfulness is, "etc. — **J.F.**

Verse 91. — Our starry monitors. They teach us,

1. To serve: though we cannot shine with their brightness.

2. To do all with strict regard to God's will.

3. To "continue" — "according to thine ordinances." — **W.B.H.**

Verse 91. — The service of nature.

1. Universal: "all are thy servants."

2. Obedient: "according to thy ordinances."

3. Perpetual: "they continue."

4. Derived: "thou hast established the earth."

Verse 92. — The sustaining power of joy in God.

Verse 92. — The word of God as a sustaining power amid the greater sorrows of life.

1. Its necessity.

   (a) For want of it, men have become drunkards to drown their sorrows, have become suicides because life was unbearable, have become broken and hopeless because they had no strength to struggle against misfortune, have become atheists in creed as, alas, they were before in practice; all, in fact, become subject to sorrow's worst bitterness and calamity's worst effects.

   (b) Nothing can supply the place of God's word. Nature throws no light on the mystery of suffering. Human philosophy is at best cold comfort, and when most needed most fails.

2. Its efficiency. Proved—

   (a) In the experience of those who have tried it.

   (b) By the character of its promises.

   (c) By the discovery it makes of a beneficent providence working through calamity and sorrow.

(d) By the revelation it gives of the pity of God and the sympathy of Christ.

(e) By its record of the "Man of sorrows, "who through suffering wrought out man's salvation, and entered into glory.

(f) By its teaching concerning the Incarnate Word; thus showing a suffering God, which may well be a solace to suffering men.

(g) By displaying the glory of heaven and the eternal felicity awaiting those who overcome through the blood of the Lamb. — **J.F.**

Verse 92. — The Godly Man's Ark; or, City of Refuge in the day of his Distress. Discovered in divers (five) Sermons...By Edmund Calamy, B.D...Eighteenth edition. 1709. 12mo.

Verse 92. — We have here set before us by the Psalmist,

1. The case which he had been in, and which he now refers to— one sad and sinking. He was under such affliction that he was ready to perish; which seems to include inward and outward trouble at once; trials without and pressure within.

2. What it was that gave him relief, and this when nothing else could, etc., the law of God.

3. How he looked back upon this relief received, namely, with thankfulness to God, to whom he speaks, and records it for the encouragement and direction of others: "Unless thy law had been my delights, I should then have perished in mine affliction." — Daniel Wilcox, 1676-1733.

Verse 92. — The life buoy. Under the form of the narrative of a shipwrecked mariner, describe the experience of the soul struggling in the sea of affliction; almost overwhelmed: yet buoyed up over each successive billow: and finally saved by clinging to the Word of God. — **C.A.D.**

Verse 92. — The Psalmist's shudder at recollected danger.

1. Sore peril: affliction tending to despair and ruin.

2. Fearful crisis: "then."

3. Many handed help: "thy law my delights." — **W.B.H.**

Verse 93. — Experience fixes the word upon the memory.

Verse 93. —

1. A good resolve: "I will never forget thy precepts."

   (a) The precepts are worth remembering.

   (b) Safety lies in remembering them.

   (c) Fidelity to God cannot be without remembering them.

   (d) Not to remember them is shameful ingratitude.

2. An excellent reason for making it: "For with them thou hast quickened me."

    (a) A reason founded upon personal experience: "me."

    (b) A reason appreciative of the benefit received: "quickened."

    (c) A reason indicative of gratitude to God: "thou." — **J.F.**

Verse 93. — Never forget; an often uttered phrase. Here golden.

1. Something that could not be forgotten: life and pardon received. How could it?

2. Something that should not be forgotten: the precious instrumentality. — **W.B.H.**

Verse 93. —

1. The instrumental power of truth.

    (a) Used by God in our regeneration: Jas 1:18 Ps 19:7.

    (b) Used in our liberation: Joh 8:32.

    (c) Used in our sanctification: Joh 17:7.

2. Our consequent affection for it. We cannot forget.

    (a) Our past obligations to it.

    (b) Our present dependence upon it.

    (c) Our future needs of it. — W.W.

Verse 95. — Wicked men patient in carrying out their evil designs. Good men patient in considering the ways of the Lord.

Verse 95. — The hatred of the wicked towards the righteous.

1. Show that it ever has been, and still is.

    (a) Select Scriptural instances, beginning with Abel.

    (b) Notice the persecutions of the church.

    (c) Treatment in the workshop.

    (d) Often in the home.

    (e) The contemptuous manner the "saints" are spoken of, etc.

2. Enquire as to why it is so.

    (a) The enmity of the carnal heart to God.

    (b) The jealousy excited by the Christian's assurance of eternal blessedness.

(c) The consciousness of being rebuked by a holy life.

(d) Excited to it by Satan.

(e) The restless mischievousness of sin which, if it cannot hinder holiness, will maliciously hurt its advocates.

3. Direct how to act when exposed to it: "I will consider thy testimonies." That means—

(a) Be the more obedient to God.

(b) Have the more watchful control over words and feelings.

(c) Love your enemies.

(d) Pray for those who hate you.

(e) Do good to them on every opportunity.

(f) Be thankful that you are among the hated and not the haters.

(g) Especially consider the holy testimony of Christ's forbearing patience. — **J.F.**

Verse 95. — Waiting counter wrought by waiting.

1. Temptations in ambush.

2. The saint with his Lord. — **W.B.H.**

Verse 95. — Immunity.

1. I am in danger.

2. I will attend to my duty.

3. I will trust thee to deliver me. — **C.A.D.**

Verse 96. —

1. An end: — "seen"; seen by one man; seen where it should not have been; seen where there was no end of boasting; seen in all perfection.

2. No end: — to the extent, spirituality, perpetuity, and perfectness of the law.

Verse 96. —

1. The Finite explored.

2. The Infinite unexplored. — **W.D.**

Verse 96. — Perfectionism disproved by experience and inspiration. — **W.B.H.**

Verse 96. — Perfection — perfect and imperfect.

1. Loud professions of perfection arise from ignorance (of self, or of God's requirements).

2. Are peculiarly liable to collapse: "I have seen an end."

3. Are best corrected by a survey of the breadth of the divine law. — **C.A.D.**

Verse 97. —

1. Unusual Exclamation.

2. Unusual Application. — **W.D.**

Verse 97. — Indescribable love and insatiable thought. The action and reaction of affection and meditation.

Verse 97. —

1. The object of love: "thy law."

2. The degree of that love: "oh, how love I, "etc.

3. The evidence of that love: "it is my meditation, "etc. — **G.R.**

Verse 97. — Love to the law.

1. An ardent confession of love.

2. An unanswerable evidence of love. — **C.A.D.**

Verse 97 (first clause). — Vehemency of love for God's word.

1. Its recognizable marks.

    (a) Profound reverence for the authority of the word.

    (b) Admiration for its holiness.

    (c) Jealousy. For its Honor; God's servant feels acute pain when men show it any slight.

    (d) Respect for its wholeness; he would not divorce precepts from promises, nor ignore a single statement in it.

    (e) Indefatigability in its study.

    (f) Eager desire to obey it.

    (g) Forwardness in praising it.

    (h) Activity in spreading it abroad.

2. Its reasonableness.

    (a) The word well deserves it.

(b) It is a proof of true intelligence.

(c) It is not less than a regard for our own interest demands.

3. Its requisiteness to the true worship of God. Men sneeringly call such an affection bibliolatry, as though it were the worship of a book. In truth, it is an essential element in the due worship of God. For—

(a) Without it there cannot be the faith which Honors God.

(b) It is involved in that love to God which constitutes the very essence of worship.

(c) It is itself an act of homage, that a worshipper dare not withhold. — **J.F.**

Verse 97-100. — Spiritual wisdom.

1. God's word the source of surpassing wisdom— excelling that of "mine enemies, ""my teachers, ""the ancients."

2. The three methods of acquiring this wisdom— love, meditation, practice.

3. The one Giver of this wisdom: "Thou:" Ps 119:98. — **C.A.D.**

Verse 98. — Constant communion with truth the student's road to proficiency.

Verse 98-100. — The truly wise man.

1. The source of his wisdom. The word of "the only wise God, "here described as

(a) Thy commandments.

(b) Thy testimonies.

(c) Thy precepts.

2. The increase of his wisdom. It arises from

(a) The abiding indwelling of the word: "ever with me, " Ps 119:98.

(b) Meditation upon the word, Ps 119:99.

(c) Obedience to the word, Ps 119:100.

3. The measure of his wisdom.

(a) Wiser than his enemies, whose wisdom was "not from above, but earthly, sensual, devilish."

(b) Wiser than his teachers, whose wisdom was "of this world."

(c) Wiser than the ancients, whose wisdom was that of unsanctified age and experience. — W.H.J. Page, of Chelsea, 1882.

Verse 99. — The surest way to excellence.

1. A good subject: "thy testimonies."

2. A good method: "are my meditations."

Verse 100. — Antiquity no security for truth as contrasted with revelation: old age no proof of wisdom as contrasted with holy living: open confession no evidence of boasting as contrasted with sullen pride.

Verse 100. — Obedience the high road to understanding. — **W.B.H.**

Verse 100. — Obedience the key of knowledge. Joh 7:17.

Verse 101. — Self restraint needful to piety.

Verse 102. — Divine teaching necessary to secure perseverance, and effectual to that end.

Verse 102. — Consider, —

1. The path appointed for men to walk in: "Thy judgments."

    (a) Right path.

    (b) Clean path.

    (c) Pleasant path.

    (d) Safe path.

    (e) The end — eternal glory.

2. The persistent pursuit of it: "I have not departed."

    (a) Persecution would drive from it.

    (b) Pleasures would allure from it.

    (c) The flesh would weary in it.

    (d) But the true believer determines to hold on his way to the end.

    (e) And carefully watches his steps lest they depart.

3. The preserving power that holds the traveller to it: "For thou hast taught me."

    (a) The traveller walks with God, and receives instruction by the special illumination of the Holy Spirit.

    (b) The choice property of this teaching is, not only that it makes wise, but that it captivates the soul, strengthens it, and holds it to a holy obedience. — **J.F.**

Verse 103. — Experience in religion the source of enjoyment in it; or,

1. Tasting the word: its sweetness.

2. Declaring the word with the mouth: its greater sweetness.

Verse 103. —

1. The word is positively sweet:" sweet to my taste."

2. Comparatively sweet: "sweeter the honey."

3. Superlatively sweet: "how sweet, "etc. — **G.R.**

Verse 103. — The comparison, setting forth the precious property of sweetness in the word: "Sweeter than honey." "Better than honey, " would not do as well. It is—

1. The purest sweetness; even precepts and rebukes.

2. Uncloying sweetness.

3. Always a beneficial sweetness.

4. A specially grateful sweetness— in affliction, in the hour of death. — **J.F.**

Verse 103. — Spiritual delicacy.

1. The taste needed to relish it.

2. The life that alone is nourished by it.

3. The rare enjoyment derived from it. — G.A.D.

Verse 103. —

1. It is sweet.

2. Let us enjoy it.

3. The best effects will follow. George Herbert says: —

"O Book! infinite sweetness! let my heart

Suck every letter, and a honey gain,

Precious for any grief in any part;

To clear the breast, to mollify all pain."

Verse 103. — If we would taste the honey of God, we must have the palate of faith. — **A.R. Fausset**.

Verse 104. — The influence of the precepts.

1. Upon the understanding.

2. Upon the affections.

3. Upon the life.

Verse 104. —

1. The intellectual effect of the Scriptures: "I get understanding."

2. Their moral effect: "I hate, "etc. — **G.R.**

Verse 104. — The understanding derived from God's precepts begets holy hatred.

1. To the false ways of conventional morality.

2. To the false ways of a formal religiousness.

3. To the false ways of an erring theology.

4. To the false ways of hypocritical practice.

5. To the false ways of sinful suggestions.

6. To the false ways of one's own deceitful heart. — **J.F.**

Outlines Upon Keywords of The Psalm, by Pastor C. A. Davis.

Verses 105-112. — The word a lamp. For guidance (Ps 119:105-106). For life in affliction (Ps 119:107). For preservation in peril of enemies (Ps 119:109-110). For joy of heart (Ps 119:111-112).

Verse 105-108. —

1. Illumination (Ps 119:105).

2. Decision (Ps 119:106).

3. Testing: "I am afflicted" (Ps 119:107).

4. Consecration (Ps 119:108).

5. Education: "teach me, "etc. (Ps 119:108).

Verse 105. — The practical, personal, everyday use of the word of God.

Verse 105. — Lamp light.

1. The believer's dangerous night journey through the world.

2. The lamp that illumines his path.

3. The eternal day towards which he travels (when the lamp will be laid aside: Re 22:5). — **C.A.D.**

Verse 106. — Decision for God, and fit modes of expressing it.

Verse 106. —

1. Veneration for the word.

2. Consecration to the word.

3. Fidelity to the word. — **G.R.**

Verse 106. — Swearing and performing.

1. The usefulness of religious vows. To quicken perception; to rouse conscience; (seen in Jewish nation: Ex 24:37 2Ch 15:12-15 Ne 5:28,29; in Scottish nation— Solemn League and Covenant).

2. The danger of religious vows. A vow unfulfilled, or receded from, is a moral injury: Ec 5:4-7.

3. The safeguard of religious vows: dependence on the Spirit of God: Eze 11:19-20 2Co 4:5. — **C.A.D.**

Verse 107. —

1. A good man greatly afflicted.

2. A sure cute for the ills of affliction: "Quicken me."

3. A safe rule to pray by when afflicted: "according unto thy word."

Verse 107. —

1. The "very much" afflicted.

    (a) The world has such— widows, orphans, etc., etc.

    (b) Most take their turn.

2. But there is "very much" grace.

    (a) God's word promises the needed quickening.

    (b) Himself very much greater than all our needs.

    (c) Christ died "in all points" has all help.

3. Therefore bring "very much" faith, as the Psalmist here.

    (a) Keen eyed for promises.

    (b) Fervent in pleading them.

    (c) Strong in expectation. — **W.B.H.**

Verse 108. — Consider, —

1. The instructive title given to prayer and praise: "The free will offerings of my mouth."

(a) It shows the believer to be a priest: "offerings."

(b) It shows the peculiarity of his service: "free will."

(c) It implies wholehearted consecration.

2. The humility portrayed in the prayer: "Accept, I beseech thee."

(a) Here is no pharisaic boasting.

(b) Even the free will offering is felt to need an "I beseech thee."

3. The longing desire for further instruction in order to a more perfect obedience: "Teach me thy judgments." — J.P.

Verse 108. — Free will seeking free grace. — **W.D.**

Verse 108. — Work for "Free willers".

1. Offerings of Prayer— for each of the blessings of salvation.

2. Offerings of Repudiation— of all claim to unassisted good.

3. Offerings of Praise— for sovereign grace. — **W.B.H.**

Verse 109. — The soul's life in jeopardy. The life of the soul secured.

Verse 109-110. — Here is, —

1. David in danger of losing his life. There is but a step between him and death; for "the wicked have laid a snare" for him. Wherever he was he found some design or other laid against him; which made him say, "My soul is continually in my hand." It was not so only as a man— it is true of us all that we are exposed to the strokes of death— but as a man of war, and especially as "a man after God's own heart."

2. David in no danger of losing his religion through this peril; for,

(a) He "doth not forget the law, "and therefore is likely to persevere.

(b) He hath not yet erred from God's precepts, and therefore it is to be hoped he will not. — **M. Henry.**

Verse 110. — Various kinds of snares, and the one way of escaping them.

Verse 110. — Consider, —

1. Some of the snares set for saints by sinners.

(a) Doctrinal snares, by intellectual sinners.

(b) False accusations, by malignant sinners.

(c) False flatteries, by deceitful sinners.

(d) False charity, by a large number of sinners nowadays.

2. The secure safeguard for a saint's safety: "I erred not from thy precepts." Obedience to God gives security, because—

    (a) The snares are then suspected and watched against.

    (b) The feet cannot become entangled by them.

    (c) God keeps him who keeps his word. — **J.F.**

Verse 111. —

1. Estate.

2. Entering upon it.

3. Entail upon it.

4. Enjoyment of it.

Verse 111. — Notice, —

1. How rich the Psalmist was determined to be: "Thy testimonies have I taken as a heritage." Rich, —

    (a) In knowledge.

    (b) In holiness.

    (c) In comfort.

    (d) In companionship, for God's company goes with his word.

    (e) In hope.

2. How he clung to his wealth: "Forever."

    (a) He hurt none by so doing; he could give generously his portion, and yet not waste.

    (b) He was right; for he had the only wealth of which an everlasting possession is possible.

    (c) He was wise.

3. How he rejoiced in his wealth: "They are the rejoicing of my heart."

    (a) Here is internal and deep joy; not always possible to the possession of wealth.

    (b) Pure, unalloyed joy; it is never so with other wealth.

    (c) Safe joy; other joy is dangerous.

(d) Unloseable joy. — **J.F.**

Verse 112. — Heart leanings. Personality, pressure, inclination, performance, constancy, perpetuity.

Verse 112. — The godly man's obedience.

1. Its reality

    (a) "To perform"; not words or feelings merely; but deeds.

    (b) "Thy statutes"; not human inventions, nor self conceits, nor conventional maxims.

2. Its cordiality: "inclined my heart."

    (a) Heart inclination is requisite for pleasing a heart searching God.

    (b) And to make obedience easy and even delightful.

    (c) "I have, "he says; was it therefore his doing? Yes. Was it his work alone No. See Ps 119:36.

    (d) The proofs. (1) Universality: "statutes, "the whole of them. (2) Uniformity: "alway."

3. Its constancy: "even unto the end."

    (a) Though a man should be cautious when planning for the future, yet this life long purpose is right, wise, and safe.

    (b) Nor can he purpose less, if holy fervency fill the heart.

    (c) It is no more than what God and consistency demand. — **J.F.**

Outlines Upon Keywords of The Psalm, by Pastor C. A. Davis.

Verse 113-120. — Vain thoughts contrasted with God's law. The believer takes sides (Ps 119:113-115); prays for upholding in the law (Ps 119:116-117); contemplates the fate of the followers of vain thoughts (Ps 119:118-119); and expresses the godly fear thereby inspired (Ps 119:120).

Verse 113. — The thought of the age, and the truth of all ages.

Verse 113. —

1. The object of hatred.

2. The object of love.

OR

1. Love the cause of hatred.

2. Hatred the effect of love. — **G.R.**

Verse 113. — Vain thoughts. What they are. Whence they arise. The mischief they cause. How they should be treated. — **W.H.J.P.**

Verse 113. — How the believer—

1. Is troubled by vain thoughts. A frequent and painful experience:

2. Does not tolerate vain, thoughts. Some, suffer them to lodge within; he is anxious to expel them.

3. Triumphs over vain thoughts. By his love to the law of God. His prayer is—"With thoughts of Christ and things divine, Fill up this foolish heart of mine." — **W.H.J.P.**

Verse 114. — Our protection from danger— "hiding-place"; in danger — "shield"; before danger— "I hope."

Verse 114. — Hiding place. Secrecy to conceal us. Capacity to hold us. Safety. Comfort. — T. Manton.

Verse 114. — Hiding and hoping.

1. A hiding place needed.

2. A hiding place provided (Isa 25:14 32:2).

3. A hiding place used. — **C.A.D.**

Verse 114. —

1. The refuge provided: "Thou art, "etc.

2. The refuge revealed: "In thy word."

3. The refuge found: "I hope, "etc. — **G.R.**

Verse 114. — Thou art my hiding place.

1. In thy grace, from condemnation.

2. In thy compassion, from sorrow.

3. In thy succour, from temptation.

4. In thy power, from opposition.

5. In thy fulness, from want. — W.J.

Verse 115. —

1. Ill company hinders piety.

2. Piety quits ill company.

3. Piety, in compelling this departure, acts as God will do at the last.

Verse 115. — Evil companionship incompatible with genuine righteousness.

1. They necessitate concealment and compromise.

2. They destroy the capability of communion with God, and the relish for spiritual things.

3. They blunt the sensitiveness of conscience.

4. They involve deliberate disobedience to God. — **J.F.**

Verse 116. —

1. Upholding promised.

2. Needful for holy living.

3. The preventive of shameful acts.

Verse 116. — Uphold me according unto thy word, etc.

1. The Psalmist pleads the promise of God, his dependence upon the promise, and his expectation from it :"Uphold me according unto thy word, "which word I hope in and if it be not performed I shall be "ashamed of my hope."

2. He pleads the great need he had of God's grace, and the great advantage it would be to him: "Uphold me, that I may live"; intimating that he could not live without the grace of God. — **M. Henry.**

Verse 117. —

1. Upholding — God's holding us up. It implies a danger, and that danger takes many forms. The believer's life may be described as walking in uprightness; he is a pilgrim. He needs upholding, for —

   (a) The way is slippery.

   (b) Our feet make the danger as well as the way.

   (c) Cunning foes seek to trip us up.

   (d) Sometimes the difficulty is not caused by the way, but by the height to which God may elevate us.

   (e) The prayer is all the more needful because the most of people do not keep upright.

2. Two blessed things that come out of this holding up.

   (a) We shall be safe for ourselves, as examples, and as pillars of the church.

(b) We shall be watchful and sensitive: "I will have respect unto thy statutes continually." Without this no man is safe. See "Spurgeon's Sermons, "No. 1657: "My Hourly Prayer."

Verse 117. — Hold thou me up, etc.

1. The good man is up.

2. The good man wishes to keep up.

3. The good man prays to be held up.

4. The good man knows that divine support is abundantly sufficient. — W.J.

Verse 117. —

1. Dependence for the future: "Hold, "etc.

2. Resolution for the future: "I will have, "etc. — **G.R.**

Verse 118. — Sin and falsehood: their connection, punishment, and cure.

Verse 118. —

1. Hearken to the tramp of God's armies. In nature; providence; angelic hosts of last day.

2. The mangled victims. Cunning deceivers specially obnoxious to God. Examples: Balaam, Pharaoh, Rome, the deceiver of the nations.

3. The warnings to us of this Aceldama. Repent. Avoid deceit. Mind God's landmarks. Hide in Christ. — **W.B.H.**

Verse 118. — God's punishment of the wicked though awfully severe is just and necessary.

1. It is due as the merited wages of iniquity.

2. It is demanded by the position of God as moral governor, and by his character as righteous.

3. It is necessary to mark the real worth of righteousness and its reward. If the wicked are not punished, the full worth of righteousness cannot appear.

4. In the nature of the case, it is absolutely unavoidable, except upon one condition, namely, the gift of genuine repentance and holiness after death; that no man has any right to expect, nor has God given the slightest intimation that he will bestow if.
5. Hell lies in the bosom of sin; and if the wicked were taken to heaven, they would carry hell thither. Heaven supplies not the things in which the wicked delight, while it abounds in those they can neither understand nor sympathise with. — **J.F.**

Verse 118 (second clause). — The deceits of the wicked are all falsehoods.

1. The world they embrace is a false Delilah.

2. The pleasure they enjoy is a Satanic snare.

3. Their formal religiousness is a vain delusion.

4. Their conceits of God are self invented lies. — **J.F.**

Verse 118-120. — Saved by fear.

1. The wrath of God revealed against sin.

2. The judgment of God executed upon sinners.

3. The fear of God created in the heart. — G.A.D.

Verse 119. — An insight into the divine will, the best assistance in our journey through the earth. Or, what I am; where I am; where I am going; how am I to get there?

Verse 119 (first clause). — The stranger in the earth.

1. A short exposition. The text means, —

    (a) That the saint is not born of the earth.

    (b) That the saint is not known on earth.

    (c) The saint's portion is not upon the earth.

    (d) The saint is compassed with sorrows and trials upon earth.

    (e) The saint is soon to leave the earth.

2. A short application.

    (a) Do not be like the world.

    (b) Be prepared to be a sufferer on the earth.

    (c) Sit loose to the world.

    (d) Correspond with home.

    (e) Cherish brotherly love for your fellow strangers on the earth.

    (f) Hasten home.

    (g) Press others to come with you.

    — Duncan Macgregor's Sermon in "The Shepherd in Israel, "1869.

Verse 119. — The stranger's prayer.

1. How he came to be a stranger in the earth. He was born again. He learned the manners of his foreign home. He spoke the language of his Fatherland; and so was misunderstood and rejected on earth.

2. How he longed after everything homelike. Home rules: "thy commandments." Home teaching: "hide not." Specially his Father's voice.

3. How in his loneliness he solaced himself by communication with his Father.

4. Would you not like to be a stranger? — **C.A.D.**

Verse 119. — The saint's acquiescence in God's judgments. — **W.B.H.**

Verse 119. —

1. Comparison of the wicked to dross.

2. Comparison of their doom to the putting away of dross.

3. The saint's admiration of divine justice as seen in the rejection of the wicked.

Verse 119. — God's putting away the wicked like dross.

1. God's judgments are a searching and separating fire.

2. The final judgment of the great day will complete the separating process.

3. The great result will be, the true metal and the dross, each gathered to its own place. — **J. F.**

Verse 120. — The judgments of God on the wicked cause in the righteous,

1. Love.

2. Awe.

3. Fear.

Verse 120. —

1. Describe the true character of the fear.

   (a) It is the fear of reverence for God's authority and power.

   (b) It is the fear of horror against sin as meriting judgment.

2. Show its compatibility with filial love.

   (a) The more we love God the more firmly we believe in the certainty and awfulness of his judgments.

   (b) The more we love God the more will we fear to arouse his chastising rod against ourselves.

   (c) In fact, if we love not God, we shall have no fear lest sin should involve us in judgment.

3. Commend it.

(a) As it proves a just sense of sin's desert.

(b) As it shows a true appreciation of God's righteousness.

(c) As it is not a fear that hath torment, but a fear which increases watchfulness, and walks hand in hand with perfect confidence in saying grace. — **J.F.**

PSALM 119 (part 3 vv. 121-176)

Verses 121-128. — The just man's prayer against injustice. Out of the prison of oppression he appeals to God to be his surely (Ps 119:121-122); utters his weary longing for deliverance (Ps 119:123-125); points to the "time" (Ps 119:126); and professes his supreme love for God's law in contrast to the oppressors' contempt of it (Ps 119:127-128).

Outlines Upon Keywords of The Psalm, by Pastor C. A. Davis.

Verse 121-122. — The double appeal.

1. Of conscious integrity: "I have done judgment, "etc.

2. Of conscious deficiency: "Be surety for thy servant for good." — **C.A.D.**

Verse 122. —

1. Suretyship entreated.

2. Good expected.

3. Obligation acknowledged: "thy servant."

Verse 122 (first clause). — After explaining the Psalmist's meaning as shown in the preceding **Verse**, this sentence may be used for a sermon upon the Suretyship of Christ, by a reference to Heb 7:22.

1. A Surety for good wanted — the deeply felt, though, perhaps, undefined want of a sin burdened soul.

> (a) The mere statement of a gratuitous pardon on the part of God is not thoroughly believable to such a soul, nor, if it could be believed in, would it give peace to the conscience. For, on the one hand, the pardon could not be perceived as just, nor as consistent with God's necessary hatred of sin, yet the conscience demands this perception; on the other hand, mere pardon does not show how the obligation to a perfect fulfilment of God's law, as righteousness, can be met, yet the conscience demands to see this before it can be satisfied to realize peace Luther's experience.

> (b) Now the Scriptures tell us that God "justifies the ungodly, "and that his "righteousness" is declared in his justifying sinners: Ro 3:25. He can forgive sins with justice. He can treat sinners as righteous persons, and yet bo righteous in doing so. How? By a Surety. Therefore, a Surety is the real want.

2. A Surety existent. Jesus is the Surety.

> (a) He undertook to bear our obligation to the law's penalty, and fulfilled it in death. Thus pardon, though mercy to us, is an act of justice to Christ.

> (b) He undertook our obligation to a perfect obedience, and satisfied for that in his fulfilment of the law; thus for God to treat us as righteous is only just to Christ.

(c) God has shown his satisfaction with the office of Christ, and with his work, by the resurrection and glorification of Christ. Hence a well accredited and efficient Surety exists.

3. A Surety nigh at hand.

(a) In the gospel, Christ as Surety comes to the sinner as truly as though he himself left his throne and came in his own person.

(b) Thus, he is so close that a sinner has but to receive the gospel into his heart and he receives Christ.

(c) Christ received as a Surety is the Surety for whosoever receives him. — **J.F.**

Verse 123. — Holy expectation — long maintained, in danger of failing; this fact pleaded; reasons for never renouncing it.

Verse 124-125. — The servant of God.

1. Making profession: "I am thy servant."

2. Making confession — of guilt, dulness, ignorance.

3. Making petition — for mercy, understanding, and teaching. — **C.A.D.**

Verse 124. — Heavenly instruction a great mercy.

Verse 124. —

1. His confidence in divine mercy.

2. His submission to divine authority.

3. His prayer for divine teaching. — **G.R.**

Verse 124. — A Perfect Prayer.

1. As to the matter of it.

(a) Here is nothing superfluous; no petition for wealth, nor for Honors, nor for anything the worldling covets.

(b) Here is nothing wanting; "Deal with thy servant according to thy mercy" comprehends everything the guilty soul needs; "Teach me thy statutes" comprehends all a saint needs to be anxious for.

2. As to the manner of it.

(a) It is direct and definite.

(b) It is simple and fervent.

(c) It is reverent yet bold.

3. As to the spirit of it.

(a) "Deal with thy servant"; a sense of obligation; a feeling of devotedness; a spirit of consecration to holy work.

(b) "Deal...according to thy mercy"; a sense of unworthiness; becoming humility; submissiveness to the divine will as to what form the mercy shall take; great faith in the mercy, its freeness and sufficiency.

(c) "Teach me thy statutes." Longing for holiness, sense of ignorance, of weakness, of dependence upon special divine spiritual influence. — **J.F.**

Verse 125. —

1. An office accepted.

2. Fitness requested.

3. Discernment desired.

Verse 125. —

1. A cheerful acknowledgment: "I am thy servant."

2. A desire implied — to serve more perfectly.

3. A need recognized — Divine instruction in holy service.

4. A plea urged: "I am thy servant, "therefore "Teach me, "etc. — **W.H.J.P.**

Verse 126-128. —

1. A terrible fact: "They have made void thy law": Ps 119:126.

2. Two blessed inferences: "Therefore, ""Therefore, "etc.: Ps 119:127-128.

Verse 126. — They make void the law, by denying inspiration, by exalting tradition, by antinomianism, by scepticism, by indifference, etc.

Verse 126. —

1. There are times when sin is specially active and dominant.

2. Such times reveal the dependence of the church upon God.

3. Such times awaken the desires of the church for the intervention of God.

4. Such times are the times when God does arise to plead his own cause. — **W.H.J.P.**

Verse 126. —

1. The work anticipated — the vindication of the divine law.

2. The work delayed.

3. The work executed: "It is time," etc. — **G.R.**

Verse 127. — The world's assault upon the truth a reason for our loving it.

Verse 127. —

1. The object of love: "Thy commandments."

2. The degree of love: "above gold, "etc.

3. The reason of this love: "therefore, "etc., because its object must ultimately prevail. — **G.R.**

Verse 127. — God's will versus the golden idol.

1. God's commandments are better than gold.

2. The love of them is proportionably nobler.

3. The unmeasurable superiority of character they produce. — **W.B.H.**

Verse 128 (first clause). — This view should be taken of all divine precepts in their bearing,

1. Toward Christ.

2. Toward Self.

3. Toward the World.

4. Toward the Church.

5. Toward Heaven. — W.J.

Verse 128. — The Bible right.

1. Its science is correct.

2. Its history is true.

3. Its promises are genuine.

4. Its morality is perfect.

5. Its doctrines are divine. — W.J.

Verse 128. Learn four lessons, —

1. It is a good thing when wicked men do not praise the truth they cannot love.

2. It is a suspicious circumstance when they are found speaking well of any part of it; it is a Judas' kiss in order to betray its interests.

3. It must be right to accept and love what the wicked oppose.

4. It is always safe to be on the opposite side to them. — J.F

Outlines Upon Keywords of The Psalm, by Pastor C. A. Davis.

Verse 129-136. — The wonderfulness of God's testimonies. (Ps 119:129), instanced as light giving (Ps 119:130), pantingly longed (Ps 119:131). An appeal for divine ordering in the word (Ps 119:132-135) at its rejection by others (Ps 119:136).

Verse 129-136. — In this division the Psalmist —

1. Praises God's word.

2. Shows his affection to it.

3. Prays for grace to keep it.

4. Mourns for those who do not. — **Adam Clarke.**

Verse 129. — The wonderful character of the word a reason for obedience. So wonderfully pure, just, balanced, elevating. So much for our own benefit, for the good of society, and for the divine glory.

Verse 129. —

1. What is wonderful in God's word should be believed.

2. What is believed should be obeyed. — **G.R.**

Verse 129. — Thy testimonies are wonderful.

1. The facts which they record are wonderful — so wonderful, that, if the book recording them were now published for the first time, there would be no bounds to the avidity and curiosity with which it would be sought and perused.

2. The morality which they inculcate is wonderful.

3. If you turn from the morality to the doctrines of the Bible, your admiration will rather increase than diminish at the contents of the singular book.

4. These testimonies are wonderful for the style in which they are written.

5. They are wonderful for their preservation in the world.

6. They are wonderful for the effects which they have produced. — Hugh Hughes, 1838.

Verse 129. —

1. Thy testimonies are wonderful. The ceremonial law is wonderful, because the mystery of our redemption by the blood of Christ is pointed out in it.

2. The prophecies are wonderful, as predicting things, humanly speaking, so uncertain, and at such great distance of time, with so much accuracy.

3. The decalogue is wonderful, as containing in a very few words all the principles of justice and charity.

4. Were we to go to the New Testament, here wonders rise on wonders! All is astonishing; but the Psalmist could not have had this in view. — Adam Clarke.

Verse 129 (first clause). —

1. Let us look at five of the wonders of the Bible.

> (a) Its authority. It prefaces every statement with a "Thus saith the Lord."
>
> (b) Its light.
>
> (c) Its power — it has a convincing, awakening, drawing, life giving power.
>
> (d) Its depth.
>
> (e) Its universal adaptation.

2. Indicate three practical uses.

> (a) Study the Bible daily.
>
> (b) Pray for the Spirit to grave it on your heart with a pen of iron.
>
> (c) Practice it daily. — D. Macgregor.

Verse 129. — To whom and in what respects are God's testimonies wonderful?

1. To whom? To those, and those only, who through grace do know, believe, and experience the truth and power of them for themselves.

2. In what respects wonderful, i.e., astonishingly pleasing, delightful, and profitable (see Ps 119:174).

> (a) In respect of the Author and origin of them, whose they are and from whence they come.
>
> (b) In respect of the subject matter of them, which they contain and reveal.
>
> (c) In respect of the manner of language in which they are revealed and declared.
>
> (d) In respect of the multitude and variety of them suited to every case.
>
> (e) In respect of the usefulness of them, and the great benefit and advantage he received from them.
>
> (f) In the respect of the pleasure and delight he finds in them (see Ps 119:111).

(g) In respect of the final design, intent, and end of them: viz., eternal life, salvation, and glory. — Samuel Medley, 1738-1799.

Verse 130. —

1. The essential light of the word.

2. The dawn of it in the soul.

3. The great benefit of its advancing day.

Verse 130. —

1. The source of divine light to man: "Thy words."

2. Its force. It forces an entrance into the heart.

3. Its direction: "unto the simple."

4. Its effect: "it giveth understanding." — **G.R.**

Verse 130. — A Bible Society Sermon.

1. Evidence from history and from personal experience that God's word has imparted the light of civilization, liberty, holiness.

2. Argument drawn from hence for the further spread of the word of God. — G.A.D.

Verse 130. — The Self evidencing Virtue of God's Word.

1. Prove it. "Entrance of thy word giveth light." If this be true, God's word is light for only light can give light. But light is self evidencing; it needs nothing to show its presence and its value but itself; so the word of God, show its own truth and divinity to the belie **Verse**

(a) His conscience it; in its convictions of sin; in its peace through the stoning blood.

(b) heart proves it; in its outgoings of love to the God, the Christ, and righteousness revealed.

(c) His experience in affliction and temptation it; in the solace and in the strength given by the word.

2. Answer an objection. "If God's word were self evidencing as light is, then everyone would acknowledge it to be truth." Answer, No; for the law holds good universal experience, that the "entrance" only of light gives light. Light cannot enter a blind man.

(a) The Scriptures teach that men by nature blind.

(b) If all men did perceive, by merely reading and hearing word, that it was light and truth, paradoxical as it may seem, the would not be truth.

(c) Hence the want of universal acknowledgment is an objection, but a confirmation.

3. Show its importance.

    (a) It the believer independent of church authority for his faith.

    (b) He need trouble to examine books of evidence; his faith is valid enough them.

    (c) He who receives the word into his soul shall be satisfied of truth and value. — **J.F.**

Verse 131. — Panting for holiness. A rare hunger; the evidence of much grace, and the pledge of glory.

Verse 132. —

1. Look.

2. Love.

3. Use and wont.

Verse 132. — Fellowship with the righteous.

1. There are some who love God's name.

2. His mercy is the source of all the goodness they experience.

3. The Lord has been always accustomed to deal mercifully with them.

4. His mercy towards them should encourage us to implore mercy for ourselves.

5. We should be anxious to secure the mercy that is peculiar to them.

6. We should be content if God deals with us as he has always dealt with his people. — W. Jay.

Verse 132. — Divine use and wont.

1. God is accustomed to look upon and be merciful toward his people.

2. We are stirred up to specially desire such merciful dealings in time of affliction.

3. Love to God qualifies us for these loving looks and merciful dealings. — **C.A.D.**

Verse 132. — Notice, —

1. The mark of true believers: "Those that love thy name."

2. God's custom of dealing with them: "Be merciful as thou usest to do."

3. Their individual and earnest solicitude: "Look thou upon me." — **J.F.**

Verse 133. —

1. A holy life is no work of chance, it is a masterpiece of order— the order of conformity to the prescribed rule; there is arithmetical and geometrical order; the proportional order; the order of relation; an order of period: holiness, as to its order, is seasonable, suitable.

2. The rule of this order: "in thy word."

3. The director chosen. See "Spurgeon's Sermons, "No. 878: "A Well ordered Life."

Verse 133. —

1. Order in outward life desired.

2. Order according to the divine idea.

3. Order in the government within.

Verse 133. —

1. Help needed.

    (a) To avoid sin.

    (b) To be holy.

2. Help sought.

    (a) From below: "thy word."

    (b) From above: "order, "etc., and "let not, "etc. — **G.R.**

Verse 133. — Sin's sway in the soul.

1. Fervently deprecated.

    (a) Realization of the horrors of its rule.

    (b) Recognition of the better power.

    (c) Thorough exclusion sought.

2. Wisely combated.

    (a) Practicalness as well as prayerfulness.

    (b) Regard had to little "steps."

3. Steps to be governed by divine rule.

4. System not trusted apart from God. — **W.B.H.**

Verse 133. — Notice, —

1. The right path for human feet: "In thy word."

2. The needed help to control the steps: "Order my steps."

3. The perverting power of a dominant sin: "Let not any, "etc. — **J.F.**

Verse 134. — What sins may be produced by oppression. What obedience ought to come from those who are set free.

Verse 134. —

1. The course to he pursued: "thy precepts."

2. The opposition to that course: "the oppression of men."

    (a) Human opinions.

    (b) Human examples.

3. Human sympathies.

4. Interests.

5. Persecutions.

6. The resistance to that opposition: "Deliver me, so will I, "etc. — **G.R.**

Verse 134. — Hindrances removed.

1. The impeding influence of persecution.

2. The prayer of the persecuted one.

3. The conduct of the delivered one (Lu 1:74,75). — **G.A.D.**

Verse 134. —

1. How some men oppress their fellows. By the laws they make — as statesmen. By the books they write — as authors. By the tyranny they exercise — as masters. By the lives they live — as professors. By the sermons they deliver — as ministers!

2. How the prayer of the oppressed may be answered. By the gift of wise and good statesmen. By increase of sound literature. By the conversion or removal of hard masters. By a baptism of the Spirit on the church. — **W.W.**

Verse 135. —

1. A choice position: "thy servant."

2. A choice delight: "thy face to shine."

3. A choice privilege: "teach me thy statutes."

Verse 135. —

1. God in the word: "Thy word."

2. God for the word: "Teach me, "etc.

3. God with the word: "Make thy face, "etc. — **G.R.**

Verse 135. — Sunshine.

1. The light in which we can best learn our lessons — God's Favor shown in pardon, justification, adoption, assurance, etc.

2. The lessons we should learn in the light — grace is productive of holiness. — **C.A.D.**

Verse 135. —

1. A rich historic promise (Nu 6:25). Its sublime origin and associations.

2. The new prayer born of it.

    (a) Looks up for the face Divine; the same in its majestic sweetness that has watched generations decay since the word was first spoken.

    (b) Asks to know its shining. Light of fatherhood, etc.

3. The old prayer repeated: "Teach me thy statutes." Last time in the psalm.

    (a) Our need of teaching — oft repeated prayer.

    (b) The intimate connection between obedience and the shining of God's face. — **W.B.H.**

Verse 136. — Abundant sorrow for abounding sin. Other men's sins the saint's own sorrows. He thinks of the good God provoked, of the sinners themselves debased, of their death, and their perdition.

Verse 136. —

1. Occasion of his grief: "they keep not thy law."

2. Extent of his grief: "rivers, "etc. See examples in Jeremiah, Ezra, Paul, Christ himself.

3. Effect of his grief. To warn, teach, invite, and exhort them — as in his psalms. — **G.R.**

Verse 136. — Sacred tears.

1. The world sinning.

2. The church weeping.

3. It is time the world began to weep for itself. — **C.A.D.**

Verse 136.

I weep, because,

1. Of the disHonor done to the Law gi**Verse**

2. Of the injury done to the law breaker.

3. Of the wrong done to the law abiding.

"That kingly prophet, that wept so plentifully for his own offences (Ps 6:6), had yet floods of tears left to bewail his people's" (Ps 119:136). — Thomas Adams.

"Benedetti, a Franciscan monk, author of the Stabat Mater, one day was found weeping, and when asked the reason of his tears, he exclaimed, I weep because Love goes about unloved." — **W.H.J.P.**

Outlines Upon Keywords of The Psalm, by Pastor C. A. Davis.

Verse 137-144. — The righteousness of God and his word. (Ps 119:137-138). Indignation at the forgetfulness of the enemies (Ps 119:139) The purity of the word (Ps 119:140-141). This righteousness of God and his testimonies is everlasting (Ps 119:142-144).

Verse 137-138. — Solemn contemplation.

1. The contemplation of the deep and awful display of the divine character is good for the soul.

2. It will lead to a conviction of the righteousness of God's character and administration.

3. It will result in loyal submission. — **C.A.D.**

Verse 137. — A consideration of divine righteousness. Convinces us of sin, reconciles us to trying providence, excites a desire to imitate, arouses to reverent adoration.

Verse 137. — God is righteous.

1. In his commands.

2. In his threatenings.

3. In his chastisement.

4. In his judgments.

5. In his promises. — **G.R.**

Verse 138. — Very faithful. Based on a faithful covenant; confirmed by faithful promises; carried out by a faithful Redeemer; enjoyed hitherto; relied on for the future. "Though we believe not, yet he abideth faithful."

Verse 139. — Zeal.

1. Consuming self.

2. Inflamed by that which would naturally quench it.

3. Fed upon God's words.

Verse 139. — Zeal.

1. Flourishing in an unpromising atmosphere.

2. Attaining an astonishing growth.

3. Accomplishing a blessed work — the consumption of self. — **C.A.D.**

Verse 139. —

1. The object of his zeal: "Thy words."

2. The occasion of his zeal: "Mine enemies, "etc.

3. The fervour of his zeal: "My zeal hath consumed me." — **G.R.**

Verse 140. —

1. An awakened sinner adoring the holy law.

2. A saint loving it because the pure love the pure.

3. A saint among sinners loving the law all the more for its contrast.

Verse 140. —

1. The crystal stream.

    (a) Flows from under the throne.

    (b) Mirrors heaven.

    (c) Undefiled through the ages.

    (d) Nourishes holiness as it flows.

2. The enraptured pilgrim.

    (a) Keeping by its brink.

    (b) Delighted with its lucid depths.

3. Pleased with its mirrored revelations — self, heaven, God.

4. Cleansed and refreshed by its waters. — **W.B.H.**

Verse 140. —

1. The purity of God's Word.

    (a) It proceeds from a perfectly pure source: "Thy word."

(b) It reveals a purity otherwise unknown.

(c) It treats impure subjects with absolute purity.

(d) It inculcates the most perfect purity.

(e) It produces such purity in those who are subject to its power. —

2. The love which its purity inspires in gracious souls.

(a) They love it because, while it reveals their natural impurity, it shows them how to escape from it.

(b) They love it because it conforms them to its own purity.

(c) They love it because to a pure heart the purity of the word is one of its chief commendations. —

3. The evidences of this love to the pure word.

(a) Desire to possess it in its purity.

(b) Subjection to its spirit and teachings.

(c) Zeal for its Honor and diffusion. — **W.H.J.P.**

Verse 141-144. — A mournful song arid a joyful refrain. Stanza 1: "I am small and despised." Refrain. The everlasting righteousness of God. Stanza 2: "Trouble and anguish have seized me." Refrain: The everlasting righteousness of God. — **C.A.D.**

Verse 141. — Here is—

1. David pious, and yet poor. He was a man after God's own heart, and yet "small and despised" in his own account and in account of many others.

2. David poor and yet pious; "small and despised" for his strict and serious godliness; yet his conscience can witness for him, that he "did not forget God's precepts." — **M. Henry.**

Verse 141. —

1. The source of man's littleness is in himself.

2. The source of his greatness is in the Divine word. Hence the greatest philosopher is a small man compared with the most uneducated whose delight is in the law of God, and who meditates, etc. — **G.R.**

Verse 141. —

1. A little scholar.

2. A quick learner.

3. A firm reminder.

Verse 141. — Unknown, yet well known.

1. The estimate formed of the believer by the world.

2. The estimate formed of the believer by himself.

3. The profession made by the believer to God.

4. On a review, a revised estimate of the believer: 1Co 1:27 Jas 4:5. — **C.A.D.**

Verse 142. — Righteousness, immutability, and truth combined in the revelation of God.

Verse 143. — Mingled emotions.

Verse 143. —

1. The dark cloud. Trouble, etc.

2. His silver lining. Yet, etc.

Verse 143. —

1. The Saint cast into prison.

   (a) The jailers: "Trouble and anguish."

   (b) Their proceeding: "take hold" and make him fast.

2. Songs in the night.

   (a) Blessed theme: "thy commandments."

   (b) Ecstatic melodies: "delights."

3. Let the prisoners hear them.

   (a) Pain held, sin held, despair held.

   (b) It is matter and melody to open prisons. — **W.B.H.**

Verse 143. — Consider, —

1. The excellency of the word, in that it gives delight when trouble and anguish oppress.

2. The great kindness of God in so framing his word that it can give delight at such a time, and under such circumstances.

3. The disposition of the believer to resort to the word for delight, when others give themselves over to vain grief and despondency.

4. The blessed position of the believer, in that he need never be without joy. — **J.F.**

Verse 144. — Everlasting righteousness revealed in the word, and producing everlasting life in believers.

Verse 144. —

1. Eternal truths.

2. Eternal life dependent upon them.

3. A cry from amid these everlasting hills. — **W.B.H.**

Verse 144 (last clause). —

1. Consider the prayer in its simplicity.

   (a) It is suitable for the awakened sinner.

   (b) For the Christian struggling against temptation.

   (c) For the suffering believers.

   (d) For the worker

   (e) For aspiring minds in the church of God.

   (f) For expiring saints.

2. The prayer more fully opened up.

   (a) Here is want confessed.

   (b) The prayer is evidently put upon the footing of free grace: "Give."

3. Lay bare the argument in the prayer.

1. The word of God, when practically and experimentally understood, is a pledge of life.

2. The word of God is the incorruptible "seed" which liveth and abideth forever.

3. It is the food of life.

4. It is the very flower and crown and glory of true life.

5. It is righteous.

6. It is everlasting. See "Spurgeon's Sermons, "No. 1572: "Alive."

Outlines Upon Keywords of The Psalm, by Pastor C. A. Davis.

Verse 145-152. — The believer's cry. The reiterated cry (Ps 119:145-148) An appeal for audience (Ps 119:149). The nearness of the enemy (Ps 119:150). But, in response to the cry, God is also near (Ps 119:151).

Verse 145-148. — The cry.

1. Whence it came: from my heart.

2. Whither it went: to the Lord.

3. When it was heard: at dawn and dark.

4. What it sought: hearing, salvation.

5. What it promised: obedience.

6. How it was sustained: by hope in God's word. — **C.A.D.**

Verse 145,146. — The souls cry.

1. The depth from which it rose.

2. The height it reached.

Verse 145,146. — Childlike prayer.

1. In its ring: "I cried."

2. In its directness: "to thee."

3. In its outburst: "whole heart."

4. In its outcries: "hear me"; "save me."

5. In its promise of better behaviour: "I will keep thy statutes." — **W.B.H.**

Verse 145. —

1. The model of player: "I cried with my whole heart."

2. The object of prayer: "Hear me, O Lord."

3. The accompaniment of prayer: "I will keep thy statutes."

Verse 146. —

1. Prayer remembered.

2. Prayer continued: "Save me."

3. Prayer yielding fruit: "I shall keep, "etc.

Verse 146. — Salvation.

1. A likely path to it— prayer: cry on.

2. The proper place for it: "unto thee"; not man, not the heart.

3. A sound view of it: "keep thy testimonies." Not to escape hell, or gain heaven, but to please and love God. — **W.B.H.**

Verse 147,148. —

1. The heavenly Companions: prayer and meditation. Inseparable. Mutually helpful.

2. Their Favorite seasons: times of stillness; night; the hour before day.

3. Their volume and night lamp: "Thy word;" "Hope." Or—

> a) A grand plea: "Thy lovingkindness." Who can match it? Who can measure it? Who can mar it?
>
> b) An insignificant pleader: "my voice.' What can "my voice" ever say to keep step with "thy loving kindness"? Asking too much out of the question.
>
> c) A clever petition ("according to thy judgment"); requesting life; stolen from God's mouth. God's lovingkindness is matched by God's own promise. W. B. H.

Verse 147. Observe in this David's diligence. 1) That it was a personal, closet, or secret prayer; "I cried"; I alone, with thee in secret. 2) That it was an early morning prayer: "I prevented the dawning of the morning." 3) That it was a vehement and earnest prayer; for it is expressed by crying. — T. Manton

Verse 147— Early rising commended.

1) A fit time for prayer.

2) For reading the word.

3) For indulging the emotions excited by it: "I hoped in they word."

Verse 148. — The Inexhaustibleness of the Bible. A sermon by Henry Melvill, at "The Golden Lecture." 1850.

Verse 148. — Meditation. Appropriate time, and fruitful subject.

Verse 148. — Meditation in the word well worth self denial and care on the part of the Christian.

1. Without meditation reading is a waste of time and an indignity offered to the word.

2. Meditation with prayer, but not prayer without meditation, will discover the sense of the word, when all other means fail; and it has this advantage, that the meaning sinks into the mind.

3. Meditation extracts sweetness from the promises, and nourishment from the whole truth.

4. Meditation makes a wise teacher and an efficient worker of one who has little natural skill or learning.

5. Meditation subjects the soul to the sanctifying power of the word.

6. Meditation is an invitation to the Holy Spirit to bless the soul, for he is closely associated with the truth, and delights to see the truth honored. — **J.F.**

Verse 149. — Prayer — hearing the result of love; prayer — answering ruled by wisdom.

Verse 149. — Quickening.

1. A prayer of unquestionable necessity: "quicken me."

2. Twin pleas of irresistible power: "thy lovingkindness:" "thy judgment." — **C.A.D.**

Verse 149. — The two accordings.

1. The "according, "to which a believer hopes to be heard by God: "Hear my voice according unto thy loving kindness."

   (a) The believer is fully aware of his own unworthiness, and the imperfections of his prayers, therefore he would have God to accept him and interpret them after the rule of his own lovingkindness.

   (b) Nor does he hope in vain; God's loving kindness overlooks the imperfections, and supplies the omissions.

   (c) What a blessed thing it is, that while the Holy Spirit helps our infirmities, the groanings that cannot be uttered are read in their true meaning by divine lovingkindness!

2. The "according" to which he expects to be answered by God: "Quicken me according to thy judgment." "Judgment" here may mean the revealed word. Then—

   (a) He expects to be answered certainly.

   (b) He expects to be answered wisely.

   (c) He expects to be answered fully, as all his needs require.

   (d) He expects that every answer should quicken spiritual life, making him holy. — **J.F.**

Verse 150,151. — Against mischief makers.

1. They press as near as they can to, harm us.

2. They get far from right to get more liberty to injure us.

3. The Lord is nearer than they.

4. God's truth is our shield and sword.

Verse 150,151. — Foes near: the Friend nearer.

1. The believer viewing with alarm the approach of his foes: "They draw near."

2. The believer recollecting with comfort the presence of his friend: "Thou art near:" Ge 15:1; 2Ki 6:14-17. — **C.A.D.**

Verse 150,151. — Two beleaguering hosts.

1. The host of evil: NEAR—

    (a) Demons, godless men, spiritual foes of world and heart.

    (b) Mischief in their van.

    (c) Law and truth left far behind.

    (d) Seeking to narrow their lines.

    (e) Thus are all saints beset.

2. The host of God: NEARER— Jehovah, his angels, and battalions of truths holy and immortal: "Thou and all thy commandments."

    (a) Entrenched in the reason: "are truth."

    (b) Camped in the heart's pavilion: "near."

    (c) Forming impregnable lines within those of the foe. — **W.B.H.**

Verse 150. — Consider—

1. Whether the description here given does not apply, more or less, to all unbelievers in Christ: "They that follow after mischief."

    (a) Some men undoubtedly and of set purpose do follow after mischief; they make themselves the tempters of others, and delight in it.

    (b) Others, who do not delight in it, yet cannot help the mischievous effect of their example.

    (c) The very morality of many unbelievers enables them to carry the pernicious influence of their unbelief Where the immorally wicked cannot come.

    (d) Even regular attendants at public worship may by their indecision encourage others in delay.

2. The dangerous position of all to whom the description, in any measure, belongs: "They are far from thy law."

    (a) They are so, in that they are unbelievers; for "this is his commandment, that we shall believe, "etc.

    (b) They are so, in that they are a cause of evil to others; for we are commanded to love and do good.

(c) To be far from God's law is to be nigh unto God's righteous wrath.

(d) For the sake of others, as well as their own, men should believe in Christ, and through faith become sanctified. — **J.F.**

Verse 151 (last clause). — The commandments of the Lord are true in principle; they lead to true living, if carried out; they truly reward the obedient; they never lead to falsehood, nor cause to be deluded.

Verse 152. — Knowledge of the word.

1. It is well to know it as God's own word.

2. As founded in truth.

3. As founded fore**Verse**

4. The earlier we know this the better.

Verses 153-160. — Divine consideration besought. "Consider my affliction" (Ps 119:153); my cause (Ps 119:154); "for thy mercies' sake" (Ps 119:156). Consider my persecutors (Ps 119:157-158), and my love to thy precepts (Ps 119:160) and act accordingly.

Verse 153-159. — The two considers. The subjects, the prayers, the arguments.

Verse 153,154. — Here—

1. David prays for succour in distress. "Is any afflicted? let him pray"; let him pray as David doth here.

> (a) He hath an eye to God's pity, and prays, "Consider mine affliction"; take it unto thy thoughts, and all the circumstances, and sit not by as one unconcerned. God is never unmindful of his people's afflictions, but he will have us to "put him in remembrance" (Isa 43:26), to spread our case before him, and then leave it to his compassionate consideration to do in it as in his wisdom he shall think fit, in his own time and way.
>
> (b) He has an eye to God's power, and prays, "Deliver me, " and again, "Deliver me." Consider my troubles and bring me out of them. God has promised deliverance (Ps 1:15), and we may pray for it with submission to his will, and with regard to his glory, that we may serve him the better.
>
> (c) He has an eye to God's righteousness, and prays, "Plead my cause": be thou my patron and advocate, and take me for thy client. David had a just cause, but his adversaries were many and mighty, and he was in danger of being run down by them: he therefore begs of God to clear his integrity, and silence their false accusations. If God do not plead his people's cause, who will? He is righteous, and they commit themselves to him, and therefore he will do it, and do it effectually: Isa 51:22; Jer 1:34.

(d) He has an eye to God's grace, and prays, "Quicken me." Lord, I am weak, and unable to bear my troubles; my spirit is apt to droop and sink: Oh, that thou wouldst revive and comfort me, till the deliverance is wrought!

2. He pleads his dependence upon the word of God, and his devotedness to his conduct. "Quicken" and "deliver me according to thy word" of promise; "for I do not forget thy precepts." The closer we cleave to the word of God, both as our rule and as our stay, the more assurance we may have of deliverance in due time. — **M. Henry.**

Verse 153. — The sick man's prayer.

1. The medicine remembered.

2. The physician sent for.

3. The physician considering the case.

4. The healing wrought. — **C.A.D.**

Verse 153. —

1. Lord, do not forget my sorrow.

2. I do not forget thy law.

Outlines Upon Keywords of The Psalm, by Pastor C. A. Davis.

Verse 154,156,159. — The threefold quickening. A capital subject, if the contexts are carefully considered.

Verse 154. — Intercession, deliverance, quickening, and all in faithfulness to the word.

Verse 154. — A prayer.

1. For promised defense.

2. For promised deliverance.

3. For promised revival

— **G.R.**

Verse 154. — The Advocate.

1. The soul hard pressed by the accuser— in the conscience (1Jo 3:20); before the world; at the throne of grace (Zec 3:1-10); at the bar of judgment.

2. The accused soul committing its case to the Advocate: 1Jo 2:2; 2Ti 1:12.

3. How the case will go. He never lost one yet.

— **C.A.D.**

Verse 155. —

1. An awful distance.

2. A distance never decreased by seeking.

3. A distance increased by sinning.

Verse 155. —

1. When salvation is far off.

2. When it is near.

OR

1. When the word is far off salvation is far off.

2. When the word is near salvation is near. — **G.R.**

Verse 155. — How to avoid salvation.

1. Salvation is inseparable from conformity to God's law: Le 18:5; Lu 5:25-28; Mt 19:17.

2. Salvation is brought to lawbreakers by the Law giver condescending to become the Law keeper and the Law victim. Salvation is avoided by those who refuse to be conformed to the eternal law or will of God. They perish themselves: their own sin punishes them: necessity punishes them. — **C.A.D.**

Verse 155. — A syllogism on salvation.

1. Salvation and obedience go together.

    (a) Have a common centre — God, his arm and his lips.

    (b) A mutual relation: we are saved in order to obedience.

In obeying we are being saved. Without obedience there is no salvation.

    (c) An identical aim — our good and God's glory.

    (d) Obedience and salvation are inseparable forever.

2. The godless are far from obedience.

    (a) Commands avoided.

    (b) Submission excluded.

3. Therefore they are far from salvation. They will not have the one; they cannot have the other. — **W.B.H.**

Verse 156. —

1. A great need.

2. Laid before a great Lord.

3. Great Favors pleaded.

4. A great mercy sought: "quicken me."

Verse 156. — Just, and the Quickener.

1. Spiritual life is the gift of God's mercy.

2. Its continuance depends on the exercise of God's power.

3. We may therefore plead for quickening on the ground of God's justice. — **C.A.D.**

Verse 156. — The saint,

1. Lost in admiration.

    (a) Of God's tender mercies.

    (b) He cries out at their greatness. They are numerous.

    Greatly tender. Great and tender; (exquisite combination!).

2. Filled with animation. The child of his admiration.

    (a) The arrow like prayer: "Quicken me:" To be like, to be true to, such a God.

    (b) The bow in the hand: "according to thy judgments." — **W.B.H.**

Verse 156. —

1. The tenderness of God's greatness.

2. The greatness of God's tenderness.

3. The stimulus to life found in his great and tender presence.

Verse 157. —

1. A word of multitude: "many."

2. A tendency of dread, viz., a tendency to decline.

3. A note of consolation: "yet do I not decline, "

Verse 158. — A grievous sight.

1. Transgressors beyond God's bounds.

2. Bounds so kindly set: "thy word."

3. Transgressions so wantonly ungrateful, so terribly dangerous, so fatal.

Verse 158. — Sorrow over sinners.

1. A sight we cannot avoid seeing.

2. A sorrow we ought not to avoid feeling. (See Lot: 2Pe 2:7,8. Moses: De 9:18,19. Samuel: 1Sa 15:11 Jer 9:1. Paul: Phm 3:18. Christ: Lu 19:41).

3. A reason we will not avoid endorsing.

Verse 158. — A righteous man cannot but be grieved at the sins of the wicked. He sees in them, —

1. The violation of the divine law which he loves.

2. Ungrateful rebellion against the God he worships.

3. Contempt for the gospel of salvation and the blood of Christ.

4. The dominion of Satan, the enemy of his God.

5. The degradation of souls which might have been sacred temples.

6. Prophetic signs of an awful, everlasting retribution. — **J.F.**

Verse 159. —

1. His own love avowed.

2. God's love pleaded.

3. Renewed life implored.

Verse 159. —

1. Attention invited: "Consider how."

2. Profession made: "I love thy precepts."

3. Petition offered: "quicken me, "etc.

4. Plea suggested: "according to, "etc. — **G.R.**

Verse 159. — My love and thy lovingkindness. The saint's love.

1. Avowed. "Thou knowest all things, "etc.

2. Submitted. In humble insistence on its sincerity. In sense of its insufficiency. In prayer to God not to over look it.

3. Lost sight of in the sudden glory of God's lovingkindness. Where is my love now?

4. Recovered and humbly brought for quickening. Lord, I'll say no more about it: "Quicken me." — **W.B.H.**

Verse 159. — Quicken, me for love's sake.

1. A prayer for quickened life.

2. Awakened by love to the divine rule of life.

3. Enforced by the plea of that love.

4. Addressed to the God of love. — **C.A.D.**

Verse 159. — Consider, —

1. The holy unsatisfaction of the believer: "Quicken me, "etc.

    (a) A prayer frequently occurring in the psalm, and always urged with great earnestness.

    (b) Its importunity proves the possession of spiritual life; in fact, none but the living ones crave quickening.

    (c) The most earnest feel the most acutely their indwelling sin, and appreciate most highly thorough sanctification.

    (d) Thus, this is, perhaps, the only unsatisfaction perfectly pure in its character.

2. The assuring Divine attribute to which he can appeal: "According to thy lovingkindness."

    (a) An attribute, not only made known in tile word, but made manifest to us in our experience of its gentle dealing.

    (b) An attribute that covers sin, and is touched with a feeling of our infirmities.

    (c) An attribute that must be affected with the cry for quickening grace.

3. The consideration he ought to be able to lay before God: "Consider how I love thy precepts."

    (a) Because from the word he learnt of the lovingkindness, and through it received life.

    (b) Without it the prayer cannot be genuine.

    (c) It is a good reason for expecting more grace; for "whosoever hath, to him shall be given, "etc. — **J.F.**

Verse 160. —

1. Early: "true from the beginning."

2. Late: "endureth forever" Or, Truth and immutability the believer's Jachin and Boaz.

Outlines Upon Keywords of The Psalm, by Pastor C. A. Davis.

Verses 161-168. — What the word is to the believer. The object of (**Verse** 161), joy (**Verse** 162), love (**Verse** 163), praise (**Verse** 164), the producer peace (**Verse** 165), and hope (**Verse** 166); therefore exceedingly loved (**Verse** 167), faithfully kept (**Verse** 168).

Verse 161,162. — God's word, the object of godly fear and godly joy.

1. It makes the heart quake by its purity and power.

2. It makes the heart rejoice by its grace and truth. — **W.H.J.P.**

Verse 161. —

1. Wrong without cause.

2. Right with abundant cause.

Verse 161 (second clause). — Awe of God's word — its propriety, its hallowed influence, the evil of its absence.

Verse 161. — Restrained by awe.

1. The causelessness of persecution.

2. The temptations to evil occasioned thereby — to revenge: to apostasy.

3. The safeguard against falling: awe of God's word. 1Sa 24:6 Da 3:16-18 Ac 4:19 5:29 — **C.A.D.**

Verse 162. —

1. The treasure hid: "great spoil" hidden in the divine word.

2. The treasure found: "as one that findeth, "etc.

    (a) By reading.

    (b) By meditation.

    (c) By prayer.

3. The treasure enjoyed: "I rejoice, "etc. — **G.R.**

Verse 162. — David's joy over God's word he compares to the joy of the warrior when he finds great spoil.

1. This great joy is sometimes aroused by the fact that there is a word of God.

    (a) The Scriptures are a revealing of God.

    (b) The guide of our life.

    (c) A sure pledge of mercy.

    (d) The beginning of communion with God.

(e) The instrument of usefulness.

2. Frequently the joy of the believer in the word arises out of his having had to battle to obtain a grasp of it.

(a) We have had to fight over certain doctrines before we could really come at them.

(b) The same may be said of the promises.

(c) Of the precepts.

(d) Of the threatenings.

(e) Even about the word which reveals Christ.

3. At times the joy of the believer lies in enjoying God's word without any fighting at all: "One that findeth."

4. There is a joy arising out of the very fact that Holy Scripture may be considered to be a spoil.

(a) A spoil is the end of uncertainty.

(b) It is the weakening of the adversary for any future attacks.

(c) It gives a sense of victory.

(d) There is, in dividing the spoil, profit, pleasure, and Honor.

(e) The spoiling of the enemy is a prophecy of rest. See "Spurgeon's Sermons, "No. 1641: "Great Spoil."

Verse 163. — Opposite poles of the Christian character.

1. Why I hate lying, because it comes from the devil (Pr 8:44, Ac 5:3): it leads to the devil (Re 11:8, 22:15): it is base, dangerous, degrading (Pr 19:5, 1Ti 4:2, 2Ti 3:13): it is hated by the Lord (Pr 6:16,17, 7:22).

2. Why I love the law. Because it emanates from God; is the reflection of his character; is the ideal of my character.

3. How I came thus to hate and love. By the grace of God: **Verse** 29. — G.A.D.

Verse 163. —

1. Opposite things.

2. Opposite feelings.

Verse 164. — Praise rendered. Frequently, statedly, heartily, intelligently.

Verse 164. — Perpetual praise.

1. True praise is ever warranted.

2. True praise is ever welcome.

3. True praise is never weary. — **C.A.D.**

Verse 164. —

1. Some never praise thee; but, "seven times a day, "etc.; for I delight to do so. "Thy righteous judgments" are a terror to them, a joy to me.

2. Some feebly and coldly praise thee, while, "seven times, "etc. My warm devotion must frequently express itself in praise.

3. Some are content with occasionally praising thee, but, "seven times, "etc. They think it enough to begin and end the day with praise, while all the day long I am in the spirit of praise.

4. Some soon cease to praise thee, but, "seven times, "etc. Not seven times only, but "unto seventy times seven." Even without ceasing, will I praise thee. — **W.H.J.P.**

Verse 165. —

1. Great love to a great law.

2. Great peace under great disquietude.

3. Great upholding from all stumblingblocks.

Verse 165. — Perfect peace.

1. The law of God should be regarded with love.

2. Love to the law is productive of great peace. Peace with God through the blood of reconciliation: peace with self by good conscience and suppression of evil desires: peace with men by charity.

3. The peace which springs from love to the law is a security against stumbling: "nothing shall offend them; "neither the daily cross (Mr 5:21,22) nor the fiery trial (Mr 4:7); nor the humbling doctrine (Joh 6:60,66, etc.). — C.A.D

Verse 165.

1. The characters described— "they which love thy law."

2. The blessing they enjoy: "great peace."

3. The evils they escape: "nothing shall offend them."— **G.R.**

Verse 165. — The peace and security of the godly.

1. Their peace. It arises from—

    (a) Freedom from an accusing conscience.

(b) Conformity to the requirements of the law.

(c) Enjoyment of the privileges revealed in the law.

(d) Assurance of divine approval and benediction.

2. Their security.

(a) They are prepared for every duty.

(b) They are proof against every temptation.

(c) They are pledged to final perseverance.

(d) They have the promise of divine protection. — **W.H.J.P.**

Verse 165. —

1. An Honorable title: "They which love thy law."

2. A good possession: "Great peace have they."

3. A blessed immunity: "Nothing shall offend them." — **J.F.**

Verse 166. —

1. A hope which is not ashamed.

2. A life which is not ashamed.

3. A God of whom he is not ashamed.

Verse 166. — A good hope through grace.

1. Salvation is God's gift: "thy salvation."

2. Is apprehended by hope: "I have hoped."

3. Is accompanied by obedience: "and done thy commandments." Heb 6:9. — **C.A.D.**

Verse 167. — Past and present.

Verse 167. —

1. The more we keep God's testimonies the more we shall love them.

2. The more we love them the more we shall keep them. — **G.R.**

Verse 167.

1. The jewels: "Thy testimonies."

(a) Rare; none like them.

(b) Rich; surpassing valuation.

(c) Beautifying those who wear them.

(d) Glittering with an internal and essential splendour, in the darkness of this world.

(e) Realising in truth the old superstitions regarding precious stones having medicinal and magic virtues.

2. The cabinet: "My soul."

(a) Exactly made to receive the jewels.

(b) A wonderful piece of divine workmanship; but all ruined and marred unless applied to the use designed.

(c) The only receptacle out of which the genuine beauty o fGod's testimonies can so shine as to excite the admiration of beholders.

3. The lock that keeps all safe: "I love them exceedingly."

(a) Love is the strongest hold fast in the uni**Verse**.

(b) It is needed, for ten thousand thieves prowl around to steal from us the treasure.

(c) A love "exceedingly" is a heavenly patent; no ingenuity can pick it; it is fire proof and burglar proof against hell itself.— **J.F.**

Verse 168. —

1. The claim of God's word upon our utmost obedience." I have kept thy precepts and thy testimonies." He does not mean that he had kept them perfectly; for that were to contradict other expressions in the psalm. He means that he kept them sincerely and strove to keep them perfectly, as one who realized their claim upon him.

(a) The whole word is divine: an equal authority pervades every precept; no distinction should be made of more or less obligation.

(b) The whole word is pure and right; expediency, or making the measure and manner of obedience suitable to our own purpose, is a false principle; to be carefully distinguished from righteous expediency, which is the foregoing of a personal right in consideration of another's benefit.

(c) The moral code of the word is a unity; obedience is like a connected chain, a wilful flaw in one link renders all useless.

2. The consciousness which greatly helps obedience: "For all my ways are before thee."

(a) "Are before thee, "as plainly seen by thee.

(b) "Are before thee, "constantly observed.

(c) "Are before thee; "deliberately placed before thee by me, that they may be corrected and directed. — **J.F.**

Verse 168. — All my ways are before thee.

1. The saint's delight.

2. The sinner's distress. — W.W.

Verse 168 (second clause). —

1. Necessarily so: for thou art the omniscient God: Ps 134:3.

2. Voluntarily so: for I choose to walk in thy sight. See Ps 16:9

3. Consciously and blessedly so. For the light of thy countenance inspires and gladdens me. See Ps 89:15. — **W.H.J.P.**

Verse 168 (second clause). — Living in the sight of God Actually the case with all; designedly the case of the godly; happily the case of the Favored; preeminently the case of those who abide in fellowship.

Verse 168. —

1. The practical and doctrinal teachings of God before us.

2. All our ways before him.

3. The sort of conduct which these two causes will produce.

Outlines Upon Keywords of The Psalm, by Pastor C. A. Davis.

Verses 169-176. — The concluding cry. Bespeaking audience for his the Psalmist asks for understanding and deliverance (**Verse** 169, 170); raises to praise God (**Verse** 171), and to speak of God (**Verse** 172), and cries for help (**Verse** 173), salvation (**Verse** 174), life (**Verse** 175), and (**Verse** 176).

Verse 169,170. —

1. The singular dignity of prayer. We are on earth, but our prayers pass the seraphim and "come near before God."

2. The powerful right of prayer — to urge with God his own word: "according to thy word."

3. The triumphant possibilities of prayer. Blessing us in mind and estate. For time and eternity. "Give me understanding." "Deliver me."

4. The amazing license accorded to prayer. To double and reiterate its requests (as here). — **W.B.H.**

Verse 169. —

1. Admission to the royal court.

2. Instruction from the royal throne.

3. Reliance on the royal word.

Verse 170-174. — The pleader: Ps 119:170. The singer: Ps 119:171. The preacher: Ps 119:172. The worker: Ps 119:173. The waiter: Ps 119:174.

Verse 170. —

1. Access sought.

2. Answer entreated.

3. Argument employed.

Verse 171. — Taught; taught to praise; praising; praising for being taught.

Verse 171. — Learning to sing by learning to obey.

Verse 171. — The Happy Scholar.

1. He rejoices in the lesson he has learnt.

2. In the Teacher who has taught him.

3. Looks forward to the end of his lesson as the time for the full singing of his song. — **C.A.D.**

Verse 171. — Lessons in Praise. —

1. It is saints' work.

2. It is sacred work, not to be hurriedly rushed into.

3. It needs Spirit instructed singers. — **W.B.H.**

Verse 172. —

1. The orator: "My tongue shall speak."

2. His chosen theme: "of thy word."

3. His inward impulse: "for all thy commandments are righteousness."

Verse 172. — Savory Speech.

1. A resolution all believers should make.

2. The qualification all believers should seek (Ps 45:1; Mt 7:34,35)

3. The edification believers would thus secure. — **C.A.D.**

Verse 173. —

1. "To will is present with me."

2. "How to perform that which I would, I find not."

3. "Help. Lord."

Verse 173. —

1. Help needed to keep the divine precepts.

2. Help sought: "Let thy hand, "etc. We should choose nothing and do nothing in which we cannot ask help from God. — **G.R.**

Verse 173. —

1. God's Hand.

    (a) Its warm hold (Joh 5:29).

    (b) Its wealth of contents (Ps 104:28).

    (c) Its heavy blow (Ps 39:10).

    (d) Its weight (1Sa 5:11).

    (e) Its saving reach (Isa 54:1).

    (f) Its sweet shadow (Isa 49:2), etc.

2. The saint plucks him by the sleeve: "Let thy hand help me."

    (a) His humble representation.

    (b) His down drawing of the hand of God. — **W.B.H.**

Verse 173. — Let Thy hand help me.

1. Thy reconciling hand: "stretched out."

2. Thy comforting hand; like that which touched Daniel and John.

3. Thy supplying hand. "Thou openest thy hand, "etc.

4. Thy protecting hand: "all his saints are in thy hand": De 33:3. "Great Shepherd of the sheep."

5. Thy supporting hand: "I will uphold thee."

6. Thy governing hand: "all my times are in thy hand."

7. Thy chastening hand: "Thy hand was heavy upon me."

8. Thy prospering hand: "the hand of the Lord was with, "etc. — **W.J.**

Verse 174. —

1. Jacob's longings.

2. Moses' choice.

Verse 174. — God's servant drinking at salvation's well, but unsated.

1. Longing yielding to delight.

    (a) At God's salvation.

    (b) At the rich Scripture inventory.

2. Delight bringing forth further longing.

    (a) For deeper discoveries in the word.

    (b) Richer experiences in the life.

    (c) Heaven's consummation. — **W.B.H.**

Verse 174. —

1. Sighings for heaven. Holiness, happiness, God.

2. Sips by the way. The word of God, the will of God, service of God, the God in all.

— **W.B.H.**

Verse 174. — I have longed for thy salvation. Thy holy salvation. Thy full salvation. Thy free salvation. Thy present salvation. Thy permanent salvation. — **W.J.**

Verse 174. — I have longed, etc. This longing arises,

1. From a painful consciousness of the need of salvation.

2. From a perception of the glories of God's salvation.

3. From the promises which give assurance of the possibility of obtaining this salvation.

4. From the gracious promptings of the Holy Ghost. — **W.H.J.P.**

Verse 175. —

1. The highest life.

2. The highest occupation.

3. Both dependent on the highest aid.

Verse 175. — Praise.

1. The noblest employment of life — to praise God.

2. The noblest presentation of praise — the holy life.

3. The noblest application of divine judgments — to inspire praise.

Verse 176. —

1. My confession: "I have gone astray."

2. My profession: "thy servant."

3. My petition: "seek thy servant."

4. My plea: "for I do not forget, "etc.

Verse 176. —

1. The confession: "I have gone astray."

2. The petition: "Seek thy servant."

3. The plea: "For I do not, "etc. — **G.R.**

Verse 176. — The last **Verse** as such. The closing minor cadence.

1. The highest flights of human devotion must end in confession of sin: "I have gone astray."

2. The sincerest professions of human fidelity must give place to the acknowledgment of helplessness: "seek thy servant."

3. The loftiest human declarations of love to God's law must come down to The mournful acknowledgment that we have only not forgotten it. — **C.A.D.**

PSALM 120

SERMON OUTLINES AND HELPFUL TIPS

Verse 1. A reminiscence.

1. It is threefold; distress, prayer, deliverance.

2. It has a threefold bearing: it excites my hope, stimulates my petitions, and arouses my gratitude.

Verse 1.

1. Special trouble: "In my distress."
2. Special prayer: "I cried unto the Lord."
3. Special Favor: "He heard me." —G.R.

Verse 2. The unjustly slandered have, besides the avenging majesty of their God to protect them, many other consolations, as

1. The consciousness of innocence to sustain them.

2. The promise of divine Favor to support them: "I will hide thee from the scourge of the tongue."

3. There is the consideration to soothe: "Blessed are ye when men shall revile you and persecute you, "etc.

4. That a lie has not usually a long life.

5. There is, lastly, for comfort, the repairing influence of time. —R. Nisbet.

Verse 2. A prayer against slander. We are liable to it; it would do us great injury and cause us great pain; yet none but the Lord can protect us from it, or deliver us out of it.

Verse 3. The rewards of calumny. What can they be? What ought they to be? What have they been?

Verse 3.

1. What the reviler does for others.
2. What he does to himself.
3. What God will do with him.

Verse 4. The nature of slander and the punishment of slander.

Verse 4.

1. The tongue is sharper than an arrow.

    (a) It is shot in private.
    (b) It is tipped with poison.

(c) It is polished with seeming kindness.
(d) It is aimed at the most tender part.

2. The tongue is more destructive than fire. Its scandals spread with greater rapidity. They consume that which other fires cannot touch, and they are less easily quenched. "The tongue", says an Apostle, "is a fire...and setteth on fire the course of nature; and it is set on fire of hell". A fiery dart of the wicked one.—G.R.

Verse 5. Bad lodgings. Only the wicked can be at home with the wicked. Our dwelling with them is trying, and yet it may be useful

(1) to them,

(2) to us: it tries our graces, reveals our character, abates our pride, drives us to prayer, and makes us long to be home.

Verse 5.

1. None but the wicked enjoy the company of the wicked.
2. None but the worldly enjoy the company of worldlings.
3. None but the righteous enjoy the company of the righteous.—G.R.

Verse 6.

1. Trying company.

2. Admirable behavior.

3. Undesirable consequences: "When I speak, they are for war".

Verse 7. The character of the man of God. He is at peace. He is for peace. He is peace. He shall have peace.

Verse 7.

1. Piety and peace are united.
2. So are wickedness and war.—G.R.

PSALM 121

SERMON OUTLINES AND HELPFUL TIPS

Verse 1. The window opened towards Jerusalem.

1. The hills we look to.
2. The help we look for.
3. The eyes we look with.

Verse 1. *Whence cometh my help?* A grave question; for,

1. I need it, greatly, in varied forms, constantly, and now.
2. In few directions can I look for it, for men are feeble, changeable, hostile, etc.
3. I must look above. To Providence, to Grace, to my God.

Verse 2. The Creator the creature's helper.

Verse 2.

1. God is his people's "help."

2. He helps them in proportion as they feel their need of his help.

3. His help is never ill vain. "My help cometh." not from the earth merely, or the skies, but "from the Lord, which made heaven and earth". Isa 40:26-31. —*G.R.*

Verse 3 (First clause). The preservation of saintly character the care of the Creator.

Verse 3. Comfort for a pilgrim along the 'mauvais pas' of life. We have a Guide omniscient, omnipotent, never slumbering, unchanging.

Verse 3. *He that keepeth thee will not slumber.*

1. The Lord's care is personal in its objects. The keeper of Israel is the keeper of the individual. God deals with us individually.

> (a) This is implied in his care of the church, which is composed of individuals.

> (b) It is involved in the nature of our religion, which is a personal thing.

> (c) It is affirmed in Scripture. Examples; promises; experiences. "He loved me, "etc., etc.

> (d) It is confirmed by experience.

2. The Lord's care is unwearied in its exercise: "Will not slumber."

> (a) He is never unacquainted with our condition.

> (b) He is never indifferent to it.

> (c) He is never weary of helping us. We sometimes think he sleeps, but this is our folly.

—*Frederick J. Benskin*, of Reading, 1882.

Verse 4.

1. The suspicion—that God sleeps.
2. The denial.
3. The implied opposite—he is ever on the watch to bless.

Verse 4. He keepeth Israel,

1. As his chief treasure, most watchfully.
2. As his dearest spouse, most tenderly.
3. As the apple of his eye, most charily and warily.
—*Daniel Featley*, 1582-1645.

Verse 5. The Lord Keeper.

1. Blessings included in this title.
2. Necessities which demand it.
3. Offices which imply it,—Shepherd, King, Husband, Father, etc.
4. Conduct suggested by it.

Verse 5 (last clause). God as near us, and as indivisible from us as our shadow.

Verse 5. *The Lord is thy keeper,* not angels.

1. He is able to keep thee. He has infinite knowledge, power, etc.

2. He has engaged to keep thee.

3. He has kept thee.

4. He will keep thee. In his love; in his covenant, etc., as his sheep, his children, his treasures, as the apple of his eye, etc.—*F.J.B.*

Verse 5. *The Lord is thy keeper.*

1. Wakeful: "Will not slumber."
2. Universal: "Thy going out and thy coming in:" "From all evil."
3. Perpetual: "Day:" "night: ...evermore."
4. Special: "Thy:" "Israel."—*W.J.*

Verse 6. The highest powers, under God, prevented from hurting believers, and even made to serve them.

Verse 6. Our Horoscope.

1. Superstitious fears removed.
2. Sacred assurances supplied.

Verse 7.

1. Personal agency of God in providence.
2. Personal regard of providence to the Favored individual.
3. Special care over the center of the personality—"thy soul."

Verse 8. Who? "The Lord." What? "Shall preserve thee." When? "Going out and coming in from this time forth." How long? "For evermore." What then? "I will lift up mine eyes."

Verse 8.

1. Changing—going out and coming in.
2. Unchanging—"The Lord shall preserve," etc.

PSALM 122

SERMON OUTLINES AND HELPFUL TIPS

Whole Psalm. Observe,

1. The joy with which they were to go up to Jerusalem: Ps 122:1-2.

2. The great esteem they were to have of Jerusalem: Ps 122:3-5.

3. The great concern they were to have for Jerusalem, and the prayers they were to put up for its welfare. *M. Henry.*

Verse 1.

1. David was glad to go to the house of the Lord. It was the house of the Lord therefore he desired to go. He preferred it to his own house.

2. He was glad when others said to him, "Let us go." The distance may be great, the weather may be rough, still, "Let us go."

3. He was glad to say it to others, "Let us go, "and to persuade others to accompany him. *G. R.*

Verse 1.

1. Joy in prospect of religious worship.

> (a) Because of the instruction we receive.
> (b) Because of the exercises in which we engage.
> (c) Because of the society in which we mingle.
> (d) Because of the sacred interests we promote.

2. Joy in the invitation to religious worship.

> (a) Because it shows others are interested in the service of God.
> (b) Because it shows their interest in us.
> (c) Because it furthers the interests of Zion. *F.J.B.*

Verse 1. Gladness of God's house. Are you "glad when, "etc.? Why glad?

1. That I have a house of the Lord to which I may go.
2. That any feel enough interest in me to say, "Let us go, " etc.
3. That I am able to go to God's house.
4. That I am disposed to go.
—J. G. Butler, in "The Preacher's Monthly, "1882.

Verse 1. *I was glad,* etc. So says,

1. *The devout worshipper,* who is glad to be invited to God's earthly house. It is his home, his school, his hospital, his bank.

2. *The adhesive Christian, who is glad to be invited to God's spiritual house.* Church is builded together, etc. There would he find a settled rest. Has no sympathies with religious gypsies, or no church people.

3. The *dying saint, who is glad to be invited to God's heavenly house.* Simeon—Stephen—Peter—Paul. W. J.

Verse 1.

1. The duty of attending the services of God's house.
2. The duty of exciting one another to go.
3. The benefit of being thus excited. F.J.B.

Verse 2. Here is,

1. Personal attendance: "*My* feet shall stand," etc.
2. Personal security: "My feet shall *stand*."
3. Personal fellowship: "O Jerusalem." G. R.

Verse 2. The inside of the church. The Honor, privilege, joy, and fellowship of standing there.

Verse 3.

1. A type of the New Jerusalem.

    (a) As chosen by God.
    (b) As founded upon a rock.
    (c) As taken from an enemy.

2. A type of its prosperity: "Builded as a city."

3. A type of its perfection: "Compact together." G. R.

Verse 3. The unity of the church.

1. Implied in all covenant dealings.
2. Suggested by all Scriptural metaphors.
3. Prayed for by our Lord.
4. Promoted by the gifts of the Spirit.
5. To be maintained by us all.

Verses 3-4. The united church the growing church.

Verse 4.

1. The duty of public worship.

    (a) In one place: "*Whither* the tribes go up."
    (b) In one company, though of many tribes: "Whither the *tribes* go up."

2. The design.

(a) For instruction: "Unto the testimony of Israel."
(b) For praise: "To give thanks unto the name of the Lord." *G. R.*

Verse 5.

1. There are thrones of judgment in the sanctuary. Men are judged there.

>(a) By the law.
>(b) By their own consciences.
>(c) By the gospel.

2. There are thrones of grace: "Of the house of David."

>(a) Of David's Son in the hearts of his people.
>(b) Of his people in David's Son. *G.R.*

Verse 6.

1. The prayer,

>(a) "For Jerusalem": not for ourselves merely, or for the world; but for the church. For the babes in grace; for the young men, and for the fathers. For the pastors, with the deacons and elders.
>
>(b) For the "peace" of Jerusalem. Inward peace and outward peace.

2. The promise.

>(a) To whom given: "They that love thee."
>
>(b) The promise itself: "They shall prosper"—individually and collectively.

Or,

1. Love to Jerusalem is the effect of true piety.
2. Prayer for Jerusalem is the effect of that love.
3. The peace of Jerusalem is the effect of that prayer; and,
4. The prosperity of Jerusalem is the effect of that peace. *G.R.*

Verse 6. God has connected giving and receiving, scattering and increasing, sowing and reaping, praying and prospering.

1. What we must do if we would prosper—"Pray for the peace of Jerusalem."

>(a) Comprehensively: "Peace"—spiritual, social, ecclesiastical, national.
>
>(b) Supremely: "Prefer Jerusalem above, "etc.
>
>(c) Practically: "Let peace rule in your hearts." "Seek peace and pursue it."

2. What we shall gain if we pray thus—"Prosperity."

(a) Temporal prosperity may thus come. God turned again the captivity of Job when he prayed for his friends.

(b) Spiritual prosperity shall thus come. Affairs of soul—holy exercises and services.

(c) Numerical prosperity will thus come. "Increased with men as a flock." *W. J.*

Verses 6-9.

1. The blessings desired for the church.

    (a) Peace.
    (b) Prosperity. Notice the order and connection of these two.

2. The way to secure them.

    (a) Prayer: "Pray for the peace of Jerusalem."
    (b) Delight in the service of God: "I was glad, "etc.
    (c) Practical effort: "I will seek thy good."

3. Reasons for seeking them.

    (a) For our own sake: "They shall prosper," etc.
    (b) For our companions' sake.
    (c) For the sake of the "house of the Lord." *F. J. B.*

Verse 7.

1. Where peace is most desirable: "Within thy walls." Within town walls, within house walls, but principally within temple walls.

2. Where prosperity is most desirable.

    (a) In the closet.

    (b) In the church. These are the palaces of the Great King; "The ivory palaces whereby they have made thee glad." *G. R.*

Verse 7. The connection between peace and prosperity.

Verse 7. *Thy walls.*

1. Enquire why the church needs walls.
2. Enquire what are the walls of a church.
3. Enquire on which side of them we are.

Verse 7. The church a palace.

1. Intended for the great King.
2. Inhabited by the royal family.
3. Adorned with regal splendor.

4. Guarded by special power.
5. Known as the court of the blessed and only potentate.

Verses 8-9. Two great principles are here laid down why we should pray for the church,

1. Love to the brethren: "For my brethren and companions' sakes."

2. Love to God: "Because of the house of the Lord our God I will seek thy good." *N. M`michael.*

Verse 9. *I will seek thy good.*

1. By prayer for the church.
2. By service in the church.
3. By bringing others to attend.
4. By keeping the peace.
5. By living so as to commend religion.

PSALM 123

SERMON OUTLINES AND HELPFUL TIPS

Whole Psalm. We have here,

1. The prayer of dependence, Ps 123:2.
2. The prayer of apprehension: "Unto thee", etc.
3. The spirit of obedience: "As the eyes of servants:" etc.
4. The patience of the saints: "Until he have mercy upon us."
—*R. Nisbet.*

Whole Psalm. Eyes and no eyes.

1. EYES.

    (a) Upward, in confidence, in prayer, in thought.
    (b) "Unto, "in reverence, watchfulness, obedience.
    (c) Inward, producing a cry for mercy.

2. No EYES.

    (a) NO sight of the excellence of the godly.
    (b) No sense of their own danger: "at ease."
    (c) No humility before God: "proud."
    (d) No uplifted eyes in hope, prayer, expectation.

Verse 1. The eyes of faith.

1. Need uplifting.

2. See best upward.

3. Have always something to see upward.

4. Let us look up, and so turn our eyes from too much introspection and retrospection.

Verse 1.

1. The language of Adoration: "Thou that dwellest in the heavens."

2. The language of Confession.

    (a) Of need.
    (b) Of Helplessness.

3. The language of Supplication: "Unto thee, "etc.

4. The language of Expectation; as shown in Ps 123:2.—*G.R.*

Verse 2. (Ps 121:4 with this **Verse**.) Two beholds.

1. God's watchful eye over us.
2. The saint's watchful eye upon God.

Verse 2. "Our eyes wait upon the Lord our God."

1. What it is to wait with the eye.

2. What peculiar aspect of the Lord suggests such waiting: "Jehovah our God." The covenant God is the trusted God.

3. What comes of such waiting—"mercy."

Verse 2. The guiding hand.

1. A beckoning hand—to go near.
2. A directing hand—to go here and there.
3. A quiescent hand—to remain where we are.—G.R.

Verse 2. Homely metaphors, or what may be learned from maids and their mistresses.

Verse 3 (first portion). The Sinner's Litany. The Saint's Entreaty.

Verse 3 (second portion). The world's contempt, the abundance of it, the reason of it, the bitterness of it, the comfort under it.

Verses 3, 4.

1. The occasion of the prayer: the contempt of men. This is often the most difficult to bear.

   (a) Because it is most unreasonable. Why ridicule men for yielding to their own convictions of what is right?

   (b) Most undeserved. True religion injures no man, but seeks the good of all.

   (c) Most profane. To reproach the people of God because they are his people is to reproach God himself.

2. The subject of the prayer.

   (a) The prayer: is not for justice, which might be desired, but for mercy.

   (b) The plea: "For we are, "etc. The reproaches of men are an encouragement to look for special help from God. The harp hung upon the willows sends forth its sweetest tones. The less it is in human hands the more freely it is played upon by the Spirit of God.—G.R.

Verse 4. *Those that are at ease.*

1. Explain their state: "at ease."
2. Show their ordinary state of mind: "proud."
3. Denounce their frequent sin: scorn of the godly.
4. Exhibit their terrible danger.

PSALM 124

SERMON OUTLINES AND HELPFUL TIPS

Verse 1. *The LORD who was on our side.* Who is he? Why on our side? How does he prove it? What are we bound to do?

Verses 1-3. Regard the text,

1. From the life of Jacob or Israel.
2. From the history of the nation.
3. From the annals of the church.
4. From our personal biography.

Verses 1-5.

1. What might have been.

2. Why it has not been.

Verses 1-5.

1. What the people of God would have been if the Lord had not been on their side.

> (a) What if left to their enemies? Ps 124:2,3. Israel left to Pharaoh and his host in the time of Moses: left to the Caananites in the time of Joshua: to the Midianites in the time of Gideon: Judah to the Assyrians in the time of Hezekiah: "Then they had swallowed us up," etc.

> (b) What if left to themselves? "The stream had gone over our soul": Ps 124:4, 5.

2. What the people of God are with the Lord on their side.

> (a) All the designs of their enemies against them are frustrated.

> (b) Their inward sorrow is turned into joy.

> (c) Both their inward and then outward troubles work together for their good. — G. R.

Verse 2, 3.

1. To swallow us alive — the desire of our wrathful enemies.
2. To save us alive — the work of our faithful God.

Verse 6.

1. The Lamb.
2. The Lion.
3. The Lord.

Verse 6.

1. They would gladly devour us.
2. They cannot devour unless the Lord will.
3. God is to be praised since he does not permit them to injure us.

Verse 6.

1. The ill will of men against the righteous.

>(a) For their spoliation.
>(b) For their destruction: "As a prey to their teeth."

2. The goodwill of God. "Blessed be the Lord, "etc.

>(a) What it supposes—that good men, in a measure and for a time, may be given into the hands of the wicked.
>(b) What it affirms—that they are not given entirely into their hands:—G.R.

Verse 7.

1. The soul ensnared.

>(a) By whom? Wicked men are fowlers. By Satan. "Satan, the fowler, who betrays Unguarded souls a thousand ways."
>(b) How? By temptations—to pride, worldliness, drunkenness, error, or lust, according to the tastes and habits of the individual.

2. The soul escaped: "Our soul is escaped, "etc. "The snare is broken, "not by ourselves, but by the hand of God.—G.R.

Verse 7.

1. A bird.
2. A snare.
3. A capture.
4. An escape.

Verse 8. Our Creator, our Helper. Special comfort to be drawn from creation in this matter.

Verse 8.

1. The Helper: "The Lord, who made heaven and earth, "who in his works has given ample proofs of what he can do.

2. The helped. "Our help" is,

>(a) Promise in his name.
>(b) Sought in his name: these make it ours.—G.R.

Verse 8.

1. We have help. As troubled sinners, as dull scholars, as trembling professors, as inexperienced travelers, as feeble workers.

2. We have help in God's name. In his perfections—"They shall put my name upon the children of Israel." In his Gospel—"A chosen vessel to bear my name." In his authority—"In the name of Jesus Christ rise up, "etc.

3. Therefore we exert ourselves.—*W.J.*

PSALM 125

SERMON OUTLINES AND HELPFUL TIPS

Whole Psalm.

1. The mark of the covenant: "They that trust."
2. The security of the covenant (Ps 125:1-2).
3. The rod of the covenant (Ps 125:3).
4. The tenor of the covenant (Ps 125:4).
5. The spirit of the covenant,—"peace."

Verse 1. See "Spurgeon's Sermons," No. 1,450: "The Immortality of the Believer."

Verses 1-2.

1. The believer's singularity: he trusts in Jehovah.
2. The believer's stability: "abideth forever."
3. The believer's safety: "As the mountains," etc.

Verse 2. The all surrounding presence of Jehovah the glory, safety, and eternal blessedness of his people. Yet this to the wicked would be hell.

Verse 2. See "Spurgeon's Sermons," Nos. 161-2: "The Security of the Church."

Verse 2. The endurance of mercy: "From henceforth even forever."

Verse 2. Saints hemmed in by infinite love.

1. *The City and the Girdle, or the symbols separated.*

    (a) Jerusalem imaging God's people. Anciently chosen; singularly honored; much beloved; the shrine of Deity.

    (b) The Mountain Girdle setting forth Jehovah: Strength; All sidedness; Sentinel through day and night.

2. *The City within the Girdle, or the symbols related.*

    (a) Delightful Entanglement. The view from the windows! (Jehovah "round about.") To be lost must break through God! Sound sleep and safe labor.

    (b) Omnipotent Circumvallation, suggesting—God's determination; Satan's dismay. This mountain ring immutable.—*W. B. Haynes, of Stafford.*

Verse 3. Observe,

1. The Permission implied. The rod of the wicked may come upon the lot of the righteous. Why?

    (a) That wickedness may be free to manifest itself.
    (b) That the righteous may be made to hate sin.

(c) That the righteousness of God's retribution may be seen.
(d) That the consolations of the righteous may abound. 2Co 1:5.

2. The Permanency denied: "The rod...shall *not rest*", etc. Illustrate by history of Job, Joseph, David, Daniel, Christ, martyrs, etc.

3. The Probity tried and preserved: "Lest the righteous put forth", etc., by rebelling, sinful compromise, etc.

    (a) God will have it tried, to prove its worth, beauty, etc.
    (b) But no more than sufficiently tried.—*John Field, of Sevenoaks.*

Verses 3-4.

1. The good defined: "The upright in heart"; such as do not "turn aside", and are not "workers of iniquity."

2. The good distressed: by "the rod of the wicked."

3. The good delivered: "Do good"; fulfil thy promise (Ps 125:3).—*W. H. J. Page.*

Verse 4.

1. What it is to be good.
2. What it is for God to do us good.

Verse 5. Temporary Professors.

1. The crucial test: "They turn aside."
2. The crooked policy: they make crooked ways their own.
3. The crushing doom: "led forth with workers of iniquity."

Verse 5. Hypocrites.

1. Their ways: "crooked."

    (a) Like the way of a winding stream, seeking out the fair level, or the easy descent.

    (b) Like the course of a tacking ship, which skillfully makes every wind to drive her forward.

    (c) Ways constructed upon no principle but that of pure selfishness.

2. Their conduct under trial. They "turn aside."

    (a) From their religious profession.

    (b) From their former companions.

    (c) To become the worst scorners of spiritual things, and the most violent calumniators of spiritually minded men.

3. Their doom: "The Lord shall," etc.

>(a) In the judgment they shall be classed with the most flagrant of sinners; "with the workers of iniquity."
>
>(b) They shall be exposed by an irresistible power: "The Lord shall lead them forth."
>
>(c) They shall meet with terrible execution with the wicked in hell.—*J. Field.*

Verse 5. (*last clause*). To whom peace belongs. To "Israel"; the chosen, the once wrestler, the now prevailing prince. Consider Jacob's life after he obtained the name of Israel; note his trials, and his security under them as illustrating this text. Then take the text as a sure promise.

Verse 5. (*last clause*). Enquire,

1. Who are the Israel?

>(a) Converted ones.
>(b) Circumcised in heart.
>(c) True worshippers.

2. What is the peace?

>(a) Peace of conscience.
>(b) Of friendship with God.
>(c) Of a settled and satisfied heart.
>(d) Of eternal glory, in reversion.

3. Why the certainty ("shall be")?

>(a) Christ has made peace for them.
>(b) The Holy Spirit brings peace to them.
>(c) They walk in the way of peace.
>—*J. Field.*

PSALM 126

SERMON OUTLINES AND HELPFUL TIPS

Verse 1.

1. Sunny memories of what the Lord did, "he turned again the captivity", etc.
2. Singular impressions,—we could not believe it to be true.
3. Special discoveries—it was true, abiding, etc.

Verse 1. A comparison and a contrast.

1. The saved like them that dream.

    (a) In the strangeness of their experience.
    (b) In the ecstasy of their joy.

2. The saved unlike them that dream.

    (a) In the reality of their experience. Dreams are unsubstantial things, but "the Lord turned"—an actual fact.
    (b) In their freedom from disappointment. No awakening to find it "but a dream": see Isa 29:8.

3. In the endurance of their joy. The joy of dreams is soon forgotten, but this is "everlasting joy."—W. H. J. P.

Verse 2. Saintly laughter. What creates it, and how it is justified.

Verse 2. *Recipe for holy laughter.*

1. Lie in prison a few weeks.
2. Hear the Lord turning the key.
3. Follow him into the high road.
4. Your sky will burst with sunshine, and your heart with song and laughter.
5. If this recipe is thought too expensive, try *keeping in the high road.*—W. B. H.

Verses 2-3.

1. Reports of God's doings.
2. Experience of God's doings.

Verses 2-3.

1. The Lord does great things for his people.
2. These great things command the attention of the world.
3. They inspire the joyful devotion of the saints.—W. H. J. P.

Verse 3. *The LORD hath done great things for us.* In this acknowledgment and confession there are three noteworthy points of thankfulness.

1. That they were "*great things*" which were done.
2. Who it was who did them: "*the Lord.*"
3. That they are done: not against us, but "*for us.*"
—Alexander Henderson, 1583-1646.

Verse 4. Believers, rejoicing in their own deliverance, solicitous for a flood of prosperity to overflow the church. See the connection, Ps 126:1-3. Remark,

1. The doubting and despondent are too concerned about themselves, and too busy seeking comfort, to have either solicitude or energy to spare for the church's welfare; but the joyful heart is free to be earnest for the church's good.

2. Joyful believers, other things being equal, know more of the constraining power of Christ's love, which makes them anxious for his glory and the success of his cause.

3. The joyful can appreciate more fully the contrast of their condition to that of the undelivered, and for their sake cannot fail to be anxious for the church through whose ministry their deliverance comes.

4. The joyful are, in general, the most believing and the most hopeful; their expectation of success leads them to prayer, and impels them to effort.—*J. F.*

Verse 4.

1. The dried up Christian.
2. His unhappy condition.
3. His one hope.
4. Result when realized.

Verse 5. *The Christian Husbandman.*

1. Illustrate the metaphor. The husbandman has a great variety of work before him; every season and every day brings its proper business. So the Christian has duties in the closet, in the family, in the church, in the world, etc., etc.

2. Whence it is that many Christians sow in tears.

    (a) It may be owing to the badness of the soil.
    (b) The inclemency of the season.
    (c) The malice and opposition of enemies.
    (d) Past disappointments.

3. What connection there is between sowing in tears and reaping in joy.

    (a) A joyful harvest, by God's blessing, is the natural consequence of a dripping seed time.
    (b) God, who cannot lie, hath promised it.

4. When this joyful harvest may be expected. It must not be expected in our wintry world, for there is not sun enough to ripen it. Heaven is the Christian's summer. When you come to reap the fruits of your present trials, you will bless God, who made you sow in tears. *Improvement.*

 (a) How greatly are they to blame who in this busy time stand all the day idle!

 (b) How greatly have Christians the advantage of the rest of the world!

 (c) Let the hope and prospect of this joyful harvest support us under all the glooms and distresses of this vale of tears.—*Outline of a Sermon by Samuel Lavington,* 1726-1807.

Verse 5. Two pictures. The connecting "*shall.*"

Verse 5.

1. There must be sowing before reaping.

2. What men sow they will reap. If they sow precious seed, they will reap precious seed.

3. In proportion as they sow they will reap. "He that soweth sparingly", etc.

4. The sowing may be with sorrow, but the reaping will be with joy.

5. In proportion to the sorrow of sowing will be the joy of reaping.—G. R.

Verse 6. In the two parts of this **Verse** we may behold a threefold antithesis or opposition; in the *progress*,

1. A sojourning: "He that now goeth on his way."

2. A sorrowing: "weeping."

3. A sowing: "and beareth forth good seed." In the regress there are three opposites unto these.

1. Returning: "He shall doubtless come again."
2. A Rejoicing: "with joy."
3. A Reaping: "and bring his sheaves with him."
—*John Hume.*

Verse 6. "*Doubtless.*" Or the reasons why our labor cannot be in vain in the Lord.

Verse 6. *Bringing his sheaves with him.* The faithful sower's return to his Lord. Successful, knowing it, personally honored, abundantly recompensed.

Verse 6. See "Spurgeon's Sermons" No. 867: "Tearful Sowing and Joyful Reaping."

Verse 6.

1. The sorrowful sower.

    (a) His activity—"he goeth forth."
    (b) His humility—"and weepeth."
    (c) His fidelity—"bearing precious seed."

2. The joyful reaper.

    (a) His certain harvest time—"shall doubtless come again."
    (b) His abundant joy—"with rejoicing."
    (c) His rich rewards—"bringing his sheaves with him."
—W. H. J. P.

PSALM 127

SERMON OUTLINES AND HELPFUL TIPS

Verse 1.

1. The human hand without the hand of God is in vain.

2. The human eye without the eye of God is in vain.

—Or—

1. God is to be acknowledged in all our works.

    (a) By seeking his direction before them.
    (b) By depending upon his help in them.
    (c) By giving him the glory of them.

2. In all our cares.

    (a) By owning our short sight.
    (b) By trusting to his foresight.—G. R.

Verse 1. (*first part*).—Illustrate the principles:

1. In building up character.
2. In constructing plans of life and of work.
3. In framing schemes of happiness.
4. In rearing a hope of eternal life.
5. In raising and enlarging the church.—J. F.

Verses 1-2.

1. What we may not expect: namely, God to work without our building, watching, etc.

2. What we may expect: Failure if we are without God.

3. What we should not do: Fret, worry, etc.

4. What we may do: So trust as to rest in peace.

Verse 2. *The bread of sorrows.*

1. When God sends it, it is good to eat it.
2. When we bake it ourselves, it is vain to eat it.
3. When the devil brings it, it is deadly meat.

Verse 2. (*last clause*).—Blessings that come to us in sleep.

1. Renewed health and vigor of body.

2. Mental repose and refreshment.

3. Sweeter thoughts and holier purposes.

4. Providential gifts. The rains fall, the fruits of the earth grow and ripen, the mill wheel goes round, the ship pursues her voyage, etc., while we slumber. Often when we are doing nothing for ourselves God is doing most.—*W. H. J.P.*

Verse 3. Sermon by Thomas Manton. Works: vol. 18. pp. 84-95. *Nichol's Edition.*

Verses 3-5. Children. Consider:

1. The effects of receiving them as a heritage from the Lord.

> (a) Parents will trust in the Lord for their provision and safety.
> (b) Will regard them as a sacred trust from the Lord, of whose care they must render an account.
> (c) Will train them up in the fear of the Lord.
> (d) Will often consult God concerning them.
> (e) Will render them up uncomplainingly when the Lord calls them to himself by death.

2. The effects of their right training.

> (a) They become the parents' joy.
> (b) The permanent record of the parents' wisdom.
> (c) The support and solace of the parents' old age.
> (d) The transmitters of their parents' virtues to another generation; for well-trained children become, in their turn, wise parents.—J. F.

Verse 4. The spiritual uses of children.

1. When they die in infancy, awakening parents.
2. When they go home from Sunday school carrying holy influences.
3. When they become converted.
4. When they grow up and become useful men and women.

Verses 4-5.

1. The dependence of children upon parents.

> (a) For safety. They are in their quiver.
> (b) For direction. They are sent forth by them.
> (c) For support. They are in the hands of the mighty.

2. The dependence of parents upon children.

> (a) For defense. Who will hear a parent spoken against?
>
> (b) For happiness. "A wise son maketh", etc. Children elicit some of the noblest and most tender emotions of human nature. Happy is the Christian minister who with a full quiver can say, "Here am I, and the children which thou hast given me."—G. R.

Verse 6. "The Reward of Well doing Sure." Sermon by Henry Melvill, in "The Pulpit," 1856.

PSALM 128

SERMON OUTLINES AND HELPFUL TIPS

Verse 1. The universality of the blessedness of God fearing men. Circumstances, personal or relative, cannot alter the blessing; nor age, nor public opinion, nor even their own sense of unworthiness.

Verse 1. Consider:

1. The union of a right fear with a right walk.

>   (a) There is a wrong fear, because slavish; this never can lead to genuine obedience, which must be willingly and cheerfully rendered.
>   (b) But the fear of reverence and filial love will surely turn the feet to God's ways, keep them steadfast therein, and wing them with speed.

2. The blessedness of him in whom they are united.

>   (a) It is blessedness of life; for that is prospered.
>   (b) It is blessedness of domestic happiness; for where the head of a family is holy, the family is the home of peace.
>   (c) It is the blessedness of a holy influence in every sphere of his activity.
>   (d) It is deep felt heart blessedness in walking with God.
>   (e) And all is but a prelude to the everlasting blessedness of heaven. —J. F.

Verse 2. The blessedness of the righteous are first generalized, then particularized. Here they are divided into three particulars.

1. The fruit of past labors.

2. Present enjoyment.

3. Future welfare: "It shall be well with thee." Well in time; well in death; well at the last judgment; well forever. —G. R.

Verse 2.

1. Labor a blessing to him who fears God.
2. The fruits of labor the result of God's blessing.
3. The enjoyment of the fruits of labor a further blessing from God.
—W. H. J. P.

Verse 2. (*first clause*). Success in life.

1. Its source—God's blessing.

2. Its channels—our own labor.

3. The measure in which it is promised—as much as we can eat. More is above the promise.

4. The enjoyment. We are permitted to eat or enjoy our labor.

Verse 2. (*second clause*). Godly happiness.

1. Follows upon God's blessing.
2. Grows out of character: "feareth the Lord."
3. Follows labor: see preceding sentence.
4. It is supported by wellbeing: see following sentence.

Verse 2. (*last clause*).

1. It shall be well with thee while thou livest.
2. It shall be better with thee when thou diest.
3. It shall be best of all with thee in eternity.
—*Adapted from Matthew Henry.*

Verse 3. The blessing of children.

1. They are round our table—expense, anxiety, responsibility, pleasure.

2. They are like olive plants—strong, planted in order, coming on to succeed us, fruitful for God—as the olive provided oil for the lamp.

Verse 3. A complete family picture. Here are the husband, the wife, the children, the house, the rooms in the side, the table. We should ask a blessing upon each, bless God for each, and use each in a blessed manner.

Verse 4. Domestic happiness the peculiar blessing of piety. Show how it produces and maintains it.

Verse 5. The blessing out of Zion. See Nu 6:24-26.

Verse 5. Two priceless mercies.

1. The house of God a blessing to our house. It is connected with our own salvation, edification, consolation, etc. It is our hope for the conversion of our children and servants, etc. It is the place of their education, and for the formation of helpful friendship, etc.

2. Our house a blessing to God's house. Personal interest in the church, hospitality, generosity, service, etc. Children aiding holy work. Wife useful, etc.

Verse 6. Old age blessed when

1. Life has been spent in the fear of God.
2. When it is surrounded to its close by human affection.
3. When it maintains its interest in the cause of God.
—*W. H. J. P.*

Verse 6. (*last clause*). Church peace—its excellence, its enemies, its friends, its fruits.

PSALM 129

SERMON OUTLINES AND HELPFUL TIPS

Verse 1. Affliction as it comes to saints from men of the world.

1. Reason for it—enmity of the serpent's seed.

2. Modes of its display—persecution, ridicule, slander, disdain, etc.

3. Comfort under it. So persecuted they the prophets: so the Master. It is their nature. They cannot kill the soul. It is but for a time, etc.

Verses 1-2.

1. How far persecution for righteousness' sake may go.

>   (a) It may be great: "afflicted", "afflicted."
>   (b) It may be frequent: "Many a time."
>   (c) It may be early: "From my youth."

2. How far it cannot go.

>   (a) It may seem to prevail.
>   (b) It may prevail in some degree.
>   (c) It cannot ultimately prevail.
>   (d) It shall cause that to which it is opposed increasingly to prevail.—G. R.

Verses 1-4. Israel persecuted but not forsaken. Persecution.

1. Whence it came: "they."

2. How it came: "Many a time", "from my youth", severely: "afflicted", "ploughed."

3. Why it came. Human and Satanic hatred, and Divine permission.

4. What came of it: "not prevailed"—to destroy, to drive to despair, to lead to sin. God's righteousness manifested in upholding his people, baffling their foes, etc.

Verses 1-4. The enemies of God's church.

1. Their violence: "The plowers plowed", etc.
2. Their persistency: "Many a time...from my youth."
3. Their failure: "Yet they have not prevailed."
4. Their great opponent: "The Lord...hath cut asunder."
—J. F.

Verse 3.

1. Literally fulfilled.

(a) In Christ. Mt 27:26 20:19 Mr 15:15 Lu 18:33 Joh 19:1.
(b) In his followers. Mt 10:17 Ac 16:23 2Co 6:5 2Co 11:23-24 Heb 11:36. And frequently in subsequent persecutions.

2. Figuratively. In secret calumnies both in Christ and his followers.—*G. R.*

Verse 4. Israel's song of triumph.

1. The Lord is righteous in permitting these afflictions to come upon his people.

2. He is righteous in keeping his promise of deliverance to his people.

3. He is righteous in visiting the enemies of his people with judgment.—*W. H. J. P.*

Verse 5.

1. An inexcusable hatred described: "hate Zion", God's church and cause. For,

   (a) Her people are righteous.
   (b) Her faith is a gospel.
   (c) Her mission is peace.
   (d) Her very existence is the world's preservation.

2. An inveterate sinfulness indicated: "Them that hate Zion." For, whatever moral virtues they may boast of, they must be,

   (a) Enemies to the human race.
   (b) In defiant opposition to God.
   (c) Perversely blind, as Saul, or radically vile.
   (d) Devil like.

3. An instinctive feeling of a good man expressed: "Let them all be", etc. Prompted by,

   (a) His love to God.
   (b) Love to man.
   (c) Love to righteousness. Hence, its existence is in itself a pledge that the righteous God will respect and comply with it.—*J. F.*

Verses 5-8.

1. The characters described.

   (a) They do not love Zion. They say not, "Lord, I have loved the habitation of thine house", etc.
   (b) They hate Zion—both its King and its subjects.

2. Their prosperity: "As the grass", etc.

3. Their end.

(a) Shame: "Let them be confounded."
(b) Loss: "Turned back."
(c) Disappointment. No mowing; no reaping.
(d) Dishonor. Unblessed by others as well as in themselves. —G. R.

Verses 6-9. The wicked flourishing and perishing.

1. Eminent in position.
2. Envied in prosperity.
3. Evanescent in duration.
4. Empty as to solidity.
5. Excepted from blessing.

PSALM 130

SERMON OUTLINES AND HELPFUL TIPS

Verse 1. The assertion of an experienced believer.

1. I have cried—that is, I have earnestly, constantly, truthfully prayed.

2. I have cried only unto thee. Nothing could draw me to other confidences, or make me despair of thee.

3. I have cried in distress. At my worst, temporally or spiritually, I have cried out of the depths.

4. I therefore infer—that I am thy child, no hypocrite, no apostate; and that thou hast heard and wilt hear me evermore.

Verse 1.

1. What we are to understand by "the depths." Great misery and distress.

2. How men get into "the depths." By sin and unbelief.

3. What gracious souls do when in "the depths." Cry unto the Lord.

4. How the Lord lifts praying souls out of "the depths"; "He shall redeem, "etc., Ps 130:8.—W. H. J. P.

Verse 1.

1. In the pit.
2. The morning star seen: "Thee, O Lord."
3. Prayer flutters up "out of the depths."—W. B. H.

Verses 1-2.

1. The depths from which prayer may rise.

    (a) Of affliction.
    (b) Of conviction.
    (c) Of desertion.

2. The height to which it may ascend.

    (a) To the hearing of God.
    (b) To a patient hearing. "Hear my voice."
    (c) To an attentive hearing.

Or,

1. We should pray at all times.

2. We should pray that our prayers may be heard.

3. We should pray until we know we are heard.

4. We should pray in faith that when heard we have the thing we have asked. "That which thou hast prayed to me against the King of Assyria I have heard." God had heard. That was enough. It was the death of Sennacherib and the overthrow of his host. —G. R.

Verses 1-2. Consider,

1. The Psalmist's condition in the light of a warning. Evidently, through sin, he came into the depths; see Ps 130:3-4. Learn,

> (a) The need of watchfulness on the part of all.
> (b) That backsliding will, sooner or later, bring great trouble of soul.

2. His sometime continuance in that condition, in the light of a Divine judgment: "I have cried." Certainly his first cry had not brought deliverance.

> (a) The realization of pardon is a Divine work, dependent upon God's pleasure. Ps 85:8.
>
> (b) But he will not always nor often speak pardon at the first asking; for He will make His people reverence his holiness, feel the bitterness of sinning, learn caution, etc.

3. His conduct while in that condition in the light of a direction. He,

> (a) Seeks deliverance only of God.
> (b) Is intensely earnest in his application: "I cried."
> (c) Is inopportune in his pleading: "Hear my voice, "etc. —J. F.

Verse 2. Attention from God to us—how to gain it.

1. Let us plead the name which commands attention.
2. Let us ourselves pay attention to God's word.
3. Let us give earnest attention to what we ask, and how we ask.
4. Let us attentively watch for a reply.

Verse 2. *Lord, hear my voice.*

1. Though it be faint by reason of distance—hear it.
2. Though it be broken because of my distress—hear it.
3. Though it be unworthy on account of my iniquities—hear it. —W. H. J. P.

Verse 3.

1. The supposition: "If thou, Lord, shouldest mark iniquities"

(a) It is scriptural.

(b) It is reasonable. If God is not indifferent towards men, he must observe their sins. If he is holy, he must manifest indignation against sin. If he is the Creator of conscience, he must certainly uphold its verdict against sin. If he is not wholly on the side of sin, how can he fail to avenge the mischiefs and miseries sin has caused?

2. The question it suggests: "Who shall stand?" A question,

    (a) Not difficult to answer.
    (b) Of solemn import to all.
    (c) Which ought to be seriously pondered without delay.

3. The possibility it hints at. "If thou, Lord." The "if" hints at the possibility that God may not mark sin. The possibility,

    (a) Is reasonable, providing it can be without damage to God's righteousness; for the Creator and Preserver of men cannot delight in condemning and punishing.

    (b) Is a God Honoring reality, through the blood of Christ, Ro 3:21-26.

    (c) Becomes a glorious certainty in the experience of penitent and believing souls. — J. F.

Verses 3-4.

1. The Confession. He could not stand.
2. The Confidence. "There is forgiveness."
3. The Consequence. "That thou mayest be feared."

Verses 3-4.

1. The fearful supposition.
2. The solemn interrogation.
3. The Divine consolation. — W. J.

Verse 4. Forgiveness with God.

1. The proofs of it.

    (a) Divine declarations.
    (b) Invitations and promises, Isa 1:18.
    (c) The bestowment of pardon so effectually as to give assurance and joy. 2Sa 12:13 Ps 32:5 Lu 7:47-8. 1Jo 2:12.

2. The reason of it.

    (a) In God's nature there is the desire to forgive; the gift of Christ is sufficient evidence for it.

    (b) But, the text speaks not so much of a desire as it asserts the existence of a forgiveness being "with" God, therefore ready to be dispensed. The blood of Christ is the reason (Col 1:14); by it the disposition to forgive righteously manifests itself in the forgiving act: Ro 3:25-26.

    (c) Hence, forgiveness for all who believe is sure: Ro 3:25 1Jo 2:1-2.

3. The result of its realization: "That thou mayest be feared": with a reverential fear, and spiritual worship.

(a) The possibility of forgiveness begets in an anxious soul true penitence, as opposed to terror and despair.

(b) The hope of receiving it begets earnest seeking and prayerfulness.

(c) A believing reception of it gives peace and rest, and, exciting grateful love, leads to spiritual worship and filial service. —J. F.

Verse 4. *There is forgiveness.*

1. It is needed.
2. God alone can give it.
3. It may be had.
4. We may know that we have it.

Verse 4.

1. A most cheering announcement: "There is forgiveness with thee."

   (a) A fact certain.
   (b) A fact in the present tense.
   (c) A fact which arises out of God himself.
   (d) A fact stated in general terms.
   (e) A fact to be meditated upon with delight.

2. A most admirable design: "That thou mayest be feared."

   (a) Very contrary to the abuse made of it by rebels, triflers, and procrastinators.
   (b) Very different from the pretended fears of legalists.
   (c) No pardon, no fear of God—devils, reprobates.
   (d) No pardon, none survive to fear him.
   (e) But the means of pardon encourage faith, repentance, prayer; and the receipt of pardon creates love, suggests obedience, inflames zeal.

Verse 4. See "Spurgeon's Sermons", No. 351: "Plenteous Redemption."

Verse 4. Tender Light.

1. The Angel by the Throne: "Forgiveness with Thee."

2. The shadow that enhances his sweet majesty: "If", "But."

3. The homage resultant from his ministry; universal from highest to least. —W.B. H.

Verses 5-6. Three postures: Waiting, Hoping, Watching.

Verses 5-6.

1. The seeking sinner.
2. The Christian mourner.
3. The loving intercessor.

4. The spiritual laborer.
5. The dying believer.—W. J.

Verses 5-6.

1. We are to wait on God.

   (a) By faith: "In his word do I hope."
   (b) By prayer. Prayer can wait when it has a promise to rest upon.

2. We are to wait for God: "I wait for the Lord." "My soul waiteth for the Lord more", etc.

   (a) Because he has his own time for giving.
   (b) Because what he gives is worth waiting for.—G. R.

Verse 6. *More than they.*

1. For the darker sorrow his absence causes.
2. For the richer splendor Iris coming must bring.
3. For the greater might of our indwelling love.—W. B. H.

Verse 6.

1. A long, dark night: The Lord absent.
2. An eager, hopeful watcher: Waiting the Lord's return.
3. A bright, blessed morning: The time of the Lord's appearing.—W. H. J. P.

Verse 7. Redeeming grace the sole hope of the holiest.—W. B. H.

Verse 7.

1. A divine exhortation: "Let Israel hope in the LORD."
2. A spiritual reason: "For with the LORD there is mercy", etc.
3. A gracious promise: "He shall redeem Israel from, all his iniquities."—J. C. Philpot.

Verses 7-8. It is our wisdom to have personal dealings with God.

1. The first exercise of faith must be upon the Lord himself. This is the natural order, the necessary order, easiest, wisest, and most profitable order. Begin where all begins.

2. Exercises of faith about other things must still be in connection with the Lord. Mercy—"with the Lord." Plenteous redemption "with him."

3. Exercises of faith, whatever their object, must all settle on him. "He shall redeem", etc.

Verse 8.

1. The Redemption: "From all iniquities."
2. The Redeemer: "The Lord." See Tit 2:14.
3. The Redeemed: "Israel."—W. H. J. P.

PSALM 131

SERMON OUTLINES AND HELPFUL TIPS

Verse 1. *Humility.*

1. A profession which ought to befit every child of God.

2. A profession which nevertheless many children of God cannot truthfully make. Point out the prevalence of pride and ambition even in the church.

3. A profession which can only be justified through the possession of the spirit of Christ (Mt 11:29-30 Mt 18:1-5). —*C.A. D.*

Verse 2. *Surely I have behaved and quieted myself.* The original bears somewhat of the form of an oath, and therefore our translators exhibited great judgment in introducing the word "surely"; it is not a literal version, but it correctly gives the meaning. The Psalmist had been upon his best behavior, and had smoothed down the roughness of his self-will; by holy effort he had mastered his own spirit, so that towards God he was not rebellious, even as towards man he was not haughty. It is no easy thing to quiet yourself: sooner may a man calm the sea, or rule the wind, or tame a tiger, than quiet himself. We are clamorous, uneasy, petulant; and nothing but grace can make us quiet under afflictions, irritations, and disappointments. *As a child that is weaned of afflictions mother.* He had become as subdued and content as a child whose weaning is fully accomplished. The Easterners put off the time of weaning far later than we do, and we may conclude that the process grows none the easier by being postponed. At last there must be an end to the suckling period, and then a battle begins: the child is denied his comfort, and therefore frets and worries, flies into pets, or sinks into sulks. It is facing its first great sorrow and it is in sore distress. Yet time brings not only alleviations, but the ending of the conflict; the boy ere long is quite content to find his nourishment at the table with his brothers, and he feels no lingering, wish to return to those dear fountains from which he once sustained his life. He is no longer angry with his mother, but buries his head in that very bosom after which he pined so grievously: he is weaned *on* his mother rather than *from* her.

"My soul doth like a weanling rest,
I cease to weep;
So mother's lap, though dried her breast,
Can lull to sleep."

To the weaned child his mother is his comfort though she has denied him comfort. It is a blessed mark of growth out of spiritual infancy when we can forego the joys which once appeared to be essential, and can find our solace in him who denies them to us: then we behave manfully, and every childish complaint is hushed. If the Lord removes our dearest delight we bow to his will without a murmuring thought; in fact, we find a delight in giving up our delight. This is no spontaneous fruit of nature, but a well-tended product of divine grace: it grows out of humility and lowliness, and it is the stem upon which peace blooms as a fair flower. *My soul is even as a weaned child*; or it may be read, "as a weaned child on me my soul", as if his soul leaned upon him in mute submission, neither boasting nor complaining. It is not every child of God who arrives at this weanedness speedily. Some are sucklings when they ought to be fathers; others are hard to wean, and cry, and fight, and rage against their heavenly parent's discipline. When we think ourselves safely through the weaning, we sadly discover that the old appetites are rather wounded than slain, and we begin crying again for the breasts which we had given up. It is easy to begin shouting before we are out of the wood, and no doubt hundreds have sung this Psalm long before they have understood it. Blessed are those afflictions which subdue our affections, which wean us from self-sufficiency, which educate us into Christian manliness, which teach us to love God not merely when he comforts us, but even when he tries us. Well might the sacred poet repeat his figure of the weaned child; it is worthy of admiration and imitation; it is doubly desirable and difficult of attainment. Such weanedness from self springs from the gentle humility declared in the former verse, and partly accounts for its existence. If pride is gone, submission will be sure to follow; and, on the other hand, if pride is to be driven out, self must also be vanquished.

Verse 2. The soul is as a weaned child:

1. In conversion.
2. In sanctification, which is a continual weaning from the world and sin.
3. In bereavement.
4. In affliction of every kind.
5. In death. —G. R.

Verse 2.

1. The soul has to be weaned as well as the body.

> (a) It is first nourished by others.
> (b) It is afterward thrown upon its own resources.

2. The soul is weaned from one thing by giving its attention to another.

> (a) From worldly things by heavenly.
> (b) From self-righteousness by the righteousness of another.
> (c) From sin to holiness.
> (d) From the world to Christ.
> (e) From self to God. —G.R.

Verse 2.

1. A desirable condition: "As a weaned child."
2. A difficult task—to subdue and quiet self.
3. A delightful result: "Surely... my soul is as a weaned child." —W. H. J. P.

Verse 2.

1. Soul fretfulness: weak, dishonorable, rebellious.

2. Soul government; throne often abdicated; God gives each the scepter of self-rule; necessary to successful life.

3. Soul quiet: its sweetness; its power. Come, Holy Spirit, breathe it upon us! —*W. B. H.*

Verse 2. See "Spurgeon's Sermons", No. 1210: "The Weaned Child."

Verses 2-3. The weaned child hoping in the Lord:

1. The first weaning of the soul, the grand event of a man's history.

2. The joy in the Lord that springs up in every weaned soul: "My soul is even as a weaned child; let Israel hope in the Lord from henceforth and forever."

3. The daily weaning of the soul through life.

4. The earnest desires and the fruitful work of every weaned soul. —*A. Moody Stuart.*

Verse 3.

1. The encouragement to hope in God.

    (a) As a covenant God, "the God of Israel."
    (b) As a covenant keeping God: "From henceforth", etc.

2. The effect of this hope.

    (a) The humility and dependence in the first **Verse**.

    (b) The contentment and weaning in the second **Verse**. Would Israel be thus humble and obedient as a little child? "Let Israel hope," etc. —*G. R.*

Verse 3. *The Voice of Hope heard in the Calm.*

1. Calmed souls appreciate God. Quiet Favors contemplation. God's majesty, perfection, and praise so discovered.

2. Calmed souls confide in God; seen to be so worthy of trust.

3. Calmed souls look fearlessly into eternity; "from henceforth and for ever." —*W. B. H.*

Verse 3. *Hope on, hope ever.*

1. For the past warrants such confidence.
2. For the present demands such confidence.
3. For the future will justify confidence. —*W. H. J. P.*

PSALM 132

SERMON OUTLINES AND HELPFUL TIPS

Verse 1.

1. The Lord remembers Jesus, our David: he loves him, he delights in him, he is with him.

2. In that memory his griefs have a prominent place—"all his afflictions."

3. Yet the Lord would be put in remembrance by his people.

Verses 1-2. Concerning his people,

1. The Lord remembers,

    (a) Their persons.
    (b) Their afflictions.
    (c) Their vows.

2. The Lord remembers them,

    (a) To accept them.
    (b) To sympathize with them.
    (c) To assist them.

Verses 1-2.

1. God remembers his people, each one: "Remember David." The Spirit maketh intercession within us according to the will of God.

2. He remembers their afflictions: "David and all his afflictions." "I know thy works and thy tribulation."

3. He remembers their vows, especially,

    (a) Those which relate to his service.
    (b) Those which are solemnly made.
    (c) Those which are faithfully performed.—*G. R.*

Verses 1-5. Notice,

1. How painfully David felt what he conceived to be a disHonoring of God, which he thought he might be able to remedy. Consider "his afflictions",—because the ark dwelt within curtains, while he himself dwelt in a house of cedar: 2Sa 7:2.

2. Consider,

    (a) Its singularity. Most find affliction in personal losses; very few suffer from a cause like this.

(b) The little sympathy such a feeling meets with from the most of men. "If God means to convert the heathen, he can do it without you, young man", was said to Dr., then Mr. Carey, when heathenism was an affliction to him.

(c) Its fittingness to a really God fearing man.

(d) Its pleasingness to God: 1Sa 2:30.

2. How earnestly he set himself to remedy the evil he deplored: "He sware", etc. There cannot be the least doubt that he would have foregone the enjoyment of temporal luxuries until he had accomplished the work dear to his heart, if he had been permitted of God. Remark,

(a) There is little zeal for God's Honor when self-denial is not exercised for the sake of his cause.

(b) Were a like zeal generally shown by God's people, there would be more givers and more liberal gifts; more workers, and the work more heartily and better done.

(c) It would be well to astonish the world, and deserve the commendations of the righteous by becoming enthusiasts for the Honor of God.—J. F.

Verses 3-5.

1. We should desire a habitation for God more than for ourselves. God should have the best of everything. "See, now, I dwell in a house of cedar, but the ark of God dwelleth within curtains."

2. We should be guided by the house of God in seeking a house for ourselves: "Surely I will not come", etc.

3. We should labor for the prosperity of God's house even more than of our own. Nothing should make sleep more sweet to us than when the church of God prospers; nothing keep us more awake than when it declines: "I will not give sleep", etc. (Ps 132:4); "Is it time for you, O ye, to dwell in your ceiled houses, and this house lie waste?"—G. R.

Verse 5. Something to live for—to find fresh habitations for God.

1. The Condescension implied: God *with us*.

2. The Districts explored: hearts, homes, "dark places of the earth."

3. The Royalty of the Work. It makes King David busy, and is labor worthy of a king.—W. B. H.

Verse 5. "*A place for the LORD.*" In the heart, the home, the assembly, the life. Everywhere we must find or make a place for the Lord.

Verse 5. "*The mighty God of Jacob.*"

1. Mighty, and therefore he joined heaven and earth at Bethel.
2. Mighty, and therefore brought Jacob back from Mesopotamia.
3. Mighty, and yet wrestled with him at Jabbok.

4. Mighty, and yet allowed him to be afflicted.

5. Mighty, and therefore gave him full deliverance.

Verses 6-7. We shall use this for practical purposes. A soul longing to meet with God. God has appointed a meeting place.

1. *We know what it is.* A mercy seat, a throne of grace, a place of revealed glory. Within it the law preserved. Heavenly food—pot of manna. Holy rule—Aaron's rod.

2. *We desire to find it.* Intensely. Immediately. Reverently. Longing to receive it.

3. *We heard of it.* In our young days. We almost forget where. From ministers, from holy men, from those who loved us.

4. *We found it.* Where we least expected it. In a despised place. In a lonely place. Where we lost ourselves. Very near us—where we hid like Adam among the trees.

5. *We will go.* To God in Christ. For all he gives. To dwell with him. To learn of him.

6. *We will worship.* Humbly. Solemnly. Gratefully. Preparing for heaven.

Verse 7.

1. The Place: "His tabernacles."

a) Built for God.

b) Accepted by God: present everywhere, he is especially present here.

2. The Attendance: "We will go", etc. There God is present to meet us, and there we should be present to meet him.

3. The Design:

a) For adoration.

b) For self-consecration: "We will worship at his footstool."—G. R.

Verses 8-9.

1. The Presence of God desired—

   (a) That it may be signally manifested: "Arise" and enter.

   (b) That it may be gracious: "Thou and the ark"—that he may be present on the mercy seat.

   (c) That it may be felt: accompanied with power: "The ark of thy strength."

   (d) That it may be abiding: "Arise into thy rest."

2. The reasons for this desire.

(a) With respect to the priests or ministers: "Let thy priests", etc.: not their own righteousness, but as a clothing: let them speak of "garments of salvation" and "robes of righteousness."

(b) With respect to the worshippers: "And let thy saints", etc. Let ministers preach the gift of righteousness; not that which grows out of man's nature, but that which is "unto all and upon all them that believe", and saints will shout for joy.—G. R.

Verse 9. Consider,

1. The importance of a righteous ministry in the church.
2. The connection between such a ministry and a joyous people.
3. The dependence of both on the gracious working of God.—J. F.

Verse 9. (*second clause*).

1. Saints.
2. Shouting.
3. Explaining—"for joy."
4. Encouraging—"Let thy saints shout."

Verse 9. (*second clause*).—The connection between holiness and joy.

Verses 9, 16. *The Spiritual Vestry.*

1. The Vestments:

    (a) Righteousness; for which the costliest stole is a poor substitute.
    (b) Salvation: learning, oratory, etc., of small account in comparison.

2. The Procuring of the vestments:

    (a) Must be from God.
    (b) Earnest prayer should constantly arise from all saints.

3. The Robing:

    (a) By God's own hand!
    (b) Their beauty and power who are so invested.
    (c) The persons are "thy priests."—W. B. H.

Verses 9, 16.

1. Priests and Saints.
2. Vestments.
3. "Hymns Ancient and Modern."
4. The Real Presence: God giving the garments and the joy.

Verse 10.

1. An evil to be deprecated: "Turn not away the face"—so that he cannot see thee, or be seen of thee, or accepted, or allowed to hope.

2. A plea to be employed, "for thy servant David's sake"—thy covenant with him, his zeal, his consecration, his afflictions, his service. Good gospel pleading, such as may be used on many occasions.

Verse 11.

1. The divine oath.
2. Its eternal stability.
3. The everlasting Kingship.

Verse 11. (*middle clause*).—Our confidence: "He will not turn from it." He is not a changing God. He foreknew everything. He is able to carry out his purpose. His Honor is bound up in it. His oath can never be broken.

Verse 12. Family Favor may be perpetual, but the conditions must be observed.

Verse 13.

1. Sovereign choice.
2. Condescending indwelling.
3. Eternal rest.
4. Gracious reason—"I have desired it."

Verse 14.

1. God finding rest in his church.

   (a) The three persons honored.
   (b) The divine nature exercised.
   (c) Eternal purposes fulfilled.
   (d) Almighty energies rewarded.
   (e) Tremendous sacrifices remembered.
   (f) Glorious attributes extolled.
   (g) Dearest relationships indulged.

2. This rest enduring forever.

   (a) There will always be a church.
   (b) That church will always be such as God can rest in.
   (c) That church will therefore be secure on earth.
   (d) That church will be glorified eternally in heaven.

Verse 15.

1. Blessed provision.
2. Satisfied people—"satisfy her poor."

3. Glorified God — "I will."
4. Happy place — Zion.

Verse 16, 18. Two forms of clothing: salvation and shame, prepared for his priests and Iris enemies. Which will you wear?

Verse 17. A Lamp ordained for God's Anointed. Being the Substance of Two Sermons, by Ebenezer Erskine. *Works, Vol. 3, pp. 3-41.*

Verses 17-18.

1. The budding horn of growing power.
2. The perpetual lamp of constant brightness.
3. The sordid array of defeated foes.
4. The unfading wreath of glorious sovereignty.

Verse 18.

1. His enemies clothed.

   (a) Who are they? The openly profane. The moral but irreligious. The self-righteous. The hypocritical.

   (b) How clothed with shame? In repentance, in disappointment, in remorse, in destruction. Sin detected. Self-defeated. Hopes scattered.

   (c) Who clothes them The Lord. He will shame them thoroughly.

2. Himself crowned.

   (a) His crown: his dominion and glory.

   (b) Its flourishing. Glory extending. Subjects increasing. Wealth growing. Foes fearing, etc.

Verse 18. (*last clause*). The Lord Jesus himself the source, sustenance, and centre of the prosperity of his kingdom.

PSALM 133

SERMON OUTLINES AND HELPFUL TIPS

Verse 1. Christian unity.

1. Its admirable excellences.
2. The signs of its existence.
3. The causes of its decay.
4. The means of its renewal.

Verse 1. The saints are here contemplated,

1. In their brotherhood.
2. In their concord.
3. In their felicity. —W. J.

Verses 1-3. Six blessings which dwell with unity.

1. Goodness.
2. Pleasure.
3. Anointing.
4. Dew.
5. God's blessing.
6. Eternal life.

Verses 1-3.

1. The contemplation: brethren dwelling together in unity.

    (a) In a family.
    (b) In a Christian church.
    (c) Brethren of the same denomination.
    (d) Of different denominations.

2. Its commendation.

    (a) Literally: "good and pleasant."

    (b) Figuratively: fragrant as the priestly anointing; fruitful as the dew on Hermon.

    (c) Spiritually, it has a blessing from God, that gives life, and continues for evermore! —G. R.

Verses 1-3. On Christians dwelling together in unity as a church.

1. *Its propriety*, on account of fraternal relationship: "*For brethren.*" The Christian brotherhood is so unique, sacred and lasting, that a lack of unity is a disgrace. They are brethren,

    (a) Because born of God, who is "the God of peace." Their claim to the brotherhood is dependent upon likeness to Him: Mt 5:9.

(b) Because united to Christ, who as elder brother desires unity: Joh 17:20-21. Not to seek it is virtually to disown Him.

(c) Because "by one Spirit are we all baptized into one body" (1Co 12:13), wherein unity must be kept: Eph 4:3.

(d) Because destined to "dwell together in unity", forever in heaven; therefore we should aim at it here.

2. *Its peculiar excellency*: both "good and pleasant."

(a) Good, in respect of church work and influence; of mutual edification and growth in grace (2Co 13:11); of the success of prayer (Mt 18:19); of recommending the gospel to others.

(b) Pleasant, as productive of happiness: as pleasing to God.

3. *Its promotion* and maintenance.

(a) Seeking the glory of God unites; in opposition to self-honor which divides.

(b) Love to Christ as a constraining power unites each to the other as it binds all closely to Christ.

(c) Activity in ministering to others, rather than desiring to be ministered unto, binds heart to heart.—J. F.

Verse 2. There must have been special reasons why a priestly anointing should be selected for the comparison, and why that of Aaron, rather than of any other of the high priests. They are these—

1. *The ointment was "holy"*, prepared in accordance with the Divine prescription: Ex 30:23-25. Church union is sacred. It must spring from the love commanded by God; be based on the principles laid down by God; and exist for the ends appointed of God.

2. *The anointing was from God through Moses*, who acted on behalf of God in the matter. Church unity is of the Holy Spirit (1Co 13:13), through Jesus as mediator. Therefore it should be prayed for, and thankfully acknowledged.

3. *By the anointing, Aaron became consecrated*, and officially qualified to act as priest. By unity the Church, as a whole, lives its life of consecration, and effectively ministers in the priesthood assigned it.

4. *The oil was diffusive*; it rested not on Aaron's head, but flowed down to the skirts of his garments. Unity will, in time, make its way from a few to the whole, especially from the leaders in a church to the rest of its members. Hence, it is a personal matter. Each should realize it, and by love and wise conduct diffuse it.—J. F.

Verses 2-3. Christian love scatters blessing by the way of coming down: "ran down", "went down", "descended."

1. God to his saints.
2. Saint to saint.
3. Saint to sinner.

Verse 3. The chosen place for blessing. A church; a church united, a church bedewed of the Spirit. What a blessing for the world that there is a commanded place of blessing!

Verse 3. (*first clause*). This should be rendered, "As the dew of Hermon, that cometh down on the mountains of Zion." From the snows upon the lofty Hermon, the moisture raised by the sun is carried in the form of vapor, by the wind towards the lesser elevations of Zion, upon which it falls as a copious dew. Thus, Christian concord in church fellowship—

1. Despises not the little ones, i.e. the mean, poor, and less gifted. It,

   (a) Recognizes that God is the Father, and Christ is the Redeemer of all believers alike.

   (b) Acknowledges oneness of faith as the true basis of fellowship; not wealth, social position or talent.

   (c) Believes that the least member is essential to the completeness of Christ's body.

   (d) Realizes that everything which renders one in any way superior to another is the gift of God.

2. Distributes of its abundance to the needy: Ac 4:32-37.

   (a) The wealthy to the poor: 1Jo 3:17.
   (b) The learned to the ignorant.
   (c) The joyful to the sorrowing.
   (d) The steadfast to the erring: Jas 5:19.

3. Displays its value more by loving generosity, than by a conspicuous appearance before the world. As Hermon was more valuable to Zion for its dew than for its adornment of the landscape.

   (a) A generous activity exhibits and requires more real grace than showy architecture or ornate worship does.

   (b) Through it, godliness flourishes more than by a vaunted respectability. Zion was fertilized by the dew, not by the grandeur of Hermon.

   (c) By it the heart of Christ is touched and his reward secured: Mr 9:40,42.—*J. F.*

Verse 3. *Commanded Mercy.* Elsewhere goodness is bestowed, but in Zion it is commanded.

1. Commanded mercy implies that it must necessarily be given.

2. Commanded mercy attends commanded unity.

3. Commanded mercy secures life more abundantly, "life for evermore."—*W. B. H.*

PSALM 134

SERMON OUTLINES AND HELPFUL TIPS

Whole Psalm. There are two things in this Psalm.

1. Our blessing God: Ps 134:1-2.

    (a) How? By gratitude, by love, by obedience, by prayer, by praise.

    (b) Where? "in the house of the Lord", "in the sanctuary."

    (c) When? Not in the day merely, but at night. Some of old spent the whole night, others part of the night, in the temple, praising God. As Christ spent whole nights in prayer for his people, they should not think it too much occasionally to spend whole nights in praise of him. Evening services should not be neglected on the Sabbath, nor on other days of the week.

2. God blessing us: Ps 134:3.

    (a) The persons blessed: "bless thee"—everyone who blesses him.

    (b) The condition: "out of Zion." In the fulfillment of religious duties, not in the neglect of them.

    (c) The blessing itself: of the Lord. They are blessed whom he blesses.—*R.*

Whole Psalm.

1. God—Jehovah—the fountain of blessing.

2. The heavens and the earth, evidence of divine capacity to bless.

3. The church, a channel of blessing.

4. The saints, the means of spreading blessing, through the spirit of blessing.

5. The riches involved in the divine benediction.—*Samuel Martin.*

Whole Psalm.

1. Unique service: temple watching, night sentinelship.

2 Sublime society: the awful things of the sanctuary.

3. Holy uplifting: hands, hearts, eyes.

4. Praise in the darkness heard far up in the light.

5. Response from the stars fulfilling the prayer: "The Creator Lord bless thee."—*W.B.H.*

Verse 1.

1. Night settles on the holy place: dark periods of church story.

2. But God has his guards: Wycliffe and his band watching for the Reformation; Waldenses, etc. Never a night so dark but God is praised and served.

3. Be it night or day, let the Levites fulfill their courses. —*W.B.H.*

Verse 1. The Lord's servants exhorted to be,

1. Devout and joyful in their service. Sing at your work, though it be in the dark.

2. Zealous to employ every season of service aright. "By night", as by day, "bless the Lord."

3. Careful to avoid all hindrances to devotion in their service. When tempted to indolence and drowsiness, say:

"Wake, and lift up thyself, my heart,
And with the angels bear thy part,
Who all night long, unwearied, sing
High praise to the Eternal King." *W.H.J.P.*

Verse 1. Directions for worship.

1. It should be with great care: "Behold."
2. With grateful joy: "Bless ye the Lord."
3. Unanimously: "all ye."
4. With holy reverence, as by "servants of the Lord."
5. With unflagging constancy: "stand by night."

Verse 1. *Ye that stand by night.* The night watchmen of the Lord's house, their value, their obscurity, their danger slumber, their consolation, their dignity, their reward.

Verse 2. Ingredients of worship.

1. Uplifted hands. Energy, courage, prayer, aspiration.
2. Uplifted hearts. Thank, praise, adore, and love the Lord.

Verse 3. The Divine Benediction.

1. From the Creator: ample, new, varied, boundless, enduring—all illustrated by his making heaven and earth.

2. From the Redeemer: blessings most needful, rich, effectual, abiding,—all illustrated and guaranteed by his dwelling among men, purchasing a church, building an abode, revealing his glory, reigning on his throne.

PSALM 135

SERMON OUTLINES AND HELPFUL TIPS

Verses 1-4.

1. The Employment. Praise three times commended, and in three respects.

(a) With respect to God: not his works merely, but himself.

(b) With respect to ourselves: it is pleasant and profitable.

(c) With respect to others: it best recommends our religion to all who hear it. All others are religions of fear, ours of joy and praise.

2. The Persons: servants in attendance at his house, who stand there by appointment, ready to hear, ready to obey.

3. The Motives.

(a) In general. It is due to God, because he is good; and it is pleasant to us: Ps 135:3.

(b) In particular. Those who are specially privileged by God should specially praise him. Ps 135:4. "This people have I formed for myself; they shall show forth my praise."—G. R.

Verse 1. *Praise ye the LORD.*

1. The Lord ought to be praised.
2. He ought to be praised *by you*.
3. He ought to be praised *now*: let us remember his present Favors.
4. He ought to be praised in everything forever.

Verse 1. *Praise him, O ye servants of the LORD.*

1. Praise him for the privilege of serving him.
2. Praise him for the power to serve him.
3. Praise him for the acceptance of your service.
4. Praise him as the chief part of your service.
5. Praise him that others may be induced to engage in his service.
—W. H. J. P.

Verse 2. What is at this day "the house of the Lord"? Who may be said to stand in it? What special reasons have they for praise?

Verse 2. The nearer to God, the dearer to God; and the better our place, the sweeter our praise.—W. B. H.

Verse 2-5. *Our God, Our Lord.* Sweet subject. See our Exposition.

Verse 3. Praise the Lord,

1. For the excellence of his nature.
2. For the revelation of his name.
3. For the pleasantness of his worship.

Verse 4. It is a song of praise, and therefore election is mentioned because it is a motive for song.

1. *The Choice*—"The Lord hath chosen." Divine. Sovereign. Gracious. Immutable.

2. *The Consecration*—"Chosen Jacob to himself." To know him. To preserve his truth. To maintain his worship. To manifest his grace. To keep alive the hope of the Coming One.

3. *The Separation*—implied in the special choice. By being taken into covenant: Abraham and his seed. By receiving the covenant inheritance: Canaan. By redemption. By power and by blood out of Egypt. Wilderness separation. Settled establishment in their own land.

4. *The Elevation.* In name—from Jacob to Israel. In value—from worthless to precious. In purpose and use—crown jewels. In preservation kept as treasures. In delight—God rejoices in his people as his heritage.

Verse 5. *I know that the LORD is great.*

1. By observing nature and providence.
2. By reading his word.
3. By my own conversion, comfort, and regeneration.
4. By my after experience.
5. By my overpowering communion with him.

Verse 5. Delicious dogmatism. "*I know,*" etc.

1. What I know.

    (a) The Lord,
    (b) That he is great.
    (c) That he is above all.

2. Why I know it.

    (a) Because he is "our Lord."
    (b) By his operations in nature, providence, and grace (Ps 135:6-13).

3. My incorrigible obstinacy in this regard is proof against worshippers of all other gods: which gods are effeminate; without sovereignty; no god, or any god. —W. B. H.

Verse 6. *Whatsoever the LORD pleased, that did he.* God's good pleasure in the work of grace. Seen, not in the death of the wicked, Eze 33:11; but in the election of his people, 1Sa 12:22; in the infliction of suffering on the substitute, Isa 53:10; in the provision of all fullness for his people in Christ, Col 1:19; in the arrangement of salvation by faith in Christ, Joh 6:39; in instituting preaching as the means of salvation, 1Co 1:21; in the adoption of believers as his children, Eph 1:5; in their sanctification, 1Th 4:3; in their ultimate triumph and reign, Lu 12:32. —C. A. D.

Verse 6. (*last words*). The power of God in places of trouble, change, and danger—*seas*; and in conditions of sin, weakness, despair, perplexity—in all *deep places*.

Verses 6-12. The Resistless Pleasure of Jehovah.

1. Behold it as here exemplified:

>   (a) Ruling all nature.
>   (b) Overturning a rebellious nation.
>   (c) Making sport of kings and crowns.
>   (d) Laying a fertile country at the feet of the chosen.

2. Be wise in view thereof.

>   (a) Submit to it: it sweeps the seas, and lays hands on earth and heaven.
>
>   (b) Think not to hide from it: the "ends of the earth" and "all deep places" are open to it; it is swifter than its own lightnings.
>
>   (c) Be awed by its majesty: God's way is strewn with crowns and the bones of kings.
>
>   (d) Seek its protection: its mightiest efforts are in defense of those it Favors.
>
>   (e) Let the Lord's people fear not with so great a God, and so exhaustless an armory.—W. B. H.

Verse 13. *Thy name, O LORD, endureth forever.*

1. As *the embodiment of perfection*: God's attributes and glory.

2. As *the object of veneration*:"Holy and reverent is his name."

3. As *the cause of salvation*: "For my name's sake", etc.

4. As *the center of attraction*: "In his name shall the Gentiles trust." "Our desire is to the remembrance of thy name." "Where two or three are gathered in my name", etc.

5. As *a plea in supplication*:"For thy name's sake, pardon", etc. "Hitherto ye have asked nothing in my name."

6. As *a warrant for action*: "Whatsoever ye do, do all in the name", etc.

7. As *a refuge in tribulation*: "The name of the Lord is a strong tower: the righteous runneth into it, and is safe." "I have kept them in thy name."

8. As *a mark of glorification*: "I will write upon him the name of my God."

9. As *a terror to transgressors*: "My name is dreadful among the heathen."—W. J.

Verse 14. *The LORD will judge his people.* Others would like to do it, but must not. The world has seven judgment days in every week, but shall not be able to condemn the saints. He himself will judge. How will he judge them

1. Their persons, as to whether they are in or out of Christ.
2. Their principles, as to whether they are genuine or spurious.
3. Their prayers, as to whether they are availing or useless.
4. Their profession, as to whether it is true or false.
5. Their procedure, as to whether it is good or bad. —W. J.

Verse 14.

1. The position of believers his people.
2. The discipline of God's family.
3. The tenderness of the Lord to them.
4. The safety of believers: they are still the Lord's.

Verse 15. *Silver and gold.* These are idols in our own land, among worldlings, and with some professors. Show the folly and wickedness of loving riches, and the evils which come of it.

Verses 16-17. The Portrait of many,

1. "*Mouths, but they speak not.*" No prayer, praise, confession.

2. "*Eyes, but they see not.*" Discern not, understand not, take no warning; do not look to Christ.

3. "*Ears, but they hear not.*" Attend no ministry, or are present but unaffected; hear not God.

4. "*Neither is there any breath in their mouths.*" No life, no tokens of life, no prayer and praise which are the breath of spiritual life.

Verse 18.

1. Men make idols like themselves.

2. The idols make their makers like themselves. Describe both processes.

Verse 19. *House of Israel.* The Lord's great goodness to all his people, perceived and proclaimed, and the Lord praised for it.

Verse 19. *House of Aaron.* God's blessing on Aaron's house typical of his grace to those who are priests unto God.

Verses 19-21.

1. The Exhortation.

    (a) To bless the Lord.

    (b) To bless him in his own house.

2. To whom it is addressed.

    (a) To the house of Israel, or the whole church.

    (b) To the house of Aaron, or ministers of the sanctuary.

(c) To the house of Levi, or the attendants upon ministers, and assistants in the services.

(d) To all who fear God, wherever they may be. Even they who fear God are invited to praise him, which is a sure sign that he delighteth in mercy.—G. R.

Verse 20. The Levites, their history, duties, rewards, and obligations to bless God.

Verse 20. (*second clause*).

1. The fear of God includes all religion.
2. The fear of the Lord suggests praise.
3. The fear of the Lord renders praise acceptable.

Verse 21.

1. The double fact.

   (a) Blessing perpetually ascending from Zion to God.
   (b) God perpetually blessing his people by dwelling with them in Zion.

2. The double reason for praise, which is found in the double fact, and concerns every member of the church.

PSALM 136

SERMON OUTLINES AND HELPFUL TIPS

Verse 1.

1. Consider his name—"Jehovah."
2. Carry out your joyful duty: "O give thanks."
3. Contemplate the two reasons given—goodness and enduring mercy.

Verse 1.

1. Many subjects for praise.

    (a) For the goodness of God: "He is good" (Ps 136:1).
    (b) For his supremacy: "God of gods; Lord of lords" (Ps 136:2-3).
    (c) For his works in general (Ps 136:4).
    (d) For his works of creation in particular (Ps 136:5-9).
    (e) For his works of Providence (Ps 136:10-26).

2. The chief subject for praise: For his mercy endureth forever.

    (a) For mercy. This is the sinner's principal need.
    (b) For mercy in God. This is the sinner's attribute, and is as essential to God as justice.
    (c) For mercy enduring forever. If they who have sinned need mercy forever, they must exist for ever; and their guilt must be forever.—G. R.

Verse 1. The Lord is good. God is originally good—good of himself. He is infinitely good. He is perfectly good, because infinitely good. He is immutably good.—Charnock.

Verses 1-3.

1. The triplet of names: "Jehovah", "the God of gods", "the Lord of lords."

2. The threefold adjuration, "O give thanks."

3. The irrepressible attribute and argument "for his mercy", etc.—W.B.H.

Verses 1-26. For his mercy endureth forever. See "Spurgeon's Sermons", No. 787: "A Song, a Solace, a Sermon, and a Summons."

Verse 4.

1. The Lord does great wonders of mercy.
2. He does them unaided.
3. He does them as none else can do.
4. He should have unique praise.

Verse 4. The great lone Wonder worker.

1. God was alone in the wonderwork of Creation: Ge 1:1-31.
2. Alone in the wonderwork of Redemption: Isa 63:5.

3. Is alone in the wonderwork of Providence: Ps 104:27-28.
4. Alone in the wonderwork of Sanctification: 1Th 5:23-24.
5. Will be alone in the wonderwork of Universal Triumph: 1Co 15:25. —C.A.D.

Verse 4. The merciful in the wonderful. The wonderful in the merciful.

Verse 7. The mercy which dwells in the creation and distribution of light.

Verses 7-9.

1. The constancy of rule.
2. The association of light with rule.
3. The perpetuity of mercy in this matter.

Verses 8-9.

1. The glory of the day of joy.
2. The comforts of the night of sorrow.
3. The hand of God in each.

Verse 10. Mercy and judgment. In the stroke that filled Egypt with anguish there was conspicuous mercy.

1. Even to Egypt; the sharp stroke should have wrought repentance. So God still strives with men.

2. Evidently to Israel; they being thus delivered; their firstborn saved.

3. Emphatically to the who world: power made known, Christ foreshadowed, an important link in the chain of redemption. —W.B.H.

Verse 11. The bringing out of God's people from their natural state, from their misery, and from association with the ungodly, a great marvel of everlasting mercy.

Versc 11. Effectual calling; the intervention at the determined moment of the mercy of infinite ages. —W.B.H.

Verse 12. Displays of divine power in the history of the saints a reason for song.

Verses 13-14. God to be praised not only,

1. For clearing our way; but also,
2. For giving faith to traverse it. The last as great a mercy as the first.

Verses 13-15. Mercy queen of the Exodus.

1. Her scepter upon the sea. What cannot Love divine conquer for its chosen!
2. Her standard in the van. Whither shall saints fear to follow her?
3. Her frown upon the pursuers; life to the beloved, fatal to the foe.
4. To her let there be brought the chaplet of our praises. —W.B.H.

Verse 15. Final victory.

1. Battalions of evil annihilated.
2. Love unharmed mounting immortal above the wave: "for his mercy endureth forever."
3. Heaven resonant with the song of Moses and the Lamb, to him give thanks.—W.B.H.

Verse 16.

1. Personal care: "To him which led."
2. Peculiar interest: "His people."
3. Persevering goodness: "Through the wilderness."

Verse 16. Led through the Wilderness.

1. God's people must enter the wilderness for trial, for self-knowledge, for development of graces, for preparation for Canaan.

2. God leads his people while in the wilderness. Their route, their provision, their discipline, their protection.

3. God will bring his people out of the wilderness.—C.A.D.

Verses 17-22. See "Spurgeon's Sermons", No. 1285: "Sihon and Og; or, Mercies in Detail."

Verse 21.

1. Our portion, a heritage.
2. Our title deed, a royal grant: "And gave."
3. Our praise, due to enduring mercy.

Verse 23. Prayer of the dying thief turned into a song.

Verses 23-24. The gracious remembrance and the glorious redemption.—C.A.D.

Verse 24. Our enemies, our accomplished redemption, the author of it, and his reason for effecting it.

Verse 24. The multiplied redemptions of the Christian life, and their inexhaustible spring.—W.B.H.

Verse 25. Divine housekeeping.

1. The Royal Commissariat.
2. Its spiritual counterpart: God's august providing for our immortal nature.
3. The queenly grace that hath the keeping of the keys: "for his mercy", etc.
—W.B.H.

Verse 26. Consider,

1. How he rules in heaven.
2. How he rules earth from heaven.
3. How mercy is the eternal element of that rule, and therefore he is the eternal object of praise.

PSALM 137

SERMON OUTLINES AND HELPFUL TIPS

Verse 1.

1. A duty once the source of joy: "remember Zion."
2. Circumstances which make the remembrance sorrowful.
3. Peculiar persons who feel this joy or sorrow: "we."

Verse 1.

1. Zion forsaken in prosperity. Its services neglected; its priests demoralized; the worship of Baal and of Ashtaroth preferred to the worship of the true God.

2. Zion remembered in adversity. In Babylon more than in Jerusalem; on the banks of the Euphrates more than on the banks of Jordan; with tears when they might have remembered it with joy. "I spake unto thee in thy prosperity, and thou saidst, I will not hear." "Lord, in trouble they have visited thee. They poured out a prayer when thy chastening was upon them."—G. R.

Verse 2.

1. Harps—or capacities for praise.
2. Harps on willows, or song suspended.
3. Harps retuned, or joys to come.

Verse 2.

1. A confession of joy being turned into sorrow: "we hanged, "etc. The moaning of their harps upon weeping willows better harmonized with their feelings than any tunes which they had been accustomed to play.

2. A holm of sorrow being turned into joy. They took their harps with them into captivity, and hung them up for future use.—G. J.

Verse 2. *We hanged our harps,* etc.

1. In remembrance of lost joys. Their harps were associated with a glorious past. They could not afford to forget that past. They kept up the good old custom. There are always means of remembrance at hand.

2. In manifestation of present sorrow. They could not play on account of,

    (a) Their sinfulness.
    (a) Their circumstances.
    (c) Their home.

3. In anticipation of future blessing. They did not dash their harps to pieces. Term of exile limited. Return expressly foretold. We shall want our harps in the good times coming. Sinners play their harps now, but must soon lay them aside for ever.—W. J.

Verse 3. (*last clause*). Taken away from the text this is a very pleasant and praiseworthy request. Why do we wish for such a song?

1. It is sure to be pure.
2. It will certainly be elevating.
3. It will probably be glad some.
4. It will comfort and enliven us.
5. It will help to express our gratitude.

Verses 3-4.

1. The cruel demand.

    (a) A song when we are captives.
    (b) A song to please our adversaries.
    (c) A holy song for unholy purposes.

2. The motive for it. Sometimes mere ridicule; at others, mistaken kindness seeking by sharpness to arouse us from despondency; often mere levity.

3. The answer to it, "How can?" etc.

Verses 3-4.

1. When God calls for joy we ought not to sorrow. The songs of Zion should be sung in Zion.

2. When God calls for sorrow we ought not to rejoice. "How shall we sing?" etc. See Isa 5:12.—G. R.

Verses 3-4.

1. The unreasonable request: "Sing us one of the songs of Zion." This was—

    (a) A striking testimony to the joyful character of Jehovah's worship. Even the heathen had heard of "the songs of Zion."

    (b) A severe trial of the fidelity of captive Israel. It might have been to their present advantage to have complied with the request.

    (c) A cruel taunt of the sad and desponding condition of the captives.

2. The indignant refusal. "How shall we sing the Lord's song in a strange land?" There is no singing this song by true Israelites—

    (a) When the heart is out of tune, as it must necessarily be when in "a strange land."

    (b) In uncongenial society—amongst unsympathetic strangers.

3. For unsanctified purposes—to make mirth for the heathen. Many so called sacred concerts pain devout Christians as much as the demand to sing the Lord's song did the devout Israelites. The Lord's song must be sung only "to the Lord."—W.H J.P.

Verses 3-4. The burlesque of holy things.

1. The servants of God are in an unsympathetic world.

2. The demand to be amused and entertained. Temple songs to pass an idle hour! Such the popular demand today. Men would have us burlesque religion to tickle them.

3. The justly indignant reply of all true men, "How shall we?" Christian workers have more serious if less popular business on hand.—W. B. H.

Verse 5. The person who remembers; the thing remembered; the solemn imprecation.

Verse 5. No harp but for Jesus.

1. The harp consecrated. At conversion.

"One sword, at least, thy rights shall guard,
One faithful harp shall praise thee."

2. The harp silent:

"Thy songs were made for the brave and free,
They shall never sound in slavery."

3. The harp restrung above:

"And I heard the voice of harpers
Harping with their harps."—W. B. H.

Verses 5-6.

1. To rejoice with the world is to forget the church.
2. To love the church we must prefer her above everything.
3. To serve the church we must be prepared to suffer anything.

Verse 7. The hatred of the ungodly to true religion.

1. Its cause.
2. Its extent. "Rase it", etc.
3. Its season for display: "in the day of Jerusalem"—trouble, etc.
4. Its reward: "Remember, O Lord."

PSALM 138

SERMON OUTLINES AND HELPFUL TIPS

Verses 1-3. David vexed with rival gods, as we are with rival gospels. How will he act?

1. *Sing with whole hearted praise.*

   (a) It would generously show his contempt of the false.
   (b) It would evince his strong faith in the true.
   (c) It would declare his joyful zeal for God.
   (d) It would shield him from evil from those about him.

2. *Worship by the despised rule.*

   (a) Quietly ignoring all will worship.
   (b) Looking to the person of Christ, which was typified by the temple.
   (c) Trusting in sacrifice.
   (d) Realizing God himself, for it is to God he speaks.

3. *Praise the questioned attributes.*

   (a) Lovingkindness in its universality, in its specialty. Grace in everything.

   (b) Truth. Historic accuracy. Certainty of promises. Correctness of prophecies. Assured of the love of God and the truth of his word, let us cling the closer to these.

4. *Reverence the honored word.* It is beyond all revelation by creation and providence, for it is—

   (a) More clear.
   (b) More sure.
   (c) More sovereign.
   (d) More complete, unique.
   (e) More lasting.
   (f) More glorifying to God.

5. *Prove it by experience.*

   (a) By offering prayer.
   (b) By narrating the answer.
   (c) By exhibiting the strength in soul which was given in answer to prayer.

Verse 2. The Christward position.

1. Worship and praise are to be blended.

2. They are to be presented with an eye to God in Christ, for he is the temple: the place of divine indwelling, sacrifice, intercession, priesthood, oracle, and manifestation.

Verse 2. (*first clause*). —

1. The soul's noblest attitude: "Toward thy temple."
2. The soul's noblest exercise: "worship," "praise."
—W.W.

Verse 2.

1. *The worshipper's contemplation.* Gaze fixed on Holy Temple. Material temple not yet built. Christ the sanctuary. Heb 8:2 All worship through him. Eye of worshippers fixed on him.

2. *The worshipper's song.* Love and truth. Note the combination. Truth by Moses. Grace and truth Jesus Christ.

3. *The worshipper's argument.* Because Christ "The Word" is the embodiment and most glorious manifestation of God. Heb 1:2-3.—*Archibald G. Brown.*

Verse 3.

1. Prayer answered *in* the day.

2. Prayer answered by giving strength *for* the day. See 2Co 12:8-9.

—A.G.B.

Verse 3.

1. Answers to prayer should be noted and acknowledged: "Thou answeredst me."

2. Speedy answers should have special praise: "In the when I cried, thou", etc.

3. A strengthened soul is sometimes the best answer to prayer: "Strengthened me with strength."

—J.F.

Verse 3. Remarkable answer to prayer.

1. The prayer: feeble, earnest, sorrowful, inarticulate.
2. The answer: prompt, divine, effectual, certain.
3. The praise deserved by such grace. See preceding **Verse**s.

Verse 3.

1. A special day.
2. A specific form of prayer: "I cried."
3. A special method of response.
—W.W.

Verse 4.

1. A royal audience.
2. A royal orchestra.

Verses 4-5.

1. They who hear the words of God will know God.

2. They who know God will praise him, however exalted they may be amongst men: "All the kings, "etc.

3. They who praise God will walk in his ways.

4. They who walk in the ways of the Lord will glorify him, and he will be glorified in them.

—G.R.

Verse 5. See "Spurgeon's Sermons", No. 1615: "Singing in the Ways of the Lord."

Verse 5. This is spoken of kings, but it is true of the humblest pilgrims. The Lord hath respect unto the lowly, and will make them sing.

1. *They shall sing in the ways.*

    (a) They take pleasure in them.

    (b) They do not go out of them to find pleasure.

    (c) They sing as they proceed in service, in worship, in holiness, in suffering.

    (d) They are in a case for singing. They have strength, safety, guidance, provision, comfort.

2. *They sing of the ways of the Lord.*

    (a) Of God's ways to them.

    (b) Of their way to God. They know whence they came out. They know where they are going. It is a good road; prophets went by it, and the Lord of the prophets. Therein we have good company, good accommodation, good prospects, good daylight.

3. *They sing of the Lord of the way.* His loving kindness. His truth. Answers to prayer. His condescension. His reviving us in trouble. His delivering us. His perfecting us. His everlasting mercy.

4. *They shall sing to the Lord of the way.*

    (a) To his Honor.
    (b) To the extending of that Honor.
    (c) As a preparation to eternally Honoring him.

Verse 6. Divine inversions.

1. Lowliness honored to its great surprise.
2. Pride passed by to its eternal mortification.
—W.B.H.

Verse 7. (*first clause*).

1. The Psalmist's dismal excursion: walking "in the midst of trouble"; this is not a spectator, but one assailed. Troubles—personal, social, ecclesiastical, national.

2. His cheering anticipation—of revival, defense, deliverance.—W.J.

Verse 7.

1. Good men are sometimes in the midst of troubles: these are many, and continue long.

2. They interfere not with their progress. They "walk in the midst" of them; faint, yet pursuing; sometimes they "run with patience", etc.

3. They have comfort in them: "Though I walk", etc., "thou wilt revive me."

4. They are benefited by them.

a) Their enemies are overthrown.
b) Their deliverance is complete.—G.R.

Verse 7. The child of God often revived *out* of trouble; more frequently *in* trouble; not seldom *through* trouble. Delivered from, sustained in, sanctified through, trouble.—A.G.B.

Verse 7. An incident of the road to the city.

1. Pilgrims beset by thieves and struck down.
2. The arrival of Great heart and flight of the enemy.
3. The flask to the lips: "thou wilt revive me." Sweet awakening to know the beauty of his face and strength of his hand!—W.B.H.

Verse 7. (*third clause*). Right hand salvation.

1. It shall be wrought of God.
2. He shall throw his strength into the deed.
3. His utmost dexterity shall be displayed.

Verse 8. (*first clause*).

1. A wide subject "That which concerneth me." Not necessarily that which gives me concern.

2. A promise that covers it: "the Lord will perfect."—A.G.B.

Verse 8. (*first and last clauses*). Faith in divine purpose no hindrance to prayer, but rather an encouragement in it: "The Lord will perfect." "Forsake not."—A.G.B

Verse 8. See "Spurgeon's Sermons", Nos. 231 and 1506: "Faith in Perfection", and, "Choice Comfort for a Young Believer."

Verse 8. The grace of God makes a man thoughtful, and leads him to concern about himself, his life, his future, and the completeness of the work of grace. This might lead us to sadness and despair, but the Lord worketh in us for other ends.

1. *He fills us with assurance.*

> (a) That the Lord will work for us.
> (b) That he will complete his work.
> (c) That he will do this in providence; if it be properly a concern of ours.
> (d) That he will do this within us. Our graces shall grow. Our soul shall become Christly. Our whole nature perfect.
> (e) That he will do this with our work for him.

2. *He gives us rest in his mercy.*

> (a) Thou wilt forgive my sins.
> (b) Thou wilt bear with my nature.
> (c) Thou wilt support me in suffering.
> (d) Thou wilt supply me in need.
> (e) Thou wilt succor me in death.

3. *He puts prayer into our hearts.*

> (a) That he will not forsake me.
> (b) That he will not leave his own work in me undone.
> (c) Nor his work by me unfinished. Why did he begin? Why carry so far? Why not complete?

Verse 8.

1. Faith's full assurance: "The Lord will perfect that which concerneth me."

2. Faith's firm foundation: "Thy mercy, O Lord, endureth forever."

3. Faith's fervent prayer: "Forsake not the works of thine own hands."

PSALM 139

SERMON OUTLINES AND HELPFUL TIPS

Verses 1, 23. A matter of fact made a matter of prayer.

Verse 1.

1. A cheering thought for sinners. If God knew them not perfectly, how could he have prepared a perfect salvation for them?

2. A comfortable truth for saints. "Your heavenly Father knoweth that ye have need of all these things."—*G.R.*

Verses 1-5. In these **Verses** we have God's Omniscience,

1. Described.

    (a) As observing minute and comparatively unimportant actions: "My downsitting and uprising."

    (b) As taking note of our thoughts and the motives behind them: "Understandest my thought."

    (c) As investigating all our ways: "Thou compassest", etc.; better rendered, "Thou triest my walking and lying down", *i.e.*, my activities and restings.

    (d) Accurately estimating every word at the instant of its utterance: "For there is not a word", etc.

    (e) As being "behind" men, remembering their past, and "before" men, acquainted with their future: "Thou hast beset me", etc.

    (f) As every instant holding men under watchful scrutiny: "And laid", etc.

2. Personally realized and pondered: "Thou hast searched *me*." *Me* and *my* run through the whole set of statements. Thus felt and used, the fact of God's omniscience,

    (a) Begets reverence.

    (b) Inspires confidence.

    (c) Produces carefulness of conduct.—*J.F.*

Verse 2-4. The knowledge of God extends,

1. To our movements, our "down sitting and uprising"—when we sit down to read, write, or converse, and when we rise up to active service.

2. To our thoughts: "Thou understandest my thoughts afar off." What they have been, what they now are, what they will be, what under all circumstances they would have been. He who made

minds knows what their thoughts will be at all times, or he could not predict future events, or govern the world. He can know our thoughts without being the Author of them.

3. To our actions: Ps 139:3. Every step we take by day, and all we purpose to do in wakeful hours of the night: all our private, social, and public ways, are compassed or sifted by him, to distinguish the good from the bad, as wheat from the chaff.

4. To our words: Ps 139:4. It has been said that the words of all men and from all time are registered in the atmosphere, and may be faithfully recalled. Whether it be so or not, they are phonographed in the mind of God.—G.R.

Verse 2. (*first clause*). The importance of the commonest acts of life.

Verse 2. (*second clause*). The serious nature of thoughts. Known to God; seen through, their drift perceived; and attention given to them while as yet in the distance.

Verse 3. The encircling Presence, in our activities, meditations, secrecies, and movements.

Verse 4.

1. Words on the tongue first *in* it, and in that stage known to God.

2. Words on the tongue very numerous, yet all known.

3. Word on the tongue have wide meaning, yet known "altogether."

Lesson: Take heed of your words not yet spoken.

Verse 5. A soul captured. Stopped, overtaken, arrested. What has it done? What shall it do?

Verse 6.

1. God imperfectly known to man.

2. Man perfectly known to God. It has been said that wise men never wonder; to us it appears they are always wondering.—G.R.

Verse 6. Theme: the facts of our religion, too wonderful to understand, are just those in which we have most reason to rejoice.

1. Prove it.

   (a) The incomprehensible attributes of God give unspeakable value to his promises.

   (b) The Incarnation is at once the most complete and most endearing manifestation of God we possess, yet it is the most inexplicable.

   c) Redemption by the death of Christ is the highest guarantee of salvation we can conceive; but who can explain it?

   (d) Inspiration makes the Bible the word of God, though none can give an account of its mode of operation in the minds of those "moved by the Holy Ghost."

(e) The resurrection of the body, and its glorification, satisfy the deepest yearning of our soul (Ro 8:23 2Co 5:2-4); but none can conceive the how.

2. Apply its lessons.

(a) Let us not stumble at doctrines simply because they are mysterious.

(b) Let us be thankful God has not kept back the great mysteries of our religion simply because there would be some offended at them.

(c) Let us readily receive all the joy which the mysteries bring, and calmly wait the light of heaven to make them better understood.—J.F.

Verses 7-10.

1. God is wherever I am. I fill but a small part of space; he fills all space.

2. He is wherever I shall be. He does not move with me, but I move in him. "In him we live, and move", etc.

3. God is wherever I could be. "If I ascend to heaven", etc. "If I descend to Sheol", etc. If I travel with the sunbeams to the most distant part of the earth, or heavens, or the sea, I shall be in thy hand. No mention is here made of annihilation, as though that were possible; which would be the only escape from the Divine Presence; for he is not the God of the dead, of the annihilated, in the Sadducean meaning of the word, but of the living. Man is always somewhere, and God is always everywhere.—G.R.

Verse 8. The glory of heaven and the terror of hell: "*Thou.*"

Verses 9-10.

1. The greatest security and encouragement to a sinner supposed.

(a) The place—the remotest part of the sea; by which you are to understand the most obscure nook in the creation.

(b) His swift and speedy flight after the commission of sin, to this supposed refuge and sanctuary: "If I take the wings of the morning."

2. This supposed security and encouragement is utterly destroyed (Ps 139:10).

—See Flavel's "*Seaman's Preservative in Foreign Countries.*"

Verses 11-12. Darkness and light are both alike to God.

1. Naturally. "I form the light, and I create the darkness."

2. Providentially. Providential dispensations that are dark to us are light to him. We change with respect to him, not he to us.

3. Spiritually. "Let him that walketh in darkness", etc. "Yea, though I walk", etc. He went before them in a pillar of cloud to guide them by day, and a pillar of fire to guide them by night. It was the same God in the day cloud and in the night light. —G.R.

Verse 14. *I am fearfully and wonderfully made.* This is true of man in his fourfold state.

1. In his primitive integrity.
2. In his deplorable depravity.
3. In his regeneration.
4. In his fixed state in hell or heaven.
—W.W.

Verses 17-18. The Psalm dilates upon the omniscience of God. In no mournful manner, but the reverse.

1. *God's thoughts of us.*

    (a) How certain.
    (b) How numerous.
    (c) How condescending.
    (d) How tender.
    (e) How wise.
    (f) How practical.
    (g) How constant.

2. *Our thoughts upon his thoughts.*

    (a) How late and yet how due to the subject.
    (b) How delightful.
    (d) How consoling.
    (e) How strengthening to faith.
    (f) How arousing to love.

3. *Our thoughts upon God himself.*

    (a) They place us near God.

    (b) They keep us near God.

    (c) They restore us to him. We are with God when we awake from sleep, from lethargy, from death.

Verses 17-18.

1. The saint precious to God. He thinks of him tenderly; in countless ways; perpetually.

2. God precious to the saints. Noting God's loving kindnesses, numbering them, newly awakening to them.

3. The mingling of these loves: "I am still with thee." —W.B.H.

Verse 18. *When I awake I am still with thee.*

1. Awaking is sometimes, yea, most commonly, taken in the *natural signification,* for the recovery from bodily sleep.

2. *Morally,* for recovery from sin.

3. *Mystically;* "when I shall awake", that is, from the sleep of death. —*T. Horton.*

Verse 18. *A Christian on Earth still in Heaven* (an Appendix to "A Christian on the Mount; or, A Treatise concerning Meditation"), by *Thomas Watson,* 1660.

Verse 18. *I am still with thee.*

1. By way of meditation.

2. In respect to communion.

3. In regard of action, and the businesses which are done by us. —*T. Horton.*

Verse 19.

1. The doctrine of punishment the necessary outcome of omniscience.

2. Inevitable judgment an argument for separation from sinners. —*W.B.H.*

Verse 20. Two scandalous offences against God.

1. To speak slanderously of him.

2. To speak irreverently of him. These are committed only by his enemies.

Verses 21-22.

1. Such hatred one need not be ashamed of.

2. Such hatred one should be able to define: "grieved."

3. Such hatred one must labor to keep right. "Perfect hatred" is a form of hate consistent with all the virtues.

Verses 23-24. The language,

1. Of self-examination.

    (a) As in the sight of God.

    (b) With a desire for the help of God: Ps 139:23. Look me through, and through, and tell me what thou thinkest of me.

2. Of self renunciation: "See if", etc. (Ps 139:24); any sin unpardoned, any evil disposition unsubdued, any evil habit unrestrained, that I may renounce it.

3. Of self dedication: "Lead me", etc.: a submission entirely to divine guidance in the future.—G.R.

Verse 24.

1. The evil way. Naturally in us; may be of different kinds; must be removed; removal needs Divine help.

2. The everlasting way. There is but one, we need leading in it. It is the good old way, it does not come to an end, it leads to blessedness without end.

Verse 24. (*last clause*).—See "Spurgeon's Sermons," No. 903: "The Way Everlasting."

PSALM 140

SERMON OUTLINES AND HELPFUL TIPS

Verses 1-5.

1. The particular source of David's affliction: it was from men. In this he was a type of Christ.

   (a) Their wickedness: "the evil man."

   (b) Their violence: "the violent man."

   (c) Their malicious designs: "which imagine mischiefs in their heart."

   (d) Their confederacy: "continually are they gathered together for war."

   (e) Their false accusations: "They have sharpened their tongues like a serpent", etc. (Ps 140:3).

   (f) Their avowed design: "they have purposed to overthrow my goings" (Ps 140:4).

   (g) Their intrigues (Ps 140:5).

2. His universal remedy: "Deliver me, O Lord"; "preserve" and help me. His defense is,

   (a) In God.
   (b) In prayer to God. —*G. R.*

Verses 1-5. In our position, age, and country, we are not in danger of violence from men, as was David; still, no man is absolutely safe front the danger.

1. Mention some eases not yet impossible.

   (a) A Christian workman, because he cannot comply with unrighteous customs, excites the animosity of his fellow workers. They will do him mischief, spoil his work, steal his tools, speak evil of him, until his employer discharges him to restore peace in the factory.

   (b) A Christian clerk or shop assistant, because his presence is a check upon his sinful companions, may have snares laid for him, etc.

2. Suggest advice, useful, should such a case arise.

   (a) Resort to God with a "Deliver me", and a "Preserve me."

   (b) Maintain integrity and uprightness.

   (c) Should the mischievous ones succeed, still trust in God, who can make their mischief lead to your profit, and make his goodness outwit their devices. —*J. F.*

Verse 3. The depraved state of the natural man as to his speech.

Verse 4. (*first clause*). A wise prayer. The wicked will slander, and oppress, or mislead, flatter and defile. No one can keep us but the Lord.

Verse 5. The Dangers of Society.

1. The secrecy of the attacks of the ungodly: "hid a snare."
2. The variety of their weapons: "and cords."
3. The cunning choice of position: "by the wayside."
4. The object of their designs: "for me": they desire to destroy the man himself.

Verse 5. *The Net by the Wayside*, or, covert temptations; temptations brought near, and made applicable to daily life.

Verse 6.

1. The language of assurance.
2. The plea for acceptance in prayer.

Verses 6-7. David comforted himself,

1. In his interest in God: "I said...thou art my God."

2. In his access to God: he had leave to speak to him, and might expect an answer of peace: "Hear", etc.

3. In the assurance he had of help from God, and happiness in him (Ps 140:7).

4. In the experience he had formerly of God's care of him: "Thou hast covered my head in the day of battle."—*Matthew Henry.*

Verses 6-8. Three arguments to be pleaded in a prayer for protection.

1. The believer's covenanted property in God. "I said... thou art my God."

2. The past mercies of God. "Thou hast covered", etc.

3. The impropriety of the wicked being encouraged in their wickedness, Ps 140:8.—*J. F.*

Verses 6-12. The Consolations of the Believer in Time of Trouble.

1. What he can say.
2. What he can remember.
3. What he is assured of.

Verses 6-7, 12-13. Times of Assault, Slander, and Temptation should be special times of Prayer and Faith. David here makes prominent five things.

1. *Possession asserted.*

> (a) The Possession: "My God." Opposed to idols. Beloved by self.
> (b) The Claim published.

(c) The Witness selected. Secret. Sacred. Searching.
(d) The Occasion chosen.

2. *Petition presented.*

(a) His prayers were frequent.
(b) His prayers were full of meaning.
(c) His prayers were meant for God.
(d) His prayers needed divine attention.

3. *Preservation experienced.*

(a) God had been his Armor bearer.
(b) God had guarded his most vital part.
(c) God had saved him.
(d) God's strength had been displayed.

4. *Protection expected.*

(a) God is a righteous Judge.
(b) God is a compassionate Friend.
(c) God is a well-known Guardian.

5. *Praise predicted.*

(a) Praise assured by gratitude.
(b) Praise expressed by words.
(c) Praise implied by confidence.
(d) Praise practiced by communion.

Verse 9. How the sin of evil speakers comes home to them. —W. B. H.

Verse 11. (*first clause.*)

1. Notice a few varieties of evil speakers.

(a) Liars; the common liar, the trade liar, the stock exchange liar, the political liar, etc.

(b) Scandal mongers.

(c) Blasphemers and swearers.

(d) Libertines and seducers.

(e) Skeptics and new theology inventors.

2. The propriety of the prayer.

(a) Because evil speaking is intrinsically an evil thing.

(b) It is an extensively injurious thing.

(c) He who would have God's truth established must needs desire that evil speaking must fail.

3. The limitation of the prayer: "In the earth."

(a) It is certain an evil speaker cannot be established in heaven, nor in hell.

(b) The earth is the only sphere of his influence; but, alas! men on the earth are too prone to be influenced by him.

(c) Then, become righteous and true, by faith in the Righteous One and the "Truth."—*J. F.*

Verse 11. (*second clause.*) The Cruel Hunter pursued by his own Dogs.

Verse 11. (*second clause.*) Theme—Sins committed, and not repented of, pursue men to their ruin.

1. Illustrate.

(a) They may raise a force of opposition from men. Tarquin, Napoleon, etc.

(b) They may precipitate ruin, as Haman was hunted by his own sin to the gallows.

(c) They may arouse destructive remorse, as in Judas.

(d) Certainly they will pursue to the judgment seat, and hunt the soul into hell.

2. Apply.

(a) How fearful a thing must sin be.

(b) The mole terrible because self-created.

(c) Flee from the avenging pursuers to Christ, the only and safe refuge.—*J. F.*

Verse 11. (*second clause.*) The hunt and pursuit of the violent sinner.

1. The progress of the chase.

(a) At first the victim is ignorant of it.

(b) But ere long he finds Scripture, conscience, God, Death, at his heels.

(c) His own sins cry loudest after him.

2. The issue of the hunt. Hemmed in, overthrown, lost forever, unless he repent.

3. Another Huntsman. "The Son of man is come to seek and save that which was lost."—*W. B. H.*

Verse 12.

1. The known fact.
2. The reasons for being so assured of it.
3. The conduct arising out of the knowledge.

Verse 12. Something worth knowing.

1. By the afflicted and the poor who trust in the Lord.

2. By the oppressors who afflict and do the wrong.

3. By all men, that they may trust in the Lord, and praise him for his compassion towards the needy, and for his even handed justice.—J. F.

Verses 12-13.

1. Trust under all circumstances (Ps 140:12).

2. Gratitude for all things: "The righteous shall give thanks unto thy name."

3. Safety at all times: "The upright shall dwell in thy presence."—G. R.

Verse 13. One of the noblest forms of praise,—dwelling in the presence of God. Or, reverent regard to God's presence, holy communion with the Lord, confiding rest in God's dealings, obedient doing of the heavenly will—the best way of giving thanks to God.

Verse 13. Two assertions beyond contradiction.

1. The righteous are sure to give thanks to God, let others be as thankless as they will. For,

> (a) They recognize all their good as coming from God.
> (b) They realize themselves as unworthy of the good they receive.
> (c) They are anxious to do right, because they are righteous; and that involves thanksgiving.
> (d) Thankfulness is a part of the joy derived from what they enjoy.

2. The upright are sure to dwell in God's presence.

> (a) In the sense of setting the Lord before them.
> (b) In the sense of an abiding present fellowship with God.
> (c) In the sense of enjoying God's approval.
> (d) In the sense of dwelling in heaven forever.—J. F.

PSALM 141

SERMON OUTLINES AND HELPFUL TIPS

Verse 1.

1. The Perpetuity of Prayer: "I cry. I cry."
2. The Personality: "unto thee", "unto me."
3. The Practicalness: "Make haste; give ear."

Verse 1. Holy haste.

1. The saint hasting to God.
2. The saint hastening God.
3. God's sure hastening to his help. —W. B. H.

Verses 1-2.

1. Prayer put forth:

    (a) With urgency: "Make haste unto me."
    (b) With fervency: "Give ear", etc.

2. Prayer set forth: "Let my prayer be set forth", etc. When hearing is obtained there is composure and order in prayer. When the fire is kindled the incense rises.

3. Prayer held forth: "The lifting up of my hands as the evening sacrifice", as constant and accepted. —G. R.

Verse 2. True prayer acceptable as incense and as the evening sacrifice. It is spiritual, solemn, ordained of God, brings Christ to remembrance.

Verse 3.

1. The mouth a door.
2. A watchman needed.
3. The Lord fulfilling that office.

Verse 4. Total abstinence from evil desires, practices, and delights.

Verse 4. A prayer,

1. For the repression of every evil tendency in the heart: "Incline not my heart", etc.

2. For the prevention of any association with the wicked in their sinful works: "To practice", etc.

3. For a holy contempt of the temporal pleasure or profit placed in our way through the sin of others: "Let me not eat", etc. Note, many who will not engage in a wicked act do not object to participate in its gains. —J. F.

Verse 4. Deprecation of,

1. Devil's desires.
2. Devil's deeds.
3. Devil's dainties. —W. B. H.

Verse 5. Rebukes of good men.

1. Invited.
2. Appreciated: "it shall be a kindness."
3. Utilized: "an excellent oil."
4. Cheerfully endured: "not break my head."
5. Repaid, by our prayers for them in time of trouble.

Verse 5. (*last clause.*) "Intercessory Prayer." See" Spurgeon's Sermons", No. 1,049.

Verse 6.

1. Times of trouble will come to the careless.
2. Then they will be more ready to hear the gospel.
3. Then they will find sweetness in that which they formerly refused.

Verse 6. A Desert Oasis.

1. The world is a stony place, hard, barren.
2. Often pride and self-trust suffer overthrowing there.
3. Then words of God by his sent servant make an oasis in the desert.
—W. B. H.

Verses 7-8. A cemetery scene.

1. Dry bones of the dead about the grave.
2. Weary bones of the aged and sick around the grave.
3. All bones being from day to day made ready for the grave.
4. Bones finding rest in God: "mine eyes are unto thee, O God", etc.

PSALM 142

SERMON OUTLINES AND HELPFUL TIPS

Verse 1.

1. A vivid memory—of what he did, and how, and when.

2. A public declaration; from which we infer that his prayer cheered him, brought him succor in trouble, and deliverance out of it.

3. A reasonable inference: he prays again.

Verses 1-2.

1. Special seasons for prayer: times of complaint and trouble.

2. Special prayer on such occasions; "I cried", "I make my supplication", "I poured out my complaint", "I showed before him my trouble." Spread the whole case before God, as Hezekiah did the letter from Sennacherib.—G.R.

Verse 2.

1. The true place for prayer—"before him."
2. The freedom of prayer—"poured out."
3. The unveiling of the heart in prayer—"shewed before him my trouble."

Verse 3. (*first clause*).

1. When.
2. Then.

Verse 3. (*latter clause*). Temptations.

1. What form they take?—"snares."

2. Who lay them?—"they."

3. How do they lay them? Secretly, craftily "in the way", frequently.

4. What becomes of the tempted believer? He lives to tell the tale, to warn others, to glorify God.

Verse 4. (*last clause*). The soul considered of no value.

1. Consider the worth of the soul.

   (a) The soul will continue forever.
   (b) The righteous will grow more happy, and the wicked more miserable.
   (c) A great price has been paid for it.

2. Contrast the care we take of our souls, and our anxiety about worldly objects.

(a) The solicitude we manifest for riches.
(b) Our care in educating the intellects of our children.
(c) Eagerness in pursuit of business, Honor—even trifles.
(d) How anxious about a human life! Describe the search for a lost child.
(e) Contrast our care for souls and our Savior's care for them: Paul's, Luther's, Whitefield's.

3. Remember some things which show that this care does not exist.

(a) If you do not statedly observe secret prayer.
(b) If your soul is not burdened with the souls of others.
(c) If you neglect family prayer, or observe it as a mere form.
(d) If you do not regularly go to prayer meetings.

Remark: The great responsibility resting upon every Christian.
—*Jacob Knapp, in "The Homiletic Monthly", 1882.*

Verse 4. (*last clause*). The burden of souls.

1. What is meant by care for souls?

(a) To have a firm conviction of their value.
(b) To cherish tender solicitude for their welfare.
(c) To feel alarming apprehensions of their danger.
(d) To make zealous exertions for their salvation.

2. Who ought specially to exercise this care?

(a) Parents.
(b) Teachers.
(c) Ministers.
(d) Members.

3. The criminality of neglect.

(a) It is ungrateful.
(b) It is cruel.
(c) It is fatal.

—*W.W. Wythe, in "The Pulpit Analyst", 1870.*

Verses 4-5.

1. A terrible plight; no friend, no helper, no pitying heart.
2. A touching prayer. A cry and a saying.

Verses 4-5.

1. Human help fails most when most needed.

  (a) In outward troubles: "I looked", etc.
  (b) In soul troubles: "No man cared for my soul."

2. Divine help is most given when most needed. A refuge and a portion when all others fail. Man has many friends in prosperity, one only in adversity.—*G.R.*

Verses 4-5.

1. Why the saints make God their refuge, and the object of their faith and hope in their greatest afflictions.

  (a) God has given himself to the saints, in the covenant of grace, to be their God, and has promised that they shall be his people.

  (b) God stands in a most near relation to the saints, and condescends to sustain many endearing characters of love, which he fulfils to their advantage.

  (c) The saints, through the power of God's grace upon their souls, have chosen him for their portion, and their highest felicity.

2. What perfections there are in God that render him a safe refuge for the saints, and a proper object of their confidence.

  (a) God is infinite in mercy.

  (b) God is infallible in wisdom.

  (c) God is boundless in power.

  (d) God is omniscient and omnipresent.

  (d) God is a Being whose love never changes.

  (e) God is an independent Being, and the Governor and Director of all things.

3. The many sweet advantages, arising to the saints, from this practice of making God their refuge, in their greatest troubles.

  (a) They have been preserved from fainting under their heavy burdens.

  (b) They have derived from God new and seasonable supplies of divine grace and strength for service.

  (c) God has refreshed his saints with divine consolations for the future.—*John Farmer,* 1744.

Verse 5. The soul choosing God.

1. Deliberately: "I cried unto thee, I said."

2. For all in all: "refuge", "portion."

3. Before every other "in the land of the living."—*W.B.H.*

Verse 5. "How we may bring our Hearts to bear Reproofs." See John Owen's Sermon in "The Morning Exercises", vol. 2, page 600, etc.; and in his "Works", vol. 16, p. 23, etc.

Verse 6. Two petitions and two arguments.

Verses 6-7.

1. The language of Despondency. "I am brought very low." "My enemies are stronger than I." "My soul is in prison."

2. Of Prayer. "Attend unto me." "Deliver me." "Bring me out of prison."

3. Of Praise.

> (a) For the congratulation of others.
> (b) For his own deliverance and prosperity.—*G.R.*

Verse 6. Low and Lowly. Here is David,

1. In a low place; the depths of a cave.

2. In a low way: "very low"; "stronger than I."

3. But see, "with the lowly is wisdom" (Pr 11:2); he prays.

4. The Lord "hath respect to the lowly", Ps 138:6. He will not pray in vain.—*W.B.H.*

Verse 7. A prisoner. A freedman. A singer. A center. A wonder.

Verse 7. Prison Dreams.

1. What we image in our fetters.

> (a) Christ's brow girt about with rare praise.
> (b) Christ's people compassing and accompanying us in costliest service.
> (c) A new life of bounty and blessing—when we get out.

2. How far do our dreamings come true? Before peril and after; under conviction, and after conversion; sick room, and active service.

3. The duty of fidelity to prison vows and lessons.—*W.B.H.*

Verse 7. (*middle clause*). A Queen Bee. An under shepherd. A warm hearth. A Museum of wonders. Or, they shall surround me, interested in my story—"out of prison"; drawn by my song—"praise thy name"; attracted by likeness of character, and admiring the goodness of the Lord.

Verse 7. (*last clause*). Take this with Ps 116:7. "The Lord hath dealt bountifully with thee." Infer the future from the past.

PSALM 143

SERMON OUTLINES AND HELPFUL TIPS

Verse 1. Three threes.

1. As to his devotions, — prayers, supplications, requests.

2. As to his success, — hear, give ear, answer me.

3. As to his argument, — because thou art Jehovah, faithful, righteous.

Verses 1-2. A suitable prayer for a believer who has reason to suppose that he is suffering chastening for sin.

1. Here is earnest importunity, as of one depending entirely upon divine Favor for a hearing.

2. Here is believing fervency laying hold of divine faithfulness and justice; see 1Jo 1:9.

3. Here is a deep consciousness of the vanity of self-justification pleading for pure mercy, Ps 143:2. — J. F.

Verse 2.

1. Who he is. "Thy servant."
2. What he knows. "In thy sight shall no man living be justified."
3. What he asks. "Enter not into judgment."

Verses 3-6. Consider,

1. The great lengths God may sometimes permit the enemy to go, Ps 143:3. The case of Job a good illustration.

2. The deep depression of spirit he may even permit his saints to experience, Ps 143:4.

3. The good things he has provided for their meditation when even at their worst, Ps 143:5.

4. The two things his grace will never suffer to die, whose existence is a pledge of near approaching joy, —

    (a) The thirsting after himself.

    (b) The practice of prayer. The whole is a good text for a lecture on the life and experience of Job. — J. F.

Verses 4-6.

1. Down in Despondency.
2. Deep in Meditation.
3. Determined in Supplication.

Verses 5-6. I muse on the work of thy hands. I stretch forth my hands *unto thee*. Hand in hand: or the child of God admiring the work of God's hands, and praying with uplifted hands to be wrought upon by the like power.

Verse 5. David's method.

1. He gathered materials; facts and evidence concerning God: "I remember."

2. He thought out his subject and arranged his matter: "I meditate."

3. He discoursed thereon, and was brought nearer to God: "I muse"—discourse.

4. Let us close by viewing all this as an example for preachers and others.—W. B. H.

Verse 6. God alone the desire of his people.

Verse 6. Deep calling to deep.

1. The insatiable craving of the heart.
2. The vast riches in glory.
3. The rushing together of the seas: "My soul is to thee."
—W. B. H.

Verse 7. Reasons for speedy answers.

Verse 7. Never despair.

1. Because you have the Lord to plead with.
2. Because you may freely tell him the desperateness of your case.
3. Because you may be urgent with him for deliverance.—J. F.

Verse 7. Cordial for the swooning heart.

1. God's beloved fainting.
2. The best restorative; her Lord's face.
3. She has the presence of mind to call him as she falls.—W. B. H.

Verse 8. The two prayers "*Cause me to hear*", and "*Cause me to know.*" The two pleas—"*In thee do I trust*", and "*I lift up my soul unto thee.*"

Verse 8. Ps 142:3. "*Thou knewest my path.*" Ps 143:8.—"*Cause me to know the way.*"

1. Trusting Omniscience in everything.
2. Following conscience in everything.

Verse 8. On fixing a time for the answering of our prayer.

1. By whom it may be done. Not by all believers, but by those who through dwelling with God have attained to a holy boldness.

2. When it may be done.

(a) When the case is specially urgent.
(b) When God's Honor is concerned.
(c) What renders it pleasing to God when done. Great faith. "For in thee do I trust."—*J. F.*

Verse 8. Listening for Loving kindness.

1. Where to listen. At the gates of Scripture; in the halls of meditation; nigh the footsteps of Jesus.

2. When to listen. "In the morning"; as early and as often as possible.

3. How to listen. In trustful dependence: "Cause me to hear thy loving kindness in the morning, for in thee do I trust."

4. Why to listen. To "know the way wherein I should walk."—*W. B. H.*

Verse 9. Admirable points in this prayer to be imitated by us. There is,

1. A sense of danger.

2. A confession of weakness.

3. A prudent foresight.

4. A solid confidence:—he expects to be hidden from his foes.

Verse 9.

1. Looking up.
2. Lying close.—*W. B. H.*

Verse 10. Two childlike requests—"Teach me...lead me."

Verse 10. See "Spurgeon's Sermons", No. 1519, "At School."

Verse 10. (*first half.*)

1. The best instructions: "Teach me to do thy will." Not merely to know, but "to do."

2. The only efficient Instructor.

3. The best reason for asking and expecting instruction: "For thou art my God."—*J. F.*

Verse 10. *Teach me to do thy will.* We may call this sentence a description of David's school; and it is a very complete one; at least, it hath in it the three best things that belong to a school.

1. The best teacher.

2. The best scholar.

3. The best lesson; for who so good a teacher as God? who so good a scholar as David? what so good a lesson as to do God's will?—*Sir Richard Baker.*

Verse 10. (*latter half.*)

1. Utopia—"the land of uprightness." Describe it, and declare its glories.
2. The difficult paths to that upland country.
3. The divine Guide,—"thy Spirit is good."

Verse 11. (*first clause.*)

1. What is this blessing? "Quicken me."
2. In what way will it glorify God, so that we may plead for the sake of his name?

Verse 11. (*second clause.*) How is the righteousness of God concerned in our deliverance from trouble?

Verse 12.

1. To the Master: "I am thy servant."
2. For the servant: he seeks protection because he belongs to his master.

PSALM 144

SERMON OUTLINES AND HELPFUL TIPS

Verse 1.

1. Two things needful in our holy war—strength and skill; for the hands and the fingers, for the difficult and the delicate.

2. In what way God supplies us with both. He is the one, and teaches the other. Impartation and Instruction. The teaching comes by illumination, experience, distinct guidance.

Verse 1. Things not to be forgotten by the Christian Soldier.

1. The true source of his strength: "The Lord my strength." If remembered,

> (a) He will not be found trusting in self.
> (b) He will never be wanting in courage.
> (c) He will always anticipate victory.
> (d) He will never be worsted in the conflict.

2. His constant need of instruction, and the Teacher who never forgets him: "Which teacheth my hands", etc. If remembered,

> (a) He will gird on the armor provided and commended by God.

> (b) He will select for his weapon the sword of the Spirit.

> (c) He will study the divinely given text book of military tactics and discipline, that he may learn (1) the devices of the enemy; (2) methods of attack and defense; (3) how to bear himself in the thick of the fight.

> (d) He will wait upon God for understanding.

3. The praise due to God, both for victories won and skill displayed: "Blessed be", etc. If remembered,

> (a) He will wear his Honors humbly.
> (b) Glorify the Honor of his King.
> (c) Twice taste the sweets of victory in the happiness of gratitude.—*J.F.*

Verse 2. Double flowers.

1. Good preserved from evil: "goodness" and "fortress."

2. Safety enlarged into liberty: "tower", "deliverer."

3. Security attended with rest: "shield, in whom I trust."

4. Sufficiency to maintain superiority: "subdueth my people under me." View God as working all.

Verse 2. A Group of Titles. Notice,

1. Which comes first. "Goodness." *Heb.* "Mercy."

    (a) It is right and natural that a saved sinner should make the most of "mercy", and place it in the foreground.

    (b) Mercy is the ground and reason of the other titles named. For whatever God is to us, it is a special manifestation of his mercy.

    (c) It is a good thing to see a believer ripe in experience making mercy the leading note in his song of praise.

2. Which comes last: "He in whom I trust." It suggests,

    (a) That what God is makes him worthy of trust.

    (b) That meditation upon what he is strengthens our trust.

3. What peculiar force the word "my" gives to each. It makes it,

    (a) A record of experience.

    (b) An ascription of praise.

    (c) A blessed boasting.

    (d) An incentive, enough to set others longing. —J.F.

Verse 3. A note of interrogation, exclamation, and admiration.

Verse 3. The question,

1. Denies any right in man to claim the regard of God.

2. Asserts the great Honor God has nevertheless put upon him.

3. Suggests that the true reason of God's generous dealings is the graciousness of his own heart.

4. Implies the becomingness of gratitude and humility.

5. Encourages the most unworthy to put their confidence in God. —J.F.

Verse 3.

1. What was man as he came from the hands of his Creator?

    (a) Rational.
    (b) Responsible.
    (c) Immortal.
    (d) Holy and happy.

2. What is man in his present condition?

(a) Fallen.
(b) Guilty.
(c) Sinful.
(d) Miserable, and helpless in his misery.

3. What is man when he has believed in Christ?

(a) Restored to a right relation to God.
(b) Restored to a right disposition toward God.
(c) He enjoys the influences of the Holy Spirit.
(d) He is in process of preparation for the heavenly world.

4. What shall man be when he is admitted into heaven?

(a) Free from sin and sorrow.
(b) Advanced to the perfection of his nature.
(c) Associated with angels.
(d) Near to his Savior and his God.

—*George Brooks, in "The Homiletic Commentary,"* 1879.

Verse 3. Worthless man much regarded by the mighty God. Sermon by Ebenezer Erskine. Works 3, pp. 141-162.

Verse 3. It is a wonder above all wonders, that ever the great God should make such account of such a thing as man.

1. It will appear if you consider what a great God the Lord is.
2. What a poor thing man is.
3. What a great account the great God hath of this poor thing, man.
—*Joseph Alleine.*

Verse 4. He is nothing, he pretends to be something, he is soon gone, he ends in nothing as to this life; yet there is a light somewhere.

Verse 4. The Shadow World.

1. Our lives are like shadows.

2. But God's light casts these shadows. Our being is of God. The brevity and mystery of life are a part of providence.

3. The destiny of the shadows; eternal night; or eternal light.—*W.B.H.*

Verse 4. The brevity of our earthly life.

1. A profitable subject for meditation.

2. A rebuke to those who provide for this life alone.

3. A trumpet call to prepare for eternity.

4. An incentive to the Christian to make the best of this life for the glory of God. —*J.F.*

Verse 5. Condescension, visitation, contact, and conflagration.

Verses 7-8, 11. Repetitions, not vain. Repetitions in prayer are vain when they result from form, thoughtlessness, or superstition; but not, *e.g.*,

1. When they are the utterance of genuine fervor.

2. When the danger prayed against is imminent.

3. When the fear which prompts the prayer is urgent.

4. When the repetition is prompted by a new motive, Ps 144:7-8; by God's condescension, Ps 144:3,11; by God's former deliverance, Ps 144:10; and by the results which will flow from the answer, Ps 144:12-14. —*C.A.D.*

Verse 8. What is "a right hand of falsehood"? Ask the hypocrite, the schemer, the man of false doctrine, the boaster, the slanderer, the man who forgets his promise, the apostate.

Verse 9. For God's Ear.

1. The Singer. A grateful heart.

2. The Song. Full of Praise. New.

3. The Accompaniment: "Psaltery." Helps to devotion. Give God the best.

4. The Auditor and Object of the eulogium: "Thee, O God." —*W.B.H.*

Verse 11. Persons from whom it is a mercy to escape: those alien to God, vain in conversation, false in deed.

Verses 11-12. The Nature and Necessity of early Piety. A Sermon preached to a Society of Young People, at Willingham, Cambridgeshire, on the First Day of the Year 1772. —*Robert Robinson.*

Verse 12. Youth attended with development, stability, usefulness, and spiritual health.

Verse 12. (*first clause*). To Young Men. Consider,

1. What is desired on your behalf: "Sons may be as plants", etc.

    (a) That you may be respected and valued.
    (b) That you may have settled principles and virtues. Plants are not blown hither and thither.
    (c) That you may be vigorous and strong in moral power.

2. What is requisite on your part to the accomplishment of this desire.

    (a) A good rooting in Christ.
    (b) Constant nourishment from the word of God.
    (c) The dews of divine grace obtained by prayer.

(d) A resolute tendency within to answer the God appointed purpose of your existence.—J.F.

Verse 12. (*second clause*). To Young Women. Consider,

1. The important position you may occupy in the social fabric: "As cornerstones."

    (a) The moral and religious tone of society is determined more by your character and influence than by those of men.
    (b) The complexion of home life will be a reflex of your conduct and character, either as daughters, sisters, or wives.
    (c) The molding of the character of the next generation, remember, begins with the mother's influence.
    (d) Let these facts weigh with you as a motive in seeking the grace of God, without which you can never fulfill your mission worthily.

2. The beauty which ought to belong to you in your position. "Polished after", etc. The beauty of,

    (a) Heart purity: "The King's daughter is all glorious within."
    (b) A noble and modest conduct: "wrought gold", no imitation; real gold.
    (c) Gracious and gentle demeanor.

3. How both the right position and right beauty are obtained.

    (a) By yielding yourselves to God.
    (b) By Christ dwelling in your heart.
    (c) By becoming living stones and polished stones under the workmanship of the Holy Spirit.—J.F.

Verse 14. A prayer for our ministers, and for the security, unity, and happiness of the church.

Verse 14. The prosperous Church. There—

1. Labor is cheerfully performed.
2. The enemy is kept without the gate.
3. There are few or no departures.
4. Faith and content silence complaint.
5. Pray that such may be our case as a church.—W.B.H.

Verse 15. The peculiar happiness of those whose God is the Lord.

PSALM 145

SERMON OUTLINES AND HELPFUL TIPS

Verses 1-2. Praise.

1. Personal praise.
2. Daily praise.
3. Enthusiastic praise.
4. Perpetual praise.

Or:

1. The attractive theme of the song.
2. The increasing fulness of the song.
3. The unending life of the singer. —C. A. D.

Verses 1-2. The four "I wills" of praise. Praise to the King; praise to the divine character; praise for all time; praise for all eternity.

Verse 2. *Every day; forever.*

1. Day by day forever God and I will endure.

2. Day by day forever our present relations will continue. He the God, I the creature; he the Father, I the child; he the blessing, I the blest.

3. Day by day forever he shall have my homage. —W. B. H.

Verse 3.

1. The dignity of man is here implied in his capacity for praising God greatly.

2. His immortality in his capacity for praising his unsearchable greatness. —G. R.

Verse 3. (*last clause.*) The unsearchable greatness of God. Consider it,

1. As a fact amply demonstrated.

2. As a rebuke to despondency: see Isa 40:28.

3. As the stay of a soul oppressed by mysteries.

4. As indicating a subject for our everlasting study. —J. F.

Verse 4.

1. Our obligation to past generations.
2. Our duty to generations to come. —G. R.

Verses 5-7. The Antiphon.

1. To praise God is a personal duty: "I will."

2. Its right performance will excite others to engage in it: "And men shall."

3. The accompaniment of others in praise will react upon ourselves. "And I will"; "And they shall abundantly", etc.

4. Such praise widens and expands a it rolls along. Beginning with God's majesty and works, it extends to his acts, greatness, goodness, and righteousness.—*C. A. D.*

Verses 5-7.

1. Subjects for praise.

    (a) Divine majesty.
    (b) Divine works.
    (c) Divine judgments.
    (d) Divine greatness.
    (e) Divine goodness.
    (f) Divine righteousness.

2. Of whom is it required.

    (a) Personal; "I will speak."
    (b) Universal; "men shall speak."—*G. R.*

Verses 6-7.

1. *The awe struck talk.* Silent as to mercies and promises, men must speak when God's terrible acts are among them.

2. *The bold avowal.* One individual declares God's greatness in power, wisdom, truth and grace. This leads others to the same conclusion, and hence—

3. *The grateful outpouring.* Many bless the Lord's great goodness in a song fresh, free, constant, joyous, refreshing, abundant, like the gush of a spring.

4. *The select song.* They *utter* goodness but *sing* of righteousness. This is a noteworthy topic for a discourse.

Verse 7. See "Spurgeon's Sermons", No. 1468: "The Philosophy and Propriety of Abundant Praise."

Verse 8.

1. Grace to the unworthy.
2. Compassion to the afflicted.
3. Forbearance to the guilty.
4. Mercy to the penitent.—*G. R.*

Verse 9. The universal goodness of God in no degree a contradiction to the special election of grace.

Verse 10. See "Spurgeon's Sermons", No. 1796: "Concerning Saints."

Verse 11. The glory of Christ's kingdom. The glory of this kingdom is manifested,

1. In its origin.
2. In the manner and spirit of its administration.
3. In the character of its subjects.
4. In the privileges that are attached to it. —*Robert Hall.*

Verses 11-12. Talk transfigured.

1. The faculty of talk is extensively possessed.
2. Is commonly misused.
3. May be nobly employed.
4. Will then be gloriously useful. —*C. A. D.*

Verses 11-13. To show the greatness of God's kingdom, David observes,

1. The pomp of it. Would we by faith look within the veil, we should "speak of the glory of his kingdom" (Ps 145:11); "and the glorious majesty of it" (Ps 145:12).

2. The power of it. When "they speak of the glory of God's kingdom", they must "talk of his power", the extent of it, the efficacy of it.

3. The perpetuity of it (Ps 145:13). The thrones of earthly princes totter, and the flowers of their crowns wither, monarchs come to an end; but, Lord, "thy kingdom is an everlasting kingdom." —*Matthew Henry.*

Verse 14. The grace of God in his kindness to the undeserving and the miserable, who look to him for help.

1. He "upholdeth all that fall."

>(a) A description, embracing (1) Sinners who have fallen lowest: (2) Backsliders who have tripped most foully.

>(b) An act implying (1) Pity which draws nigh; (2) Power which places the fallen upon their feet; (3) Preservation which keeps them standing.

2. He "raiseth up all those that are bowed down." Consolation for those who are—

>(a) Bowed down with shame and penitence.
>(b) Oppressed with perplexities and cares.
>(c) Weighted with a sense of weakness in the presence of onerous duties.
>(d) Depressed because of prevailing error and sin around them. —*J. F.*

Verse 14. Help for the fallible.

1. Whatever our present position we are liable to fall. Sickness. Loss. Friendlessness. Sin.

2. However low we fall we are not below the reach of God's hand.

3. Within the reach of God's hand we shall experience the action of God's love. "Upholdeth." "Raiseth up." —*C.A.D.*

Verses 15-16. Universal dependence and divine support. The Psalmist here teaches—

1. The Universality of Dependence amongst creatures: "The eyes of all wait upon thee." We depend upon God for "life, and breath, and all things." Entire dependence should beget deep humility.

2. The Infinitude of the Divine Resources: "And thou givest them their meat." His resources must be,

>   (a) Infinitely vast.
>   (b) Infinitely various. Both sufficient and adapted for all.

3. The Timeliness of the Divine Communications: "In due season. "A reason for patience if his gifts seem delayed.

4. The Sublime Ease of the Divine Communications: "Thou openest thine hand", and the countless needs of the universe are satisfied. An encouragement to believing prayer.

5. The Sufficiency of the Divine Communications: "And satisfiest the desire of every living thing." "God giveth to all liberally." Our subject urges all men to,

>   (a) Gratitude. Constant provision should lead to constant thankfulness and consecration.

>   (b) Trust. (1) For temporal supplies. (2) For spiritual supplies. "Grace to help in time of need" will surely be given to all who look to him. —*William Jones, in "The Homiletic Quarterly"*, 1878.

Verse 17.

1. What God declares himself to be.
2. What his people find him to be.
3. What all creatures will ultimately acknowledge him to be. —*G. R.*

Verses 18-20. Gather from these **Verse**s the character of God's people.

1. They call upon God.
2. They fear God.
3. They have desires towards God.
4. They have answers from God.
5. They love God.

Verse 18. (*last clause.*) True prayer, in what it differs essentially from mere formalism.

Verse 18. At the palace gates.

1. Directions to callers.

>   (a) "Call upon him"; let the repetition suggest pertinacity.

(b) Call "in truth"; sincerely, with promises, in appointed way.

2. Encouragement for callers. Jehovah is nigh, with his ready ear, sympathizing heart, and helpful hand.—*W. B. H.*

Verses 18-19. The blessedness of prayer.

1. Definition of prayer: "calling upon God."

2. Variety in prayer: "call, desire, cry."

3. Essential characteristic of prayer: "truth."

4. God's nearness in prayer.

5. Assured success of prayer. "He will fulfil, hear, save."—*C. A. D.*

Verse 20. Those who love God are preserved *from* excessive temptation, falling into sin, despair, apostasy, remorse, famishing; preserved *in* trial, persecution, depression, death; preserved *to* activity, holiness, victory, glory.

Verse 20. Solemn Contrasts.

1. Between human characters. "Them that love him." "The wicked."

2. Between human destinies. "Preserveth." "Destroy."—*C. A. D.*

Verse 20. How the love of God is the opposite of wickedness, and wickedness inconsistent with the love of God.

Verse 21. Individual praise suggests the desire for universal praise. We like company in a good deed; we perceive the inadequacy of our own song; we desire others to be happy; we long to see that done which is right and good.

PSALM 146

SERMON OUTLINES AND HELPFUL TIPS

Verse 1.

1. An exhortation: it is addressed to ourselves: "Praise ye the Lord."
2. An example: the Psalmist cries to himself, "Praise the Lord."
3. An echo: "Praise the Lord, O my soul." Let us say this to our own souls.

Verse 1. Whom should I praise? And why? And when? And how?

Verse 1. Public worship.

1. Should be with a sense of fellowship: "Praise *ye*": pleasures of communion in praise.

2. Should never lose its individuality: "O my soul." God is only praised by individual hearts. Temptations to wandering in public services.

3. Should be full of Jehovah's felt presence: each and all should worship *him* alone. —W.B.H.

Verse 2. Work for here and hereafter.

1. "While I live"; or a period of uncertainty and mystery.

2. "I will praise the Lord"; or a service definite, determined, due, and delightful. Certainty amid uncertainty.

3. "While I have any being"; or an enthusiastic pre-engagement of eternity. —W.B.H.

Verse 3.

1. It dishonors God.
2. It degrades you.
3. It disappoints in every case.

Verse 4. Decease, Decay, Defeat.

Verse 4. (*second clause*). The failure of man's projects, the disappearance of his philosophies, the disproving of his boastings.

Verse 5. The secret of true happiness.

1. *What it is not.* The man here mentioned has his work and warfare, for he needs help; and he has not all he desires, for he is a man of hope.

2. *What it is.* It lies in the *hath,* the *help,* and the *hope,* and these are all in God.

Verses 6-7. The God of our hope is,

1. Creator.
2. Truth keeper.

3. Vindicator.
4. Provider.
5. Deliverer.

Verse 7. (*last clause*).—See "Spurgeon's Sermons", No. 484: "The Lord—the Liberator."

Verse 7. The People's Rights.

1. Three rights of humanity. Justice, Bread, Freedom.

2. God's interventions in their behalf. Revolutions, Reforms, Regenerations. Christ's war with Satan.

3. The magnificent supply of the three blessings in Christ's kingdom.

4. The men who are fashioned and trained under this *regime*.—W.B.H.

Verse 8. (*first clause*). Spiritual blindness, its curse, cause, and cure.

Verse 8. (*second clause*). Who are the people? Who raises them? How he does it. And what then?

Verse 8. (*third clause*). God's love to the righteous.

1. He made them righteous.
2. They are like him.
3. They love him.
4. Their purposes are one with his own.

Verse 9. Observe the provision made in the Jewish law for the stranger. The way in which strangers were received by God. The truth that his chosen are strangers in the world. His design to gather in strangers in the latter days.

Verse 9. (*center clause*). The claims of orphans and widows upon the people of God.

Verse 9. (*last clause*). Illustrated by Joseph's brethren, Haman, and others.

Verse 10.

1. A cause for praise—"The Lord shall reign forever."
2. A center of praise: "O Zion."
3. A cycle of praise: "all generations."
4. A call to praise; "Praise ye the Lord."

PSALM 147

SERMON OUTLINES AND HELPFUL TIPS

Verse 1. Praise. Its profit, pleasure, and propriety. —J.F.

Verse 1. The Reasonable Service.

1. The methods of praise: by word, song, life; individually, socially.

2. The offerers of praise: "ye."

3. The objects of praise: "the Lord, our God."

4. The reasons for praise: it is "good", "pleasant", "becoming." —C.A.D.

Verses 1-3.

1. The Privilege of Praising God.

(a) It is good.
(b) Pleasant.
(c) Becoming.

2. The Duty of Praising God.

(a) For gathering a church for himself among men: "The Lord doth build up Jerusalem."
(b) For the materials of which it is composed: "The outcasts", etc.
(c) For the preparation of those materials for his purpose: "He healeth", etc. Ps 147:3. —G.R.

Verse 2. The Lord is Architect, Builder, Sustainer, Restorer, and Owner of the Church. In each relation let him be praised.

Verse 2. The Great Gatherer.

1. Strange persons sought for.
2. Special search and means made use of.
3. Selected center to which he brings them.
4. Singular exhibition of them for ever and ever in heaven.

Verse 2. First the church built and then the sinners gathered into it. A prosperous state of the church within necessary to her increase from without.

Verse 2. See "Spurgeon's Sermons", No. 1302: "Good Cheer for Outcasts."

Verse 2. Upbuilding and Ingathering.

1. The church may be in a fallen condition.
2. Its upbuilding is the Lord's work.
3. He accomplishes it by gathering together its outcast citizens. —C.A.D.

Verse 3. See "Spurgeon's Sermons", No. 53: "Healing for the Wounded."

Verse 3. God a true physician, and a tender nurse.—*J.F.*

Verses 3-4. Heaven's Brilliants, and Earth's Broken Hearts.

1. The Proprietor of the Stars with the Wounded. The stars left kingless for broken hearts. Jehovah! with lint and liniment and a woman's hand. Who binds together the stars, shall bind firmly grieved hearts.

2. The Gentle Heart healer with the Stars. Be all power entrusted to such tenderness. Its comely splendor. God guides the stars with an eye on wounded hearts. The hopefulness of prayer.

3. Hearts, Stars, and Eternity. Some hearts shall "shine as the stars." Some stars shall expire in "blackness of darkness." God's hand and eye are everywhere making justice certain. Trust and sing.—*W.B.H.*

Verses 3-4. God's Compassion and Power.

1. Striking diversity of God's cares: "hearts" and "stars."

2. Wonderful variety of God's operations. Gently caring for human hearts. Preserving the order, regularity, and stability of creation.

3. Blessed results of God's work. Broken hearts healed; wounds bound up. Light, harmony, and beauty in the heavens.

4. Mighty encouragement to trust in God. God takes care of the universe; may I not entrust my life, my soul, to him? Where he rules unquestioned there is light and harmony; let me not resist his will in my life.—*C.A.D.*

Verse 5. A contemplation of God's greatness.

1. Great in his essential nature.

2. Great in Power.

3. Great in wisdom. Let us draw inferences concerning the insignificance of man, & c.

Verse 6. Reversal.

1. In the estimate of the world the meek are cast down and the wicked lifted up.

2. In the judgment of heaven the meek are lifted up and the wicked cast down.

3. The judgment of heaven will, in the end, be found the true one.—*C.A.D.*

Verse 7. The use and benefit of singing.

Verse 8. God in all. The unity of his plan; the cooperation of divine forces; the condescending mercy of the result.

Verse 9. See "Spurgeon's Sermons", No. 672: "The Ravens' Cry."

Verse 11. The singularity of our God, and of his Favor. For which he is to be praised.

1. *The objects of that Favor distinguished.*

>   (a) From physical strength.
>   (b) From mental vigor.
>   (c) From self-reliance.
>   (d) From mere capacity for service.

2. *The objects of that Favor described.*

>   (a) By emotions relating to God.
>   (b) By the weakest forms of spiritual life.
>   (c) By the highest degrees of it; for the most mature saint fears and hopes.
>   (d) By the sacred blend of it. Fear of our guilt, hope of his mercy. Fear of self, confidence in God. Hope of perseverance, fear of sinning. Hope of heaven, fear of coming short. Hope of perfection, mourning defects.

3. *The blessing of that Favor implied.*

(a) God loves to think of them.
(b) To be with them.
(c) To minister to them.
(d) To meet them in their fears and their hopes.
(e) To reward them forever.

Verse 11. He takes pleasure in their persons, emotions, desires, devotions, hopes, and characters.—*W.W.*

Verse 12.

1. The Lord whom we praise.
2. His praise in our houses—Jerusalem.
3. Our praise in his house—Zion.

Verse 13. A Strong Church.

1. The utility and value of a strong church.

2. The marks which distinguish it.

>   (a) Gates well kept.
>   (b) Increase of membership.
>   (c) The converts blessed to others.

3. The important care of a strong church: to trace all blessing to Zion's God.—*W.B.H.*

Verses 14-15. See "Spurgeon's Sermons", No. 425: "Peace at Home, and Prosperity Abroad."

Verses 14-15. Church blessings.

1. Peace.
2. Food.
3. Missionary energy.
4. The presence of God: the source of all blessing.

Verse 15. (*second clause*). See "Spurgeon's Sermons", No. 1607: "The Swiftly Running Word."

Verse 16. The unexpected results of adversity: snow acting as wool.

Verses 16-18. See "Spurgeon's Sermons, "No. 670: "Frost and Thaw."

Verse 19.

1. God's people.
2. God's Word.
3. God's revelation to the soul.
4. God's praise for this special revelation.

Verse 20. *He hath not dealt so with any nation... Praise ye the Lord.* The sweet Psalmist of Israel, a man skillful in praises, doth begin and end this Psalm with *Hallelujah*. In the body of the Psalm he doth set forth the mercy of God, both towards all *creatures* in general in his common providence, and towards his *church* in particular. So in this close of the Psalm: "He sheweth his word unto Jacob, and his statutes to Israel. He hath not dealt so with any nation." In the original 'tis, "He hath not dealt so with *every nation*": that is, with *any* nation. In the text you may observe *a position* and *a conclusion*. A position; and that is, that God deals in a singular way of mercy with his people above all other people. And then the *conclusion:* "*Praise ye the Lord.*" Doctrine. That God deals in a singular way of mercy with his people, and therefore expects singular praises from his people. — *Joseph Alleine* (1633-1668), *in* "A Thanksgiving Sermon."

Verse 20. See the wonderful goodness of God, who besides the light of nature, has committed to us the sacred Scriptures. The heathen are enveloped in ignorance. *As for his judgments, they have not known them.* They have the oracles of the Sybils, but not the writings of Moses and the apostles. How many live in the region of death, where the bright star of Scripture has never appeared! We have the blessed Book of God to resolve all our doubts, and to point out a way of life to us. "Lord, how is it thou wilt manifest thyself unto us, and not unto the world?" Joh 14:22. — *Thomas Watson.*

Verse 20. Electing Grace inspires the Heart with Praise.

1. God's love has chosen us. Hallelujah.
2. God has entrusted us with his truth. Hallelujah.
3. God has made us almoners of his bounty. Hallelujah.
4. God through us is to save the world. Hallelujah. — *W.B.H.*

PSALM 148

SERMON OUTLINES AND HELPFUL TIPS

Whole Psalm.

1. What is implied in the invitation to the natural creation to praise God.

   (a) That praise is due to God on its account.

   (b) That it is due from those for whose benefit it was created.

   (c) That it is a reproof to those who do not praise God who are actually capable of it. "If these should hold their peace, the stones would immediately cry out."

2. What is implied in the invitation to innocent beings to praise God. "Praise ye the Lord from the heavens. Praise ye him all his angels, praise ye him all his hosts": Ps 148:1-2.

   (a) That they owe their creation in innocence to God.
   (b) That they owe their preservation in innocence to him.
   (c) That they owe the reward of their innocence to him.

3. What is implied in the invitation to fallen beings to praise God: "Kings of the earth and all people", etc.: Ps 148:11-13.

   (a) That God is merciful and ready to forgive. "Not willing that any should perish", etc. They would not be called upon to praise God if they were irrecoverably lost. Our Lord would not when on earth accept praise from an evil spirit.

   (b) That means of restoration from the fall are provided by God for men. Without this they would have no hope, and could offer no praise.

4. What is implied in the invitation to the redeemed to praise God: Ps 148:14.

   (a) That God is their God.

   (b) That all his perfections are engaged for their present and eternal welfare.—G.R.

Verse 1. *Praise ye the Lord.*

1. The Voice—of Scripture, of nature, of grace, of duty.

2. The Ear on which it rightly falls—of saints and sinners, old and young, healthy and sick. It falls on our ear.

3. The Time when it is heard. Now, ever, yet also at special times.

4. The Response which we will give. Let us now praise with heart, life, lip.

Verse 1. (*second and third clauses*).

1. The character of the praises of heaven.
2. How far they influence us who are here below.
3. The hope which we have of uniting in them.

Verse 2.

1. The angels as praiseful servants.

2. The other hosts of God, and how they praise him.

3. The rule without exception: "*all — all.*" Imagine one heavenly being living without praising the Lord!

Verse 3.

1. God's praise continual both day and night.
2. Light the leading fountain of this praise.
3. Life behind all, calling for the praise.

Verses 5-6. Creation and conservation, two chief reasons for praise.

Verse 7. God's praise from dark, deep, and mysterious things.

Verse 8. Canon Liddon preached in St. Paul's on Sunday afternoon, December 23, 1883, and took for his text Ps 148:8, *Wind and storm fulfilling his word.* He spoke of the divine use of destructive forces.

1. In the physical world we see wind and storm fulfilling God's word.

   (a) The Bible occasionally lifts the veil, and shows us how destructive forces of Nature have been the servants of God.

   (b) Modern history illustrates this vividly.

2. In the human, spiritual, and moral world, we find new and rich application of the words of the text.

   (a) In the State we see the storm of invasion and the storm of revolution fulfilling God's word.

   (b) In the Church we see the storm of persecution and the storm of controversy fulfilling God's word.

   (c) In the experience of individual life we see outward troubles, and inward storms of religious doubts fulfilling God's word. — *The Contemporary Pulpit,* 1884.

Verse 9. *Trees.* The glory of God as seen in trees.

Verse 10. The wildest, the quietest, the most depressed, and the most aspiring should each have its song.

Verses 11-18.

1. The universal King. Alone in excelling. Supreme in glory.

2. The universal summons. Of all nations, ranks, classes and ages. Foreshadowing the Judgment.

3. The universal duty: praise,—constant, emphatic, growing.—W.B.H.

Verse 12. God to be served by strength and beauty, experience and expectation.

Verse 12. *And children.* A Children's Address.

1. Where the children are found (Ps 148:11-12). In royal and distinguished society: yet not lost or overlooked.

2. What they are called to. "Praise the Lord." Even they have abundant reason.

3. What are the lessons of the subject?

    (a) Children should come up with their parents on the Sabbath.
    (b) Children should unite in heart and voice in God's praises.
    (c) Children should seek fitness for this praise by believing in Christ.—W.B.H.

Verse 14. The Favored People and their God.

1. What he does for them.
2. What he makes them: "Saints."
3. Who they are: "Children of Israel."
4. Where they are: "Near unto him."
5. What they do for him: "Praise ye the Lord."

PSALM 149

SERMON OUTLINES AND HELPFUL TIPS

Verse 1. *Praise ye the lord.*

1. The one work of a life.
2. The work of the truly living of all degrees.
3. Their work in many and various forms.
4. A work for which there is abundant cause, reason, and argument.

Verse 1.

1. A wonderful gift—to be a saint.
2. A wonderful people—who are saints.
3. A wonderful assembly—a congregation of saints.
4. A wonderful God—the object of their song.

Verses 1-2. The new song of the saints.

1. The saints are God's children by the new birth.
2. The new birth has given them a new heart.
3. The new heart utters itself in a new song.—*C.A.D.*

Verses 1, 5.

1. We must praise God in public, "in the congregation of the saints": the more the better; it is like to heaven.

2. We must praise him in private. "Let the saints" be so transported with their joy in God as to "sing aloud upon their beds", when they awake in the night, as David; Ps 119:62.—*Matthew Henry.*

Verse 2. The duty, reasonableness, and benefit of holy joy.

Verse 2. A peculiar people, their peculiar God, and their peculiar joy in him.

Verse 2. (*second clause*). Christ's people may well rejoice:

1. In the majesty of his person.
2. In the righteousness of his rule.
3. In the extent of his conquests.
4. In the protection they enjoy under him.
5. In the glory to which he will raise them.
—*From "The Homiletical Library," 1882.*

Verses 2, 4. The cause given to God's Israel for Praise. Consider,

1. God's doings for them. They have reason to rejoice in God, and employ themselves in his service; for it is he that "made" them.

2. God's dominion over them. This follows upon the former: if he made them he is their King.

3. God's delight in them. He is a King that rules by love, and therefore to be praised.

4. God's designs concerning them. Besides the present complacency he hath in them, he hath prepared for their future glory. "He will beautify the meek", etc. —*Matthew Henry.*

Verse 4. The text bears other renderings. Read as in Authorized Version.

1. *The character to be aimed at—the meek.*

   (a) Submissive to God. To his truth. To his dealings.

   (b) Gentle towards men. Bearing with patience. Forgiving with heartiness. Loving with perseverance.

   (c) Lowly in ourselves.

2. *The Favor to be enjoyed—beautify.*

   (a) The beauty of gentleness.
   (b) The beauty of peace.
   (c) The beauty of content.
   (d) The beauty of joy.
   (e) The beauty of holiness.
   (f) The beauty of respect and influence.

3. *The good results to be expected.*

   (a) God will be glorified and Christ manifested.
   (b) Men will be attracted.
   (c) Heaven will be anticipated.

Verse 4. (*first clause*). The Lord's taking pleasure in his people is,

1. A wonderful evidence of his grace.
2. The highest Honor they can desire.
3. Their security for time and eternity. —*J.F.*

Verse 5. *Saintly joy.*

1. The state to which God has lifted the saints: "glory", in contrast with sin, reproach, affliction.

2. The emotion which accordingly befits the saints: "be joyful."

3. The utterance of that emotion incumbent on the saints: "sing aloud." —*C.A.D.*

Verse 5. (*second clause*). Let them praise God—

1. Upon their beds of *rest*, upon their *nightly* couch.

   (a) Because of what God has done for them during the day.

(b) Because sleep is the gift of God.

(c) Because they have a bed to lie upon.

(d) Because the Lord is their keeper (Ps 4:5,8).

2. Upon their beds of *sickness.*

(a) Because it is God's will they should suffer.

(b) Because affliction is often a proof of God's love.

(c) Because, if sanctified, sickness is a great blessing.

(d) Because praise offered upon a bed of sickness is a testimony to the power of religion.

3. Upon their beds of *death.*

(a) Because the sting of death is removed.

(b) Because their Lord has passed through death.

(c) Because Christ is with them while they suffer.

(d) Because of what awaits them.

(e) Because they have the glorious hope of resurrection. —*C.W. Townsend, of Inskip,* 1885.

Verse 6.

1. The Christian life a combination of adoration and conflict.

2. In each case it should be at its best: "high praises", "two edged sword."

3. In each case holiness should be conspicuous: it is of saints that the text speaks.

Verse 8. The restraining and subduing power of the gospel.

Verse 9. The Honor common to all saints.

PSALM 150

SERMON OUTLINES AND HELPFUL TIPS

Verse 1. *Praise God in his sanctuary.*

1. In his personal holiness.
2. In the person of his Son.
3. In heaven.
4. In the assembly of saints.
5. In the silence of the heart.

Verses 1-6. God should be praised. Where? (Ps 150:1). Wherefore? (Ps 150:2). Wherewith? (Ps 150:3-5). By whom? (Ps 150:6).—*C.A.D.*

Verse 2. *His excellent greatness.* Wherein the greatness of God is specially excellent, and where it is best seen.

Verse 2. *Praise him for his mighty acts.*

1. For us. Election. Redemption. Inspiration.

2. In us. The work of enlightenment in the understanding; purification in the heart; quickening in the conscience; subjugation in the will.

3. By us. Thought through us; felt through us; spoke through us; worked through us. To him be all the glory!—*W.J.*

Verse 2. *Praise him according to his excellent greatness.*

1. Reverently, according to the greatness of his being.
2. Gratefully, according to the greatness of his love.
3. Retrospectively, according to the greatness of his gifts.
4. Prospectively, according to the greatness of his promises.—*W.J.*

Verse 2. What the exhortation requires.

1. That men should study God's works, and observe the glory of God in them.
2. That they should meditate on his greatness till they realize its excellence.
3. That they should openly proclaim the Honor due to him.
4. That they should not contradict in their life the praise they speak.—*J.F.*

Verse 3. *Praise him with the sound of the trumpet.*

1. When you fight.
2. When you conquer.
3. When you assemble.
4. When you proclaim his Word.
5. When you welcome Jubilee.

Verses 3-6.

1. The variety of the ancient service of worship necessitating serious expenditure; consecration of high talent; hard and constant toil.

2. The lessons of such service.

    (a) God should be worshipped royally.
    (b) The efforts of the best genius are his rightful tribute.
    (c) All human ability cannot place a worthy offering at his feet.

3. The soul and essential of true worship.

4. God's requirements as to worship in these present times. —W.B.H.

Verse 6.

1. The august Giver of "life, and breath, and all things."

2. The due and true use of the gifts of life.

3. The resultant swathing of earth in consecrated atmosphere, and millennial hallelujahs. —W.B.H.

Verse 6. A fitting close to the psalter, considered as a desire, a prayer, or an exhortation.

1. As a desire, it realizes the glory due to God, the worship ennobling to man, the disposition of heart which would make all the world into a holy brotherhood.

2. As a prayer, it seeks the downfall of every superstition, the universal spread of the truth, the conversion of every soul.

3. As an exhortation, it is plain, pertinent, pure in its piety, perfect in its charity. —J.F.

HALLELUJAH!

Printed in Great Britain
by Amazon